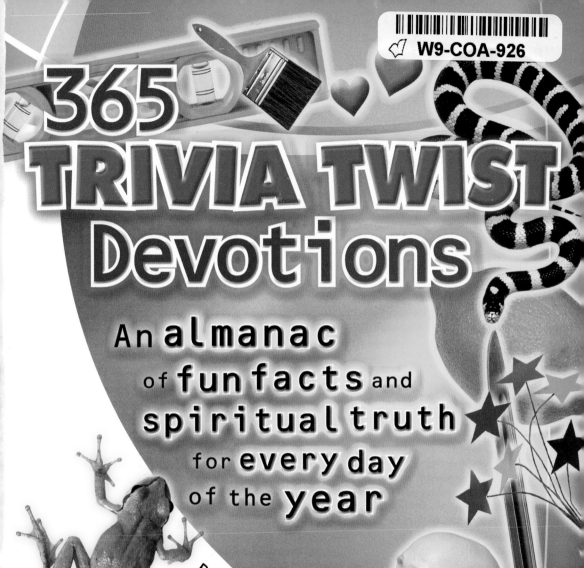

365 TRIVIA TWIST Devotions

An almanac of fun facts and spiritual truth for every day of the year

Betsy Schmitt & David Veerman

Standard PUBLISHING
Bringing The Word to Life

Cincinnati, Ohio

Published by Standard Publishing, Cincinnati, Ohio
www.standardpub.com

Copyright © 2005 by The Livingstone Corporation.

Project editors: Greg Holder and Betsy Todt Schmitt.
Cover design: Robert Glover. Interior design: Mark Wainwright.
Produced with the assistance of The Livingstone Corporation (www.LivingstoneCorporation.com).
Project staff includes Betsy Todt Schmitt, David R. Veerman, Phoebe Blaustein, Mary Horner Collins, Madeleine Garber, Mary Larsen, Kirk Luttrell, Joel Bartlett, and Allison Schmitt.

ISBN-13: 978-0-7847-1737-0
ISBN-10: 0-7847-1737-0

12 11 10 09
5 4

introduction

Dear Reader,

Welcome to the *365 Trivia Twist Devotions*! Get set for a wild, and sometimes wacky, look at the historical happenings, intriguing inventions, and offbeat holidays that take place every day of the year. From Thomas Edison's birthday to the day that Cracker Jack® first put a prize in the box, you will discover a fascinating bunch of fun facts associated with every calendar day. Adding to the fun is an insightful devotion, which gives a spiritual twist to the main trivia fact for the day. So not only will you have lots of random facts for impressing your friends, but you also will be learning how God's Word has something to say about everything—including National Sticky Bun Day!

At the end of each devotion, you will also find a challenge—something to help you put the day's spiritual truth into practice. Use these suggestions as a fun spin to your daily time with God. Our prayer is that through this fun-packed and engaging devotional you will begin a lifelong habit of spending time with God—and enjoying it!

We hope that you will have as much fun reading *365 Trivia Twist Devotions* as we have had doing the research and writing! After all, we never would have known that April 16th is National Weed Day, or that on June 13, 1825, Walter Hunt patented the safety pin. Did we mention that September 19th is National Talk Like a Pirate Day? Go ahead, dig in, and find your own favorite trivia twists to share!

God Bless,
Betsy Schmitt
Dave Veerman

happy new year!

Today starts a brand new year! Celebrate!

New Year's Day is one of the world's oldest holidays. In fact, it was first observed nearly 4,000 years ago by the ancient Babylonians (that's a lot of New Year's Day celebrations!). But it was not always celebrated on the first of January. The Babylonians observed the start of the new year on the first day of spring, as did many other cultures. It wasn't until much later when the Romans came to power that January 1 was set as the official start of the new year.

The date may have changed, but one New Year's Day tradition has remained the same—making New Year's resolutions. Even the early Babylonians marked the start of a new year with making resolutions. But while our modern resolutions tend to be about losing weight or exercising more, the most popular ancient Babylonian resolution was to return borrowed farm equipment!

Almost everyone makes resolutions. Maybe you resolve to read your Bible every day. Maybe you promise to finish *all* your homework before you go online or watch television. Perhaps your resolution is to be nicer to your brother or sister. Or maybe *you* have something borrowed that needs to be returned!

New Year's resolutions are fun to make; sometimes we even keep them. But more often than not, our resolve weakens after a few days. By the time February rolls around, those promises are long forgotten. But before you get too discouraged, there is good news. There is one whose Word you can count on, day in and day out. God's promises will never change. His resolutions will stay strong from January 1 through December 31, each and every year. Depend on *his* promises to help you keep yours.

Without wavering, let us hold **tightly** to the hope we say we have, for God can be **trusted** to **keep** his promise.

[Hebrews 10:23]

also on this day

1735
Paul Revere was born.

1840
The first bowling match in the U.S. was recorded.

1892
Ellis Island Immigrant Station formally opened in New York.

to do ☑

GO AHEAD AND MAKE A RESOLUTION ON THIS NEW YEAR'S DAY. WRITE IT DOWN IN YOUR BIBLE AND ASK GOD EVERY DAY TO HELP YOU KEEP IT.

a penny saved

Today is Thrift with Flair Day!

Bet you didn't know that there was a day to celebrate being thrifty! The First Annual National Thrift with Flair Day was created in 2000 to help families who had spent too much money on stuff they didn't need to make a fresh start on getting control of the family budget.

Actually, that's not a bad idea. How are you doing in the money department? Maybe you get a weekly allowance. Or maybe you just received some money as a Christmas gift. Whatever your financial situation, this is a good time to consider how you spend your money. Consider the following questions: What was the last item you purchased? Did you really need it? How much money do you save? How much do you give to God as offering?

It's tempting when you have some money in your pocket to pick up the latest CD of your favorite band, or to buy another pair of jeans before your old ones are worn out. But what happens when you really need something, or the offering plate comes around on Sunday, and you have nothing left?

The fact is God has given us everything that we have or own. How we spend our money reflects how we feel about God. If we put God first, then we will try to honor him with the way we spend and use our money. That means making good decisions about what to buy and when, how much to save, and how much to give back to God. But if we spend money as if we love it more than God, watch out! We'll be joining the ranks of those people who inspired Thrift with Flair Day in the first place!

As Jesus put it, we can't love God and money equally. Who do you love?

to do ☑

CELEBRATE THRIFT WITH FLAIR DAY BY MAKING A BUDGET (OR SPENDING PLAN) FOR YOURSELF. HERE'S ONE SIMPLE WAY TO DO THAT. TAKE THREE ENVELOPES. MARK ONE SAVE, MARK ANOTHER ONE SPEND, AND MARK THE THIRD GIVE. THEN DECIDE HOW MUCH YOU PLAN TO PUT INTO EACH ENVELOPE ON A WEEKLY OR MONTHLY BASIS.

also on this day 1910

* The first junior high school was opened in Berkeley, California.

"**No one** can serve **two** masters. For you will **hate** one and **love** the other, or **be devoted** to one and **despise** the other. You **cannot** serve both **God** and **money.**" [Luke 16:13]

Sleepy Time

Today is the Festival of Sleep Day.

It's probably safe to say that we don't give much thought to our sleep habits—certainly not enough to devote a day to celebrate sleeping! We all know it's something we have to do in order to stay healthy. Most of us know that we don't feel well when we don't get enough sleep. But that's about as far as our thinking on the subject goes.

Consider the following facts:

- We will spend about a third of our life sleeping.
- Teens need an average of 10 hours of sleep each night—as much as a young child.
- If it takes you less than five minutes to fall asleep at night, you're sleep deprived. The ideal period of time for falling asleep is between 10 and 15 minutes, meaning you're still tired enough to sleep deeply but not so exhausted that you feel sleepy by morning.
- Lack of sleep can affect our moods, our performance, and our ability to think.
- The 1989 Exxon Valdez oil spill off Alaska, the Challenger space shuttle disaster, and the Chernobyl nuclear accident have all been attributed to human errors in which sleep-deprivation played a role.

Getting a good night's sleep is important! Jesus knew that. On frequent occasions, Jesus and his disciples broke away from the crowds to rest (Matthew 8:18 and Mark 6:31). And one time, Jesus was sound asleep while his disciples were battling a fierce storm (Mark 4:35-41). The Bible tells us that rest is a gift from God. So before your head hits the pillow tonight, make sure to thank him for a sleep-filled night!

to do ☑

TRY KEEPING A SLEEP DIARY FOR THE NEXT WEEK. RECORD WHEN YOU GO TO BED, WHAT TIME YOU WAKE UP, YOUR GENERAL MOOD THAT DAY, OR ANY FACTORS AFFECTING YOUR SLEEP. SEE WHAT A DIFFERENCE A GOOD NIGHT'S SLEEP MAKES IN YOUR DAILY LIFE.

It is **useless** for you to work **so hard** from early morning until **late** at night, anxiously **working** for food to eat; for **God** gives **rest** to his **loved** ones.

[Psalm 127:2]

also on this day

1892 J.R.R. Tolkien's birthday

1888 The drinking straw was patented by Marvin C. Stone.

1924 English explorer Howard Carter discovered the sarcophagus of Tutankhamen in the Valley of the Kings, near Luxor, Egypt.

trivial pursuit

About 20 years ago two friends got into a friendly argument over who was the better game player. In order to settle the argument fairly, the two created their own board game based on answering a series of, well, trivial questions. Eventually, they decided they had a moneymaking idea, and the Trivial Pursuit® game was born. At first the game received a less than enthusiastic reception, selling only a few hundred copies when it debuted in 1982. But by 1984 word of mouth took over, and in that year alone, 20 million games were sold. There are now more than a half dozen spin-offs on this popular game, including Trivial Pursuit® Junior.

Trivia has become a national pastime. There are Web sites devoted to trivia of every imaginable sort—movies, books, sports, celebrities, food, animals. There are even books and games devoted to Bible trivia. Considering that trivia often has to do with unimportant, obscure facts, do you ever wonder why we are so obsessed with it?

Well, it is fun. And there's that certain sense of personal satisfaction when you are the only one who knows which birds have been trained to tend sheep or what the biggest selling restaurant food happens to be (OK, the answers are geese and french fries). Still, Jesus reminds us that only one thing is truly important—and that's to make God's concerns our No. 1 priority. When we fill our minds with God's thoughts, his desires, and the concerns of his heart, everything else becomes, well, trivial.

to do ☑

CREATE A TRIVIA TEST BASED ON FACTS ABOUT YOURSELF. GIVE IT TO YOUR BEST FRIEND OR A FAMILY MEMBER. AFTER SHARING THE ANSWERS, MAKE SURE TO TELL THAT PERSON ABOUT THE ONE THING THAT IS TRULY MOST IMPORTANT.

"He will give you all you need from day to day if you live for him and make the Kingdom of God your primary concern." [Matthew 6:33]

also on this day

1850 The first American ice-skating club was formed in Philadelphia, Pennsylvania.

1896 Utah became America's 45th state.

birds of a feather
Today is National Bird Day.

National Bird Day was created in 2003 as a day to celebrate and reflect on what we can learn from our fine-feathered friends. If you wish, you can get a book about birds at your local bookstore or library and try to identify the different types of birds that fly into your backyard. Or you can check out some interesting Web sites about birds. But did you know that you can learn much about—and from—birds just by reading the Bible?

There are more than 50 different references to birds in the Bible, and more than 34 different types are mentioned. The Bible tells us that God created birds for his own glory (Psalm 148:5, 7-10), that he provides them with food and shelter (Psalm 104:10-12, 16, 17), and that all the birds of this world belong to him (Psalm 50:11). God created birds to sing (Song of Songs 2:12), to soar (Isaiah 40:31; Hosea 11:11), and to be tamed (James 3:7). Birds provide a source of food (Genesis 9:2, 3), provide a source of wisdom (Job 12:7), and on one special occasion, provided airborne meals for God's prophet Elijah (1 Kings 17:2-6).

But the most important lesson we can learn from birds is how much God cares. In Matthew 10:29 we learn that God knows when even one sparrow falls to the ground. Think of all the birds in the world or even in your backyard. God cares specifically and tenderly for each one. So why is that important to know? Mathew 10:31 says, "So don't be afraid; you are more valuable to him [God] than a whole flock of sparrows." If God cares so much for just one little sparrow, imagine how much more he cares for you!

also on this day 1956

In the *Peanuts* comic strip, Snoopy walked on two legs for the first time.

to do ☑

BUY OR MAKE A BIRD FEEDER AND PUT IT IN YOUR YARD. WATCH THE BIRDS COME TO FEED. LET EACH BIRD THAT FLIES INTO YOUR YARD REMIND YOU HOW MUCH GOD LOVES YOU.

The first female governor in the United States, Mrs. Nellie Taylor Ross, was sworn in as the governor of Wyoming. 1910

"Not even a **sparrow**, worth **only** half a penny, can **fall** to the ground without your **Father knowing** it."

[Matthew 10:29]

Construction of the Golden Gate Bridge began. 1933

instant messaging

Samuel Morse demonstrates the telegraph for the first time in public.

In 1838 Samuel Morse unveiled the telegraph, demonstrating for the first time how signals could be transmitted by wire. Using a system of dots and dashes—now known as Morse code—the New York University professor showed how people could communicate over long distances nearly instantaneously. In some ways, you could call this the earliest form of today's instant message—or IM.

The telegraph wasn't, however, an instant success. It took Congress five years to agree to give Morse the money to build an experimental telegraph line from Washington to Baltimore, a distance of 40 miles.

The message, "What hath God wrought?" sent later by Morse code from the old Supreme Court chamber in the United States Capitol to Baltimore, officially opened the completed line on May 24, 1844. Morse allowed Annie Ellsworth, the young daughter of a friend, to choose the words of the message, and she selected this now well-known verse from Numbers 23:23.

Morse's invention revolutionized communication. Being able to communicate rapidly opened up a whole range of possibilities that before had been impossible. Imagine your world without cell phones, emails, or IMs. You would have to walk to your friend's house to tell him anything, or send him or her a letter by good old snail mail. Thankfully, we don't need any type of electronic device to help us communicate with God. All we need to do is speak or think and instantaneously God hears us. Prayer has been, and always will be, our IM to God. Use it today!

also on this day

1412
Joan of Arc was born.

1912
New Mexico became America's 47th state.

1942
The first commercial around-the-world airline flight took place.

The **LORD** is **close** to all who **call** on him, yes, to **all** who call on him **sincerely**.

[Psalm 145:18]

to do ☑
INSTANT MESSAGE GOD TODAY THROUGH PRAYER. TELL HIM WHAT'S ON YOUR MIND.

Jean-Pierre Blanchard, a Frenchman, and his American passenger, Dr. John Jeffries, became the first people to cross the English Channel by air balloon when they traveled from Dover to Calais. The trip was not without its perils. The two had to shed their clothes as the wind died and the balloon's airbag began to cool too quickly over the sea. For Blanchard, who had an avid interest in aviation, this was the beginning of many "firsts" for him. In 1793, Blanchard made the first ever balloon ascent in America, carrying a letter from President George Washington from Pennsylvania to New Jersey (the first airmail!). Blanchard also made first balloon flights in Germany, Belgium, Poland, and the Netherlands.

But that's not his only claim to fame. The story goes that Blanchard also owns the record for the most consecutive number of times saying, "Gosh, I hope we make it," during one particular hazardous trip. Hope certainly had to be a major part of every one of Blanchard's flights. But his hope was based on uncertainty. Blanchard really didn't know whether his balloon would land safely, or if the wind would die, or if the airbag would cool too quickly. He just wanted them to.

That's quite different from the hope we have as Christians. In the Bible *hope* is defined as looking forward to something you expect to happen. We can have that kind of confidence because of God's character. What God has done for us in the past is the guarantee of what he will do in the future. We have *real* hope because it is based in God himself.

O Lord, you alone are my hope. I've trusted you, O LORD, from childhood. [Psalm 71:5]

to do ☑

MAKE AN ACROSTIC OF THE WORD **HOPE**, MAKING A LIST OF WHAT WE HAVE HOPE FOR IN GOD. HERE'S A START: H—HEAVEN. YOU DO THE REST!

also on this day

I'm Not Going to Take It Anymore Day

1789 The first national presidential election was held.

Galileo discovered four of Jupiter's moons. 1610

you gotta have hope

In 1785, a hot air balloon successfully crossed the English Channel for the first time.

Outstanding Young People

In 1981, Elvis Presley Day was declared in Alabama, Florida, Georgia, Illinois, Kansas, North and South Carolina, Pennsylvania, and Virginia.

to do ☑

READ THE STORY OF DANIEL AND HIS THREE FRIENDS IN DANIEL 1–4. WRITE DOWN AS MANY DESCRIPTIONS AS YOU CAN FIND OF WAYS IN WHICH THESE FOUR YOUNG MEN WERE OUTSTANDING.

In all matters requiring **wisdom** and balanced judgment, the king found the **advice** of these **young** men to be **ten** times better than that of **all** the magicians and enchanters in his **entire** kingdom.

[Daniel 1:20]

Elvis Presley was only 19 years old when he began his singing career in 1954. Two years later he was an international sensation. Over the span of his 23-year career, Elvis sold over one billion records worldwide, more than anyone else in record industry history. He received 14 Grammy nominations (won three), 149 of his songs appeared on Billboard's Top 100 Pop Chart in America, and he won the Grammy Lifetime Achievement Award when he was only 36 years old. He starred in 33 successful movies and made history with his television appearances and specials. But of all his many accomplishments, the one Elvis reportedly treasured the most was being named one of the Ten Outstanding Young Men of the Nation in 1970—an award based on outstanding personal achievement, patriotism, humanitarianism, and community service.

Had there been such an award given back in 553 BC, certainly Daniel and his three friends would have been shoo-ins. Consider their accomplishments. The four Israelites were deported to a foreign country where they were forced into the king's service. Alone, serving an arrogant king who worshiped idols, Daniel made up his mind to remain obedient to God despite his circumstances. He refused to accept the king's food and wine, and his friends followed his example. God blessed their obedience and gave these young men special skills and abilities so that they found favor with the king. So it was not surprising that of all the young men in his service, the king chose Daniel and his friends as outstanding young men of the day.

You don't have to become an internationally-known pop star to be an outstanding young man or woman. All it takes is what Daniel and his friends did—trusting and obeying God in whatever you do.

also on this day

National Bubble Bath Day

1958

Bobby Fisher won the U.S. Chess Championship for the first time at the age of 14.

the blind will see

In 1929, the Seeing Eye was incorporated in Nashville, Tennessee, with the purpose of training dogs to guide the blind.

Dorothy Harrison Eustis, an American living in Switzerland, was breeding and training German shepherd dogs for service to the Swiss Army and European police departments. While Mrs. Eustis realized the desirable characteristics of the breed—its alertness, stamina, and responsibility—she didn't know the dog's full potential. On a visit to a school, she saw German shepherds being trained as guides for blinded veterans of World War I. Deeply impressed, she wrote an article about the dogs, entitled "The Seeing Eye."

That article reached a young man from Tennessee, Morris Frank, who wrote, "Thousands of blind like me abhor being dependent on others. . . . Train me and I will bring back my dog and show people here how a blind man can be absolutely on his own." After training Mr. Frank in Switzerland with his dog Buddy, the three returned to the states and opened the Seeing Eye school in Nashville, Tennessee. Since 1929, the school has matched nearly 13,000 specially bred and trained dogs with nearly 6,000 men and women in North America.

During his three-year ministry on earth, Jesus didn't just train the blind—he completely restored their sight (Matthew 9:27-31; 12:22; Mark 10:46-52). But Jesus' mission was far more than just healing the physically blind. Jesus called those who were blind to their sins—the spiritually blind—to recognize their sins and turn to him for forgiveness. How is your spiritual eyesight?

also on this day

1913
Richard M. Nixon was born.

1902
New York State introduced a bill to outlaw public flirting.

1953
The United Nations opened its headquarters in New York City.

Then **Jesus** told him, "I have come to **judge** the world. I have come to **give sight** to the **blind** and to show those who **think** they see that they are **blind**." [John 9:39]

to do ☑

TAKE A LOOK AT 2 PETER 1:3-9. MAKE A LIST OF ALL THE WAYS WE ARE TO GROW IF WE HAVE "SPIRITUAL SIGHT."

Ray Bolger, the son of a housepainter, began his career as a song-and-dance man in Vaudeville back in the early 1930s. He brought his act to Broadway and eventually began making movies in 1936. Over the years he became known for his "rubbery" dancing style, which made him a natural when it came time to cast *The Wizard of Oz*. But Bolger at first refused the role assigned him—the Tin Man. Bolger said the part was too limiting for his talents, and thankfully, the directors agreed. Ray Bolger went on to make movie history as the endearing Scarecrow—a role that he became closely identified with in his lifetime.

As the Scarecrow, Bolger's performance was unforgettable. We laughed at his clumsiness as he fell over himself trying to help Dorothy and the others. Our hearts were won over by his great concern for Dorothy's situation and his cleverness in rescuing her from the Wicked Witch. Yet the Scarecrow believed, "I'm a failure because I haven't got a brain."

Sometimes we can fall into that same trap—believing that we are a failure because we aren't smart enough, or fast enough, or tall enough, or whatever. But the truth is that God has created you and me exactly the way he planned from the very beginning of time. He has given us unique abilities and gifts to use for his work. So think about it. Are you like the Scarecrow, thinking you lack something that you already have? Ask God to help you see the unique gifts he has given to you.

Ray Bolger was born in Dorchester, Massachusetts, in 1904.

I praise you because I am fearfully and wonderfully made; your works are wonderful, I know that full well [Psalm 139:14, NIV]

if only I had

to do ☑

ASK ONE OR TWO PEOPLE WHO KNOW YOU WELL (A PARENT, A TEACHER, OR FRIEND) TO WRITE DOWN THREE THINGS THEY ADMIRE MOST ABOUT YOU. HOW DO THEIR LISTS MATCH WITH WHAT YOU WOULD WRITE?

also on this day

Volunteer Fireman's Day

1928 Children's author Maurice Sendak was born.

The first underground passenger railway system opened in London.

UNDERGROUND

Donald Howard Rogers piloted the first passenger jet on a trip from Chicago to New York.

1863

1951

just say thanks

Today is International Thank-You Day!

How are you at telling others thank you? Let's take a quick thankfulness quiz. You just received lots of Christmas presents. Your thank-you notes are . . .

❑ In the mail.
❑ In the thought-process stage.
❑ What thank-you notes?

You've been sick and your friend brought you some schoolwork. You say . . .

❑ Thanks! I didn't want to fall too far behind in my work.
❑ Can you stay and explain it to me?
❑ What did you do that for?

You have a loving family, a warm house to live in, clothes, and food to eat. You . . .

❑ Thank God each day.
❑ Think of all the things that you don't have.
❑ Think, "Hey, I deserve this!"

Expressing thanks is not always our first response. Remember the 10 lepers? Check out the Bible account in Luke 17:12-19. Jesus healed 10 men who had leprosy, but only 1 returned to say thank you!

God is pleased when we say thanks and will teach us more about himself when we come to him with grateful hearts. Saying thank you to God and to others should be a part of our daily routine, like brushing our teeth or making our beds. Make it your habit today.

to do ☑

WHO DO YOU NEED TO THANK? TELL THAT PERSON TODAY—BY EMAIL, PHONE, OR HANDWRITTEN NOTE! YOU'LL BE GLAD YOU DID.

also on this day

1755
✵ Alexander Hamilton was born.

1770
✵ The first shipment of rhubarb was sent to the United States from London.

No matter **what** happens, **always** be **thankful**, for this is **God's will** for **you** who belong to **Christ Jesus**.

[1 Thessalonians 5:18]

Hattie Caraway became the first woman elected to the U.S. Senate in 1932.

You Da Woman!

Born in Tennessee, Hattie Wyatt attended Dickson Normal College, where she met and married fellow student Thaddeus Horatius Caraway. The couple soon moved to Arkansas. While her husband practiced law, Hattie cared for the family farm and the children. Thaddeus was elected to Congress in 1912, but Hattie couldn't vote for him until women won the right to vote in 1920. Thaddeus was elected to the Senate but died unexpectedly during his term in 1932. The Arkansas governor appointed Hattie to her husband's seat, which was confirmed in a special election held on January 12, 1932, making her the first elected woman senator.

Although Hattie maintained a "housewife" image in the Senate and made no speeches on the floor—earning her the nickname "Silent Hattie"—she learned much from her husband's years of public service. Hattie took her legislator's responsibilities seriously and built a reputation for integrity.

Centuries before Hattie Caraway lived, God had appointed a woman to represent him before the people. Deborah was the fourth and only female judge that God had appointed. All of Israel came under her jurisdiction, and from under a palm tree, she dispensed wisdom and justice to the people. In addition, Deborah was a prophetess, an advocate for her people, and a warrior who helped her people successfully defeat a much stronger enemy. Deborah, like Hattie, took her responsibilities seriously and ruled with integrity.

When you have an opportunity to lead others, you can learn from both Hattie and Deborah. As they did, take your responsibilities seriously and exercise your leadership with integrity and courage.

to do ☑

THINK OF A WOMAN WHOM YOU ADMIRE THE MOST (IT CAN EVEN BE YOUR MOM). WRITE DOWN ALL THE QUALITIES THAT YOU ADMIRE THE MOST IN THAT PERSON.

The **godly** walk with **integrity**; **blessed** are **their** children after them.
[Proverbs 20:7]

also on this day

National Pharmacist Day

·1915 Congress established the Rocky Mountain National Park.

The first public museum in America was established in Charleston, South Carolina. 1773

Batman debuted on television. 1966

Who's to blame?

Today is Blame Someone Else Day.

Do we really need a day devoted to blaming someone else? People have been blaming others since the very beginning of time. Remember Adam and Eve? When God confronted Adam in the garden and asked him if he had eaten fruit from the tree God had forbidden, what did Adam do? He blamed Eve. Then Eve blamed the serpent (check it out in Genesis 3:1-13). And the blame game continued on long after that. How about Aaron's response when Moses asked why he had helped the people make a golden calf to worship? Here's Aaron's story: "They said to me, 'Make us some gods to lead us, for something has happened to this man Moses, who led us out of Egypt.' So I told them, 'Bring me your gold earrings.' When they brought them to me, I threw them into the fire—and out came this calf" (Exodus 32:23, 24).

Have you ever blamed someone? For example, if you did poorly on a test, would you say, "I couldn't study because my brother's music was playing too loud," or "I didn't study enough"?

Maybe a better approach to "Blame Someone Else Day" is to step up and take responsibility for our actions. In fact, the Bible makes it very clear that we will be judged according to our *own* words and actions—not those of someone else. Jesus said, "The words you say now reflect your fate then; either you will be justified by them or you will be condemned" (Matthew 12:37).

also on this day

1845

Anthony Faas of Philadelphia patented the accordion.

1928

Ernst F. W. Alexanderson gave the first public demonstration of television.

1930

The first Mickey Mouse comic strip was published.

to do ☑

WHEN WAS THE LAST TIME YOU BLAMED SOMEONE ELSE FOR SOMETHING YOU DID? WRITE THAT PERSON A NOTE OR TELL HIM THAT YOU TAKE RESPONSIBILITY FOR WHAT YOU DID. THEN SEE WHAT KIND OF RESPONSE YOU GET.

For **we** are each **responsible** for our **own** conduct.

[Galatians 6:5]

living to serve

Albert Schweitzer was born in 1875.

Albert Schweitzer was born in a small town in Germany. During his lifetime, he was known as a philosopher, a physician, and a humanitarian. At age 21, Schweitzer decided to dedicate the first part of his life to studying the arts, sciences, music, and theology. During that time, he became a respected writer on theology, an accomplished organist, and an authority on the life of Johann Sebastian Bach. In 1905, Albert Schweitzer began to prepare for his other life—a life dedicated to serving others.

Schweitzer studied medicine, earned his degree in 1913, and then left for west Africa to establish a missionary hospital in Gabon. Except for a few short interruptions, Schweitzer spent his remaining 50 years in Africa fighting leprosy and sleeping sickness. For his work and dedication, Dr. Schweitzer won the Nobel Peace Prize in 1952. He later used the $33,000 prize to expand his missionary hospital and to build a leper colony.

But perhaps his most notable accomplishment was being called the greatest Christian of his time. Dr. Schweitzer served humanity through thought and action, what he called a "reverence for life." In a speech given in 1935, Dr. Schweitzer advised students, "Those will be happy who are looking for, and are finding, how they can serve."

Jesus said that serving others is the highest calling anyone can answer. He told his disciples that he had come not to be served but to give his very life in serving others. Should his followers do no less? Dr. Schweitzer didn't think so.

to do ☑

WRITE DOWN THREE WAYS YOU CAN SERVE OTHERS TODAY.

"For even **I**, the **Son of Man**, came here not to **be served** but **to serve** others, and to give **my** life as a ransom for **many**."

[Matthew 20:28]

also on this day

1784

The United States ratified a peace treaty with England, ending the Revolutionary War.

NBC's *Today* show premiered.

1952

It's National Clean Off Your Desk Day

Our Friend, the Enemy

Martin Luther King Jr. was born on this day in 1929.

M artin Luther King Jr. was a peacemaker. He believed that as Christians we are called to love our enemies. During his lifelong mission to gain civil rights for African Americans, Dr. King advocated nonviolent and peaceful actions as a way of change. To this end, Dr. King advocated sit-ins, boycotts, and other nonviolent strategies to end segregation laws that discriminated against African Americans. For his efforts, Dr. King was named *Time* Magazine's Man of the Year in 1963, and he received the Nobel Peace Prize in 1964.

Dr. King was well aware that this kind of love was difficult—impossible, even, if a person depended on his own efforts. Dr. King knew that love for those who hate you can come from only one source—Jesus. Dr. King called it "the love of God working in the lives of men. And when you rise to love on this level, you begin to love men, not because they are likeable, but because God loves them. You look at every man, and you love him because you know God loves him. And he might be the worst person you've ever seen."

That, according to Dr. King, is what Jesus was talking about when he told us to love our enemies. For when we love like that, Dr. King said, that love has the power to change. He wrote, "We must discover the power of love, the power, the redemptive power of love. And when we discover that we will be able to make of this old world a new world. We will be able to make men better. Love is the only way."

to do ☑

THINK OF SOMEONE YOU CONSIDER AN ENEMY. DO SOMETHING NICE FOR THAT PERSON TODAY—GIVE HER A COMPLIMENT, SAVE HIM A SEAT ON THE BUS, OR DO HIM A FAVOR. AND IN OBEDIENCE TO JESUS, PRAY FOR THAT ENEMY.

also on this day

1777 The people of New Connecticut (now the state of Vermont) declared their independence from England.

1892 Rules for a new game, involving attaching peach baskets to a suspended board, were first published in Springfield, Massachusetts. That game is now known as basketball.

•1967 The first National Football League Super Bowl was played. The Green Bay Packers defeated the Kansas City Chiefs, 35–10.

"But **I** say, **love** your enemies! **Pray** for those who persecute you!"

[Matthew 5:44]

Happy Nothing Day!

Seems like a strange idea for a holiday, doesn't it? How exactly do you celebrate nothing? Then again, consider the possibilities. For example, today you are in keeping with the spirit of the holiday if you spend it doing absolutely nothing! No presents, no festivities, no decorations, no big meal. Nothing.

Actually, there was a man in Bible times who was really big into nothing. Solomon was one of the wisest, richest, and most powerful kings around. He had everything—money, gold, treasures, cattle, palaces. He did everything— led a nation, built cities and roads, constructed the temple for God. But when it came right down to it, Solomon decided that it all meant nothing. It was all meaningless, futile, insignificant, and unimportant. He wrote about his views of life in the book Ecclesiastes. Here are just a few of King Solomon's statements: "But as I looked at everything I had worked so hard to accomplish, it was all so meaningless. It was like chasing the wind. There was nothing really worthwhile anywhere," (2:11) and, "As people come into this world, so they depart. All their hard work is for nothing. They have been working for the wind, and everything will be swept away" (5:16). Not exactly a cheery guy!

By the end of the book, however, Solomon comes to an important conclusion. The only way to find true meaning and satisfaction in this world is through God. Nothing else can fill our lives like knowing, worshiping, and obeying the Lord.

So maybe a better way to celebrate Nothing Day is to spend some time with God and thank him for all the "something" that he has given to you.

Today is National Nothing Day.

Here is my final conclusion: Fear God and obey his commands, for this is the duty of every person. [Ecclesiastes 12:13]

it's a nothing ya'!

8203924885840398

to do ☑

MAKE A LIST OF ALL THE REASONS YOU HAVE TO WORSHIP GOD TODAY.

also on this day

1547 — **Ivan the Terrible was crowned Czar of Russia.**

The first five-player college basketball game was played at Iowa City, Iowa. 1896

early to bed, early to rise

Ben Franklin was born on this day in 1706.

Inventor, writer, diplomat, businessman, musician, scientist, humorist, civic leader, international celebrity, genius—all these titles can be used to describe one of the most remarkable people of American history, Ben Franklin. Born into the family of a Boston candle maker, Benjamin Franklin not only helped found a new nation, but he also helped define the American character.

Franklin was an inventor, credited with inventions such as the lightning rod, the Franklin stove, and bifocals. He was also an international statesman, crossing the Atlantic eight times to help negotiate the treaties that led to the formation of the United States.

Franklin was a publisher and a writer as well. His most famous publication was *Poor Richard's Almanac*, which Franklin first published in 1732 under the pseudonym Richard Saunders. The 26 editions of *Poor Richard's Almanac* were filled with calendar, weather, and astronomical information. But what Franklin's almanac was most well-known for was his collection of humorous sayings and advice, such as "Fish and visitors smell after three days"; "Necessity never made a good bargain"; and "Early to bed and early to rise, makes a man healthy, wealthy, and wise."

Of course, Franklin was not the first to write a collection of witty sayings. Solomon, the wisest man to ever live, passed on his wisdom in the book of Proverbs. Each short, concise statement conveyed a truth for practical living. But the main theme of Solomon's proverbs was that the source of all *true* wisdom was God. Centuries before Ben Franklin ever walked the earth, Solomon wrote, "Fear of the Lord is the beginning of knowledge."

Those are some wise words worth remembering!

to do ☑

READ PROVERBS 2. WRITE DOWN A LIST OF ALL THE BENEFITS OF WISDOM THAT YOU FIND THERE.

also on this day

James Madison Randolph, grandson of President Thomas Jefferson, was the first child born in the White House. 1806

1962 **Jim Carrey was born.**

Fear of the **LORD** is the beginning of **knowledge**. Only **fools** despise **wisdom** and **discipline**. [Proverbs 1:7]

going solo

In 1997, Norwegian Borge Ousland completed the first solo crossing of Antarctica via the South Pole.

Since 1915 adventurers, explorers, and polar travelers have dreamed about crossing Antarctica alone. Many tried, and just as many failed. Norwegian adventurer Børge Ousland had tried once in 1995 and had failed. Undeterred, Ousland returned to Antarctica in 1996. He was joined by polar travelers from four other nations. But in 1997, Ousland stood alone as the only man to successfully travel the 1,675 miles across the South Pole. Four years later, Ousland made a complete North Pole crossing, becoming the first man to cross both poles completely solo.

In explaining why he crossed both poles alone, Ousland said, "It must be the hard, strong nature, and the back to basic feeling I get when I am out there. When you do unsupported expeditions to the poles, there is no way to cheat; it is your own ability, strength, and preparations that will decide if you make it or not."

For Ousland, the hardest aspect of either trek was overcoming the mental obstacle—knowing that he was completely alone. "I had to break a lot of mental borders before I even could make the decisions to start. No one had even tried it before, and not many believed I would make it," he recalled.

Doing anything solo is much harder than having someone by your side. King David knew that firsthand. Many times in his life, David felt completely alone and abandoned. Many of his psalms reflected his feelings of loneliness. In Psalm 25, David wrote, "Turn to me and have mercy on me, for I am alone and in deep distress" (v. 16). But during his deepest times of distress, David remembered who was walking beside him, ready to comfort him at a moment's notice.

Read the familiar verses of David's most famous psalm. These are good words to remember when you are going solo.

Even when I walk **through** the dark valley of **death**, I will **not** be **afraid**, for **you** are close beside me. Your **rod** and your **staff protect** and **comfort** me.

[Psalm 23:4]

also on this day

Today is Winnie the Pooh Day (author A.A. Milne was born in 1882).

1896
The X-ray machine was exhibited for the first time. It cost the public 25 cents to see the machine.

1943
U.S. bakers stopped selling sliced bread. Only whole loaves were sold until the end of World War II.

to do ☑

READ PSALM 23 ALOUD. MEMORIZE IT AND RECITE IT TO SOMEONE IN YOUR HOME.

The world's greatest bicycle race was started as a way to increase the circulation of a French sports newspaper. The newspaper's cycling reporter suggested a six-day race over roads and towns rather than on a track. On January 19, 1903, it was announced that a month-long bike race would be held from Paris to Lyon to Marseille to Toulouse to Bordeaux to Nantes to Paris—and the Tour de France was born.

The first race attracted 60 riders and included six stages covering approximately 2,388 kilometers (about 1,400 miles). The most recent Tour de France included a prerace prologue, 20 stages, and covered 3,390 kilometers. The race, which runs for 22 days with only 2 days of rest, is a test of human spirit as much as physical prowess. As six-time winner Lance Armstrong explained, "I believe that the man who works the hardest is the man who deserves to win." Perseverance—working hard day after day in the rain, the heat, or up in the mountains—is the key to winning what some consider the greatest sporting event in the world.

That same characteristic is also needed living out your faith each day. In fact, the apostle Paul compared living as a Christian to a race. In 1 Corinthians 9:24 Paul writes, "Remember that in a race everyone runs, but only one person gets the prize. You also must run in such a way that you will win."What is the prize? Paul calls it the "eternal prize" of Heaven.

The persevering Christian prays consistently, gives thanks consistently, and keeps his or her focus on Jesus—the lead runner and model finisher of the race.

How's your race coming along?

"And let us run with endurance the race that God has set before us. We do this by keeping our eyes on Jesus, on whom our faith depends from start to finish." [Hebrews 12:1, 2]

In 1903, a French sports newspaper announced the inception of the Tour de France.

to do ☑

REFLECT ON THE FAITH RACE YOU ARE RUNNING. ASSESS HOW YOU ARE DOING. WHAT DO YOU NEED TO IMPROVE? WHERE DO YOU EXCEL?

also on this day

Today is National Popcorn Day.

Today is National Penguin Awareness Day.

General Robert E. Lee was born today. 1807

the great race

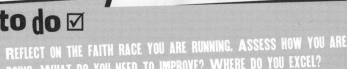

Wisdom of the Aged

At 69, Ronald Reagan was the oldest person to become U.S. President.

to do ☑

WRITE A LETTER TO AN OLDER PERSON THAT YOU KNOW—A GRANDPARENT, TEACHER, PASTOR, OR EVEN YOUR PARENT. TELL THIS PERSON THE MANY WAYS HE HAS HELPED YOU AND THE MANY REASONS FOR YOUR RESPECT.

When Ronald Reagan came to the White House in 1981 for the first of his two terms as president, he was well past the age when most people retire. When he left the White House in 1989 at age 77, President Reagan was eight years older than the next-oldest president, Dwight D. Eisenhower, was when he left office in 1961.

The president was often the first to joke about his age. At one point, he reportedly said, "Thomas Jefferson once said, 'We should never judge a president by his age, only by his works.' And ever since he told me that, I stopped worrying." But perhaps his most well-known quip about his age came during a debate with Democratic presidential candidate Walter Mondale. The president, who was some 17 years older than his opponent, asserted, "I will not make age an issue of this campaign. I am not going to exploit, for political purposes, my opponent's youth and inexperience."

We live in a society that values youthfulness. Thousands of dollars are spent each year on ways to preserve youth—plastic surgery, diet and exercise plans, laser eye surgery, hair transplants. In some cultures, however, age is a sign of wisdom and authority. Elders are to be respected and cared for. That's how the Bible says we as Christians should act. Where elders are respected, long life is a blessing, not a joke.

In Leviticus 19:32, God tells us to "Show your fear of God by standing up in the presence of elderly people and showing respect for the aged." In fact Paul wrote, "And this is the promise: If you honor your father and mother, 'you will live a long life, full of blessing'" (Ephesians 6:3).

Good advice to follow, don't you think?

Wisdom belongs to the **aged**, and **under-standing** to those who have lived **many** years.

[Job 12:12]

also on this day

1885 The roller coaster was patented by L.A. Thompson.

The album "Meet the Beatles" was released in the U.S., marking the start of the Beatles's English invasion. **1964**

1937 Franklin Delano Roosevelt became the first president to be inaugurated on January 20. The 20th Amendment of the Constitution officially set the date for the swearing in of the president and vice president.

standing in the gap

Thomas Jonathan Jackson was born on this day in 1824.

Next to Robert E. Lee, Thomas J. Jackson was probably one of the most respected generals in the Confederate Army. A graduate of West Point, Jackson first earned recognition as a war hero in the Mexican War. His experience as a military instructor at the Virginia Military Institute, coupled with his war experience, earned him the rank of brigadier general at the first major battle of the Civil War near Manassas, Virginia. But it was Jackson's conduct during that battle for which he earned his nickname "Stonewall." During the battle when lines were beginning to break, General Bernard E. Bee proclaimed, "There is Jackson standing like a stone wall." In that moment a legend was born, as Jackson became known for his fierce tenacity and steadfastness in the heat of the battle.

Through the prophet Ezekiel, God spoke about this same type of faithfulness. Despairing of Israel's lack of faith, God was searching for men and women who could be "stone walls" against evil. "I looked for someone who might rebuild the wall of righteousness that guards the land. I searched for someone to stand in the gap in the wall," the Lord said.

What does it mean to stand in the gap? For us, it means a willingness to stand up for what we know is right, even when we may be the only ones. It means befriending the kid at school who has no friends. It means sticking up for the one who is being bullied and mocked. It means making a difference for God by living according to his truth and Word.

How about you? Are you willing to stand in the gap?

> "I looked for **someone** who might **rebuild** the wall of righteousness that **guards** the land. I **searched** for someone to **stand** in the gap in the wall so I wouldn't have to **destroy** the land, but I found **no** one." [Ezekiel 22:30]

also on this day

Today is Squirrel Appreciation Day.

1799

Edward Jenner introduced the smallpox vaccine.

1846

The first issue of the *Daily News*, edited by Charles Dickens, was published.

to do ☑

HOW CAN YOU MAKE A DIFFERENCE FOR GOD TODAY? WRITE DOWN THREE WAYS YOU CAN "STAND IN THE GAP" AT SCHOOL, AT HOME, AND IN YOUR NEIGHBORHOOD.

the end of an era

Queen Victoria of England died on this day in 1901 after reigning for nearly 64 years. Edward VII, her son, succeeded her.

Imagine living in a country in which only one ruler had ever been in power. When Queen Victoria died at age 82, it marked the end of an era in which most of her British subjects had known no other king or queen. Her reign, which spanned more than half a century, was the longest in British history.

Having one ruler who governs you for the majority of your life is a strange concept for most of us. We are used to changes in those who govern us and make the laws. We are familiar with presidents and governors and mayors, not kings or queens or princes.

Yet, do you realize you are part of a kingdom that will never end and you are under the power of a king who will always rule? As a Christian, you are part of God's kingdom and Jesus is your king who will reign forever and forever.

What exactly is God's kingdom? The Bible tells us. First, the kingdom of God is not a place. Jesus told his followers, "The Kingdom of God isn't ushered in with visible signs. You won't be able to say, 'Here it is!' or 'It's over there!' For the Kingdom of God is among you" (Luke 17:20, 21). The kingdom of God was not the powerful government that the people of Israel were looking for. No, the kingdom of God is the rule of God in his people's hearts. Wherever God's people are living and obeying his Word, then that's where the kingdom of God exists. Wherever you go and whenever you share the good news of Jesus, you are spreading God's kingdom.

to do ☑

BE A KINGDOM BUILDER TODAY. TELL ONE PERSON WHO LIVES IN YOUR HOUSE OR GOES TO YOUR SCHOOL ABOUT YOUR KING.

also on this day

1879 James Shields began a term as a U.S. Senator from Missouri. He had previously served in Illinois and Minnesota—making him the first Senator to serve in three different states.

Apple introduced the Macintosh computer. It was the first computer to use point-and-click technology. 1984

For the Kingdom of God is not a matter of what we eat or drink, but of living a life of goodness and peace and joy in the Holy Spirit. [Romans 14:17]

the risk-taker

John Hancock, U.S. statesman, patriot, and president of the Continental Congress, was born on this day.

You could never accuse John Hancock of playing it safe. This popular and well-known patriot not only was the first to sign the Declaration of Independence, but he did it with a flourish that none could miss. When it came time to sign the Declaration of Independence, which was an act of treason against England, Hancock remarked, "I'll sign it in letters bold enough so the King of England can see it without his spectacles on!"

John Hancock was definitely the right man at the right time. At a time when bold leaders were needed, Hancock willingly stepped forward and risked his life for the cause of independence.

Thousands of years earlier, a young Jewish girl had been given a similar opportunity to risk her life for a greater cause. Esther had been chosen as the new queen of Persia. But even in that role, she did not have free access to the king. No one in all of Persia could approach the king without an invitation—or it meant certain death. So when Esther's cousin informed her of a plot to kill all the Jews in Persia and begged her to ask the king for mercy, Esther's first response was "I can't." But when her cousin pointed out that she was the right person at the right time and place to do so, Esther agreed. Because of her willingness to take a risk, the Jewish people were saved. She, like John Hancock and others, made a difference.

It may not be evident to you, but perhaps God has put you in a special place—at school, in your neighborhood, maybe even at home—where you can make a difference if are willing to take the risk.

to do ☑

THINK ABOUT THIS: WHAT IS THE GREATEST RISK YOU HAVE TAKEN? ASK A PARENT OR AN ADULT FRIEND ABOUT THE GREATEST RISK SHE HAS TAKEN.

also on this day

1910
* **It is National School Nurse Day.**

1845 English-born Elizabeth Blackwell became the first woman in America to receive a medical degree.

The lowest temperature ever recorded in the U.S. was reported on this day in Prospect Creek Camp, Alaska—minus 80 degrees Fahrenheit! *1971*

"If you keep quiet at a time like this, deliverance for the Jews will arise from some other place, but you and your relatives will die. What's more, who can say but that you have been elevated to the palace for just such a time as this?" [Esther 4:14]

Real Treasure

In 1848, gold was discovered in California.

J ohn Sutter was a Swiss immigrant who had come to California in 1839 with dreams, not of finding gold, but of building his own private empire. By the mid-1840s, Sutter had built a fort, had 12,000 head of cattle, and employed hundreds of workers. But it was an accidental discovery while building a sawmill that completely changed Sutter's life—and the nation's history.

While constructing the sawmill, which Sutter intended to provide lumber for his growing ranch, a glint of something caught a worker's eye. Gold! At first, Sutter and his men tried to keep the discovery a secret. But by the winter of 1848, whispers of a gold strike had drifted eastward across the country. At first, few people believed the rumors. But when President James Polk told the nation that the reports were true, the gold rush was on!

Thousands of men and women headed to California to make their fortune. Few, however, realized their dream of striking it rich.

The lure of treasure and quick wealth has always been a temptation. In fact, Jesus warned his followers about spending all their time and effort going after earthly treasure. That type of treasure, Jesus said, would eventually be destroyed or stolen. It wasn't the type of treasure that would last.

Instead, Jesus tells his followers (like us!) to store our treasures in Heaven, where it will be protected forever. So how do you store treasures in Heaven? By using all your resources—money, time, and abilities—for God's work. In fact, any time we obey God and do what he wants, we are storing up treasures in Heaven!

How much heavenly treasure do you have saved?

to do ☑

MAKE A LIST OF YOUR RESOURCES. THINK OF ONE WAY THAT YOU CAN USE EACH OF THOSE RESOURCES TO STORE UP TREASURES IN HEAVEN.

"Don't store up treasures here on earth, where they can be eaten by moths and get rusty, and where thieves break in and steal. Store your treasures in heaven, where they will never become moth-eaten or rusty and where they will be safe from thieves." [Matthew 6:19, 20]

also on this day

1908 The first Boy Scout troop was started in England.

1922 Christian K. Nelson patented the ice-cream treat known as the Eskimo Pie®.

•1985 Penny Harrington became the first woman police chief of a major U.S. city (Portland, OR).

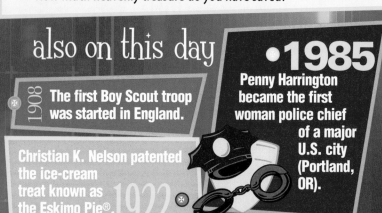

opposites!

Today is Opposite Day.

Think of the possibilities! You run downstairs in the morning and greet your family, "Good night! I can't wait to go to school. Can we have some yummy brussels sprouts for dinner? I'm going to do all my homework as soon as I get home. No TV for me tonight!" Then as soon as you pick up your mom and dad off the floor, you can gleefully announce, "Happy Opposite Day!"

The idea behind Opposite Day—where everything you say is the reverse of what you mean—is meant to be fun. But Jesus was totally serious about his followers being the exact opposite of what the world expects. For example, in his teaching that we often call the Beatitudes, Jesus said that God blesses the needy, those who mourn, who are persecuted, and who are gentle and lowly (Matthew 5:3-12). That's not what the world thinks. Our world says that people who are happy, who have a lot of stuff, who are powerful, and who are protected are the ones who are blessed.

Jesus wanted his followers to know that living for God means being different from everyone else. If we follow Jesus, then what we say and how we act will be different from the world. We will give to others instead of taking from them, help those who don't deserve our help, and love those who hate us. That's not easy to do. But in giving up our rights in order to serve others, we will receive *everything* that God has in store for us.

Compared to the world, every day is Opposite Day when you live for Jesus.

"And so it is, that **many** who are **first now** will be **last then**; and those who are **last now** will be **first then**."

[Matthew 20:16]

also on this day

1858

Mendelssohn's "Wedding March" was publicly played for the first time at the wedding of Britain's Princess Victoria.

1924

The first Winter Olympics was held in Chamonix, France.

1961

President John F. Kennedy presented the first live presidential news conference from Washington, D. C.

to do ☑

INSTEAD OF BEING THE FIRST IN LINE OR THE FIRST TO GRAB DESSERT, DO THE OPPOSITE TODAY AND BE LAST!

most valuable

A diamond weighing 114 pounds was discovered near Pretoria, South Africa, in 1905.

During a routine inspection at the Premier Diamond Mine in South Africa, a 3,106-carat diamond was discovered. Named the Cullinan Diamond, it weighed 114 pounds and was the largest diamond crystal ever found.

After examining the diamond for six months, Joseph Asscher prepared to cut the enormous stone into smaller pieces. Fearful of how his heart might react to a blunder, Asscher had a doctor stand by as he hit the first critical blow. After nearly shattering the diamond on his initial attempt, Asscher managed to divide the diamond with his second blow—and then promptly fainted. The crystal was cut into 106 polished diamonds, valued at tens of millions of dollars.

The largest of the stones is the Star of Africa, which at 530.2 carats is the largest cut diamond in the world. The gem was presented to Britain's King Edward VII and can be seen today in the Tower of London with the other crown jewels.

Imagine the excitement of discovering such a huge diamond! But do you know that the Bible tells us about something that is even more valuable than the most precious of gems? It's wise speech!

Speech that is wise reflects God's love and concern for others. It is sincere and honest. It contains words that are meant to encourage and comfort. A person who uses wise speech thinks about what he is going to say before speaking.

If you have ever been the recipient of cruel and thoughtless speech, you know how harmful unwise words can be. But if the people in your life speak to you with words that are caring and encouraging, you know the real value of wise speech!

to do ☑

WHEN WAS THE LAST TIME YOU USED UNWISE WORDS? CONSIDER WHAT YOU CAN SAY NOW TO THAT PERSON TO CORRECT THE SITUATION.

Wise speech is **rarer** and **more valuable** than gold and rubies. [Proverbs 20:15]

also on this day

1837
Michigan became America's 26th state.

1788
The first European settlers landed in Australia. This day is celebrated as Australia Day.

George F. Green patented the electric dental drill for sawing, filing, and polishing teeth.
1875

Lighting the Way

In 1880, Thomas Edison patented the electric incandescent lamp.

to do ☑

THINK OF A BIBLE VERSE THAT HAS HELPED "LIGHT" YOUR PATH. WRITE IT DOWN AND CARRY IT WITH YOU TODAY.

Thomas Edison, considered one of America's greatest inventors, has been credited with ushering in the electrical age with the refinement and development of the electric incandescent lamp—otherwise known as the lightbulb. Although people had been using electric arc lights, which produced light by creating an arc of electricity between wires, the blinding glare that these arc lights gave off made them unsuitable for use in the home. Edison came up with the idea of producing light by heating a wire (or filament) until it glowed brightly. While others had come up with a similar concept, Edison patented the first *practical* electric lightbulb, one that used only a small current and that lasted a long time before it burned out.

Incandescent lighting remains the primary way that we light our homes today. Take a walk through your home and count all the lightbulbs. You may be amazed to discover how dependent we are on this one single invention.

But just as we depend on Edison's incandescent lamp to light the way in our homes, we need to depend upon another type of lamp to light our paths for living. Psalm 119:105 says that God's Word is a "lamp for my feet and a light for my path." Just as you turn on the light before you enter a darkened room, so you turn to God's Word, the Bible, to help you see the right way to live.

Whenever you are confused or wondering about what you should do, read God's Word to help guide you and light your way.

Your **word** is a **lamp** for my **feet** and a **light** for my **path**.

[Psalm 119:105]

also on this day

1973 **The Vietnam Peace Agreement was signed.**

1926

John Baird, a Scottish inventor, demonstrated a pictorial transmission machine called television.

Composer Wolfgang Amadeus Mozart was born. 1756

The National Geographic Society was founded in Washington, D. C. 1888

the boy king

In 1547, 9-year-old Edward VI became king of England after his father, Henry VIII, died.

King Edward VI was a child when his father Henry VIII died. Expectations were high when Edward VI was crowned. It was hoped that the new king would enjoy a long and successful reign, resolving the religious problems of the day. But Edward died of tuberculosis only a few years after taking the throne, long before any of these expectations could be met. In fact, Edward never ruled the country himself. His uncle, the Duke of Somerset, governed as regent because Edward was so young.

Maybe you are 9 years old or know someone who is nine. Imagine being the ruler of an entire country! Imagine your friends and family calling you "King" or "Queen." A pretty scary thought, isn't it? But this wasn't the first time that a young person was named king. In Bible times, Joash was only 7 years old when he became king. Unlike the unfortunate Edward, Joash ruled for 40 years. At first, Joash got off to a good start. He had a wise advisor, Jehoiada, who helped him to follow God's laws. But when Jehoiada died, Joash began listening to the wrong advice. Instead of obeying and relying on God's Word, Joash led his people into evil. Eventually, his own officials killed him.

Both Edward and Joash depended on those around them for good advice. We need to do the same. But eventually we need to begin making our own decisions. As a youngster, Joash knew about God because of his wise helper, Jehoiada. But Joash needed his own relationship with God. We do too. It's OK to learn from our parents and our Sunday-school teachers about God, but at some point we need to make our own decision about following God.

Have you?

to do ☑

MAKE A TIME LINE OF YOUR PERSONAL HISTORY. START WITH THE DAY YOU WERE BORN. MARK OTHER IMPORTANT EVENTS IN YOUR LIFE. PUT STARS ON EVENTS THAT WERE SIGNIFICANT TO YOUR SPIRITUAL GROWTH, SUCH AS THE DAY YOU WERE BAPTIZED AND THE DAY YOU FIRST SHARED YOUR FAITH WITH A FRIEND.

also on this day

1878
The first telephone switchboard was installed in New Haven, Connecticut.

National Kazoo Day

"Choose to love the LORD your God and to obey him and commit yourself to him, for he is your life." [Deuteronomy 30:20]

it's a puzzle to me!

This is National Puzzle Day.

Celebrate National Puzzle Day and have fun doing this word search. Look for the following names of famous Bible characters in the puzzle below. Remember that words can be horizontal, vertical, diagonal, backwards or upside down! Have fun!

```
D Y S W N E K U L M P A B I G A I L
P E T E R T Z N L N O M O L O S R E
V E B A T N I J M O S E S Y R G O K
C A I O P T L H A I W I V J Y R A M
L H T U R S E L R O C T R U E M F U
A M O S I A K E T Y R A M D W S B G
R F S Y U L H I H K M U H E C M U H
P Y R E M A K N A W A F H W O M N S
A B H J R Y A A E N R T H P O F E L
U G H A Y S U D O D K U K K A B A H
L M S M L L H A E D K M A E R N G T
H U V E O E S T H E R I P J O H N E
D H N S A V O E I L P I J T Y N O B
K A D S H E J R R W M L E H C A R A
A N R A Y H I N T O C P W I O T Y Z
V O N D V A E R A H A B T Y S O N I
E O S S V I X N C A M E N R O E U L
J O M N A D D E R W E H T T A M S E
```

ESTHER	MARTHA	LUKE
DEBORAH	NAOMI	JESUS
SARAH	MARK	JOHN
RUTH	HABAKKUK	JAMES
ELIZABETH	JONAH	MATTHEW
ABIGAIL	PAUL	AMOS
RAHAB	PETER	NAHUM
MARY	JUDE	MICAH
EVE	MOSES	DANIEL
RACHEL	DAVID	SOLOMON
		JOSHUA

also on this day

1843
William McKinley, 25th President of the United States, was born in Niles, Ohio.

1756
R. Taylor patented the ice-cream cone rolling machine.

1861
Kansas became America's 34th state.

1900
The American Baseball League was organized in Philadelphia. It consisted of eight teams.

"Can you **solve** the **mysteries** of **God**? Can you **discover everything** there is to know about the **Almighty**?" [Job 11:7]

the real lifesaver!

In 1790, the first official lifeboat was tested at sea.

The birthplace of the lifeboat was at the River Tyne in northeast England. The mouth of the river, which opened onto the North Sea, was extremely dangerous. As one sailor described it, the entrance into the harbor was "very narrow, with dangerous rocks on one side and a steep sandbank on the other, with a hard shoal bar across, where the waves of the sea frequently run very high." In other words, it took a very skilled seaman to safely navigate a sailing ship into the harbor.

After one particularly devastating shipwreck, where more than half of the crew lost their lives as the townspeople watched helplessly on the shore, a local businessman decided something had to be done. Nicolas Fairles organized the institution for the "Preservation of Life from Shipwreck" and offered a reward for anyone who could design a boat that could rescue sailors in the worst conditions at sea. Henry Greathead took the challenge, and it was his design that became the model for the lifeboat. Greathead's boat, called the *Original*, was first tested in 1790 on the open sea, and it became a true lifesaver.

Today we have many devices designed to save lives—seatbelts, safety caps on medications, smoke detectors, fire extinguishers. But the greatest lifesaver is neither a boat, nor a restraining device, nor anything we can hold or see. It is a name—Jesus—the only name that anyone can call upon and be saved forever. The Bible tells us that without Jesus we are lost, dead in our sins. Jesus alone, through his sacrifice on the cross, offers us complete forgiveness for all our wrongdoings and saves us for all eternity.

Now that's a real lifesaver!

also on this day

1487
Bell chimes were invented.

1798
The first brawl in the U.S. House of Representatives took place. Congressmen Matthew Lyon and Roger Griswold fought on the House floor.

1847
The town of Yerba Buena was renamed San Francisco.

"There is **salvation** in **no one** else! There is **no** other **name** in all of heaven for people to call on to **save** them."

[Acts 4:12]

to do ☑

BUY A PACK OF LIFESAVERS® CANDY. HAND THEM OUT TO YOUR FRIENDS AND TELL THEM ABOUT THE REAL LIFESAVER, JESUS!

A year after the Russians had launched Sputnik, the world's first satellite, into space, the United States countered with its own earth-orbiting satellite. Weighing only 31 pounds, the Explorer I satellite was launched into space aboard a Jupiter-C rocket. The entire country waited for 90 long seconds to hear the fate of the satellite. Finally, a tracking station in California reported, "Goldstone has the bird." The launch was a success; America had entered the space age.

The country had been reeling ever since the Russians had first successfully put a satellite into space. No one knew exactly how to react to the knowledge that a man-made (and specifically Russian-made) object was possibly spying on America as it circled the earth every 90 minutes. The idea made people nervous and a bit scared.

Today the idea of man-made objects circling the earth is commonplace. In fact, many homes have satellite dishes designed to collect signals from space so that we can watch hundreds of different TV channels. The idea that someone is "watching us" from outer space is no longer the threat that it once was. But it is true that someone *is* watching us from the heavens—God.

The Bible tells us that God sits on his throne in Heaven and looks down on all of his creation. Nothing happens on our planet that God does not see or know about. But rather than fill us with dread as Sputnik did, this knowledge should make us feel secure that God knows every last detail of our lives. He is in total control of everything that goes on around us. And that's 24/7, not just an occasional pass around this earth of ours.

The LORD looks down from heaven and sees the whole human race. From his throne he observes all who live on the earth. He made their hearts, so he understands everything they do. [Psalm 33:13-15]

In 1958, the U.S. launched its first satellite, the Explorer I, into space.

eyes in the skies

to do ☑

CHECK OUT A SATELLITE TRACKING SITE ON THE INTERNET TO SEE HOW MANY SATELLITES ARE ORBITING THE WORLD AT ANY GIVEN TIME.

also on this day

1990 McDonald's opened its first restaurant in Moscow, Russia.

Composer Franz Schubert was born. **1797**

Survivor

This is Robinson Crusoe Day.

Robinson Crusoe is probably the best-known "survivor" of all time. This man ended up alone on an island after his ship wrecked. He had no TV, phone, DVDs, video games, or CDs—pretty boring, right? Absolutely not! You can read the exciting story of his adventures in the book by Daniel Defoe.

Suppose you, like Robinson Crusoe, were marooned on an island, cut off from family, friends, and the rest of civilization. What would you like to have with you to help you survive? How could you make it through those long, lonely days and nights?

A knife would come in handy. And how about dry matches, a raincoat, and fishing hooks—those sure would be good to have. But here's another suggestion: your Bible. That's right. You also would have to survive spiritually, mentally, and emotionally. Having God's Word would help you stay in close contact with him. The Bible's stories, teachings, and promises would give you hope and encouragement. In fact, many other "survivors" (including prisoners of war) have said that Bible reading and prayer helped them hold on until their rescue.

How many Bibles do you have? How often do you read God's Word? Instead of taking it for granted, pretend that, like Robinson Crusoe, you live on an island and need to survive. Then read the Bible, looking for hope and for direction and, of course, for God.

to do ☑

COMMIT TO READING THE BIBLE REGULARLY—A PASSAGE OR A CHAPTER A DAY. KEEP A RECORD OF GOD'S "SURVIVAL TIPS."

How **sweet** are your **words** to my taste, **sweeter** than **honey** to my **mouth**!

[Psalm 119:103, NIV]

also on this day

1862 "The Battle Hymn of the Republic," by Julia Ward Howe, was first published in the *Atlantic Monthly*.

The U.S. Supreme Court convened for the first time in New York City. **1790**

Eastman Kodak Co. introduced the $1 Brownie box camera. **1900**

the shadow

This is Groundhog Day.

The crowd grows larger and more excited by the minute. And as the time draws near, they push forward, each person trying to get a good look. Then the creature emerges—it's dark and furry, bigger than a squirrel, about the size of a small dog, and built close to the earth. Taking a few hesitant steps on this cloudy morning, it seems bold and in no hurry to return to its hole. And the crowd cheers.

The place? Punxsutawney, Pennsylvania. The occasion? Groundhog Day. Tradition holds that if the groundhog sees its shadow and is frightened back into its hole, then we'll have six more weeks of winter. But if it doesn't run scared, we'll have an early spring. At least that's the idea—the hope.

By February, people who have to struggle with the cold, ice, and snow of winter are tired of it all. They want spring to come early, the sooner the better. So they celebrate with Punxsutawney Phil and the crowd and hope.

Everyone needs hope. Imagine winter without spring, night without morning, school with no vacation, or sickness without the possibility of getting well. People without hope become *very discouraged*.

The Bible talks a lot about hope because God offers hope to everyone who believes—hope for forgiveness and for eternal life. And because God is the one offering the hope, we know it's true and real.

So when you feel like you're in an endless winter, remember God. Look up to him and hope. You can do this anytime—he's always available—and you don't have to wait for a furry animal to make its move.

also on this day

1802

The first leopard to be exhibited in the United States was shown by Othello Pollard in Boston, Massachusetts.

1863

Samuel Langhorne Clemens used a different name for himself for the first time. He is better remembered by that name—Mark Twain.

to do ☑

DRAW AN ARROW ON A PIECE OF PAPER. MAKE IT ABOUT 2 INCHES WIDE AND 8 INCHES LONG. WRITE **HOPE** ON THE ARROW AND PIN IT TO YOUR BULLETIN BOARD IN YOUR ROOM, POINTING UP. USE IT TO REMIND YOU TO LOOK UP TO GOD FOR HOPE.

Such things were written in the **Scriptures** long ago to **teach** us. They give us **hope** and **encouragement** as we wait patiently for God's **promises**. [Romans 15:4]

discovery

On this day in 1995, Colonel Eileen Collins became the first woman to pilot the space shuttle when the Discovery blasted off.

Exploring space has been very important to the United States for many decades. The name of the shuttle, "Discovery," accurately describes the goal of all of our rocket launches, orbital missions, visits to the moon, space walks, space stations, and space shuttles. We want to discover what's out there—in our solar system and beyond. Because of the space program, words like *launch*, *probe*, *orbit*, and *reentry* have become common. And our new heroes include Shepherd, Grissom, Glenn, Armstrong, Aldrin, Ride, McAuliffe, Husband, and many more—Eileen Collins too.

People have always been fascinated with space. Looking up on a clear night, away from city lights, can feel awesome and overwhelming. Countless twinkling stars and planets fill our field of vision. And in considering the millions of miles to the nearest star, we can feel pretty small and almost insignificant.

But get this: The creator of everything—each planet, galaxy, quasar, and quark—is also the creator of our tiny planet, Earth. And he takes a special interest in each and every one of the billions of people who live here. That includes you.

Not only did God make you, but he also loves you. To prove it, he came to earth, becoming a person just like you, to die for you (check out John 3:16). So you're pretty special after all.

Many people haven't yet made that discovery. We don't need a space shuttle to find God. We'll never be able to understand everything about God, who he is, and why he does what he does. But the real discovery is knowing that he lives and that he loves and cares for us.

So look to the skies and celebrate!

Great is the LORD! He is most worthy of praise! His greatness is beyond discovery! [Psalm 145:3]

to do ☑

TONIGHT AFTER DARK, GO OUTSIDE AND LOOK INTO THE SKIES. TRY TO COUNT THE STARS. THINK ABOUT GOD AND THANK HIM FOR LETTING YOU DISCOVER HIS LOVE.

also on this day

Norman Rockwell, the famous painter, was born.

1894

Rock singers Buddy Holly (22), Ritchie Valens (17), and the "Big Bopper" (28) died in a plane crash in Iowa.

1959

the goal

Charles Lindbergh (1902) and Rosa Parks (1913) were both born on this day.

Have you ever heard of Charles Lindbergh? What about Rosa Parks? They were very different people, but they shared a couple of important qualities. Each had a goal and the determination to reach it. And they each displayed great courage in pursuing the goal.

Charles Lindbergh was the first person to fly solo across the Atlantic Ocean. On May 21, 1927, he took off from an airport in New York in his little plane, The Spirit of St. Louis. The plane had only one engine and a propeller, and Lindbergh had none of the sophisticated navigational tools that modern pilots have. With only a magnetic compass, his airspeed indicator, and luck to navigate, Lindbergh flew the 1,000-mile trip, often through snow and sleet, and landed in Paris 33½ hours after takeoff.

Rosa Parks's journey was much shorter but took just as much courage. As an African American, she was tired of racism and of how she and other African Americans were treated. So on December 1, 1955, she refused to give up her seat on a bus to a white man. This violation of the rules sparked a controversy that was a catalyst for the civil rights movement. Rosa's convictions and courage came from her faith. She says, "I had a very spiritual background, and I believe in church and my faith, and that has helped to give me the strength and courage to live as I did."

What goals do you have? Maybe you have a big one, like Lindbergh, that you want to achieve one day. Or perhaps, like Parks, your goal involves making something right in the world.

Ask God to give you the right goals and to give you the courage to achieve them.

to do ☑

USING AN INDEX CARD, LIST YOUR GOALS IN THESE CATEGORIES: BIG LIFE GOALS, DAY-TO-DAY GOALS: PHYSICAL, SOCIAL, MENTAL, SPIRITUAL. KEEP THE CARD ON YOUR DESK AS A REMINDER AND MOTIVATOR.

also on this day

1894

J.W. Goodrich introduced rubber galoshes (boots) to the public.

1957

Smith-Corona Manufacturing Inc. of New York began selling portable electric typewriters. The first machine weighed 19 pounds.

I **strain** to reach the **end** of the **race** and receive the **prize** for which God, **through** Christ Jesus, is **calling** us up to heaven. [Philippians 3:14]

Then Disaster Struck!

This is Disaster Day.

HURRICANE EVACUATION ROUTE

Whoever decided to proclaim this disaster day probably had a good reason. Maybe a bunch of bad events piled up at this time of the year. Or maybe someone thought, "Why not have all our disasters on one day and get them over with!" (as if that were possible). But we probably wouldn't hold a Disaster Day party. If this were "No More Disasters Day," then we'd celebrate!

Everyone has experienced disasters, big and small—those times when things go wrong and life seems to be falling apart. It could be something personal like a relationship dissolving, a prized possession breaking, or a pet dying. Or it could be something really big like a tornado, fire, earthquake, or war. Terrible events can do more than ruin our day; they can wreck our lives!

But the news isn't all bad. In fact, it's very good. God turns bad events into good (see Romans 8:28) and is able to keep his people from the worst kind of disaster.

The verse for today reminds us of that promise. Jeremiah was a prophet who experienced nothing but disaster from a human point of view. Yet he tells us that God's plans are good, giving us hope for the future.

So if today, or any day, seems disastrous, remember God's promises for you and keep trusting in him.

to do ☑

TAKE A FEW MINUTES AND READ ABOUT THE LIFE OF JEREMIAH. LOOK IN THE BIBLE BOOK WITH HIS NAME AS THE TITLE OR USE ANOTHER BIBLE STUDY RESOURCE.

"For I **know** the **plans** I have for **you**," says **the LORD**. "They are plans for **good** and **not** for disaster, to give you a **future** and a **hope**."

[Jeremiah 29:11]

also on this day

1870
The first motion picture was shown to a theater audience in Philadelphia.

Ed Prescot patented the loop-the-loop roller coaster.

1901

What a nice thing to say

Today is Pay a Compliment Day.

What a switch! Yesterday we discussed disasters, and today we look at the bright side. And that's exactly what a compliment is—looking for something positive in someone else and then telling him or her about it.

Mark Twain said, "I can live a month on one good compliment." Phrases like, "That's a nice shirt," "Thank you for your thoughtfulness," "I really enjoyed your solo," and "You're such a good friend!" are music to our ears—they seem to brighten even a cloudy, rainy day. We feel affirmed and encouraged.

Compliments are easy to give, and they don't cost anything. I wonder why we don't give more of them.

The Bible passage for today introduces us to a great compliment-giver—a man named Joseph. In fact, he was such a positive person that he was given the nickname Barnabas, which means "Encourager." Read more about him in the New Testament, and you'll discover that his encouragement was very important to the apostle Paul after he became a follower of Christ. So Barnabas's nickname says a lot about the kind of person he was. It's sure better than being called Grouchy, Gloomy, or something similar.

If people who know you best were to give you a nickname based on your attitude, outlook, and actions, what do you think they would choose? Make the switch—be an encourager.

also on this day

1895 Baseball great Babe Ruth was born.

1911 Ronald Wilson Reagan, the 40th president of the United States, was born in Tampico, Illinois.

1935 The game Monopoly® first went on sale.

to do ☑

IN THE NEXT 24 HOURS, COMPLIMENT FIVE DIFFERENT PEOPLE (SUCH AS FAMILY MEMBERS, FRIENDS, OR TEACHERS). BE SINCERE AND SPECIFIC.

For instance, there was Joseph, the one the apostles nicknamed Barnabas (which means "Son of Encouragement"). He was from the tribe of Levi and came from the island of Cyprus. [Acts 4:36]

hurts like the dickens
This is Charles Dickens Day.

Charles Dickens was a famous English author who lived from 1812 to 1870. Dickens's writings include *A Christmas Carol, Great Expectations, Oliver Twist,* and *David Copperfield*. One of Dickens's most well-known books, *A Tale of Two Cities*, tells of the French Revolution and has this famous opening line: "It was the best of times, it was the worst of times."

Whenever you hear reports on the evening news, you may think that these days are both the best and the worst. All the stories of terrorism, crime, and other terrible problems and conditions make it seem as though things couldn't be worse. But when you hear of breakthroughs in medicine, technology, and nutrition, you think, "Life is good!"

The people in Jesus' day lived in similar times. When Jesus looked around him at all the disobedience and disbelief, he pronounced the times evil. But then he hinted at what would be the most significant event in history and the best news ever proclaimed. Earlier Jesus had said, "For as Jonah was in the belly of the great fish for three days and three nights, so I, the Son of Man, will be in the heart of the earth for three days and three nights" (Matthew 12:40). Jesus was predicting his death and resurrection. Through his sacrifice he would break the power of sin and death and give salvation to the evil world.

And you know what? He did it!

So whenever you hear all the bad news, remember the good news. Jesus came; Jesus lived; Jesus died for our sins; Jesus rose from the dead; Jesus loves you. That's the best news in the worst of times.

to do ☑

ASK ONE PERSON TO GIVE YOU THE GOOD NEWS FOR THE DAY. THEN SAY, "AND THE BEST NEWS IS THAT JESUS LIVES . . . AND HE ROCKS!"

[Jesus] said, "These are evil times, and this evil generation keeps asking me to show them a miraculous sign. But the only sign I will give them is the sign of the prophet Jonah. . . . What happens to me will be a sign that God has sent me, the Son of Man, to these people."

[Luke 11:29, 30]

also on this day

1817 Frederick Douglass, a leader in the anti-slavery movement and an advisor to President Lincoln, was born.

1984 Space shuttle astronauts Bruce McCandless II and Robert L. Stewart made the first untethered space walk.

1943 The U.S. government announced that shoe rationing would go into effect in two days.

Be Prepared

This is National Boy Scouts Day.

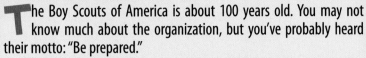

The Boy Scouts of America is about 100 years old. You may not know much about the organization, but you've probably heard their motto: "Be prepared."

That's great advice for Scouts who are hiking and camping. The equipment needs to be in good shape, the food and other supplies need to be gathered, and everyone needs to be organized. Heading out for adventure unprepared could bring serious problems.

But that motto gives great advice for non-Scouts and for the rest of life too. Good preparation is important for students in school, for athletes on teams, for workers on the job, for anyone who wants to be successful and do something well.

When talking to his followers, Jesus used the same expression: Be prepared. He was explaining that he would ascend to Heaven after his resurrection and that he would come to earth a second time in the future. He made the point that no one knows the exact time of his second coming, so they should always be prepared for it.

Being prepared for Christ's return means living as though he might come at any moment. A good way to do this is to ask, "Would I like to be doing this when Jesus returns?" If you have a close walk with God and you spend time with him through prayer and Bible reading, you can look forward to Jesus' second coming as a wonderful, exciting day and the beginning of eternity with him in Heaven.

So what about it—are you prepared?

to do ☑

READ MATTHEW 24:1–30. ON A SHEET OF PAPER, LIST ALL THE SIGNS OF THE SECOND COMING OF CHRIST.

also on this day

So be **prepared**, because you **don't know** what day your **Lord** is coming. [Matthew 24:42]

✳ This is Kite Flying Day.

A charter was granted for the College of William and Mary in Williamsburg, Virginia.

● 1693

●1922

The White House began using the radio after President Harding had it installed.

whether or not

Take a quick look outside. Is it clear or cloudy? Sunny or snowy? Wet or dry? Coolish or warmish? And here's a question for you: Does the weather match the forecast for today?

Weather affects everyone—some people much more than others. Farmers, for example, need sun and rain in the right amounts at specific times of the year. Pilots have to fly around or above storms. Those who fish, sail, and do other water activities keep their eyes on the skies. And no athlete wants the game cancelled because of inclement weather.

The weather can affect a person's mood too. How do you feel when the day is dark and cloudy compared to bright and sunny?

What frustrates many is that we have no choice. Weather is what it is, and we have to accept it and deal with it.

We can't choose a lot of things. Besides the weather, we can't choose our families, our basic physical and mental characteristics, the laws of the land, and many of the events around us.

But we can choose our attitudes. We can choose to be positive and pleasant, even when everything doesn't go our way. We can choose how we act toward other people. We can choose to move closer to God rather than away from him. We can choose to obey and believe God and trust him for the future.

In today's Bible passage, Moses is about to leave the Israelites, turning over the leadership of the nation to Joshua. So in this final speech, he challenges the people to make the right choices. Imagine yourself in that crowd, hearing these final words from this great man of God and leader. What does it mean for you to "choose life"?

Meet Moses' challenge. Regardless of the weather or anything else, make choices today that honor God.

to do ☑

FOR ONE DAY, KEEP TRACK OF THINGS AND EVENTS THAT YOU CAN'T CONTROL. MAKE A NOTE OF HOW THOSE THINGS AFFECT YOUR ATTITUDE. EACH TIME YOU WRITE ONE DOWN, THINK ABOUT MAKING A POSITIVE, GOD-HONORING CHOICE.

"Today I have given you the choice between life and death, between blessings and curses. I call on heaven and earth to witness the choice you make. Oh, that you would choose life, that you and your descendants might live!" [Deuteronomy 30:19]

also on this day

W.G. Morgan invented volleyball.

1895

1964 The Beatles appeared on the *Ed Sullivan Show*.

ups and downs

This is Umbrella Day.

Here's a riddle: What can go up the chimney down but not down the chimney up? The answer—*an umbrella*. Think about it. If the umbrella is down, you could move it up and down the chimney. If the umbrella is up or open, however, you couldn't bring it down the chimney from outside because it would be too big. Use that riddle to stump your family and friends.

Actually, the umbrella is a great invention. We can carry it around and then open it when we need to, usually in a rain shower. Or we can open one up on the deck, at the pool, or on the beach to keep us in the shade. Umbrellas protect us from rain and sun.

But umbrellas don't provide much protection against hurricanes, rockslides, rattlesnakes, volcanic eruptions, meteorites, or stampeding cattle. Umbrellas can be helpful, but sometimes we need more help than they offer.

King David the psalmist wrote songs about God's protection. At many times in his life, God had protected David. When David was a shepherd boy, God protected him from a lion and a bear that attacked his sheep. When David faced the giant Goliath, he was confident of God's protection, and he killed the giant with only a sling and stones. As commander of Israel's army, David experienced God's protection in battle and from his enemies. But David's protection didn't come from umbrellas, shelters, weapons, or even armies—it came from God. Today's verse is a good example. David trusted in God to shield him, strengthen him, and save him—in every situation. Did he use weapons in battle? Sure. Did he seek shelter in a storm? Of course. But he knew that ultimately his protection, especially from evil, had to come from the Lord.

No matter what you face, remember that God is your ultimate protector. Trust him, talk to him, and turn over your concerns to him.

to do ☑

TELL SOMEONE THE CHIMNEY RIDDLE. AND WHENEVER YOU SEE AN UMBRELLA WHISPER A PRAYER OF THANKS TO GOD FOR HIS PROTECTION.

also on this day

1763 The Treaty of Paris ended the French and Indian War. In the treaty, France yielded Canada to England.

1863 The fire extinguisher was patented by Alanson Crane.

My God is my **rock**, in whom I find **protection**. He is my **shield**, the **strength** of my **salvation**, and my **stronghold**, my **high tower**, my **savior**, the one who **saves** me from violence. [2 Samuel 22:3]

plugged in

On this day in 1847, Thomas Edison was born.

The inventions of Thomas Edison include the phonograph, generator, motor, motion pictures, and more that 600 patented products. Probably he is most famous for inventing the lightbulb. Just think of what life would be like without those amazing glass appliances that turn on at the flick of a switch or tap on a button, pushing away the darkness. Before the lightbulb, people would do most of their work between sunrise and sunset and then rely on candles. What an amazing, life-changing invention.

But that's not Edison's greatest achievement. Even more important is his fantastic system of generating and distributing electricity. Because of Thomas Edison, we can light not just one bulb, but the whole house! Without the power and the power grid, we could have a thousand lightbulbs, but they would be useless. It's one thing to have a lightbulb and a lamp. It's quite another to have it actually work. A lightbulb only works when connected to the power source.

That may seem obvious. But have you ever wondered why the lamp in your bedroom didn't work . . . or the DVD player . . . or the radio, only to discover that it was unplugged? Every electrical appliance needs to be plugged in. It needs electricity. It needs power!

The same is true for people. One day Jesus told his followers that they would receive *power* to live his way and to tell others about him. This power would come from God himself, the Holy Spirit. But they had to be plugged in.

This happens when we trust in Christ as Savior and then stay close to him through reading his Word and praying.

So how are you doing? Are you plugged in?

"But when the **Holy Spirit**
has come upon you,
you will receive **power**
and will **tell people** about me
everywhere—in **Jerusalem**,
throughout **Judea**,
in **Samaria**, and to the
ends of the **earth**." [Acts 1:8]

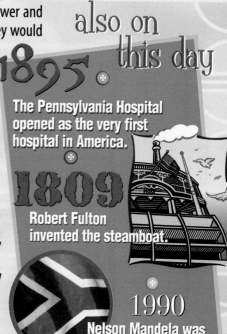

also on this day

1895 The Pennsylvania Hospital opened as the very first hospital in America.

1809 Robert Fulton invented the steamboat.

1990 Nelson Mandela was freed after 27 years in captivity.

to do ☑

MAKE A SMALL SIGN THAT SAYS, "POWER!" PUT THE SIGN ON A LAMP IN YOUR BEDROOM TO REMIND YOU TO STAY PLUGGED IN TO GOD.

When you hear the name "Abraham Lincoln," what do you think of? Great president? The one who freed the slaves? "Honest Abe"? Lincoln got that nickname because he was known for his honesty. He had a reputation for honesty.

A reputation is what a person is "known as." It reflects what the person is like, what he or she has done, or how he or she has acted. Sometimes reputations aren't fair or accurate. Someone's reputation might be based on a rumor or on one act. For example, the new kid might keep to himself and get the reputation of being stuck up, but he may just be shy. Or a girl might be caught cheating on a test one time and then be known as a cheater. But usually reputations are built over time with a pattern of behavior. So, because of the way Abraham Lincoln lived and spoke, he became known as "Honest Abe."

A good reputation is valuable. Today's verse says that having one is "better than having silver or gold." That's especially true for a Christian, a follower of Christ. A Christian's reputation reflects on God.

Think of people you know. How would you describe their reputations? funny? brainy? dishonest? angry? fun?

If others thought of you, how would they describe your character or reputation? What would you like to be known as? loyal? sincere? kind? someone close to God?

You build a reputation one day at a time and one action at a time. So start now. What can you do today and then tomorrow to be known as someone who is like Christ?

Choose a good reputation over great riches, for being held in high esteem is better than having silver or gold. [Proverbs 22:1]

On this day in 1809, Abraham Lincoln was born.

to do ☑

THINK ABOUT ONE OR TWO KIDS AT SCHOOL OR IN THE NEIGHBORHOOD WHO HAVE GOOD REPUTATIONS. THEN THINK OF HOW THEY EARNED THEM.

also on this day

This is National Lost Penny Day.

1733 **English colonist James Oglethorpe founded Savannah, Georgia.**

Frederick W. Thayer patented the baseball catcher's mask. 1878

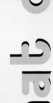

what do they say?

This is Get a Different Name Day.

Hello
my name
is:_____

Who's Who?

Johnny Cash once had a hit song entitled, "A Boy Named Sue." It tells the story of a young man who had to fight his way through life because people would make fun of his name. The end of the song reveals that the man's father named him "Sue" to make him tough.

You may have wanted to change your name. Perhaps someone with the same first or last name did something terrible, and it was all over the news. How would you like to be named "Saddam"? You'd quickly get sick of all the comments and jokes. Or maybe you think your last name is too long or confusing, like "Froomerwhipplesnitczle." Try putting that on the back of your baseball jersey!

Names are interesting because we are so attached to them. If asked, "Who are you?" we answer with our name. And if someone whispers our name, even in a noisy room, we hear it—we're tuned in.

But people are more than their names. Beyond your name, you are a student, a son or daughter, or a team member. You are a citizen, a musician, or a friend.

The truth about you and every person is that you are good, special, important, and loved by God. You were created in his image. No matter what happens or how you feel, always remember that you are not just a boy or girl. And you are much more than your name. You are a child of God, made like your heavenly Father, and you bear the family resemblance. Wow!

So **God** created **people** in his **own** image; God **patterned** them after himself; **male** and **female** he created them.

[Genesis 1:37]

also on this day

1635 The first public school in the U.S. was established.

1965 Sixteen-year-old Peggy Fleming won the ladies senior figure skating title.

the love test

Today is Valentine's Day.

This is probably the only day in the year that you eat those pastel colored hearts. You know, the ones with love messages on them, like "Be mine," "Sweetie Pie," and "Love ya." The messages aren't too deep, but, hey, how much room is there on a candy heart?

Actually, even if the writing space were much bigger, the message probably still would be pretty shallow. That's because we say "love" so easily and casually. For example, every day we proclaim love for hot dogs, puppies, warm weather, TV shows, fudge, and a host of other favorite things and activities. So when we say "I love you" to a person, do we feel the same as we do for an electronic game or a friend's hairstyle ("I *love* what you've done to your hair!")? No wonder it's confusing.

Jesus said that his followers would be known by their love for each other (check out John 13:35). And he said that soon after he had washed his disciples' feet and had told them to follow his example. So it seems that the love Jesus was talking about is more than a feeling or a sweet compliment. His type of love involves action, a decision to act for someone else's good. He did that when he chose to come to earth and to die on the cross for our sins. That's true love!

Look at the verses for today. This passage emphasizes the attitudes and actions of love.

So whom do you say that you love? mom? dad? brother? sister? friend? Think how you show it, how you act. That's the test—because actions speak louder than words.

Love is patient and kind. Love is not jealous or boastful or proud or rude. Love does not demand its own way. Love is not irritable, and it keeps no record of when it has been wronged. It is never glad about injustice but rejoices whenever the truth wins out. Love never gives up, never loses faith, is always hopeful, and endures through every circumstance.

[1 Corinthians 13:4-7]

also on this day

This is National Ferris Wheel Day.

1741 American Revolutionary War traitor Benedict Arnold was born.

to do ☑

MAKE A VALENTINE FOR A SPECIAL PERSON IN YOUR LIFE. USE PART OR ALL OF TODAY'S BIBLE PASSAGE TO THANK THAT PERSON FOR HIS LOVE ACTIONS TOWARD YOU. YOU COULD SAY, FOR EXAMPLE, "THANKS FOR BEING SUCH A GOOD FRIEND. PAUL WROTE THAT 'LOVE NEVER GIVES UP, NEVER LOSES FAITH, IS ALWAYS HOPEFUL,' AND I SEE THAT IN YOU."

profile in courage

What do you know about Susan B. Anthony, besides the fact that today is her birthday? (And the only way you know that is because you just read it. You probably haven't planned a party!) Maybe you've seen Susan B. Anthony's image on a dollar coin (you know, the one with the odd shape about the size of a quarter). Several years ago she received the honor of appearing on our money. During her lifetime, she worked hard to free slaves, improve education, get better pay and working conditions for laborers, stop drunkenness and alcoholism, and give women the right to vote. No wonder she's famous!

Every one of those actions took courage. Imagine the opposition she must have faced from people who were against those causes. In fact, just for her work against slavery, she encountered angry mobs, armed threats, and objects thrown at her. A dummy of her was hanged in one town. In another, her image was dragged through the streets. Some people were really upset at Susan. But she kept working.

Courage means doing what you know is right, regardless of the cost or danger.

It means telling the truth when others are lying, sticking up for a friend, reaching out to someone who's not popular, and taking a stand for your beliefs. It means telling someone that you trust in Jesus when you know that person might make fun of your faith.

The Bible is filled with stories of courageous men, women, boys, and girls who made a difference for God and for good in the world. You can be a person of courage, too, like Susan B. Anthony.

to do ☑

LOOK UP SUSAN B. ANTHONY ON YOUR COMPUTER AND READ ABOUT HER LIFE. IF YOU CAN, GET A SILVER DOLLAR WITH HER PICTURE ON IT AND KEEP IT AS A REMINDER TO BE A PERSON OF COURAGE.

also on this day

This is National Gumdrop Day.

Galileo was born. 1564

1758 **Mustard was advertised for the first time in America.**

Morris and Rose Michtom, Russian immigrants, introduced the first teddy bear in America. 1903

"But now take courage, . . . says the LORD. . . . Take courage, all you people still left in the land, says the LORD. Take courage and work, for I am with you, says the LORD Almighty." [Haggai 2:4]

don't win this "oscar"
This is Do a Grouch a Favor Day.

We don't know who made this up, but it's a good idea. Doing a favor for a grouch might just brighten his or her day. And if it happens more than once, the grouch might not be so grouchy.

A grouch seems always to be in a bad mood. Everything is negative to him or her. On a partly cloudy day, grouches see the clouds, not the sun. Can you think of any grouches in your life? Remember Oscar the Grouch from Sesame Street. He lives in a garbage can, for goodness sake—no wonder he has a bad attitude!

Grouches aren't fun to be around. Wouldn't you rather hang with positive people, who see the good and make you feel good about life and about yourself? Maybe you have a friend like that . . . or a relative . . . or a teacher . . . or a person at church.

But wait a second. What about you? Do you think people call you a grouch? If so, consider things you might do to become a more positive person. A good start would be to list all the good in your life and to thank God for those blessings. Then try to look for at least one good thing every day to thank him for.

to do ☑

TAKE THIS DAY SERIOUSLY AND DO SOMEONE A FAVOR. HELP SOMEONE WHO'S FEELING GROUCHY TO FEEL BETTER.

also on this day

1946

Detroit, Michigan, declared this to be Aretha Franklin Day. 1968

The first commercially designed helicopter was tested in Connecticut.

And now, **dear** brothers and sisters, let me say one **more** thing as I close this letter. **Fix** your thoughts on what is **true** and **honorable** and **right**. Think about things that are **pure** and **lovely** and **admirable**. Think about things that are **excellent** and worthy of **praise**. [Philippians 4:8]

This is Random Acts of Kindness Day.

Kinda Nice

A "random act of kindness" involves doing something nice and good for someone else, even a stranger, for no particular reason. Such kind acts catch others by surprise and brighten their day. An adult, for example, might pay for someone's gas (big bucks) or another driver's toll on the tollway (pocket change). The random action doesn't have to be big and expensive; the thought is what counts. This can be really fun when the act is done in secret, and the person receiving the kindness never learns who did it.

Usually we worry more about ourselves than others, and we're quick to point out when we have experienced something bad and "undeserved." So when someone is especially kind, considerate, generous, and helpful to us, we feel good about ourselves and about life. Then we may even pass on the kindness to someone else.

This idea isn't new—check out today's verse. Christians are to be kind and imitate Christ.

Actually, this whole idea of a random act of kindness reflects the Golden Rule. Remember that verse? Jesus said, "Do for others as you would like them to do for you" (Luke 6:31).

So just consider how you would like to be treated and then treat another person the same way. Who do you know who would appreciate a kind act? Maybe your mom, dad, brother, sister, neighbor, friend, classmate, or even a stranger. Be more like Christ as you pass on the kindness.

to do ☑

DO A RANDOM ACT OF KINDNESS TODAY. IF YOU WISH, TELL A FRIEND OR TWO ABOUT THIS DAY, AND PERFORM SOME KIND ACT TOGETHER. AND MAKE SURE THAT YOUR KIND ACT IS SOMETHING THE PERSON DOESN'T EXPECT. LET IT BE A SURPRISE.

Instead, be **kind** to each other, **tenderhearted**, **forgiving** one another, just as **God** through **Christ** has forgiven **you**.

[Ephesians 4:32]

also on this day

This is Championship Crab Races Day.

Julius Wolff was credited with being the first to can sardines.

1876

1934
The first high school automobile driver's education course was introduced in State College, Pennsylvania.

what a view

In 1930, Elm Farm Ollie became the first cow to fly in an airplane.

OK, this is a stretch, but imagine you're Ollie, the first cow to fly in an airplane. You've returned to earth and are back in the herd (stay with me here), trying to explain your experience to the other cows—Daisy, Bessie, Mookie . . . the whole gang. All they've ever known is the farm, the barn, and the field. And every day's schedule looks the same: get up, give milk, eat grass, return to the barn. But you've traveled much farther and have seen much more. How would the other cows respond?

Until your trip, you were just like them. But your point of view changed, and you saw things you never imagined—treetops, homes, cars, highways, and land to the horizon. Your life will never be the same.

That silly story is close to what humans experience. We spend our lives on this planet. Some people never travel out of the country in which they are born, and some people don't even leave their hometowns! But God is much bigger than our world—and far beyond. He sees all the people of the world all the time. He also sees everything beyond our tiny planet, throughout the universe. So when he tells us about life, the future, how to live, or anything else, we ought to listen carefully. We should try to see life from his point of view.

God says, for example, that this life is not everything. He offers eternal life in Heaven with him, if we have given our lives to his Son. He says that we can trust him for the future. And God tells us about all of this in his Word, the Bible.

So try to see life from God's point of view, and trust him in everything.

also on this day

1930

Clyde Tombaugh discovered the planet Pluto.

1987

The Girl Scout organization changed the color of their uniforms from green to blue.

Jesus turned and **looked** at his disciples and then said to **Peter** very sternly, "Get **away** from me, **Satan! You** are seeing things merely from a **human** point of view, **not** from **God's.**" [Mark 8:33]

to do ☑

THE NEXT TIME YOU'RE IN AN AIRPLANE OR ON THE TOP FLOOR OF A TALL BUILDING, LOOK DOWN AT EVERYTHING BELOW. THEN THINK OF HOW GOD SEES EVERYTHING.

surprise!

In 1913, Cracker Jack® put prizes in their boxes for the first time.

Don't you just love surprises? Good ones, that is. A card with cash from your aunt . . . a visit from an old friend . . . a good grade on a test when you thought you hadn't done very well . . . the chocolate center in a piece of candy . . . a random act of kindness.

The makers of Cracker Jack® knew that. So way back in 1913, they put prizes in their boxes to help sell their caramel-coated popcorn and peanuts snack. It worked! Kids (parents too) liked the snack, but they *loved* the surprise prize. Since then, people think "prize" and "surprise" when they hear *Cracker Jack*. Even today, the bag proclaims, "Prize inside! Whad'ya get? There are new surprises waiting for you. So open a bag and enjoy."

Surprise is a good word to associate with Jesus too. He was constantly saying and doing things that were unusual and unexpected. People thought they had him figured out, and then he would say something like, "The first will be last and the last first," or "The least in this world will be the greatest in my kingdom." And in today's verse, he proclaimed that he had come to "give life in all its fullness." Another translation of this verse says that Jesus came to give life "more abundantly." *Fullness* and *abundantly* are like having a bucket that is totally full and overflowing. So abundant life is having extra life, life overflowing, like getting a surprise prize in the box.

Today, many people think they know all about Jesus. They think following him is just religion. In fact, it's totally different because it's life overflowing. Think of the life Christ offers as "life with a prize inside!"

to do ☑

BUY A FEW BAGS OF CRACKER JACK. GIVE THEM TO FRIENDS AND SAY, "JESUS IS LIKE A CRACKER JACK BAG—HE GIVES LIFE WITH A PRIZE INSIDE. OPEN A BAG AND ENJOY."

"The **thief's** purpose is to **steal** and **kill** and **destroy**. **My** purpose is to **give life** in all its **fullness.**" [John 10:10]

also on this day

1878
Thomas Edison patented the phonograph.

The Coca-Cola Company introduced Cherry Coke®.

1473
Nicolas Copernicus was born.

1985

You Can Do It!

In 1998 when she won the ladies' figure skating competition in Nagano, Japan, American Tara Lipinski, at age 15, became the youngest gold medal winner in winter Olympics history.

Today we're going to talk about Tara and Tim—two young people who made an impact.

You know about Tara from the information you just read. As she was growing up and competing, everyone knew she was a rising star, a promising athlete, a potential champion. But to win the gold medal at 15, now that was a shock! The competition was tough, and she was so young and inexperienced. No one expected her to win. Maybe that's why she did so well. Feeling no pressure, she just went out and skated her best.

Now let's consider Tim. This young man lived hundreds of years before Tara. He was young, too, and few expected much from him. But his good friend and mentor, the apostle Paul, knew better. He knew that Tim had what it took to be a great leader in the church. Paul even wrote two letters to his young friend to encourage him and to help him do his best. Those letters are in the Bible—1 Timothy and 2 Timothy.

In today's verse, Paul gives Tim advice that you should hear too. He wrote, "Don't let anyone think less of you because you are young." In other words, just because you are young don't think you can't do something great for God—you can! And then Paul added, "Be an example." So not only can you make a difference by what you do but also by how you live.

While some people are tempted to underestimate the young, some great Christians have been quite young. They made a difference for Christ. You can too!

to do

THINK OF HOW YOU CAN BE A BETTER EXAMPLE IN "WHAT YOU TEACH," "THE WAY YOU LIVE," "YOUR LOVE," "YOUR FAITH," OR "YOUR PURITY." THEN TAKE ONE STEP TO MAKE THE CHANGE.

Don't let **anyone** think **less** of you because you are **young**. Be an **example** to all believers in what you **teach**, in the way you **live**, in your **love**, your **faith**, and your **purity**. [1 Timothy 4:12]

also on this day

1872 — The Metropolitan Museum of Art opened in New York City.

Silas Noble and J.P. Cooley patented the toothpick manufacturing machine. 1872

1962 — John Glenn became the first U.S. astronaut to orbit the earth.

a sticky situation

This is National Sticky Bun Day.

Now *this* is a great day to celebrate. Yum, yum sticky buns! "Rolled dough, spread with sugar and nuts; then sliced and baked in muffin tins with honey or sugar and butter in the bottom"—that's how one dictionary described the tasty treat. It sure sounds like good eatin', almost any time.

But you probably shouldn't grab one just before shaking hands or working on the computer or shuffling cards or handling your best shirt or bowling or applying makeup or performing surgery. That would be a bad idea—the stickiness would cause a problem.

That's just common sense. We would feel pretty foolish if we did any of those activities with hands covered in sticky honey or sugar and butter. But sometimes we make foolish decisions in other areas of life. Maybe you've heard about someone crashing a car because he or she was reading or watching TV while driving. Occasionally, the newspaper will report on a person who ignored warning signs and was seriously injured. There are always examples of people who make unwise choices and end up in trouble.

To get more personal, maybe you've done something foolish, like gossip about a friend, lie to your parents, cheat on a test, pretend to be cool or smart, or do something wrong just because other kids want you to. Not only are those actions unwise, they also lead to trouble.

The Bible talks a lot about wisdom (check out today's verse). Wisdom is like common sense plus. It involves thinking things through, comparing possible actions with what God wants, and then making the right choice.

Wise people know what to do in any sticky situation.

to do ☑

EACH TIME YOU EAT SOMETHING SWEET (SUGAR ON CEREAL, CANDY, SOFT DRINK, STICKY BUN, AND SO FORTH), THINK ABOUT STICKY SITUATIONS AND WISDOM. ASK GOD TO HELP MAKE YOU WISE.

also on this day

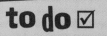

1885 The Washington Monument was dedicated.

The first International Pancake Race was held in Liberal, Kansas. **1950**

My child, eat honey, for it is good, and the honeycomb is sweet to the taste. In the same way, wisdom is sweet to your soul. If you find it, you will have a bright future, and your hopes will not be cut short. [Proverbs 24:13, 14]

the whole truth and nothing but the truth

On this day in 1732, George Washington was born.

Earlier this month we celebrated Abraham Lincoln's birthday. Kids used to get both his birthday and this day off from school. Now we have "Presidents' Day"—the third Monday in February instead, so you only get one vacation day. But it's still good to remember these two great presidents, Lincoln and Washington.

Like Lincoln, George Washington was known for his honesty. Supposedly he admitted to his father, "I cannot tell a lie. I chopped down the cherry tree." Whether that story is true or not, it's good to be known as someone who tells the truth. That's a great reputation to have!

The Bible says we should tell the truth, but that's not always easy. When caught doing something wrong, we want to make excuses instead of admitting what we did. Or in order to impress someone we might make up a story about ourselves. Or to get ahead in school, we are tempted to cheat. Many times in a variety of situations we feel the pressure to lie or to hide the truth. One of the problems with telling a lie is that it leads to other lies and then to more lies, until you're not really sure what you said to whom—a real mess.

Lying is so common that in court witnesses have to "swear to tell the truth, the whole truth, and nothing but the truth." And when people say something to someone, they have to add, "I promise."

Telling the truth may hurt (you might be punished, lose a friendship, or get a lower grade), but it will help you in the long run. You'll become a person with a clear conscience and a good reputation. And most important, you'll be obeying God.

And that's the truth!

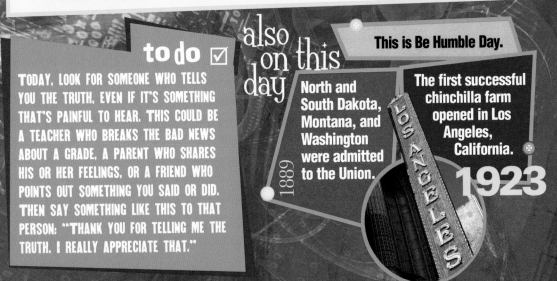

to do ☑

TODAY, LOOK FOR SOMEONE WHO TELLS YOU THE TRUTH, EVEN IF IT'S SOMETHING THAT'S PAINFUL TO HEAR. THIS COULD BE A TEACHER WHO BREAKS THE BAD NEWS ABOUT A GRADE, A PARENT WHO SHARES HIS OR HER FEELINGS, OR A FRIEND WHO POINTS OUT SOMETHING YOU SAID OR DID. THEN SAY SOMETHING LIKE THIS TO THAT PERSON: "THANK YOU FOR TELLING ME THE TRUTH. I REALLY APPRECIATE THAT."

also on this day

This is Be Humble Day.

North and South Dakota, Montana, and Washington were admitted to the Union. 1889

The first successful chinchilla farm opened in Los Angeles, California. **1923**

"Do not steal. Do not cheat one another. Do not lie." [Leviticus 19:11]

the one and only

On this day in 1685, composer George Friedrich Händel was born.

You may never have heard of Händel, but he was considered in England and by many in Germany as the greatest composer of his day. You probably *have* heard of the *Messiah*, however, his best-known work, and its famous climax, "Hallelujah," usually called the Hallelujah chorus. Every Christmas, throughout the world, church and community choirs perform this magnificent composition. It comes at the end, and usually everyone in the audience stands. It's more than a tradition. They stand to honor the one about whom the choir is singing: Jesus, the Messiah.

For hundreds of years, the Jewish people were awaiting their deliverer, their Messiah. When Jesus came, he said that Messiah was exactly who he was and that he had come to deliver people from their sins. Usually the name *Jesus* is followed by *Christ*—a Greek word that means "Messiah."

Jesus was 100 percent God and 100 percent human. That's what the Bible teaches. He was a human being, just like you, but he lived a perfect life. He faced all the temptations and pressures that humans face, but he didn't give in and sin. When Jesus died on the cross, he took the punishment for our sins on himself, in our place. And then he rose from the dead and now lives. And, as Händel's *Messiah* proclaims, "He shall reign forever and ever"!

Many people have claimed to be the Messiah and to have the truth. They have encouraged people to follow them. The Bible calls them "false prophets." Only one Messiah exists, only one Savior—Jesus. Do you know him?

also on this day

1836

The siege of the Alamo began.

1874

Walter Winfield patented the game of lawn tennis. He first called the game, "sphairistike."

1896

Tootsie Roll® candies were first sold in stores.

Simon Peter **answered**, "**You** are the **Messiah**, the **Son** of the living **God**."

[Matthew 16:16]

to do ☑

GET A CONCORDANCE (THAT'S A BOOK THAT LISTS ALL THE WORDS IN THE BIBLE AND WHERE TO FIND THEM) OR USE AN ELECTRONIC CONCORDANCE ON YOUR COMPUTER. SEARCH FOR THE WORD, "MESSIAH," AND LOOK UP ALL THE VERSES IN THE NEW TESTAMENT WHERE IT IS USED.

Question: When is it time to go to the dentist? Answer: "Tooth hurty!" (Get it? "Tooth hurty" sounds like "two-thirty.") That's a lame joke, but what better way to celebrate the first nylon bristle toothbrush?

Do you ever wonder what people did to protect their teeth before toothbrushes? Maybe they used wood or their fingers, or just chewed until their teeth wore out or fell out (Woodn't chew?—another joke). We know that some ancient people had good teeth, however.

Actually this discussion of teeth is a good reminder of the importance of taking care of our bodies. God has given us these bodies, and he wants us to serve him in the world. You have only one body. You can't return it to the hospital where you were born and ask for a replacement.

In another Bible verse, Paul says, "Don't you know that your body is the temple of the Holy Spirit, who lives in you and was given to you by God? You do not belong to yourself" (1 Corinthians 6:19). So that makes it even more important to think about our health.

Taking care of the body involves more than brushing and flossing. Diet, exercise, sleep, and, certainly, staying away from stuff that can destroy you (alcohol, drugs, cigarettes, and so forth) all play a part.

Some young people act like this isn't important because, right now, they feel good. So they veg out, eat junk food, sleep just a couple of hours a night, and smoke. But eventually all those habits cause harm.

Every year you live is another year of enjoying life and serving Christ. And remember, be true to your teeth, and they'll never be false to you!

Your teeth are as white as sheep, newly shorn and washed. They are perfectly matched. [Song of Songs 4:2]

On this day in 1938, the first nylon bristle toothbrush was made.

it's 2:30

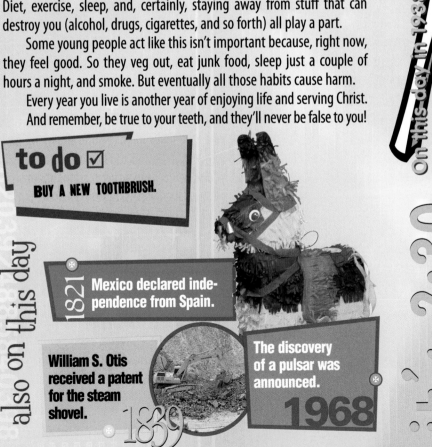

to do ☑
BUY A NEW TOOTHBRUSH.

also on this day

1821 Mexico declared independence from Spain.

William S. Otis received a patent for the steam shovel. 1839

The discovery of a pulsar was announced. **1968**

Don't Monkey Around

On this day in 1751, Edward Willet displayed the first trained monkey act in the United States.

Have you ever seen a trained monkey act? They're pretty hard to find these days. But maybe you've seen the monkeys in a zoo. If so, you know they can be very funny racing around, making weird sounds and faces, and even showing off for the crowd. No wonder we use the expression "monkeying around." Or maybe you've heard someone say, "That's more fun than a barrel of monkeys." Or how about—"Monkey see; monkey do"? That refers to the habit of monkeys to copy the actions of humans. Obviously, no one takes monkeys very seriously.

Some people act like monkeys, though. They like to have a good time and always seem to be messing around and goofing off. And they enjoy making fun of everything and everyone. The problem, however, is that no one takes them seriously either. Even if they try to be serious, we think they're making a joke.

Our passage for today points out that in life we have a time for everything, even a "time to laugh" and a "time to dance." But our laughing and cutting up should be done at the *right time*, not all the time. The Bible also says we have a time to be serious, "to cry" and "to grieve."

We laugh at the wrong time when we joke about God, his Word, and his people, or when we make fun of painful situations, and when we take lightly serious matters. God wants us to enjoy life to the full, to have "abundant life." But he also wants us to be very serious about what is important.

So have a blast—laugh, joke, sing, and celebrate. But at the right time. I'm serious.

to do ☑

THIS WEEK, NOTICE HOW MANY OF THE JOKES ON TELEVISION MAKE FUN OF OTHER PEOPLE, LAUGHING AT THEIR PROBLEMS, AND PUTTING THEM DOWN. WORK HARD AT NOT USING THAT KIND OF HUMOR.

There is a **time** for **everything**, a season for **every** activity under heaven. . . .
A time to **cry** and a time to **laugh**.
A time to **grieve** and a time to **dance**. [Ecclesiastes 3:1, 4]

also on this day

Famous French painter Pierre-Auguste Renoir was born. **1841**

•1983 The final episode of M*A*S*H aired. This was the most watched television program in history.

truly grand

On this day in 1919, the Grand Canyon in Arizona was established as a National Park by an act of the U.S. Congress.

Covering 1,217,403 acres (or 277 miles), the Grand Canyon is immense, averaging 4,000 feet deep, 6,000 feet at its deepest point, and 15 miles wide at its widest point. This awe-inspiring natural formation is home to many rare and specially protected plants and animals. Over 1,500 plant, 355 bird, 89 mammalian, 47 reptile, 9 amphibian, and 17 fish species live in the park. This place is amazing, and a person will be blown away by the view.

More impressive than the Grand Canyon, however, is our creator who made it. The Bible explains that God created the heavens and the earth. That's why we can see his touch in the natural beauty that surrounds us—a sparkling waterfall, a bright sunrise and glowing sunset, the lush green forests, the majestic mountains and mysterious deserts, the wide variety of plants and animals of every imaginable shape and color. Many who stand at the rim of the Grand Canyon break into song, proclaiming, "How Great Thou Art."

Sometimes we get so caught up in the daily routine, looking down at our problems, or inside at our struggles, that we forget to look up and around at the surrounding wonder. Check it out—God's fingerprints are everywhere.

Each butterfly, earthworm, spiderweb, grass blade, drop of rain, petunia, wispy cloud, sparrow, squirrel, snowflake, and breeze should remind us of our creator. And, as he said, the highest and best of all his creation is people . . . like you.

Our God is truly grand!

So the creation of
the **heavens** and the **earth**
and **everything** in them
was **completed.** [Genesis 2:1]

"Be **glad**; **rejoice** forever
in **my** creation!" [Isaiah 65:18]

also on this day

This is National Pistachio Day.

1846
William "Buffalo Bill" Cody was born.

1930
New York City installed traffic lights.

to do ☑

LOOK FOR EVIDENCE OF GOD IN HIS CREATION. EACH TIME YOU SEE SOMETHING, THANK HIM FOR WHAT HE HAS MADE AND FOR MAKING YOU.

eat a pancake

Pancakes for breakfast! Who doesn't love a stack of hot flapjacks, smothered in butter and syrup or fruit or sprinkled with sugar? But have you ever eaten a cold, plain pancake? It's tasteless and unappetizing. Piping hot and covered with toppings, and the combination works!

That's the case with many food items. We add sugar or other ingredients to improve the taste. So it's no wonder that we can approach other areas of life the same way. We may think, "I don't care for this class, but if I can sit next to my friend, then it might be bearable," or "I don't care for my outfit, but if I add this touch of color, then it'll be OK."

Some take it a step further, thinking, "My life is rather bland, so I'll spruce it up a bit," or "I probably should be a better person. I'll add a little God, a bit of Jesus. Then I'll be better, well-rounded, and get to Heaven too." But in our spiritual lives, that doesn't work.

We can't just sprinkle a little spiritual sugar on our lives. Instead we must be completely changed, "born again." That would be like a pancake becoming an omelet—a dramatic change would have to occur. No wonder Nicodemus had to ask Jesus to explain what it means to be born again. Becoming a follower of Christ means praying and turning over our lives to him. Then the Holy Spirit comes and lives inside and changes us from the inside out.

So enjoy your pancakes. But remember, becoming an omelet requires transformation.

Jesus replied, "I assure you, unless you are born again, you can never see the Kingdom of God." [John 3:3]

to do ☑

THE NEXT TIME YOU EAT OUT FOR BREAKFAST, ORDER PANCAKES. BEFORE POURING ON THE SYRUP, TAKE A BITE. THEN THANK GOD FOR MAKING YOU COMPLETELY DIFFERENT FROM THE INSIDE THROUGH HIS SPIRIT.

also on this day

1974 *People* magazine was first issued by Time-Life (later known as Time-Warner).

This is International Polar Bear Day. 1896

jump!

In 1912, the first parachute jump from an airplane was made.

Imagine being the first person to jump out of a plane, trusting your life to a parachute. Think of your questions: "OK, how does this work?" "What happens if I pull the cord and nothing happens?" "How 'bout I go *second*?"

Leaving the safety of the airplane would take faith, but you'd jump if you had confidence in the person who made the parachute, the one who prepared it, and your instructor. Of course asking questions would be good. You would be foolish just to take someone's word that your jump would be safe. For example, what if a complete stranger said, "Let me strap this parachute to your back and take you up in a plane. Then, when we get real high, you jump out of the plane, pull the cord, and land safely." No doubt you wouldn't go. Why should you trust *that* guy?

You've heard often that the Christian life is based on faith. That means trusting God, that his Word is true, and that he will do what he says. It doesn't mean we just "jump" without asking questions or checking everything out. Eventually, however, the moment of truth arrives and we leap.

Besides becoming a Christian, this applies to other decisions along the way. Let's say you're reading the Bible and you see where God wants you to turn over a relationship to him or to take a certain action. So, by faith, you do it. Not knowing the eventual outcome, you trust God and obey him.

How strong is your faith in God? Are you ready to take the leap?

to do ☑

GET AN OLD HYMNAL AND LOOK UP THE HYMN "TRUST AND OBEY." READ IT ALOUD OR, IF YOU KNOW IT, SING IT.

also on this day

The horse playing Mr. Ed on TV died.

A basketball game was first televised (Fordham University vs. the University of Pittsburgh) from Madison Square Garden in New York City. 1940

What is **faith**?
It is the confident **assurance** that what we **hope** for is **going** to happen.
It is the **evidence** of things we **cannot** yet **see**. [Hebrews 11:1]

Walk This Way

We're used to the "Walk/Don't Walk" signs. We know that even if we have the green light, we have to wait for the "Walk" sign to light up before we can cross the street. Someone in 1952 had that great idea to help us cross streets and tell us when it's safe to walk.

The Bible says a lot about "walking," but the references aren't about busy street corners. Most of the time, the word *walk* means "live." In other words, as you are living each day (walking through life), God says, remember this.

In today's verse, for example, Jesus tells his followers to walk in his light. And 1 John 1:7 says, "But if we are living in the light of God's presence" (many Bible versions read, "if we walk in the light"), "then we have fellowship with each other, and the blood of Jesus, his Son, cleanses us from every sin."

It always makes sense to walk in the light, doesn't it? If you're in a dark room and want to get out, you turn on the light. If you're camping in the woods and need to walk around, you turn on your flashlight. The light shows you the path and helps you take steps that are safe and sure.

Those who walk without light usually will get hurt—bump a knee, fall down, or worse. Those who walk in life without Christ's light won't do very well either.

We find his light in the Bible. When we read God's Word, the teachings, stories, and examples, it's like having a light shining on our path, showing us where to go, keeping us safe and heading in the right direction.

How's your walk?

to do ☑

TAKE A WALK AROUND THE NEIGHBORHOOD, PRAYING AT EACH HOUSE FOR THE PEOPLE WHO LIVE THERE. ASK GOD TO SHOW THEM THE LIGHT.

Jesus replied, "My light will shine out for you just a little while longer. Walk in it while you can, so you will not stumble when the darkness falls. If you walk in the darkness, you cannot see where you are going."

[John 12:35]

also on this day

This day was established in Scotland when a woman could propose to a man. If the man refused the proposal, he had to pay a fine.

1288

☀ 1940

Hattie McDaniel became the first African American to win an Oscar, which she won for her supporting role as Mammy in *Gone with the Wind*.

a true superhero

On this day in 1941, Captain America appeared for the first time in a comic book.

One of Marvel's biggest comic book successes and top-selling superheroes was Captain America. He debuted just prior to America's entry into World War II and was a symbol for the wave of public spirit and patriotism that followed Pearl Harbor. Captain America had agility, strength, speed, endurance, and reaction time superior to any human.

But the biggest attraction of this superhero was that Captain America wasn't born with great power—it had been bestowed upon him as a gift. This champion of freedom started out as Steve Rogers, a scrawny young man who had been rejected by the army as unfit for service. Then he was given a "strange seething liquid" that turned him into a superhero with extraordinary strength and power. It could happen to anyone—even an ordinary person.

As followers of Jesus Christ, we're much like Steve Rogers. Spiritually speaking, we're scrawny, powerless, and unable to save ourselves. But God offers us salvation through his Son and the power of his Spirit living in us. Through the gift of the Holy Spirit, we are strengthened and given all we need to accomplish what God has in store for us. And the best part is that this gift can be given to anyone.

So how can we have access to such a gift? All you need to do is make Jesus the Lord of your life. Becoming a Christian means that you can look forward to eternal life in Heaven.

That's much easier than downing a glass of "strange seething liquid," wouldn't you agree?

"And **now** I will send the **Holy Spirit**, just as my **Father** promised. But stay here in the city until the **Holy Spirit** comes and **fills** you with **power** from **heaven**." [Luke 24:49]

also on this day

Today is National Pig Day.

Today is Whuppity Scoorie Day—the Scottish Noise Festival welcoming spring.

1872 Yellowstone became the first national park.

to do ☑

CREATE YOUR OWN SUPERHERO. GIVE HIM OR HER A NAME, SPIRITUAL POWERS, AND A MISSION. IMAGINE THAT THIS SUPERHERO IS YOU!

just like new

Today is Old Stuff Day.

It could be that scruffy bit of blanket that you have carried around since you were a toddler. Or maybe it's the love-worn teddy bear with the torn ear and the missing eye. Or it could be that stack of treasured "art" from preschool featuring the stick people with big heads and mismatched faces. Whatever your secret stash may be, we all have old stuff that we just can't part with lying around in the closet, a desk drawer, or in the basement.

To be sure, old stuff can become quite valuable, like antique furniture, vintage cars, and jewelry that have been passed down from generation to generation. But when it comes to that old pair of jeans with the holes or the ratty sweatshirt, old stuff is, well, just old. It's valuable only to the owner. And eventually there comes a day when the old has got to go!

Spiritually speaking, we also can carry around a lot of old stuff—old habits, old attitudes, and old sins. And unless we get rid of that old stuff, our lives can become quite cluttered and sometimes even messed up. The good news is that Jesus offers us a chance to get rid of the old and become totally new! It's true. As Christians, we are brand new people on the inside. We are not the same anymore. When Jesus becomes our new master, we have new attitudes, new habits, and a new way of living.

Why not celebrate Old Stuff Day by taking an inventory of yourself? Are you still holding on to old habits that aren't very Christ-like? Maybe you have an old attitude that you know needs to be changed. Ask Jesus to help you get rid of that old stuff and bring in the new!

to do ☑

GET A SHEET OF PAPER AND ON ONE SIDE WRITE "OLD" AND ON THE OTHER SIDE, "NEW." LIST THE OLD ATTITUDES, HABITS, AND BEHAVIORS THAT YOU HAD. ON THE OTHER SIDE, RECORD WHAT HAS BEEN NEW SINCE YOU BEGAN FOLLOWING JESUS.

What this means is that **those** who become **Christians** become **new persons**. They are **not** the **same** anymore, for the **old life** is **gone**. A **new life** has **begun!** [2 Corinthians 5:17]

also on this day

Today is National Banana Cream Pie Day.

Dr. Seuss (actual name Theodor Seuss Geisel) was born. 1904

Walt Disney World® welcomed its 50 millionth visitor. 1976

A Singing Tribute

On this day in 1931, "The Star Spangled Banner" became America's national anthem.

"The Star-Spangled Banner," one of the most well-known national anthems, was originally written as a poem. During the War of 1812, Francis Scott Key and a friend were sailing down the Chesapeake Bay when the British began their attack on the city of Baltimore. Key and others with him watched the bombardment of Fort McHenry, which continued for two days. Through those long nights, the group was able to catch glimpses of the huge American flag—42-feet long—specially made to be big enough so that the British would not miss it.

When at last the shelling stopped, Key anxiously peered through the early morning fog to see if the flag was still flying. And so he wrote on the back of an envelope the poem he called "Defense of Fort M'Henry." As Key later said, "Then, in that hour of deliverance, my heart spoke: 'Does not such a country, and such defenders of their country, deserve a song?'"

As Key was inspired by the heroic defense of his country, so too were the psalm writers inspired by the acts and blessings of God. Just listen to some of their stirring tributes: "I will sing to the LORD because he has been so good to me" (Psalm 13:6); or "But as for me, I will sing about your power. I will shout with joy each morning because of your unfailing love. For you have been my refuge, a place of safety in the day of distress" (Psalm 59:16).

When we are aware of all that God has done for us, all the blessings he showers upon us daily, all the ways he guides, cares, and loves us, then we too will have to ask, "Does not such a God deserve a song?" He does!

to do ☑

GO AHEAD! SING A SONG TO GOD TODAY—EITHER ONE YOU KNOW, OR BE DARING AND WRITE YOUR OWN.

Sing about the **glory** of his **name**! **Tell** the **world** how **glorious** he is. [Psalm 66:2]

also on this day

1845 **Florida became America's 27th state.**

Alexander Graham Bell was born. 1847

1923 The first issue of *Time* magazine was published.

This is Courageous Follower Day.

come, follow me?

Leaders are the ones who take the greatest risks and who shoulder the responsibility for the success (or failure) of a venture. But where would these great leaders be if they had no followers? For example, how far would Christopher Columbus have sailed without his shipmates? What if no one followed General George Washington as he braved the cold, dark waters of the Delaware River that fateful Christmas Eve? And what if no one heeded the call to liberty by patriots such as Samuel Adams, Patrick Henry, and others? It takes courage to follow someone into uncharted waters, unknown territories, or into the face of life-threatening opposition.

Peter, James, and John faced all these uncertainties—and more—when a relatively unknown carpenter from Nazareth stood on the shores of the Sea of Galilee and asked them to "Come, be my disciples" (Mark 1:17). The three, in fact, put down their nets, left their families and only known source of income behind, and *followed*. At the time, they didn't know where this leader would take them. Even during the three years they spent with Jesus, they still had questions about who exactly this man was, what his (and their) mission was, and where he was taking them. Still they followed, willing to risk everything.

Do you have what it takes to be a courageous follower? Are you willing to follow Jesus when it means befriending the unpopular kid at school or refusing to follow the crowd? You may have questions about where Jesus is leading you, but you can be sure that following him is the right choice. It's worth the risk!

to do ☑

BE A COURAGEOUS FOLLOWER OF JESUS TODAY! DARE TO GO AGAINST THE CROWD. BE BOLD IN TELLING OTHERS ABOUT HIM.

also on this day

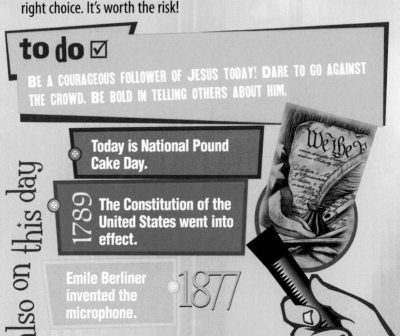

* Today is National Pound Cake Day.

1789 The Constitution of the United States went into effect.

Emile Berliner invented the microphone. 1877

"Come, follow me," Jesus said, "and I will make you fishers of men."

[Mark 1:17, NIV]

Perfect!

On this day in 1924, Frank Carauna became the first person to bowl two successive perfect 300 games.

The dream of every serious (and even the not-so-serious) bowler is to bowl the perfect game. That means throwing not one, not two, but 12 consecutive strikes. So imagine how Frank Carauna must have felt back in 1924 when he became the first to bowl two perfect 300 games—24 consecutive strikes in one afternoon. Amazing!

Perfection, particularly in sports, has always been a benchmark of the truly talented. For example, Romanian gymnast Nadia Comaneci earned the first perfect score of 10 in her sport during the 1976 summer Olympics. And she earned not just one 10, but seven. Of the thousands of pitchers who have come through the major league pipeline, only 17 have ever pitched perfect games, allowing no base-runners, no runs, hits, errors, hit batsmen, or walks over nine innings.

There's no doubt. Perfection, whether in sports, school, or other areas, is hard to achieve. And when it comes along, people take note.

So what does it mean when Jesus says, "But you are to be perfect, even as your Father in heaven is perfect" (Matthew 5:48)? Perfect? How can anyone be perfect this side of Heaven? God knows that we will never be flawless in this life. But we are to aspire to be as much like Jesus as possible. That means we need to mature as Christians. We need to keep growing in our faith through Bible study, being with other believers, prayer, and loving others as Jesus does. It also means keeping ourselves away from sinful values and activities and doing all we can to keep growing as Christians.

How can we do that? Thankfully, we don't need to rely on our own strength. Through the Holy Spirit God gives us the power and the energy to keep growing in our faith.

Perfect!

to do ☑

THINK OF ONE TASK THAT YOU FACE TODAY OR THIS WEEK. HOW COULD YOU USE GOD'S POWER AND STRENGTH TO FACE IT? ASK HIM FOR HELP RIGHT NOW!

We **proclaim** him, **admonishing** and **teaching** everyone with all **wisdom**, so that we may present **everyone perfect** in **Christ**. [Colossians 1:28, NIV]

also on this day

1770
"The Boston Massacre" took place, when British soldiers fired on a crowd of people in Boston, Massachusetts.

1845
The U.S. Congress appropriated $30,000 to ship camels to the western U.S.

1994
The world's largest milkshake was made, containing 1,955 gallons of chocolate, in Nelspruit, South Africa.

making an impression

On this day in 1950, Silly Putty® was invented.

While trying to produce a human-made rubber material, engineer James Wright came up with a gooey rubber-like substance that had a lot of bounce! While no practical use was ever found for the bouncing putty, a Connecticut toy store owner immediately recognized the fun appeal of the stuff and asked marketer Peter Hodgson to help him sell it.

Hodgson believed he had a blockbuster product on his hands and began packaging the gooey substance in plastic eggs, selling them for $1. The only thing lacking was a name. After much study, Hodgson came up with a name that he believed summed up the product perfectly—Silly Putty®!

For more than 50 years and with more than 300 million eggs sold, Silly Putty has become a staple of American childhood. Silly Putty's greatest appeal, though, goes beyond its bouncing ability. The best part is taking Silly Putty, pressing it onto newspaper, and picking up an imprint of the ink. Then you can stretch and distort the words and pictures into weird and silly shapes and images.

In a way, playing with Silly Putty is a lot like how God works with us. God has pressed into us his very image and likeness (Genesis 1:26). Obviously, we are not exactly like God. But our creativity, our feelings, and our ability to think and reason reflect God's image. We are made with the imprint of his character—his love, kindness, patience, forgiveness, and faithfulness.

Then the fun begins as he stretches and shapes us through our circumstances and our experiences. Over time, God molds and transforms us into the godly men and women that he has designed us to be. And as we spend more time with God, learning about him, we will become more and more like him!

And **we**, who with **unveiled faces** all **reflect** the **Lord's glory**, are being **transformed** into his likeness with **ever-increasing glory**, which comes from the **Lord**, who is the **Spirit**. [2 Corinthians 3:18, NIV]

also on this day

Today is Alamo Day. In 1836, the 13-day siege of the Alamo by Santa Anna and his army ended when the Mexican army of 3,000 men defeated the 189 Texas volunteers.

1475 Michelangelo was born.

1808 At Harvard University, the first college orchestra was founded.

to do ☑

IF YOU HAVEN'T PLAYED WITH SILLY PUTTY FOR A WHILE, GO AHEAD AND GET AN EGG! HAVE FUN STRETCHING IT AND MOLDING IT. AS YOU PLAY WITH YOUR SILLY PUTTY, IMAGINE THE WAYS THAT GOD IS STRETCHING AND MOLDING YOU RIGHT NOW.

Perhaps you are familiar with the story of Queen Esther—the beautiful, brave Jewish woman who won the beauty contest to become the new queen of Persia. She risked her life to approach the king and beg for the deliverance of the Jewish people from a signed death warrant and certain extermination. Because of her courage King Xerxes allowed the Jewish people to defend themselves, and the Jews of Persia were able to defeat their enemies and survive. This all happened on March 7 (the 14th day of the month of Adar of the Hebrew calendar), and to celebrate their deliverance, a new holiday was declared—Purim.

Jewish people today still celebrate Purim. In fact it is one of the most fun holidays on the Jewish calendar. Traditionally the day features carnival-like celebrations with plays and parodies, beauty contests, and much feasting. The celebration is sometimes referred to as the Jewish Mardi Gras. And of course the story of Esther is retold as a wonderful reminder of how God works in all situations—even when the circumstances seem bleak and overwhelming—to protect his people. In fact, Jewish people sometimes refer to these situations as "Purim stories"—meaning a crazy, mixed-up series of events that don't seem to make sense, but in the end all work out.

As Christians, we can celebrate that same truth. In the book of Esther, even though God is never mentioned by name, we can clearly see him at work in the lives of individuals and in the nation itself. We can be sure that God still is at work in our world as well. Even when we can't understand everything that is happening around us, we can be sure that God is faithful and that he will protect all who belong to him.

But the Lord is faithful; he will make you strong and guard you from the evil one. [2 Thessalonians 3:3]

to do ☑

CELEBRATE PURIM BY TAKING TIME TO READ THE STORY OF ESTHER (ESTHER 1–9).

also on this day

1933 The board game *Monopoly*® was invented.

Peter Pan became the first Broadway play to be televised in color. The original cast was featured. 1955

behind the scenes

Her-Story, His-Story

to do ☑

The purpose of International Women's Day is to remember women's struggles to achieve equality in the last hundred years and to recognize the achievements of women. Today it is observed by the United Nations and is a national holiday in many countries.

International Women's Day is the story of ordinary women as makers of history. One such woman in the Bible is Ruth—an ordinary woman who made history.

Ruth was the most unlikely of Bible heroines. She was from Moab, a longtime enemy of Israel. She had married an Israelite whose family had traveled from Bethlehem seeking relief from a famine. Years later, Ruth's husband died, her sister-in-law's husband had died, and her mother-in-law Naomi's husband had died. The three widows were left to fend for themselves.

Naomi told her daughters-in-law to stay in Moab and remarry, but she was going home. Ruth refused to leave Naomi. Ruth told her, "I will go wherever you go and live wherever you live. Your people will be my people, and your God will be my God."

So Ruth and Naomi returned to Bethlehem. Ruth went to the fields to gather the leftover grain so she and Naomi could eat. The field belonged to Boaz, a relative of Naomi's. Boaz, who had heard about Ruth's great devotion to her mother-in-law, took the two women under his protection and eventually married Ruth.

But the best part of the story is that Ruth and Boaz had a son named Obed. He later had a son named Jesse, whose son was David, King of Israel. And from David's family line came the most important person of all—Jesus.

Ruth was an ordinary woman doing ordinary things, but God used her to make history. Her story became *his* story.

But Ruth replied, "**Don't** ask me to **leave** you and turn **back**. I will **go** wherever **you go** and **live** wherever **you live**. **Your people** will be **my people**, and **your God** will be **my God**." [Ruth 1:16]

also on this day

1969 **The Pontiac Firebird Trans Am was introduced.**

Today is Middle Name Pride Day—tell someone your middle name and be proud!

1894

A dog license law was enacted in New York State. It was the first animal control law in the U.S.

time to PANIC?!

Today is Panic Day!

It's official. Today you have permission to lock yourself in your room, grab your security blanket or favorite stuffed animal, and stay in bed until tomorrow. It's Panic Day!

So what sends you into panic mode? A huge math test? Getting that book report done by next week? Maybe the idea of speaking in front of the class makes your hands start to sweat and puts your stomach in knots.

Whatever it is, we all face situations in which our first instinct is to hit the panic button. Tom Roy certainly knows. The Pennsylvania native came up with the idea of Panic Day in memory of his own panic attacks as a young actor. While he submitted the idea of this holiday as a joke, many people take this holiday all too seriously. Roy says, "Every year someone calls me and asks, 'Did you create Panic Day because of all the stuff that's going on in the world right now?'"

Good question. There's plenty to read about or hear in the news to make anyone panic. At times, events are enough to convince anyone that the world is out of control. You may even feel that way when you are forced to move because of a job transfer or when a loved one gets sick or when parents divorce. Life very quickly can go haywire.

So what can you do when panic begins to bubble up? First of all, remember who is in control. As the psalm writer reminds us, "The LORD is in his holy Temple; the LORD still rules from heaven. He watches everything closely, examining everyone on earth" (Psalm 11:4). Nothing happens to you that God does not know about or see. Trust him to care and guide you whenever panic hits.

I form the **light**
        and create **darkness**,
I bring **prosperity**
        and create **disaster**;
I, the LORD,
        do **all** these things.

[Isaiah 45:7, NIV]

also on this day

Happy birthday, Barbie®!

1562
Kissing in public was banned in Naples (punishable by death).

1858
Albert Potts of Philadelphia patented the street mailbox.

to do ☑

FIND OUT WHAT PUTS YOUR FRIENDS OR FAMILY MEMBERS INTO A PANIC. REMIND THEM OF WHO IS IN CONTROL.

for the love of money?

The United States issued paper money in 1862.

Paper money was first issued during the Revolutionary War by colonial governments. While some of the money was readily accepted in exchange for goods, other bills were not. During the war, the Continental Congress issued bills called "Continentals." But with no firm backing for the money, these bills essentially became worthless. As George Washington put it, "A wagonload of currency will hardly purchase a wagonload of provisions."

It wasn't until 1862 that the federal government issued Legal Tender Notes, also known as United States Notes. These new notes—issued in denominations from $1 to $1,000 (later $5,000 and $10,000)—were the first national currency used as legal tender for most public and private debts. Then in 1913, the Federal Reserve Act was passed to regulate the flow of money and stabilize the economy. These Federal Reserve Notes issued in 1914 make up more than 99 percent of today's paper money.

Today we value money for what it is able to purchase for us. People trust in their wealth to buy what they need and more—houses and cars, clothing, food, luxury items. We all understand and speak the language of money in our culture.

But King Solomon recognized an important truth: We can easily get trapped into trusting and depending on our money to meet our needs rather than God. We use money daily to solve our problems. Often it's the easiest way to get what we want. Money is necessary for survival, but if we begin to love money more than God and depend on it to meet our every need, then we will soon run into trouble. People who build their lives on money rather than God soon discover that they have nothing in their spiritual banks.

to do ☑

TAKE OUT A BILL AND LOOK FOR THE MOTTO "IN GOD WE TRUST." THINK OF ALL THE DIFFERENT WAYS YOU SHOULD TRUST IN GOD RATHER THAN IN MONEY.

Wisdom or **money** can get you almost **anything, but** it's important to know that only **wisdom** can **save** your **life.** [Ecclesiastes 7:12]

also on this day

515 BC
The building of the great Jewish temple in Jerusalem was completed.

The Salvation Army arrived in the United States from England.

1880

The Wrigley Company of Chicago raised the price of its seven-stick pack of Wrigley's chewing gum from a quarter to 30 cents.

1986

No one saw it coming. The previous day the weather had been unusually warm. The predictions were for fair weather. Then on the afternoon of March 11, light snow began to fall. Two days later, the Northeast was buried in 46.7 inches of snow.

At the time, the Blizzard of 1888 was called the "worst storm in living memory," and it still holds the distinction of the worst winter storm on record in many areas of the Northeast. The blizzard also had a long-reaching impact. The U.S. Weather Service Bureau was created to help better predict the weather, and cities began taking responsibility for snow removal.

Storms have a way of bringing our lives to a standstill. While we have better ways today of tracking and predicting storms, we often don't know where they will hit or how severe they will be.

Remember the disciples in the boat on the Sea of Galilee? There they were in the middle of the lake, when an unpredictable storm caught them off guard. They feared for their lives as they struggled to keep their boat afloat. And where was Jesus? Sleeping in the back of the boat. When the panicked disciples woke him up, Jesus rebuked the raging seas and the whipping winds. In an instant, the storm stopped. Then Jesus turned to his friends and said, "Where is your faith?"

Life's storms are like that, too. Whether you are faced with attending a new school, dealing with an illness in your family, or coping with an unexpected loss, remember Jesus' words. In the midst of the storm, we need to remember that Jesus is with us and that he can calm whatever storm we are facing.

"Where is your faith?" he asked his disciples. In fear and amazement they asked one another, "Who is this? He commands even the winds and the water, and they obey him." [Luke 8:25, NIV]

to do ☑

WHAT UNEXPECTED "STORM" HAS TAKEN YOU BY SURPRISE? BASED ON WHAT YOU JUST READ, WRITE DOWN THREE WAYS YOU CAN WEATHER THIS STORM.

also on this day

1969 Levi-Strauss started selling bell-bottomed jeans.

Today is Johnny Appleseed Day.

the great blizzard of 1888

On this day in 1888, the most famous storm in American history began.

The Girl Scouts was founded on this day in 1912.

good deeds

More than 90 years ago today, Juliette "Daisy" Gordon Low gathered 18 girls from her hometown of Savannah, Georgia, and held the first Girl Scout meeting. Juliette's vision was to form an organization that would help girls develop physically, mentally, and spiritually. The girls hiked, camped, played sports, learned first aid, and served others. Within a few years the group was organized officially as Girl Scouts, Inc. Today the group has a membership of more than four million girls. More than 50 million women in the United States today were once Girl Scouts.

At the core of Girl Scouting is the Promise. The Girl Scout Promise is the way members agree to act every day toward one another and other people. At every meeting girls affirm their commitment to the principles of Girl Scouts with these words: *On my honor, I will try: To serve God and my country, To help people at all times, And to live by the Girl Scout Law.*

At the heart of this promise is service and helping others. In much the same way, Christians need to put their faith into action by serving and helping others. James puts it this way: "Faith that doesn't show itself by good deeds is no faith at all—it is dead and useless" (James 2:17).

Our good deeds are an outward expression of our commitment to God. How do we show others what is in our hearts? By cleaning our room without being asked. Helping a classmate at school with homework. Volunteering to do the "dirty jobs" at church. Collecting canned food for the hungry. Deeds of loving service affirm our faith in Jesus.

Let your good deeds shine for God!

also on this day

Today is National Baked Scallops Day!

1789
The U.S. Post Office was established.

1894
Coca-Cola® was sold in bottles for the first time.

In the **same** way, let **your** good deeds **shine** out for **all** to see, so that **everyone** will **praise** your heavenly **Father**.

[Matthew 5:16]

to do ☑

PUT YOUR FAITH INTO ACTION WITH A GOOD DEED AT HOME, AT SCHOOL, OR IN YOUR NEIGHBORHOOD.

the family tree

Today is Genealogy Day.

Where do your ancestors come from? Where do you fit on your family tree? Are you related to some famous person in history? Maybe you haven't given much thought to questions like this, but thousands of people spend countless hours trying to discover the answers to the secrets hidden in their personal family trees.

Genealogy, the record of members of a family, is the second most popular hobby in America today—right after gardening. Genealogy is fun and educational, and everyone can join in, no matter how old. It's like a mystery—you never know who you might find belonging to your family.

Genealogies were important in biblical times. In numerous places in the Bible, you will come across long lists of names tracing biblical family trees. (For example, see Genesis 4, 5; 1 Chronicles 5, 6; Ezra 10.) It's often tempting to skip over these passages as just a long list of dead people, but genealogies were critical to the Jewish people. Why? For one thing, family trees were helpful in tracing priestly or royal descent. The genealogies also showed how God was at work through families in the Jewish nation. (Remember, the promise of a great nation had been given to a family—Abraham's—and passed down from there.) The New Testament has two genealogies that trace Jesus' family tree, showing that Jesus was related to all Jews (Matthew 1:1-17) and that Jesus was related to all humankind (Luke 3:23-38). Both Matthew's and Luke's genealogies establish without a doubt that Jesus is the Messiah and the Savior of the world.

Go ahead and read one of the two New Testament genealogies. If you are a follower of Jesus, then guess what? You belong to Jesus' family tree as well!

to do ☑

IF YOUR FAMILY HASN'T DONE SO, TAKE SOME TIME TO MAKE A FAMILY TREE AS FAR BACK AS YOU CAN GO.

A **record** of the **genealogy** of **Jesus Christ** the son of **David**, the son of **Abraham**.

[Matthew 1:1, NIV]

also on this day

1781
The planet Uranus was discovered. In 1930 the planet Pluto was discovered.

1887
Chester Greenwood of Maine patented earmuffs.

The comic strip *Dennis the Menace* appeared for the first time.

1951

Albert Einstein was born on this day in 1879.

Great Wisdom

When *Time* magazine selected the most important person who lived in the 20th century, the editors chose Albert Einstein: "He was the pre-eminent scientist in a century dominated by science. The touchstones of the era—the [atomic] Bomb, . . . quantum physics and electronics—all bear his imprint." Einstein has been hailed as a "genius among geniuses" and the greatest thinker of the 20th century.

Slow in learning to talk as a child, expelled by one school headmaster, and proclaimed by another as unlikely to amount to much, Einstein went on to develop theories that would change how we view and practice science forever. His work in quantum physics and the theory of relativity, for example, continues to impact how we view our world today.

Great minds and thinkers like Einstein inspire us, and rightfully so. Most of us can't imagine being that wise. Yet, the truth is that being wise—being able to determine right from wrong—is never out of our reach. You may not be able to come up with the latest or greatest scientific theory, but you can always know what God wants you to do. How? James tells us that all we have to do is ask God, "who gives generously to all without finding fault" (James 1:5, NIV).

Godly wisdom goes beyond just knowing facts and information. It is the ability to make the right decision in difficult situations. It is choosing what God wants instead of what we want. And it comes from learning God's will by reading his Word and then doing it.

Want to be known as a wise person? Ask God for wisdom. Then do what he tells you!

to do ☑

IN WHAT AREAS OF YOUR LIFE DO YOU NEED WISDOM? TAKE TIME RIGHT NOW TO ASK GOD FOR HIS WISDOM.

If you need **wisdom**—if you want to **know** what **God** wants you to **do—ask him,** and he will **gladly** tell you. He will **not** resent your asking. [James 1:5]

also on this day

1892 Today is National Potato Chip Day. Have a bag!

1914 Henry Ford announced the new continuous motion method to assemble cars, reducing the time it took to make a car from 12 hours to 93 minutes.

1794 Eli Whitney received a patent for his cotton gin.

Today is the Ides of March.

"Beware the Ides of March," the fortune-teller warned in Shakespeare's play, *Julius Caesar,* forever marking that day with a sense of ill will and feeling of dread. And for those who know the fate of Julius Caesar on that particular day, it's no wonder (More about that later!).

At that time, the Romans wouldn't have thought twice about the Ides of March. Even Shakespeare's audience wouldn't have blinked at the mention of that date. To the Romans, the Ides of March was simply the standard way of saying March 15. In the Roman calendar, every month had an Ides, usually on the 15th day, sometimes on the 13th. The Ides was one of three days that the Romans used as reference points for counting other days.

It was the events that occurred on that day, later immortalized in Shakespeare's *Julius Caesar,* that have forever associated the Ides of March with betrayal and evil. On that day, Julius Caesar's so-called friends and followers assassinated him while he sat on his gilded throne in the Roman Senate. As he lay dying from the many stab wounds he received, historians reported that Caesar looked up at his friend Brutus and said, "You, too, my child?"

Years later, another leader would be betrayed by another so-called friend. This time the leader would be betrayed by a kiss—a signal that led to Jesus' arrest and death on a cross. The "friend"? Judas Iscariot.

Let this day serve as a reminder of the true, real friends in your life. Friends that stick close to you, listen to you, and care about you are valuable. They are worth much more than the dozens of superficial, fair-weather friends, who vanish when life gets tough.

There are "friends" who destroy each other, but a real friend sticks closer than a brother. [Proverbs 18:24]

to do ☑

TELL A FRIEND THAT TODAY IS THE IDES OF MARCH. AND THEN EXPLAIN WHAT IT MEANS. THEN TELL YOUR FRIEND WHAT HE OR SHE MEANS TO YOU.

also on this day

1907 Finland is the first European country to give women the right to vote.

GIVE WOMEN THE VOTE

Wilt Chamberlain is the first to score 4,000 points in an NBA season. 1962

the ides of march

the truth will set you free

Freedom of Information Day is celebrated each year on the anniversary of the birth of James Madison, the fourth president of the United States and chief author of the Bill of Rights. The day's purpose is to focus on the importance of every citizen's right to obtain government information in a democratic society.

An important part of obtaining truth about the government was established in 1966 through the Freedom of Information Act. This law establishes the public's right to obtain information from agencies such as the Defense Department, the State Department, and the Central Intelligence Agency.

As James Madison wrote, "A popular Government without popular information or the means of acquiring it, is but a prologue to a farce or a tragedy or perhaps both. Knowledge will forever govern ignorance, and a people who mean to be their own governors must arm themselves with the power knowledge gives."

Madison noted that knowing the truth and having knowledge were important elements in a free society. Jesus also taught that knowing the truth was essential to being free. And what is that truth? The Bible tells us that Jesus is truth and the source of truth. John wrote, "For the law was given through Moses; grace and truth came through Jesus Christ" (John 1:17, NIV). Jesus identifies himself as the truth. "I am the way, the truth, and the life" (John 14:6).

As the source of all truth, Jesus is able to set us free from our sins, from the consequences of our sins, and from the deception of Satan. Jesus clearly shows us the way to God—and when we know God, we have true freedom.

Jesus' perfect truth gives us the freedom to be all that God intends for us to be.

to do ☑

COMPLETE THIS SENTENCE, "BECAUSE I KNOW JESUS LOVES ME AND FORGIVES ME, I AM FREE TO _____."

also on this day

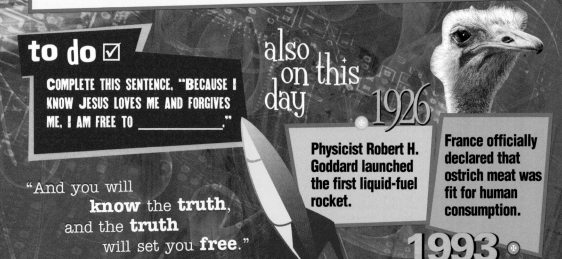

1926
Physicist Robert H. Goddard launched the first liquid-fuel rocket.

France officially declared that ostrich meat was fit for human consumption.

1993

"And you will **know** the **truth**, and the **truth** will set you **free**."

[John 8:32]

the real St. Patrick

Today is St. Patrick's Day.

So exactly who is St. Patrick?

Patrick, the patron saint of Ireland, was actually born in Wales. His name was Maewyn, and he almost didn't get the job as bishop of Ireland because he was uneducated. In fact, far from being a saint, Patrick grew up a pagan. At age 16 he was sold into slavery by a group of Irish bandits who had raided his village. During his captivity Patrick became closer to God. Patrick wrote, "and the faith grew in me, and the spirit was roused, so that, in a single day, I have said as many as a hundred prayers, and in the night nearly the same."

After six years Patrick escaped and went to Gaul where he studied in a monastery. During that time, the young man realized that his calling was to convert pagans to Christianity. Patrick's first wish was to return to Ireland and convert the pagans there. But his superiors sent another man first. Patrick was appointed as the second bishop to Ireland.

Patrick devoted his life to serving Christians already living in Ireland and to converting the pagans. He traveled throughout Ireland, establishing monasteries and opening schools and churches. By the time of his death, nearly the entire country of Ireland had become Christians. Patrick died on March 17 in 461—the day that has been commemorated as St. Patrick's Day ever since.

While most Americans celebrate St. Patrick's Day with shamrocks and wearing green, the real intent of the day was to pray for missionaries around the world. So if you want to wear green today, go ahead. But be sure to take time to thank God for the many men and women who have devoted their lives to spreading the good news of Jesus Christ.

> Then he told me, "The God of our ancestors has chosen you to know his will and to see the Righteous One and hear him speak. You are to take his message everywhere, telling the whole world what you have seen and heard." [Acts 22:14, 15]

also on this day

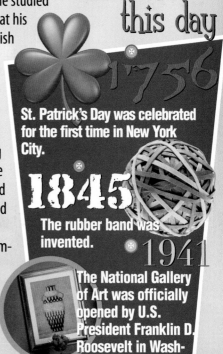

1756
St. Patrick's Day was celebrated for the first time in New York City.

1845
The rubber band was invented.

1941
The National Gallery of Art was officially opened by U.S. President Franklin D. Roosevelt in Washington, D. C.

to do ☑

SHARE WITH SOMEONE TODAY THE REAL MEANING OF ST. PATRICK'S DAY.

The first space walk took place on this day in 1965.

Mission Impossible

Imagine you are 200 miles above Earth, orbiting the planet in a spacecraft that is going about 18,000 miles an hour. Your co-astronaut helps you into a pressurized suit, makes sure your oxygen tank is operating properly, and then opens the hatch to the spacecraft. And there you are—ready to embark on your EVA—Extravehicular Activity, better known as a space walk.

Most of us wouldn't give another thought to the concept of actually walking in space (to be completely accurate, it's really more like floating in space). Astronauts perform this rather routine procedure all the time during space flights. It's no more incredible than landing on the moon or docking at a space station located hundreds of miles above us in space.

Yet when Soviet cosmonaut Alekse Leonov performed the first space walk on March 18, 1965, high above Siberia, it was an incredible feat. To many people it was unbelievable. And when a human being first stepped onto the surface of the moon four years later, it was like watching the impossible happen. Now we talk about going to Mars, and no one doubts that someday it just might happen.

Sometimes our technology and scientific knowledge make us feel as though we can do *anything*. Nothing is impossible given enough time, knowledge, and money. But if we're looking for the impossible to be done, there's only one for whom everything is possible. He is the one who spoke and the world came into being. He is the one who has power over life and death. He is the one who dared to live on this planet as a human and offer eternal life to everyone who believes.

With God, nothing—absolutely nothing—is impossible.

to do ☑

THINK ABOUT SOMETHING YOU'VE READ ABOUT OR LEARNED ABOUT THAT AMAZES YOU. NOW THINK ABOUT SOMETHING GOD HAS DONE THAT AMAZES YOU.

Jesus looked at them and said, "With **man** this is **impossible**, but with **God all** things are **possible**."

[Matthew 19:26, NIV]

also on this day

* Today is National Buzzard Day.

* Poppin' Fresh, the Pillsbury Dough-boy®, was introduced. * **1961**

* **1881** Barnum & Bailey's *Greatest Show on Earth* opened in Madison Square Garden in New York City.

It's a chocoholic's dream and a dieter's nightmare: a chocolate candy bar weighing in at over 5,000 pounds! It took three days to make, was 124 inches long, 59 inches wide, and 17.7 inches thick. According to the *Guinness World Records,* it was the largest bar of chocolate ever made.

We are fascinated with the greatest, the biggest, the longest, the fastest, the highest, or the best. Just check out the website for the *Guinness World Records.* With the click of the mouse, you can discover where to buy the world's most expensive hamburger, who has the world's longest beard, or who grew the world's tallest celery plant. And if that's not enough for you, today also marks the date in 1994 when the world's largest omelet in history was made with 160,000 eggs in Yokohama, Japan.

If you are looking for the world's best gift-giver, though, don't bother looking in the *Guinness World Records.* You're not going to find that record there. When it comes to the absolute best, nothing tops what God gives us each and every day. James tells us that "every good and perfect gift" comes from him. God specializes in giving us good things. Take a look at what God gives us: life, food, rain and fruitful seasons, wisdom, and peace. He lavishes upon us grace, love, forgiveness, compassion, kindness, rest, strength, and power.

But his very best gift—the greatest, most spectacular, most amazing gift of all—was his Son. The familiar words of John 3:16 remind us that "For God so loved the world that he gave his only Son, so that everyone who believes in him will not perish but have eternal life."

That beats any chocolate bar—no matter how big.

Every good and perfect gift is from above, coming down from the Father of the heavenly lights, who does not change like shifting shadows. [James 1:17, NIV]

The world's largest chocolate bar was made on this day in 2000.

to do ☑

WRITE A THANK-YOU NOTE TO GOD TODAY FOR THE GIFTS HE HAS GIVEN TO YOU. BE SPECIFIC.

also on this day

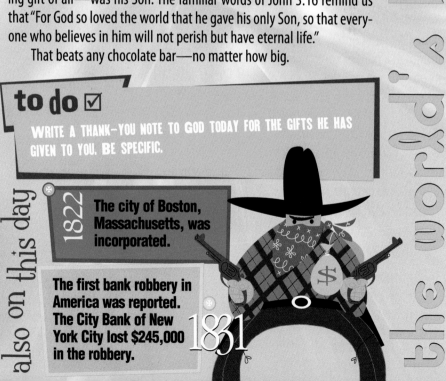

1822 The city of Boston, Massachusetts, was incorporated.

The first bank robbery in America was reported. The City Bank of New York City lost $245,000 in the robbery. **1831**

the world's best

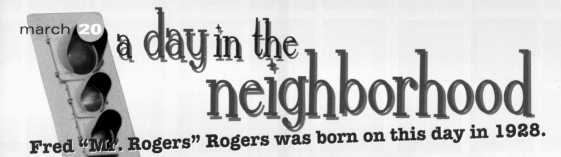

a day in the neighborhood

Fred "Mr. Rogers" Rogers was born on this day in 1928.

Many of us grew up listening to the soothing and reassuring voice of Mr. Rogers as he entered his home, took off his jacket and shoes, put on his familiar sweater and comfy sneakers, and welcomed us into his neighborhood.

Fred Rogers devoted his life to the welfare and well-being of children through the power of television. "He was so genuinely, genuinely kind, a wonderful person," said David Newell, who played Mr. McFeely on the show. "His mission was to work with families and children for television. That was his passion, his mission, and he did it from Day One."

"I got into television because I hated it so," Rogers said of his show, which became the longest running program on PBS from 1968 to 2001. "And I thought there was some way of using this fabulous instrument to be of nurture to those who would watch and listen."

In 2002, President George W. Bush awarded Rogers with the Presidential Medal of Freedom, the nation's highest civilian honor, for his contribution to the well-being of children and a career in public television that demonstrated the importance of kindness, compassion, and learning.

As an ordained minister, Fred Rogers took a page from his master and teacher, Jesus. Jesus openly welcomed even the youngest child into his presence. In fact, he scolded his disciples for keeping the children away from him (see Mark 10:14). Jesus had a special place in his heart for children and warned his disciples that anyone who harmed them would be punished severely (Matthew 18:4-6). But anyone who welcomed a little child, he said, would be welcoming him.

That's a good act to follow—show those younger than you the kindness and care you would give to Jesus.

> But when **Jesus** saw what was happening, he was **very** displeased with his disciples. He said to them, "**Let** the children **come** to me. **Don't** stop them! For the **Kingdom** of **God belongs** to such as these." [Mark 10:14]

also on this day

Today is Rotten Sneaker Day.
Today is Big Bird's Birthday.

1947

A blue whale weighing 180-metric tons was caught in the South Atlantic Ocean.

1999

Bertrand Piccard and Brian Jones became the first men to circumnavigate the Earth in a hot air balloon. The non-stop trip began on March 3 and covered 26,500 miles.

to do ☑

SPEND SOME TIME WITH A YOUNGER CHILD TODAY! TREAT HIM TO AN ICE CREAM, OR READ HIS FAVORITE BOOK. AS YOU DO THIS, REMEMBER JESUS AND HIS LOVE FOR CHILDREN.

Do you remember?

Today is Memory Day.

How good is your memory? Can you remember what you wore to school a week ago? How about the name of your preschool teacher? Our memory—the ability to recall past events, facts, people, or figures—is an important function we rely on daily.

Sometimes the information we have stuffed in our memory isn't very useful. We call that *trivia*. At other times our ability to recall facts and figures is critical. Just try taking a history test when your memory goes blank! Witnesses in court can play a crucial role in determining guilt or innocence as they recount what they saw or heard.

We have all sorts of ways to help our memory. Flash cards help us remember math facts. We have calendars, address books, assignment notebooks, PDAs, and other devices to help us remember birthdays, appointments, and other necessary information. We make lists, set alarms, and even tie strings around fingers so we won't forget an important errand.

One of the most important pieces of information we can store in our memories is God's Word. Knowing God's Word makes us wise, helps us know what to do in every situation, and keeps us from sinning. We are told to write God's Word on our hearts (Psalm 40:8), to treasure his Word as a precious gem (Psalm 119:72), and to use his Word as a weapon against Satan (Ephesians 6:17).

As important as memorizing God's Word is, however, it's just the first step. The Bible tells us that the way to keep from sinning is not only to hide God's Word in our heart but also to *obey* and *follow* God's rules (Psalm 119:9). It's a one-two punch—memorize and obey!

Don't forget!

to do ☑

CELEBRATE MEMORY DAY BY MEMORIZING TODAY'S VERSE. WHAT OTHER WORDS OF GOD CAN YOU HIDE IN YOUR HEART?

I have **hidden** your **word** in my **heart**, that I might **not sin** against **you**.

[Psalm 119:11]

also on this day

⊛ **Today is National Flower Day. Give someone special a flower!**

1685 **The great composer Johann Sebastian Bach was born.**

Nintendo released Game Boy Advance®.

2001

On this day in 1455, The Gutenburg Bible was the first book ever printed.

The Power of Print

If you have one or more Bibles in your home, take a moment to say thank you to Johann Gutenberg, who on this day in 1455 printed the world's first book, the Bible. Gutenberg was a native of Mainz, Germany. He began experimenting with casting movable type in the 1440s. By about 1450 Gutenberg had perfected a technique that allowed him to produce enough type to print small grammar books and other short works. It was soon afterward that he began work on the project to which his name would forever be linked—the Gutenberg Bible.

Gutenberg and his workmen produced close to 180 copies of the Bible. Each Bible consisted of nearly 1,300 pages, measuring about 16 inches by 12 inches (that's a big book!). Gutenberg never made a profit from his invention or from publishing the Bible. In fact, he died penniless and owing money. Today one of his surviving Bibles is worth millions of dollars.

Gutenberg's invention ushered in the print revolution. Information was now accessible to the general population. In the ensuing years, church leaders like William Tyndale worked to translate and print the Bible into the English language.

Because of the determination and creativity of men like Gutenberg, Tyndale, and others, we now have access to the Bible in any number of translations, with study notes, devotions, maps, charts, and other aids to help us understand God's Word. The power of God's Word is available in 500 different languages today and is available to more than 35 million people around the world.

Spend some time today celebrating Gutenberg's great gift to us by reading your Bible!

to do ☑

MAKE IT A PERSONAL GOAL TO READ THE BIBLE DAILY. ASK A PARENT OR YOUR SUNDAY-SCHOOL TEACHER FOR A READING PLAN. YOUR BIBLE MAY HAVE ONE IN THE BACK. CHECK IT OUT!

It is the **same** with my **word**. I **send** it out, and it **always** produces fruit. It will accomplish **all** I want it to, and it will **prosper everywhere** I send it. [Isaiah 55:11]

also on this day

Today is National Goof-Off Day.

Tara Lipinski, at 14 years and 10 months, became the youngest women's world figure skating champion. **1997**

1954 The first shopping mall opened in Southfield, Michigan.

the long journey

On this day in 1806, Lewis and Clark began their return journey from the Pacific Coast.

Imagine setting out on a journey without a map, without any directions, and without knowing your final destination. That's exactly what Meriwether Lewis and William Clark had to do when Thomas Jefferson commissioned the two to explore the newly purchased Louisiana Territory. Their mission? To discover an overland route to the Pacific Ocean, following the Missouri and Columbia rivers. When Lewis and Clark set out on May 14, 1804, it was the beginning of one of America's greatest adventures.

More than a year later the expedition stood on the beaches of the Pacific Ocean near the mouth of the Columbia River. With winter soon to arrive, the expedition set up camp and waited for spring before setting out for home. So on March 23 the expedition started back up the Columbia and headed homeward.

When Lewis and Clark started out, they didn't know where they were going to end up. They didn't know what they might encounter. They only had their mission and their supplies.

Thousands of years earlier, a man named Abraham faced a similar journey. He didn't know exactly where he was going. He certainly didn't have a map, and he didn't know what he was going to encounter on his way. He only knew that God had told him to leave his homeland and go to a new land that God would show him. There God would make Abraham the father of a great nation. Abraham trusted God and obediently went.

You may never have to explore uncharted land like Lewis and Clark did. But God may lead you to unknown places, like Abraham, where you can serve him. That's when you will need to respond like Abraham—with trust and obedience.

also on this day

1513 Ponce de Leon discovered Florida.

1775 Patrick Henry declared, "Give me liberty or give me death!"

1839 The expression "OK" [oll korrect] was first used—in Boston's *Morning Post*.

Then the LORD told Abram, "**Leave** your **country**, your **relatives**, and your father's **house**, and **go** to the **land** that I will show you."

[Genesis 12:1]

to do ☑
MAKE A MAP OF YOUR LIFE. MARK THE PLACE WHERE GOD HAS YOU TODAY. INCLUDE, IF YOU CAN, WHERE YOU THINK GOD WILL LEAD YOU IN THE FUTURE.

great escapes!

Harry Houdini, one of the world's most famous escape artists, was born this day in 1874. Houdini, whose real name was Ehrich Weiss, built his career on the notion that he could escape from anything.

Houdini became most famous for his escapes from handcuffs. During his career, the handcuffed Houdini escaped from sunken packing crates, an enormous paper bag (without tearing the paper), padded cells, coffins, a roll-top desk, burglar-proof safes, a preserved giant squid (yuck!), a giant football, a diving suit, a U.S. mail pouch, and a plate glass box.

While acts like Houdini's amaze us and leave us thinking, "How did he do that?" these feats of trickery pale in comparison to the great escapes in the Bible. Remember Paul and Silas? While in Philippi, the pair was arrested, beaten, and thrown into the dungeon of the prison. And since the jailer was ordered not to let Paul and Silas escape, he further clamped their feet into leg stocks, a type of "feet-cuffs." Get the picture?

Yet, in the middle of the night, as Paul and Silas were singing hymns of praises to God, an earthquake shook the prison. The prison doors flew open. The chains of every prisoner fell off! But Paul and Silas remained in the jail. And because they stayed, the jailer wanted to know all about the God that they worshiped. That very night the jailer and his entire family were saved.

Paul and Silas didn't have to rely on sleight of hand or illusions. Instead they relied on God. And we can too. When we focus on God, rather than our own problems, he is able to perform amazing acts right before our eyes.

His great works are too marvelous to understand. He performs miracles without number. [Job 9:10]

to do ☑

DO YOU HAVE A FAVORITE CARD TRICK? PERFORM ONE FOR A FRIEND OR FAMILY MEMBER. THEN TELL THEM WHO PERFORMS THE MOST AMAZING ACTS AND MIRACLES.

also on this day

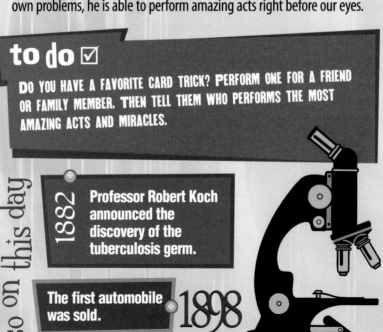

1882 Professor Robert Koch announced the discovery of the tuberculosis germ.

The first automobile was sold. **1898**

Free at Last!

In 1807, the British Parliament abolished the slave trade.

Since 1772 it had been legally recognized that individuals in Britain could not be slaves. However, that did not prevent the British from participating—and leading—the international trade in slaves. British ships loaded with cheap goods such as firearms, gunpowder, alcohol, and beads would sail to Africa and return with slaves. At the height of the slave trade, British ships were said to carry about 50,000 slaves a year.

In the late 1700s, men like William Wilberforce and Thomas Clarkson worked tirelessly to stir public opinion against this practice. Then in 1807, as the acting spokesman in parliament against slavery, Wilberforce was successful in getting the slave trade abolished throughout the British Empire. But that was only the beginning. Wilberforce spent the remaining years of his life working for the abolition of slavery itself. In 1833, as Wilberforce lay dying, he was informed that the Abolition of Slavery Act was passed. After a bloody civil war, the United States freed all its slaves and abolished slavery some 30 years later.

It's hard for us to understand the concept of slavery today. We live in a country where we are free to speak our minds, to worship as we please, and to go where we want. We consider ourselves free people. But the Bible tells us that there is another type of slavery. If we are without Jesus, we are slaves to our selfish desires and our sinful nature.

Slavery to sin is bad news. The good news is that Jesus died on the cross to set us free from sin. That doesn't mean we are free to do whatever we want. No, that would lead us right back into slavery. Jesus has set us free to live unselfishly for him and for others. Celebrate your freedom today!

to do ☑

FINISH THIS SENTENCE:
"THANK YOU GOD THAT I
AM FREE TO DO _____
_____
TODAY."

Christ has set us **free** to **live** a free life. So take your **stand!** **Never** again let **anyone** put a harness of **slavery** on **you**.

[Galatians 5:1, The Message]

also on this day

The city of Venice was founded.

421

1668

The first horse race in America took place.

It's Your Day!

This is National Make Up Your Own Holiday Day!

By now you probably have noticed that there is a holiday for just about every day of the year. There are holidays to celebrate food, animals, people, and events. Here are a few you have already missed: Happy Mew Year Day for Cats (January 2); Answer Your Cat's Question Day (January 22); or Stop Bad Service Day (March 7). But you still have time to mark your calendar for the following: Cow Appreciation Day (July 14); Raspberries and Cream Day (August 7); Elephant Appreciation Day (September 22); even Eat a Red Apple Day (December 1).

Now to be sure, the majority of holidays mark significant events such as birthdays, national milestones, and other important celebrations. In fact, holidays have been around a long time (take a look at tomorrow's entry to see one really ancient celebration). After God delivered the Israelites from slavery in Egypt, he gave them a whole list of holidays and festivals to celebrate and observe. These holidays reminded the people of God's great miracles and helped them remember what God had done for them.

That's not a bad place to start when creating your own holiday. Begin with God and how he has cared for you and your family. Maybe you can celebrate "Dad's New Job Day," or "We're All Healthy, Thank You Very Much Day." Or maybe it's time to throw a party because it's "I Have a New Friend Day" or "God Keeps Me Safe Day." Once you think about it, there are probably as many ways as days in a month—make that in a year—to celebrate God's goodness and care for you.

So go ahead. Create your own holiday. Celebrate "National Fig Day" if you want. Just start your celebration with thanks to God.

to do ☑

PLAN A FAMILY CELEBRATION TODAY FOR YOUR SPECIAL HOLIDAY. MAKE DECORATIONS. PLAN AT LEAST ONE ACTIVITY OR GAME TO GO ALONG WITH YOUR CELEBRATION. THEN HAVE FUN!

We **praise** you, LORD, for **all** your **glorious power**. With **music** and **singing** we **celebrate** your **mighty acts**.

[Psalm 21:13]

also on this day

1953
Dr. Jonas Salk announced the discovery of a new vaccine that would prevent polio.

Groundbreaking ceremonies were held in Washington, D. C., for the Vietnam Veterans Memorial.
1982

Donald Duck co-hosted the Academy Awards.
1958

get up and smell the air

Today is Smell the Breezes Day in Egypt.

You made the moon to mark the seasons and the sun that knows when to set. [Psalm 104:19]

Believe it or not, this holiday is one of Egyptian culture's oldest traditions. Known as *Sham el Nessim*, it probably was celebrated as early as 4,500 years go. Sham el Nessim literally means "sniffing the breeze" and marks the beginning of spring. According to Egyptian tradition, you are supposed to get up early, cut open an onion, and then smell it! Then during the day you are supposed to take time to go outdoors and enjoy the fresh air.

Today, celebrating Smell the Breezes Day is much the same—with the possible exception of cutting an onion! Millions of Egyptians take the opportunity to go out and have a picnic. The holiday celebration also includes special foods such as smelly fish like sardines or anchovies, dyed eggs, and greens such as green onions and lettuce. In some areas of Egypt, the day is marked with folk dances and parades.

What a great way to welcome spring, don't you think? The changing of the seasons happens without fail year in, year out. Most of us probably go from winter to spring, and spring to summer without taking much notice, except to put away our coats. Yet, each passing season is a reminder of our great God, who created this world and set into motion the pattern of each season. Immediately after the flood during Noah's time, God promised that the world would go on: "As long as the earth remains, there will be springtime and harvest, cold and heat, winter and summer, day and night" (Genesis 8:22). God promised never again to destroy the world with water, and the rainbow is a sign of that promise.

Celebrate spring this year like an Egyptian. Go outside and take a deep breath. Let the sweet smell of springtime air refresh you and remind you of God's everlasting faithfulness.

to do ☑

WEATHER PERMITTING, PACK A PICNIC LUNCH OR DINNER WITH YOUR FAMILY. THEN GO OUTSIDE AND SMELL THE BREEZES!

also on this day

1790 — The shoelace was invented.

1884 — The first long-distance phone call was made between Boston and New York City.

On this day in 1797, Nathaniel Briggs patented the washing machine.

Clean Up!

The next time you throw your laundry in the hamper, be thankful you don't have to go down to the nearest river or stream to wash your clothes by hand! Before the washing machine, people got dirt out of their clothes by pounding them on rocks and rinsing them in streams. Of course, that's better than what sailors did. They used to throw their clothes in a bag over the side of the ship and trail the bag behind them with the hopes that the rushing water would remove the dirt.

In 1797, Nathaniel Briggs came up with an invention that he believed would revolutionize this backbreaking chore for women—the predecessor of today's automatic washing machine, the washboard. While it was one step removed from lugging the clothes down to the river, this invention still required a lot of work on the part of the cleaner. Still, it was a beginning.

Today we enjoy the convenience of throwing our dirty laundry into the washing machine, adding a cupful of detergent, turning on the machine, and walking away. About 30 minutes later—clean clothes!

Now we all know it's important to keep our outer selves clean and wear clean clothes every day. But it's also important to keep our inner selves clean. You don't need a washing machine to do that. You don't even need to find the nearest stream and pound out the dirt. All you need to do is go before God, confess your "dirty laundry," and God will wash away your sins.

David knew that clean feeling that comes when we confess our sins before God and we are confident that he forgives us. Read Psalm 51, and rejoice with David that we have a God who is able to clean us daily—without scrubbing!

to do ☑

WHAT DO YOU NEED TO CONFESS TO GOD TODAY? GIVE HIM YOUR "DIRTY LAUNDRY" AND LET HIM WASH YOU CLEAN.

Purify me from my **sins**, and I will be **clean**; **wash me**, and I will be **whiter** than **snow**.

[Psalm 51:7]

also on this day

1885 The Salvation Army was officially organized.

Sally Ride became the first woman in space. 1983

⊛1979 A major accident occurred at Pennsylvania's Three Mile Island nuclear power plant. A nuclear power reactor overheated and suffered a partial meltdown.

Jammed!!

On this day in 1848, an ice jam stopped the flow of water over Niagara Falls.

Niagara Falls is the second largest waterfall in the world. Water from Lakes Michigan, Erie, Superior, and Huron empty into the Niagara River and then fall over a spectacular drop the same height as a 20-story building.

Nearly 12 million visitors make the trek yearly to view the majestic beauty of the falls. But imagine going to Niagara Falls and not seeing a drop of water trickle over. Even in the coldest of winters, the tremendous volume of water never stops flowing.

One time, however, the flow of water over the falls completely stopped for several hours because of an ice jam in the upper river. The Falls didn't freeze over, but the flow of water stopped so that people were able to walk out and recover lost items from the riverbed.

The ice jam halting the flow of water over Niagara Falls is a good word picture for what happens when we allow sin to go unconfessed in our lives. Just like the ice jam upstream completely cut off the flow of water from the falls, our sin completely cuts us off from God. If we continually ignore our wrong thoughts, attitudes, and actions, we will find ourselves separated from God. His love, grace, and forgiveness cannot flow through us because our sin is acting liking an ice jam. Remember, God is completely holy. He cannot ignore, excuse, or tolerate our sin in any form.

That's the bad news. The good news is that our sin does not prevent God from loving us. The Bible tells us that when we confess our sins to God and turn from them, he is always willing to forgive us. Just as the flow of water rushed over Niagara Falls after the ice jam was removed, so a deluge of God's forgiveness washes and removes our sins and our guilt.

But there is a problem— your sins have cut you off from God. Because of your sin, he has turned away and will not listen anymore.

[Isaiah 59:2]

also on this day

1790 John Tyler, the 10th president of the United States, was born in Virginia.

1886 Coca-Cola® was invented.

1974 *Mariner 10* became the first spacecraft to reach the planet Mercury. It had been launched on November 3, 1973.

to do ☑

FIND SOME PICTURES OF NIAGARA FALLS ON THE INTERNET. LET THEM REMIND YOU OF GOD'S OVERFLOWING LOVE FOR YOU AS YOU CONFESS YOUR SINS.

who's in control?

This is I Am in Control Day.

Who is in control at your house? At school? We all know people who are in control. They are the ones who make the decisions, come up with the plans, and get stuff done. Maybe that describes you!

In certain situations it's good to know that somebody is in control—like when you are flying in an airplane or going to the dentist. You certainly want to know that a trained and experienced pilot controls the plane, or that a professional dentist is about to fill in your cavity.

We all like to feel as though we have control. We like to feel free to make our own decisions and choices. But we can quickly get into trouble when we believe that "*I* am in control." Take for example, King Nebuchadnezzar (Daniel 1–4). He was king of the greatest empire of the world at that time. Everyone had to obey his every command. Nebuchadnezzar answered to no one, or at least he thought so.

One day as he was congratulating himself on all his great accomplishments, God said, "You are no longer ruler of this kingdom. . . . You will live in the fields of the wild animals, and will eat grass like a cow." And King Nebuchadnezzar did just that for seven long years. You see, the king had forgotten an important fact. Although he knew about the God of Israel, Nebuchadnezzar didn't really think that God was in charge. Only after living like a cow for seven years did the king come to his senses and recognize that God was truly in control.

So rather than celebrate "I Am in Control Day," take time to acknowledge and thank the one who really is in charge of everything!

to do ☑

READ KING NEBUCHADNEZZAR'S PRAISE SONG TO GOD IN DANIEL 4:34, 35. THINK ABOUT ALL THE WAYS GOD IS IN CONTROL RIGHT NOW.

All the people of the **earth** are **nothing** compared to **him**. **He** has the **power** to do as he **pleases** among the **angels** of **heaven** and with those who live on **earth**. [Daniel 4:35]

also on this day

1858 Hyman L. Lipman of Philadelphia patented the pencil.

The U.S. signed a treaty that purchased Alaska from Russia for $7.2 million. **1867**

Amelia Earhart became the first woman to make a solo flight across the Atlantic. **1932**

Tower of Pride

On this day in 1889, the Eiffel Tower opened.

The Eiffel Tower, an immense structure of exposed latticework made of iron, was built for the Paris Exposition of 1889. At the time, it was the world's tallest structure. At 984 feet, it was a soaring celebration of the science and technology achievements of the age.

The Tower was not without its critics. One group of French artists called the Eiffel Tower "useless and monstrous"—an affront to French taste and the arts. At one time it was almost torn down, saved only because of its antenna, which was used for telegraphy. Today it is completely accepted by French citizens and is internationally recognized as one of the symbols of Paris itself.

Of course, the Eiffel Tower was not the first time humans had built a structure to honor their own achievements. That distinction goes to the Tower of Babel (see Genesis 11). After the flood, and the world had been repopulated, the people of the world decided that they would erect a tower in honor of—themselves! It most likely was a ziggurat (a pyramid-looking structure with steps). Often they would be as tall as 300 feet and just as wide.

The Tower of Babel was undoubtedly an incredible sight to see. But the people built it for all the wrong reasons—for their honor and glory, not God's. We can do the same thing when we "build monuments" by using trophies, awards, report cards, clothes, or possessions to call attention to our achievements and ourselves. It's OK to be good at sports or at school, or to be honored for your achievements. But when those items or honors take God's place in your life, you may be building a monument that will never last.

to do ☑

TAKE AN INVENTORY OF YOUR ROOM OR YOUR LOCKER AT SCHOOL. WHAT "MONU-MENTS" DO YOU HAVE TO YOUR ACHIEVEMENTS? WHAT CAN YOU DO TO MAKE THOSE "MONUMENTS" A TRIBUTE TO GOD?

Before his **downfall** a man's **heart** is **proud**, but **humility** comes before **honor**.

[Proverbs 18:12, NIV]

also on this day

Today is National Bunsen Burner Day.

1918
Daylight savings time went into effect for the first time.

1870
In Perth Amboy, New Jersey, Thomas P. Munday became the first African-American to vote.

I VOTED! DID YOU?

This is April Fools' Day!

merry christmas!

also on this day

Have you ever tried to fool someone on this day? Saying it's Christmas probably won't work too well. Have you ever been fooled?

Sometimes on this day we play tricks, like setting an alarm early, telling a friend to go to the principal's office, or putting a fake spider on your mother's plate. Those are harmless pranks, and usually everyone gets a good laugh.

But there's another kind of deception that's a lot more serious. And it happens more than just one day a year.

When the apostle John wrote 1 John, he warned Christians about people he called "false prophets." These people were trying to fool people into believing lies about Jesus and God's plan of salvation. Unfortunately, some were falling for it and being led the wrong way. So John said to test everyone who claims to be teaching truth about God. The test? See if they believe that Jesus, God himself, actually lived as a man, a real human being (see 1 John 4:2).

Today we have false teachers, too. Sometimes you'll hear them on TV or radio, claiming to have special inside knowledge about how to get close to God. Or you might hear about a best-selling book that promises meaning in life, happiness, and salvation. What they say may sound good, and even true, but it's false.

Don't be fooled. Before listening to anything someone says about God, Jesus, and how to know God personally, find out if the person believes that Jesus is God *and* human. And check what they say with what the Bible teaches. It should match. That's the test.

to do ☑

ASK A PARENT OR ANOTHER RESPECTED CHRISTIAN HOW HE OR SHE CAME TO FAITH IN CHRIST.

1748 The ruins of Pompeii (a town in Italy that had been destroyed by a volcano) were found.

Oliver Pollack designed the symbol for the dollar ($). *1778*

Dear friends, do not believe everyone who claims to speak by the Spirit. You must test them to see if the spirit they have comes from God. For there are many false prophets in the world. [1 John 4:1]

a hint of mint

In 1792, the U.S. Mint began operations.

Hey, do you know what a mint is? Not the hard candy that you eat after dinner, but *mint* as in the U.S. Mint. Here's a hint. If you work there you're not allowed to take home samples.

Actually, a mint is where money is made. That's where the expression "worth a mint" comes from. At one time or another, everyone would like to be able to make his or her own money. But that would be against the law. Only the government can produce coins and bills.

But what if you could have your own mint? Imagine you had tons of money. Do you think your life would change?

Most would answer, "You bet!" And then they tell of all the stuff they'd buy and things they'd do—clothes, CDs, electronic gear, sports equipment, fabulous vacation trips, and a few gifts for friends. Sounds great, right?

Well, this is another area where it's easy to be fooled. Money looks good, but it can cause a bunch of trouble.

That's what Paul was telling young Timothy in today's verse. The love of money can lead to greed, theft, broken relationships, anger, hatred, cheating, and even murder. And worst of all, money can become an idol, taking the place of God in a person's life.

Money itself isn't bad. In fact, God gives us money and other resources to use for him. But loving it and craving it is terrible.

Stick to the candy mint!

to do ☑

LOOK AT TODAY'S PAPER AND FIND ALL THE NEWS ARTICLES ABOUT PROBLEMS CAUSED BY MONEY. JUST ABOUT EVERY SECTION, EVEN THE SPORTS SECTION, WILL HAVE SOMETHING.

also on this day 1805

Famous author Hans Christian Anderson was born.

The first Easter "egg roll" on the grounds of the White House was held. 1877

The first clear photograph of the sun was taken. 1845

For the **love** of money is at the **root** of all kinds of **evil**. And **some** people, craving money, have **wandered** from the faith and **pierced** themselves with many **sorrows.** [1 Timothy 6:10]

idle and idol

In 1953, the first issue of TV Guide was published.

About how much time do you spend watching television each day? Most Americans spend a bunch. And when you aren't sure what's on, do you channel surf with the remote, or do you check out a schedule?

Many people arrange their lives around the TV schedule. In fact, *TV Guide* is one of the nation's most-read magazines, with a circulation of about 9 million.

Television has become a huge part of our lives. And, according to people who study these things, it has changed us in two very significant areas.

First, many of us have become "couch potatoes." We sit or lie around and watch, instead of being active, moving around, going outside, and playing sports. As you might expect, this has led to more and more people being overweight and out of shape. We're idle.

The other big change involves our expectations, what we want out of life. The products we see advertised on TV look *so* good. And the TV stars are beautiful and talented and seem *extremely* happy. So these days everyone seems to want to be a celebrity. All the "reality" shows add to this, giving certain individuals a few hours on prime time. *American Idol* promises fame and fortune to each winner.

We can feel plain and ordinary when we compare ourselves to television personalities. We may even think, "What can I do? I don't have those looks and abilities. I'm a nobody, not a star."

When that feeling hits, review today's featured verse. Paul wrote that God uses ordinary people. In fact, most of the early believers were not wise, powerful, or wealthy in the world's eyes. Yet to God they were important, and they changed the world!

So forget those American idols and listen to God. Only his opinion of you matters.

Remember, dear **brothers** and **sisters**, that **few** of **you** were **wise** in the world's eyes, or **powerful**, or **wealthy** when **God** called you. [1 Corinthians 1:26]

also on this day

This is National Find a Rainbow Day.

1860
The Pony Express began delivering mail.

1868
A Hawaiian surfed on the highest wave ever—a 50-foot tidal wave.

to do ☑

TAKE A VACATION FROM TV. FOR ONE DAY, A COUPLE OF DAYS, OR A WEEK, WATCH NO TELEVISION. ASK YOUR PARENTS TO HELP YOU STICK TO THIS DECISION.

O K, you're on a trip with your family and sitting in the backseat of the car. Overhearing the conversation between your mom and dad, you sense that you may be lost—their frustration level is rising. Soon you see your mother pull out a map, point to it, and say something like, "I guess we should have turned there!"

Whenever we travel, it's good to have directions. Otherwise we'll go the wrong way and be lost. Even if we think we know the right way and are very sincere about it, we should probably check a map to make sure. We *could* be sincerely wrong!

Life is like that. People travel along, heading in a certain direction. Kids go to school, go to college, get jobs, get married, have children . . . they make a lot of decisions and turns. Wouldn't it be great to have a guidebook or map to show us the right way to travel through life?

We have one. It doesn't look like a map, but it's a guidebook all right. And you probably have one in your room.

It's the Bible—God's Word.

Look at what the verse for today promises. It says that Scripture teaches us what is true and right. In other words, the Bible puts us on the right road in life and keeps us there.

That's why reading and studying the Bible is so important. When we read a passage and then ask, "What's the point here? What does God want me to know and to do?" we will find our directions.

Don't get lost. Check God's map.

All Scripture is inspired by God and is useful to teach us what is true and to make us realize what is wrong in our lives. It straightens us out and teaches us to do what is right. [2 Timothy 3:16]

Today is National Reading a Roadmap Day.

to do ☑

IF YOU HAVEN'T ALREADY STARTED A REGULAR BIBLE READING PROGRAM, IT'S NOT TOO LATE TO START.

also on this day

1828 The process for making cocoa powder was patented.

Martin Luther King Jr. was assassinated. 1968

way to go!

In 1985, an estimated 5,000 radio stations around the world simultaneously played the song, "We Are the World."

Together

In the mid-1980s people became very aware of the problem of hunger in Africa, with powerful pictures of starving children broadcast on TV. So a group of musicians, led by Harry Belafonte, Lionel Ritchie, Stevie Wonder, and Quincy Jones, formed U.S.A. for Africa to raise money to feed those who were starving. Eventually more than 44 musicians joined to record "We Are the World." The recording quickly rose to number one, and in a tremendous show of unity, stations around the world played the song at the same time.

Wouldn't it be great if Christians were known for that kind of unity, with people from many different backgrounds, shapes, sizes, and languages joining together as one? That's what Jesus wants us to do.

In today's passage Jesus is praying for his disciples right near the end of his time on earth. As you read the verse, listen to the feeling in Jesus' voice. He knows he will be leaving soon to experience the pain of the cross. Yet he prays for those men who have remained close to him.

But check out the previous verse. Jesus said, "I am praying not only for these disciples but also for all who will ever believe in me because of their testimony" (John 17:20). Wow! That means Jesus was praying for us—for me and for *you*.

And his prayer is that we would be "as one." The unity of Jesus' followers would help the world believe that he really was sent from God and died for sins.

Do people at your school and in your neighborhood see unity among you and your fellow believers? What do you suppose they think about Jesus because of you and your relationships?

That's something to think about.

to do ☑

DO YOU KNOW ANOTHER CHRISTIAN AT YOUR SCHOOL, SOMEONE WHO GOES TO A DIFFERENT CHURCH? ASK HIM OR HER A FEW QUESTIONS LIKE THESE: WHAT DO YOU LIKE ABOUT YOUR CHURCH? WHAT'S YOUR FAVORITE BIBLE VERSE? HOW CAN I PRAY FOR YOU?

"My prayer for all of them is that they will be one, just as you and I are one, Father—that just as you are in me and I am in you, so they will be in us, and the world will believe you sent me." [John 17:21]

also on this day

1965 Lava Lamp Day was celebrated.

The Mayflower sailed from Plymouth, Massachusetts, on a return trip to England. 1621

•1614

American Indian Pocahontas married English colonist John Rolfe in Virginia.

go for the gold

In 1896, the first modern Olympic games opened in Athens, Greece.

The Olympic games are a dazzling display of athletic ability, sportsmanship, and international goodwill. Every two years, alternating summer and winter games, millions of people around the world watch their national heroes "go for the gold." Observers are thrilled as the winning athletes receive the medals, accompanied by their national anthem.

Frequently the broadcasts of the games are interrupted by "up close and personal" stories of individual competitors. We learn about each athlete's hometown, family, workout schedule, and path to the Olympics. The stories are inspiring, especially when we see the tremendous dedication, hard work, and the countless hours of working out invested in an Olympic goal. For some of the young people, a sport has become life!

Very few people get to be in the Olympics. But almost anyone can exercise and work out. And we don't have to compete for medals or awards to benefit from sports and activity. Regular exercise helps us keep our weight under control, build strength and endurance, and live longer and better. Hopefully, many who sit and watch the Olympics will be inspired to get up and work out.

In today's verse, the apostle Paul agrees that physical exercise is good. But even more important, he points out, is *spiritual* exercise. People work out spiritually by regularly spending time studying the Bible, praying, learning from godly teachers, worshiping, and sharing their faith. That's like stretching, doing sit-ups and push-ups, lifting weights, swimming, biking, and running a few miles. But the rewards are worth more than even the Olympics.

What's your workout schedule? Go for the gold!

Physical exercise has **some value**, but **spiritual** exercise is much **more** important, for **it** promises a **reward** in both **this** life and the **next**. [1 Timothy 4:8]

also on this day

This is National Library Week.

1906
The first animated cartoon was copyrighted.

1924
Four planes left Seattle on the first successful flight around the world.

to do ☑

PUT TOGETHER A DAILY PHYSICAL AND SPIRITUAL WORKOUT SCHEDULE. FOR EXAMPLE, YOU COULD START EACH DAY BY DOING 10 SIT-UPS AND THEN READING A CHAPTER OF THE BIBLE. AS YOU GAIN STRENGTH, INCREASE WHAT YOU DO IN BOTH AREAS.

teamwork

This is No Housework Day.

Whoever named this day must have been tired, or must have wanted a break from the daily routine of washing clothes, dusting furniture, vacuuming floors, cleaning up, picking up, and straightening up. But imagine if this day were to extend into a week or a month—what a mess!

The fact is someone needs to do housework. No one wants to live in disgusting filth (isn't that how your room was once described?). That's why families need to pull together and work together. So everyone is assigned jobs to do around the house.

Someone takes out the garbage. Someone sets the table. Someone takes care of the dishes. Other chores include cutting grass, shoveling snow, raking leaves, weeding, making school lunches, babysitting . . . the list seems endless. And everyone is expected to clean up his or her own messes!

Are you tired yet?

Actually, effective families are like winning teams (remember the Olympics?). And teamwork means that each person plays a role and does his or her part . . . and does it well.

You say, "Sometimes I feel like a slave!" Guess what—Paul was writing to *real* slaves when he wrote today's verse. But it applies to any kind of work we have been given: work for pay, schoolwork, and even chores. We are to work *hard* and *cheerfully*. And the secret for doing that is to know that we are working for God, not Mom, Dad, the teacher, a coach, or a boss.

Which of your chores are waiting to be done? Get going.

to do ☑

THIS WEEK, DO YOUR CHORES BEFORE YOU HAVE TO, ESPECIALLY BEFORE YOUR PARENT GETS ON YOUR CASE. AND DO YOUR WORK WITH A GOOD ATTITUDE. THAT WILL PLEASE GOD, AND—WHO KNOWS?—THE REST OF THE FAMILY MAY FALL DOWN IN SHOCK!

also on this day

1864
One of the first camel races in the United States was held in Sacramento, California.

The first steel columns were set for the Empire State Building.
1930

Work hard and cheerfully at whatever you do, as though you were working for the Lord rather than for people.

[Colossians 3:23]

Forever, it seems, people have wanted to stay young, even back in the 1400s. And people today are still looking for a "fountain of youth"—skin treatments, vitamins, and special diets—anything that can help them live better and longer.

They want to look young and feel young and to slow down the aging process. That's because old age can be a pain. Joints and muscles ache, sicknesses hit, much is spent on prescriptions and doctors, and death moves closer. In today's verse, Solomon wrote that many old people "no longer enjoy living." One version of this verse (The Living Bible) translates old age as "the evil years."

When we're young we have energy, and life is fun and exciting. So exciting, says Solomon, that we can forget about God. We can get so involved in playing games, spending time with friends, going to parties, eating, laughing, and enjoying our youth that we feel no need for our creator.

But life passes quickly, and before we know it, we're much older and wishing for our own fountain of youth.

Actually, a young person without God can become a bitter old person. Maybe you know someone like that—always complaining and griping, always feeling bad, joyless, and sad. But a young person *with* God can become a grateful and gracious old person, someone who has spent a lifetime serving the Lord and can look back with no regrets. Maybe you know someone like that: a grandparent, a neighbor, or someone at church.

Which kind of person do you want to become? It's your choice.

This is the birthday of Ponce de Leon (1460). He's the Spanish explorer who spent much of his life searching for the Fountain of Youth.

Don't let the excitement of youth cause you to forget your Creator. Honor him in your youth before you grow old and no longer enjoy living. [Ecclesiastes 12:1]

to do ☑

TALK TO ONE OR MORE ELDERLY PEOPLE WHO SEEM TO BE JOYFUL. ASK THEM THE SECRET OF THEIR HAPPINESS AND HOW THEY CAME TO FAITH IN CHRIST.

also on this day

1893 *The Critic* reported that the ice cream soda was the national drink of the U.S.

1974 Hank Aaron of the Atlanta Braves hit home run 715, surpassing Babe Ruth's record 714.

the evil years

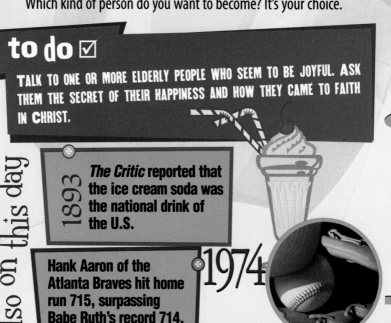

War and peace

In 1865, General Robert E. Lee and his 26,765 troops surrendered to Union General Grant at the Appomattox Court House in Virginia. This ended the U.S. Civil War.

War is terrible—always. Sometimes wars are necessary when dictators enslave, despots attack, and nations and terrorists invade. Evil people spreading evil must be stopped. But wars exact an awful price. And this day marks the end of one of our nation's costliest wars, in which Americans fought each other.

Families and friends can engage in their own "civil wars"—neighborhoods and churches, too. And most of those conflicts begin over unimportant and even silly issues. It's so sad to see people who should love each other fighting for a petty reason.

The verse for today is found in a familiar part of the Gospels called the Sermon on the Mount. In this sermon Jesus was teaching his disciples and the gathered crowds what being his follower would mean. Obviously he thought that working for peace is important, and he said that those who do so will be blessed.

Peacemaking means making an effort to get along. It may involve swallowing our pride and keeping silent when we want to yell and scream. It may mean compromising or giving in. It certainly means loving the other person and treating him as a special and loved creation of God.

With whom are you "at war" these days? Someone at school? A brother or sister? What will it take to make peace with that person?

Work for peace.

God **blesses** those
who work for **peace**,
for **they** will be called
the **children** of God.

[Matthew 5:9]

also on this day

The annual Rat Race and Parade are held in Louisville, Kentucky.

1833
Peterborough, New Hampshire, opened the first municipally supported public library.

1959
NASA announced the selection of America's first seven astronauts.

to do ☑

MAKE A LIST OF PEOPLE WITH WHOM YOU OFTEN HAVE DISAGREEMENTS, CONFLICTS, OR FIGHTS. USE THAT AS A PRAYER LIST. ASK GOD TO WORK IN THEIR HEARTS AND ON YOUR RELATIONSHIPS WITH THEM.

Looking Good!

In 1797, Claude Ambroise Seurat, the world's skinniest man, was born in Troyes, France.

Claude was so skinny he was called "the human skeleton." He probably was so skinny that he would be marked absent in class, had to move around in the shower to get wet, and would look like a zipper when he turned sideways and stuck out his tongue. Just kidding!

Have you ever felt too thin? How about too fat? We should eat the right foods and exercise, of course, but most Americans are way too concerned about their looks. Comparing ourselves to movie celebrities or magazine models, we never see our bodies and faces as just right.

But God made people of all shapes and sizes. Some people are tall, and some people are short. Some of us have dark skin, and others have light skin. Certain individuals have long noses, and others have short ones. Some are naturally athletic, and some are gifted in music. Aren't the differences great? Wouldn't it be boring if we were all alike?

We can be easily fooled by the way people look on the screen or in ads. Virtually all of those actors and models have had surgery or have taken other extraordinary measures to make themselves look that way. Most people look normal. The next time you're at a mall, amusement park, or other large gathering, look around. You'll see a wide variety of God's creations. And that's good.

Psalm 139 presents an amazing view of our lives as God sees us. And check out the good news in today's verse—God watched over us, even before we were born, putting us together just as he wanted.

Does that mean we should let ourselves go and become slobs? Of course not! It does mean, however, that we can accept the way God made us and celebrate who we are.

By the way, you look great!

to do ☑

TAKE A GOOD LOOK AT YOURSELF IN THE MIRROR. SPEND A FEW MINUTES THANKING GOD FOR WHAT YOU SEE—HAIR, EYES, NOSE, SKIN, BODY TYPE, HEIGHT—AND FOR WHAT YOU DON'T SEE—PERSONALITY, TALENTS, INTELLECT, ABILITIES, AND FAMILY.

You **watched** me
    as I was being **formed**
in **utter** seclusion,
    as I was **woven** together
in the **dark** of the **womb**.

[Psalm 139:15]

also on this day 1849

Walter Hunt of New York City patented the safety pin. He sold the rights for only $100.

This is also National Cinnamon Crescent Day (yum!).

This is National Siblings Day (be nice to yours).

On this day in 1947, Jackie Robinson became the first African-American to play baseball in the major leagues.

Safe at Home

Watch almost any major sporting event, and you'll see athletes of a variety of skin colors, races, and nationalities. So you might be surprised to learn that for a long time, the major leagues of professional baseball were open to white people only. Many black players were good enough, but they weren't allowed. So they played in the "Negro Leagues."

In 1947, however, Jackie Robinson broke the color barrier when he joined the Brooklyn Dodgers. And he was named Rookie of the Year! Just two years later he received the National League's Most Valuable Player Award. In 1957, Jackie retired from baseball, after helping the Dodgers win six National League championships and one World Series. He was elected to baseball's Hall of Fame in 1962.

Certainly Jackie was a sensational athlete; he was also courageous—that first year he endured a lot of criticism, threats, and taunts. But soon many other African-Americans followed, and the color barrier was obliterated.

Racism (treating people differently because of their race, skin color, or nationality) is wrong and should have no place in our lives. Christians especially should steer away from this sin.

The Bible is very clear about God loving all kinds of people. In fact, the apostle John reports that individuals "from every nation and tribe and people and language" will be included in God's kingdom (Revelation 7:9). And today's verse states that we should be unified in Christ.

What separates you from others? Race or skin color shouldn't. Remember Jackie Robinson and Galatians 3:28, and be the kind of person who is known for love and unity.

to do ☑

TODAY, GO OUT OF YOUR WAY TO GET TO KNOW A PERSON OF ANOTHER RACE. THIS COULD BE A STUDENT IN ONE OF YOUR CLASSES, A NEIGHBOR, OR SOMEONE AT CHURCH.

There is **no longer Jew** or **Gentile**, **slave** or **free**, **male** or **female**. For you are **all** Christians— you are **one** in **Christ Jesus**.

[Galatians 3:28]

also on this day

1986
Dodge Morgan sailed solo nonstop around the world in 150 days.

1970
Apollo 13 was launched to the moon.

Albert Einstein introduced his Theory of Relativity. **1906**

Since this is National Mathematics Education Month, here's a test: Take three apples from five apples and how many do you have? The answer: three (that's how many you took). Now that was a *trick* question.

In your very first arithmetic classes you learned to add and subtract. You found, for example, that $2 + 2 = 4$, $4 + 4 = 8$, and so forth. And you've never forgotten those lessons. They make sense. They're true. You can take it to the bank!

Things add up in other areas as well, not just in numbers and math. For example, if at a friend's house you see a dog food dish, a leash, and a bag of dog food, and you hear barking, you conclude that the family has a dog. The evidence is clear—it all adds up.

When we want answers to questions, we look for evidence. Then we add the clues together to discover the truth.

The evidence for the reality of God and Jesus works that way. People may wonder and have questions, but they need to check out the evidence. At the beginning of his Gospel, Luke wrote that he had investigated the evidence and was presenting it to his readers so they could be sure (see Luke 1:1-3).

Then, in today's passage, John, one of Jesus' closest followers and friends, says he is writing as an eyewitness. John's conclusion? "He is Jesus Christ, the Word of life."

God doesn't want us to check our brains at the door. He says to look closely, investigate, ask, check out the evidence. So don't get stressed out if you or your friends have questions about faith. When you look at the evidence, you'll find that it all adds up.

The one who existed from the beginning is the one we have heard and seen. We saw him with our own eyes and touched him with our own hands. He is Jesus Christ, the Word of life. [1 John 1:1]

This is National Mathematics Education Month.

to do ☑

READ ONE OF THE GOSPELS (MATTHEW, MARK, LUKE, OR JOHN) AND LOOK FOR EVIDENCE OF THE TRUE IDENTITY OF JESUS. KEEP TRACK OF YOUR FINDINGS AND SHARE THEM WITH A PARENT.

also on this day

1861 The Civil War begins with the attack on Fort Sumter, South Carolina.

1900 Puerto Rico becomes a U.S. territory.

it all adds up

the whole picture

In 1796, the first elephant was brought to America from Bengal, India.

Did you hear about the blind men who encountered an elephant? One man held the tail of the animal, so he thought an elephant was like a rope. Another man had his arms wrapped around a leg, so he thought an elephant was like a tree trunk. The third man had hold of the animal's trunk. There's no telling what that man thought! Because the men were blind, they couldn't see the animal and were limited to the part they encountered.

That's often how it is with people and Jesus. If a person only sees part of Jesus, one aspect of his life, that person might form a wrong opinion of him.

One time Jesus asked his disciples what people were saying about him. They had a list of answers. They reported that some people said he was a religious radical; some thought Jesus was a spiritual leader; others said he was a great teacher. Those ideas were correct, but each one gave only part of the picture. Then Jesus asked who they, his close followers, thought he was. And Peter gave the right answer: "The Messiah, the Son of the living God."

Today people probably would give similar responses. Everyone seems to have an opinion about Jesus. Some would say that he was a very good man. Others might mention his life-changing teachings and great moral example. Some might even say that Jesus was God's Son. But the whole picture includes all of that and more. The truth is that Jesus is 100% God and 100% man. He came to earth to live a perfect life, to die on the cross for our sins, and to rise from the dead. He's alive!

Do you have the whole picture?

to do ☑

GO OVER YOUR LIST FROM YESTERDAY (EVIDENCE FOR JESUS' TRUE IDENTITY). THINK OF HOW YOU WOULD HAVE ANSWERED JESUS IF YOU HAD BEEN THERE THAT DAY AND JESUS ASKED YOU, "WHO DO YOU SAY THAT I AM?"

When Jesus came to the region of Caesarea Philippi, he asked his disciples, "Who do people say that the Son of Man is?" "Well," they replied, "some say John the Baptist, some say Elijah, and others say Jeremiah or one of the other prophets." Then he asked them, "Who do you say I am?" Simon Peter answered, "You are the Messiah, the Son of the living God." [Matthew 16:13–16]

also on this day

This is National Peach Cobbler Day.

Thomas Jefferson was born.

1743

that's a laugh!

This is International Moment of Laughter Day.

Because this is International Moment of Laughter Day, go ahead—chuckle, giggle, guffaw . . . let it out.

Everyone enjoys a good laugh, but people have differing senses of humor. Some people enjoy puns or word play. Others enjoy physical humor or slapstick, like watching someone fall down or getting a pie in the face. Some people think awkward situations, such as you see in TV situation comedies, are humorous. And many enjoy jokes that tell a story and catch them by surprise. Regardless of the source of the humor, doctors report that laughter is good for our health.

So laughing, being happy, and having fun can be great. But you know what's even better? *Joy.* Happiness, laughter, and fun can be superficial and hide problems and hurts. As Proverbs 14:13 reminds us, "Laughter can conceal a heavy heart; when the laughter ends, the grief remains." But joy shines out from the inside. Laughter can only last for minutes, while joy can last a lifetime. Happiness depends on "happenings," but joy comes from knowing that God loves us and that our future is secure in him.

No wonder Paul encouraged the Philippian believers to "always be full of joy in the Lord."

So think again—what makes you laugh? And what brings you joy?

Always be **full** of **joy** in the **Lord**. I say it again— **rejoice!** [Philippians 4:4]

also on this day

This is National Pecan Day.

1853

Harriet Tubman began her underground railroad, helping slaves escape.

to do ☑

ASK A PARENT, GRANDPARENT, OR SUNDAY-SCHOOL TEACHER TO TELL YOU A GOOD JOKE. ALSO, MEMORIZE TODAY'S VERSE, PHILIPPIANS 4:4.

The Taxman Cometh

This is Income Tax Day.

1040

to do ☑

ASK A PARENT TO EXPLAIN HOW TAXES WORK AND WHAT IT MEANS TO BE A GOOD CITIZEN.

"**Well then**," he said, "give to **Caesar** what **belongs** to him. But **everything** that belongs to **God** must be given to **God**."

[Luke 20:25]

Ask any adult about April 15, and he or she will frown and mumble about income tax. This is the payment deadline. Most people have money taken out of their checks every payday, so they expect to receive refunds. But *all citizens*, even those who don't make enough to pay any taxes, are required to fill out the forms, and that can be a pain.

Every level of government has taxes. In addition to income taxes, we pay taxes on property, sales, entertainment, parking, gas, travel, and on and on. No wonder people can feel taxed to death. But how else would the government get money to operate? Our taxes pay for salaries of teachers, police officers, firefighters, and government workers. Taxes pay for the construction and maintenance of roads and highways, schools, libraries, government buildings, and much more.

The people of Jesus' day sure didn't like paying taxes, especially since they lived under the Romans, a foreign power. And the powerful Roman government could be very cruel. So one day some people who were trying to trick Jesus asked if it was right to pay taxes. Jesus simply answered, "Give to Caesar what belongs to him." But then he added, "Everything that belongs to God must be given to him."

Jesus was saying that his followers should honor the government and be good citizens whenever possible. But he was also pointing out that God is a higher authority, over *all* rulers and governments. In fact, everything belongs to God (not to us or anyone else), including our very lives, so we must give ultimate honor and devotion to him.

What can you do to give back to God what belongs to him?

also on this day

1452 Leonardo da Vinci was born.

The ocean liner *Titanic* hit an iceberg and sank. **1912**

✳ **1865** Abraham Lincoln died after being shot in a theater by John Wilkes Booth.

Every now and then a city engineer will report a bridge needing work because of "stress cracks." The daily pounding of traffic and the years of changing temperature and other forces have taken their toll. If not repaired, the bridge might collapse.

People can experience stress too. Life's pressures wear on us, making us weak and worried. The signs include headaches, sleep problems, nervousness, and a constant bad mood. Maybe you remember when a parent seemed to get mad about every little thing, and later you learned about the tough day at work. The stress led to anger that was taken out on others.

Maybe you've had a similar experience. After a rough day at school with teachers piling on the homework, you learned that a friend was in an accident. Then, on the way home, you had an argument with a friend. And just as you walked in the door, Mom reminded you of all your chores. Talk about stress! Can you feel the pressure, the cracks? No wonder you were in a bad mood.

Life is filled with anxieties, worries, and stresses—we can't escape them. But we can deal with them. The first step is to be aware of what is causing us stress. Next, the Bible tells us we should, "Give all your worries and cares to God, for he cares about what happens to you" (1 Peter 5:7). This means praying and giving our stress to our loving heavenly Father. It doesn't mean you shouldn't be concerned about your friend, dive into your school assignments, heal your relationship, or do your chores. It means realizing that God cares about you and your life situations more than you do, and he's there to help—you can count on him.

So cast your cares on the one who cares.

to do ☑

TAKE AN INDEX CARD OR A SMALL PIECE OF PAPER AND LIST ALL YOUR PRESENT CARES AND WORRIES THAT CAUSE YOU STRESS. THEN PRAY ABOUT EACH ITEM ON THE LIST ONE AT A TIME SAYING, "I KNOW, FATHER, THAT YOU CARE ABOUT _____ MORE THAN I DO, SO I GIVE THIS TO YOU. THANK YOU."

Don't worry about anything; instead, pray about everything. Tell God what you need, and thank him for all he has done. [Philippians 4:6]

This is National Stress Awareness Day.

care casting

also on this day

1867 ✹
Wilbur Wright, one half of the airplane-inventor team, was born.

Two giant pandas arrived in the United States from China. 1972

everywhere and always

On this day in 1970, the Apollo 13 space capsule splashed down into the ocean.

How'd you like to be an astronaut? Imagine blasting off into space on a NASA mission, and then, after completing the mission, returning safely to earth. If you heard or read anything about the Apollo 13 mission (or saw the movie), you know how they almost didn't make it back.

One man said he wouldn't fly in a spaceship or even in an airplane because Jesus said, "*Lo*, I am with you always" (Matthew 29:20, KJV). He was kidding, of course. *Lo* is not the same as *low*. Jesus was saying that he would always be with his disciples wherever they were and "even to the end of the world."

And check out our verses for today. Paul writes, "Whether we are high above the sky or in the deepest ocean, nothing in all creation will ever be able to separate us from the love of God that is revealed in Christ Jesus our Lord." That's great news!

Think about it. You could blast off from Cape Canaveral and fly to the edge of our solar system, and God would be there. You could get into a diving suit and be lowered deep into the ocean, and God would be there. Distance is nothing to him.

That's not all. The Bible also promises that no person, angel, or demon can come between us and God. Nothing, nobody, no place, no how can keep us from God and his love.

What an amazing promise!

So no matter what you face today or where you are, remember that God is with you and in you, helping you and giving you peace and courage.

> And I am convinced that nothing can ever separate us from his love. Death can't, and life can't. The angels can't, and the demons can't. Our fears for today, our worries about tomorrow, and even the powers of hell can't keep God's love away. Whether we are high above the sky or in the deepest ocean, nothing in all creation will ever be able to separate us from the love of God that is revealed in Christ Jesus our Lord. [Romans 8:38, 39]

also on this day

This is National Cheeseball Day.

1629

Horses were first imported into the colonies by the American Massachusetts Bay Colony.

1790

Benjamin Franklin died.

to do ☑

TELL SOMEONE THE "LO, I AM WITH YOU ALWAYS" JOKE. THEN SAY SOMETHING LIKE THIS: "ACTUALLY, GOD IS WITH ME HIGH AND LOW AND EVERYWHERE I GO. ISN'T THAT GREAT?"

warning!

On this day in 1775, Paul Revere went on his famous ride.

A flashing red light. A loud siren. The needle nearing empty on the gas gauge. A severe weather bulletin interrupting a TV show. Yellow caution signs on the highway.

Every day signals and signs alert us to watch out and take caution. Sometimes these warnings can be irritating because they interrupt us or slow us down, but we know they're important.

On this day in 1775, Paul Revere made his famous revolutionary ride. "The British are coming! The British are coming!" he shouted, warning fellow citizens about the oncoming army.

We need warnings. Without them we could rush headlong into trouble. And we're wise if we heed them. We may have to stop what we're doing, turn around, and go in another direction.

The Bible gives many warnings—statements beginning with words like, "Watch out," or "Be careful." God wants people to know what can hurt them, and he wants them to travel in the right direction.

Today's verse says to "warn each other." In other words, in addition to reading and believing the Bible for ourselves, we should pass on God's warnings to others. This verse also implies that we should encourage fellow believers to live the right way.

Do you know someone who needs to hear God's warnings? Perhaps a friend is about to do something wrong that will only lead to trouble and pain. Or maybe you know someone who is being led astray. How can you warn against these harmful actions and guide toward right ones?

What can you do to tell people the good news about following Christ and warn them of the bad news about living without him?

to do ☑

ASK GOD TO GIVE YOU THE OPPORTUNITY TO GIVE A FRIEND OR TWO HIS WARNING. THEN DO IT WHEN THE OPPORTUNITY ARISES.

You must **warn** each other **every** day, as long as it is called **"today,"** so that **none** of you will be **deceived** by **sin** and **hardened** against **God**. [Hebrews 3:13]

also on this day

This is National Animal Crackers Day.

A huge earthquake and fire hit San Francisco.

1906

The Republic of Ireland was established.

1949

april **19**

On this day in 1897, the first annual Boston Marathon was held.

Running the Race

What's the longest race you've ever run? Sprints are short, like racing a friend on the playground or running the 100-yard dash in a track meet. Some races are medium distance—a few times around the track. And some are long, measured in miles. One of the longest races is the marathon, 26.2 miles. And one of the most famous of these races is the Boston Marathon, where every year since 1897, thousands of men and women run through the streets of Boston. The fastest time for a woman in this marathon is 2 hours, 20 minutes, and 43 seconds, run by Margaret Okayo from Kenya in 2002. And another Kenyan, Cosmos Ndeti who ran the course in 2 hours, 7 minutes, and 15 seconds in 1994, holds the men's record.

The Bible compares life to a race. Hebrews 12:1 says, "let us run with endurance the race that God has set before us." And today's verse encourages us to "run in such a way that you will win."

Some people live as though life is a sprint. They go as hard and as fast as they can. But life is much more like a long-distance race, a marathon. For any race, runners need to prepare, to wear the right clothes and shoes, and to begin when the starting signal sounds. But marathon runners need to run smart so they can finish well.

Young people can find it difficult to imagine life stretching out to seven or eight decades when only the next year seems a long way off. So that's where faith comes in. We need to listen to God, our coach, and run the race he gives us according to his plan. Then we'll finish well.

How are you running these days?

to do ☑

ASK SOMEONE WHO HAS RUN A MARATHON TO TELL YOU ALL THE TRAINING AND PREPARATION NEEDED TO RUN AND FINISH WELL.

also on this day

Remember that in a **race** everyone **runs**, but only **one** person gets the **prize**. You **also** must **run** in such a way that you will **win**. [1 Corinthians 9:34]

This is National Primrose Day.

The American Revolutionary War began. **1775**

1939
Connecticut approved the Bill of Rights for the United States Constitution—148 years late!

the root of the problem

This is National Weed Day.

What is "National Weed Day"? Do you think it was established to honor weeds? Perhaps the person who named this day wanted to remind us to be aware of weeds and to get rid of them. Whatever the case, let's talk about weeds.

If you've ever had a garden or lawn, you know how frustrating weeds can be. They grow fast and thick and can choke out the flowers, grass, or vegetables that you want to grow. If you wait too long, the seeds hit the wind, and soon you have hundreds more weeds to deal with. And they're almost impossible to eliminate. You keep pulling them, but soon they're back like a monster in a bad horror movie.

Gardeners and other plant experts explain that the secret to getting rid of weeds is to attack their roots. In fact, most weeds will spring from even a part of a root left in the ground. That's why pulling them isn't always effective. We need to use special sprays and other treatments.

Weeds can grow in our lives as well. When Jesus told the parable of the sower and seeds, he explained that as seeds fall on thorny ground, "all too quickly the message is crowded out by the cares of this life and the lure of wealth, so no crop is produced" (Matthew 13:22). So if we want to grow in our faith and be productive for Christ, we need to beware of weeds.

Today's verse carries this a step further. It says that we also should help keep weeds out of the lives of other believers. And one of the worst is the weed of unbelief.

How's your life garden doing? How about your Christian friends? Ask God to help you blast those roots.

Look after each other so that none of you will **miss out** on the special **favor** of God. **Watch out** that no bitter **root** of unbelief rises up among you, for **whenever** it springs up, many are **corrupted** by its poison. [Hebrews 12:15]

also on this day

1841
Edgar Allen Poe's story, *Murders in the Rue Morgue*, was published. It is considered the first detective story.

1879
The first mobile home (horse drawn) was used in a journey from London.

1934
The movie *Stand Up and Cheer* opened. It was child star Shirley Temple's debut.

to do ☑

ASK YOUR MOM OR DAD IF YOU CAN HELP GET RID OF WEEDS IN THE GARDEN. AFTER THEY GET OVER THE SHOCK OF YOUR QUESTION AND ANSWER "YES," GET THE WEED–KILLING SPRAY AND GO TO IT. AND EACH TIME YOU SPRAY, PRAY! ASK GOD TO REMOVE ANY ROOTS OF SIN IN YOUR LIFE.

hooked!

On this day in 1959, the largest fish ever hooked by a rod and reel, a great white shark weighing 2,264 pounds, was caught.

You're fishing with your dad out in the ocean. The sky is clear, the weather warm, and the sea calm. Your line is in the water, but mostly you're just catching rays. Then *wham!* Something hits your bait and almost knocks you off your seat. And for several hours you fight what turns out to be a *huge* white shark . . . and finally you land him.

Now pretend you're the shark. You're a lean, mean, fighting and eating machine. Being gigantic, you go wherever you want and eat whatever you can gather into your wide jaws. Gliding fearlessly through the deep, you spot a delicious morsel just ahead and above. So you grab it in one big swallow. Then *wham!* Something bites into your gullet and pulls back—you're hooked. You fight like crazy, pulling the line and boat in circles, all one ton of you, but you can't get free. You're caught.

That's how temptation always works. We glide through life and spot something we want to have or do. Ignoring possible dangers, we bite and swim away. But then, *wham!*, we feel the hook. Temptations like stealing, smoking, drinking alcohol, making fun of someone, and other "tasty morsels" may seem OK, but they come with hooks.

So when you spot something that looks good but you think it may be bad, or you're not sure, don't take the bait. Leave it alone and "swim" away as fast as you can.

to do ☑

WHAT TEMPTS YOU? TALKING ABOUT SOMEONE ELSE? LOOKING AT A CLASS-MATE'S TEST PAPER TO GET A BETTER GRADE? WATCHING MOVIES YOU KNOW ARE OFF-LIMITS? GET A FISHHOOK AND GLUE IT TO THE CENTER OF AN INDEX CARD AND WRITE "JAMES 1:14, 15" AT THE BOTTOM. ON THE FLIP SIDE WRITE DOWN YOUR BIGGEST TEMPTATION. PUT YOUR CREATION ON YOUR WALL OR DESK SO YOU'LL SEE IT EVERY DAY.

also on this day

753 B.C. Tradition says that on this day Rome was founded.

John Adams was sworn in as the first U.S. Vice President. 1789

Temptation comes from the lure of our own evil desires. These evil desires lead to evil actions, and evil actions lead to death. [James 1:14, 15]

Happy Earth Day to You!

This is Earth Day.

Earth Day was established in 1970 by John McConnell to, in his words, "celebrate the wonder of life on our planet."

Some believers wonder why Christians should be concerned about "celebrating life" and taking care of the environment. Today's passage tells us why.

First, the Bible tells how God created the heavens and the earth. Then God said it was "excellent in every way." That means the earth is God's and that it's good.

Next, we read about the natural order of creation. Plants, birds, fish, grass, fruit, animals, and humans are all mentioned, and each has a place and purpose.

Then check out God's instructions to Adam and Eve: "subdue" the earth and "be masters."

So here's the deal. God has given us humans a beautiful planet on which to live. It is filled with amazing natural resources to use. But he expects us to be wise and careful in how we treat the water, soil, plants, and animals—our home and our resources. Elsewhere in the Bible God says that we must be good managers of what he has entrusted to us (see Luke 12:42-48). This means no wasting or polluting. And it certainly means taking good care of ourselves and our world.

What can you do to be a better earth manager?

to do ☑

TAKE A WALK THROUGH YOUR NEIGHBORHOOD AND PICK UP TRASH. YOU CAN ALSO ENCOURAGE YOUR FAMILY TO RECYCLE.

God blessed them and told them, "Multiply and fill the earth and subdue it. Be masters over the fish and birds and all the animals." And God said, "Look! I have given you the seed-bearing plants throughout the earth and all the fruit trees for your food. And I have given all the grasses and other green plants to the animals and birds for their food." And so it was. Then God looked over all he had made, and he saw that it was excellent in every way. This all happened on the sixth day. [Genesis 1:28-31]

also on this day

1864 The United States Congress mandated that all coins minted as U.S. currency bear the inscription, "In God We Trust."

1994 The world's largest lollipop, weighing 3,011 pounds, was made in Denmark.

On this day in 1896, the first movie was shown in a theater in New York City.

reel  life

Ever since the first silent film flickered across the silver screen, men, women, boys, and girls have watched with delighted imagination. Whether for a cartoon or a comedy, a romance, western, or space adventure, we've regularly filled theaters in every city and town across the country.

Movies are fun and entertaining because they capture us and entertain us. The professional acting, stirring music, and spectacular scenes draw us into the story. We've grown up with movies, and now we see them on televisions, videos, DVDs, and computers.

We know that movies aren't real, of course. But sometimes we can feel as though we're watching truth unfold because it is so real. Sometimes we're shocked to learn that the writer, producer, or director of a movie made up things and put them in a movie advertised as a true story. Sometimes movies based on history are more fiction than fact.

After watching a movie some people say something like, "Now I know what *really* happened." Instead, we should be thinking, "That was interesting. I wonder if that's what really happened." In other words, we shouldn't accept as fact everything projected on a screen.

That's especially important with movies and other media about Jesus and people in the Bible. Our authority should be the Bible, not a movie, book, or video. We can enjoy the presentation, but we should check the facts.

Today's passage tells about the people of Berea. After listening to Paul and Silas preach, they compared the message with Scripture, to see if it made sense and was true. God's Word was their guide.

So go ahead and enjoy your video entertainment. But know the difference between what's real and what's not.

to do ☑

CHECK OUT ONE OR TWO OF THESE WEBSITES THAT REVIEW MOVIES: WWW.PLUGGEDINONLINE.COM; WWW.GOSPELCOM.NET/IFC; WWW.BOTCW.COM; WWW.MOVIEGUIDE.ORG. USE THE REVIEWS TO HELP YOU CHOOSE A MOVIE TO SEE AND TO KNOW WHETHER OR NOT IT STICKS TO THE FACTS.

And the people of Berea were more open-minded than those in Thessalonica, and they listened eagerly to Paul's message. They searched the Scriptures day after day to check up on Paul and Silas, to see if they were really teaching the truth. [Acts 17:11]

also on this day

1564 William Shakespeare was born.

The Coca-Cola Company announced that it was changing its 99-year-old secret formula. However, New Coke® was not successful. **1985**

Dr. Allen Bussey completed 20,302 yo-yo loops. **1977**

How often do you use a computer? Before answering, remember the computers at your school, in cars and appliances, and in your PDA. These days, computers are everywhere. Not too long ago they were rare. In fact, you probably know an older person who finds computers very confusing and intimidating. But not you—they've always been part of your life. And they sure have revolutionized the way we work, learn, and relate to others.

We live in what has been called "the information age." We have more information about more things than previous generations could ever imagine. We have so many TV channels we find it difficult to choose one to watch. The Internet is amazing, and everywhere we turn we see cameras and computers. News broadcasters make sure we know just about everything that's going on in the world, and often we see it happening live.

So we might get the idea that technology is the greatest power in the world. *Wrong!*

Only God knows everything. Beyond facts and events, he knows thoughts, desires, emotions, and motives. He knows every hidden dream and sin. He knows the past, the present, and the future, and he sees everything in the universe at the same time. When he was reflecting on God's knowledge, the writer of Psalm 44 exclaimed, "God knows the secrets of every heart."

Some people may feel as though they don't want God to know all their secrets. But it's good news for those who are comforted knowing God knows what they're going through. And what makes this even better news is the fact that God *loves* us.

Did you get that? He *knows* you and still *loves* you. That means God wants the very best for your life. It means that you can trust him to guide you the right way—his way.

Now *that* computes!

to do ☑

TAKE A FEW MINUTES TO READ PSALM 139 AND THEN ROMANS 8:28–39. THANK GOD FOR KNOWING YOU, LOVING YOU, AND BEING WITH YOU EVERYWHERE.

God would surely have known it, for he knows the secrets of every heart. [Psalm 44:21]

On this day in 1981, the IBM Personal Computer was introduced.

who knows?

also on this day

1850 This is National Grilled Cheese Sandwich month.

A patent was granted for the first soda fountain. **1833**

All Nations, United!

From its very beginning, the vision of the United Nations has always been to have a place where countries could work out their differences and meet global challenges together—where all nations would be "united."

That's a good idea. And, through the years, this famous institution has had successes and setbacks in trying to reach its goals. The main roadblock to success is the simple fact that leaders of some countries don't *want* to cooperate, to compromise, or to reach a solution. They may talk about peace while planning for war. They may pretend to promote freedom while keeping people enslaved. They may act as though they're all for what's right while doing what is wrong.

Daily newscasts and other reports make it clear that wars, terrorism, and atrocities will be with us for a while. And we can get discouraged.

Eventually, however, all those terrible things will end. Peace will come, and people of every race and nation will live together as one.

"When?" you ask. When Christ returns.

The book of Revelation tells about the future. In it the apostle John wrote what God had revealed to him. When you read this book, you'll see that God is in control and that he will win the battle against Satan and evil. Today's verse tells us that "a vast crowd, too great to count, from every nation and tribe and people and language" will stand before God and worship him together. Now that's unity.

So don't get discouraged by negative news and nations divided. Remember God's promise to bring us all together under his rule.

to do ☑

TODAY, PRAY FOR PEACE. BE SPECIFIC, MENTIONING EACH OF THE TROUBLED NATIONS IN THE NEWS.

After this I saw a vast crowd, too great to count, from every nation and tribe and people and language, standing in front of the throne and before the Lamb. They were clothed in white and held palm branches in their hands.

[Revelation 7:9]

also on this day

This is World Penguin Day.

A patent was granted for the thimble. 1684

1953
U.S. Senator Wayne Morse ended the longest speech in U.S. Senate history. The speech on the Offshore Oil Bill lasted 22 hours and 26 minutes.

quite a greeting!

This is Hug an Australian Day.

You've had a rough day. According to your teachers, you couldn't do anything right. Then, one of your best friends got mad at you for something you didn't say. And to top it off, you can't find your favorite CD and are afraid it's lost. So you walk in your house, head down, frustrated and discouraged. Dropping your books on the kitchen table, you slump into a chair.

Then your mom comes in, sits next to you, and gives you a hug. Now don't you feel better?

Hugs can do that. Of course, you still have to do your homework, call your friend to make things right, and look for your CD. But for a while, your spirit would rise and you'd feel like your old self again.

Hugs work. When we hug people, we let them know that we care and that we will stand with them. Hugs also say, "I like you—you're OK" and "Welcome! We're glad you're here."

Guess what? Hugs are biblical too. Our verse today says to "greet one another with a holy embrace"—a hug!

You don't have to look for an Australian (although that would be fine). Almost anyone will do. Your mom, dad, brother, sister, friend, teacher, classmate, new student, neighbor, and many others would love it.

Greet one another with a holy embrace. [2 Corinthians 13:12, The Message]

also on this day

1514
Copernicus made his first observations of Saturn.

1607
The British established an American colony at Cape Henry, Virginia. It was the first permanent English establishment in the Western Hemisphere.

1803
Thousands of meteorites fell on the town of L'Aigle in France.

to do ☑
HUG AT LEAST THREE PEOPLE TODAY.

HELP!
This is National Volunteer Week.

We see litter on a street and wonder why the city crews haven't picked it up. We wonder why city government won't take care of that junky vacant lot, or why some social agency isn't helping the elderly or the homeless. We hear about nursery workers needed at church and think, "They should hire someone to do that." Because our government does so much for us, we may assume that someone else should do everything.

But that would be impossible—there are too many needs and not enough money. And that's where volunteers come in. These are men, women, boys, and girls who pitch in, using their own time and money to make a difference in their neighborhoods, city, and world.

This is National Volunteer Week, but Christians shouldn't need anyone to remind them to help others. Jesus said that people would be able to identify his followers by their love for one another. And throughout the Bible God tells us to reach out, especially to the poor, widows, and orphans. You'll find tons of verses, including the one for today, telling us to *serve* others.

So look around. What do you see that needs to be done that you could do? Who needs your help? When will you start?

to do ☑

ASK YOUR PASTOR OR YOUTH PASTOR ABOUT HOW YOU CAN SERVE AT CHURCH.

also on this day

1965
R.C. Duncan patented disposable diapers.

Graeme Obree, the Flying Scotsman, set a world bicycling record (52.713 km/h).

1994

If your **gift** is that of **serving others**, serve them **well**. If you are a **teacher**, do a **good job** of teaching.

[Romans 12:7]

A Day at the Beach

In 1985, the largest sand castle in the world was completed near St. Petersburg, Florida. It was four stories tall!

The sun beating down, bright and hot. A light breeze. Waves lapping against the shore. Cool, wet sand pushing up through your toes as you walk. There's nothing quite like a day at the beach.

Remember those first seashore visits and sand castle building attempts? Mom or Dad helped you scoop out sand with a plastic shovel and bucket. Then you dumped it and together shaped the pile with your hands into a "castle." As you got older, you used the tools yourself and built even bigger ones. You may have even built a sand "fort" that you could sit in.

But have you ever seen those huge sand sculptures built by professionals? They're amazing. The world record sand castle was bigger than a house—four floors.

Whether it's small buildings made by turning over sand-packed cups, or huge world-class fortresses, all of these sand structures have this in common: they don't last. Wind and waves quickly wipe them out.

No wonder Jesus used sand to make an important point. He said that building one's life on the wrong foundation is foolish and like building a house on sand—it will crumble. Instead, we should be wise, and build on solid rock. The right foundation makes all the difference.

And Jesus explained that the only solid foundation for life includes listening carefully to him and then doing what he says. Jesus said that to do otherwise would be foolish: "But anyone who hears my teaching and ignores it is foolish, like a person who builds a house on sand. When the rains and floods come and the winds beat against that house, it will fall with a mighty crash" (Matthew 7:26, 27).

How's *your* foundation?

to do ☑

ASK SOMEONE WHO IS A BUILDER, AN ARCHITECT, OR A CONSTRUCTION WORKER TO TELL YOU ABOUT FOUNDATIONS.

"**Anyone** who **listens** to my **teaching** and **obeys** me is **wise**, like a person who **builds** a **house** on **solid rock**."

[Matthew 7:24]

also on this day

✳ **This is National Cracker Day.**

W.H. Carrier patented the design for his air conditioner. **1914**

✳ **1758**
James Monroe, the fifth president of the United States, was born in Westmoreland County, Virginia.

In 1913, Gideon Sundback of Hoboken, New Jersey, patented the zipper. It's also National Zipper Day.

Think what life would be like without zippers. We have zippers on coats, pants, jackets, shoes, and other clothes. And book covers, luggage, briefcases, purses, backpacks, athletic bags, and other cases use zippers. We could find even more zippers around the house and in the car.

Zippers are safe, durable (usually), easy to use, and inexpensive. Without zippers, we'd have to tie or tape everything shut—or use Velcro® and put up with that annoying sound all day. So go ahead and let out a cheer for zippers on their special day!

We've become so familiar with this clever invention that we use the word in other ways. If your father wants you to be quiet, for example, he might say, "Zip it up!" In other words, he wants you to pretend you have a zipper on your mouth and keep it closed.

Actually that's good advice to remember, especially if you tend to say the wrong thing at the wrong time, to interrupt, or to go on and on. Your mouth gets you in trouble. It opens, and out pops the word or phrase that you later regret.

Our verse for today says that people can seem intelligent just by being quiet. You've probably seen that. You're having a conversation with a group of kids and one of them (whom you don't know very well) simply listens and nods occasionally. That kid ends up looking a lot smarter than one who asks silly questions or makes inappropriate comments.

Quietly listening when others speak also shows respect. Too often we jump in with our personal comments and stories. No one likes being interrupted. Listening could be called the language of love.

The lesson? There's a time to be quiet. And who knows? You might even learn something. So zip it up.

Even fools are thought to be wise when they keep silent; when they keep their mouths shut, they seem intelligent. [Proverbs 17:28]

to do ☑

TODAY, EVERY TIME YOU USE A ZIPPER, SAY A QUICK PRAYER, ASKING GOD TO HELP YOU LISTEN MORE AND TALK LESS.

zip it up!

also on this day

1997
American and Russian astronauts took the first joint space walk.

This is also National Shrimp Scampi Day.

1896

and that's the truth!

Would we lie to you? It's National Honesty Day!

On the last sale of the day, a woman came into the general store and asked for a half-pound of tea. The young clerk weighed out the tea and handed the parcel to the woman.

The next morning, in preparing to open the store, the clerk discovered a four-ounce weight on the scale. Instantly he remembered using this same scale while selling the woman her tea. She had been shorted by four ounces! The young man quickly weighed out the balance of the half-pound of tea, closed up the store, and delivered it to his customer.

That clerk later became the 16th president of the United States and was known as "Honest Abe." (In February we talked about him and his reputation.)

Honesty is a character trait that we admire in others. An honest person is sincere, truthful, trustworthy, honorable, fair, and genuine. We know we can trust honest friends with our deepest secrets. We know we can depend upon them to show up when they say they will. We know that whatever they say, we can count on them to keep their word. We all want those kinds of friends. We should also *be* those kinds of friends.

Do you know who else values honesty? God does! In fact, he includes honestly in his top 10 rules for living (otherwise known as the Ten Commandments). Number 9 says, "Do not testify falsely against your neighbor" (Exodus 20:16). In other words, tell the truth! Be honest! In Leviticus, when Moses gave the people God's rules for living holy and pure lives, he said, "Do not steal. Do not cheat one another. Do not lie" (Leviticus 19:11). And Proverbs 11:1 says, "The LORD hates cheating, but he delights in honesty."

If God delights in honesty, shouldn't we?

to do ☑

TO CELEBRATE NATIONAL HONESTY DAY, THANK SOMEONE FOR BEING HONEST TO YOU. AND MAKE A COMMITMENT TO TELLING THE TRUTH TODAY.

It is **better** to be **poor** and **honest** than to be a **fool** and **dishonest**.

[Proverbs 19:1]

also on this day

1789
George Washington took office as the first elected U.S. president.

The United States and France signed the Lousiana Purchase Treaty. **1803**

The ice cream cone made its debut.
1904

through thick and thin

Today is National Loyalty Day.

Here's the situation: you have promised your best friend that you will spend Friday night helping him watch his little brother. Another friend calls and invites you to attend a concert featuring your absolutely favorite band. What are you going to do? Give yourself 10 points on the Loyalty Meter if you said you were going to stick with your best friend; give yourself 5 points if you had to think about it for more than a minute; and give yourself 0 points if you decide to go to the concert.

Loyalty is all about sticking with your friends or family no matter what. In fact, the Bible tells us that the greatest evidence of genuine friendship is loyalty—loving at all times. (Take a look at 1 Corinthians 13:7.) So what does it mean to be a loyal friend? It means sticking by your friend when she is having a tough time at home. It means helping your friend with his math homework when you would rather be watching TV. It means standing by your friend when everyone else has disappeared.

Jonathan and David shared that kind of friendship. You can read about it in 1 Samuel 20. Jonathan knew that his father, King Saul, was out to get David. He knew that being David's friend was against his father's wishes. But David and Jonathan had vowed before God to remain friends, and so Jonathan did everything he could to help and support David. Later, David returned that loyalty when he took care of Jonathan's son Mephibosheth. That's the kind of loyal friends that God wants us to be.

So, on National Loyalty Day, what kind of friend are you—a fair-weather friend or one who is there through thick and thin?

A **friend** is **always loyal**, and a **brother** is **born** to **help** in time of **need**.

[Proverbs 17:17]

also on this day

Today is National Teen Day.

1941 Cheerios® hit the store shelves.

1952 Mr. Potato Head® was introduced.

to do ☑

DO YOU HAVE A FRIEND WHO HAS BEEN LOYAL TO YOU? TAKE TIME TODAY TO THANK HIM OR HER.

Be kind, you say? To *my* brother? You've got to be kidding. You don't have to live with him! Many of us have a sibling whom we would rather ship off to a deserted island than be kind to. And we may have good reasons—clothes that are borrowed and never returned, nonstop teasing, phone messages that mysteriously get lost. You know.

Sometimes it is hard to get along with those who live in the same house as we do. Did you know that even Jesus had half brothers who weren't thrilled to be related to him? In fact, Jesus' family thought that he was a bit crazy (Mark 3:21) and laughed at him for what he was doing (John 7:3). Later, after Jesus had died and rose from the dead, two of his half brothers (James and Jude) became leaders in the early church.

Joseph also encountered troubles with his brothers. Of course, some may argue that he brought it on himself by telling all his brothers that someday they would worship him. (Never a good idea to say to a sibling!) Still, Joseph's brothers reacted a bit harshly by selling him off as a slave and telling his father he was dead. Yet even in those extreme circumstances, we see Joseph and his brothers reunited at the end of the story and Joseph offering these wonderful words of forgiveness: "God turned into good what you meant for evil. . . . Indeed, I myself will take care of you and your families" (Genesis 50:20, 21).

God has placed us into our families for his purposes. And it is his desire that we get along with our brothers and sisters—no matter how difficult that may be on certain days.

to do ☑

BE NICE TO YOUR SIB TODAY. DO YOUR SIBLING'S CHORES TODAY. LET HER WEAR YOUR FAVORITE SHIRT. LET HIM RIDE YOUR BIKE! SAY SOMETHING POSITIVE ABOUT YOUR SIB.

How wonderful it is, how pleasant, when brothers live together in harmony! [Psalm 133:1]

also on this day

1919 The first U.S. air passenger service started.

The National Day of Prayer is the 1st Thursday of this month.

Leonardo da Vinci died. **1519**

no kidding—be kind to your kin

Today is Sibling Appreciation Day.

Time to Owe Up

This is Tax Freedom Day.

As the saying goes there are only two certainties in life—death and taxes. Taxes, the special fees collected by governments and rules, have been around since Bible times. And the idea of paying taxes probably has been hated just as long.

The first tax mentioned in the Old Testament was a census tax, commanded to be paid by Moses for every person 20 years and older, to be used for the care of the tabernacle. Later, when the Israelites demanded to be ruled by kings, the kings (as the prophet Samuel had warned!) began to tax the people to help pay for buildings, armies, and other government projects. Then, as invading countries conquered the Israelites, the foreign kings demanded even higher taxes.

When Jesus was born the people were paying taxes to the despised Roman Empire. Their coins, which carried Caesar's image, were a constant reminder that their hard-earned money was going to support Rome. Yet, when the Jewish leaders questioned Jesus about whether it was right for the Jews to pay taxes to Rome, Jesus reminded them that this was money due to Caesar. At the same time, however, Jesus told the people they needed to give to God what he was owed.

Think about that. What do you think you owe God right now? How about your faithfulness, your obedience, your love? What about your time and the abilities he has given to you? What might you owe God there? Just as we are expected and obligated to pay taxes to our governments, we need to "pay" God what is owed him as well. You can even take this a step further. What do you "owe" your parents, your teachers, your friends?

The Bible reminds us that we are to give to everyone what we "owe" him or her, whether it's respect, time, or our money.

to do ☑

TODAY MAKE A PRETEND BILL OF WHAT YOU OWE GOD. CONSIDER HOW YOU CAN "PAY UP."

Give to every-one what you owe them: **Pay** your **taxes** and import **duties**, and **give respect** and **honor** to **all** to whom it is **due**.

[Romans 13:7]

also on this day

1802 Washington, D.C., was incorporated as a city.

West Virginia imposed the first state sales tax. 1921

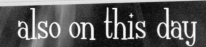

•**1966**
The game Twister® was featured on the *Tonight Show* with Johnny Carson.

be on the lookout

Today is National Weather Observer's Day.

Imagine a world without weather forecasters. We wouldn't know whether to take an umbrella, if we should bring a jacket, or if we need sunscreen. We certainly wouldn't be able to tell if a dangerous storm was approaching or if we should go ahead and plan that picnic. Such information is critical for people like pilots, farmers, or anyone whose work is dependent on weather conditions.

Thankfully, we don't have to guess about what the weather is going to be like for the next day or even the next several hours. We can tune in the nightly weather forecast or listen to the radio to quickly find out how to prepare for the predicted conditions. At times, such information can be lifesaving.

As Jesus was preparing for his return to Heaven, he urged his followers to be vigilant. But they weren't to be concerned about the weather conditions. They were to be looking for a special event—Jesus' return to earth. More than 2,000 years has passed since Jesus spoke those words, but the truth remains: Jesus is coming again, and as his followers, we need to be on constant watch.

So what does that mean? For one, it means working faithfully at the tasks that God has given you. It means keeping close to God at all times. It means being faithful to pray and meet with God daily, to read his Word, and to be actively doing his will.

Think about it. When Jesus returns, do you want to be caught napping or to be engaged in helping others? The best way to be prepared and vigilant for Jesus' return is to be doing his work. That way you can "keep a constant watch."

> "**Keep** a **constant watch**.
> And **pray** that, if possible,
> you may **escape**
> these **horrors** and **stand**
> before the **Son of Man**."

[Luke 21:36]

also on this day

Today is National Tuba Day.

1626
Dutch explorer Peter Minuit landed on Manhattan Island. Native Americans later sold the island (20,000 acres) for $24 in cloth and buttons.

1979
Margaret Thatcher, the first woman Prime Minister of Great Britain, was elected.

to do ☑

THINK OF TWO WAYS YOU CAN "KEEP A CONSTANT WATCH" SO YOU WILL BE READY FOR JESUS' RETURN.

party time!

Today is Cinco de Mayo.

Cinco de Mayo (which means the fifth of May) is one of two days that celebrates the independence of Mexico. Although Mexico's official independence day is *el Dieciseis de Septiembre* (September 16), Cinco de Mayo is also considered a day of great importance. On this day, a vastly outnumbered, untrained, and poorly equipped Mexican people defeated a much stronger and more powerful French army.

Today it has become a popular holiday in the United States. People mark the day with fiestas, parades, mariachi music, piñatas, and of course, lots of great-tasting Mexican food. At its heart, Cinco de Mayo remains a day to celebrate the Mexican people's courage, culture, and freedom.

While holidays like Cinco de Mayo are wonderful opportunities to remember important events in a nation's history, they also are a great reason to have a party and have fun!

Ezra knew that. The people of Israel had just finished rebuilding the city walls of Jerusalem. Now it was time to restore the people's faith, so Ezra and others spent several hours reading God's Word to the people. The people wept as they heard God's Word, realizing how they had strayed from obeying God. Yet Ezra reminded them: "Don't be sad! Now is the time to celebrate." Ezra sent the people home to "celebrate with great joy because they had heard God's words and understood them" (Nehemiah 8:12).

Some people like to think that God is all about dos and don'ts and is just looking for ways to stop us from having fun. That couldn't be further from the truth. God wants us to celebrate and to be joyful. That's why he has commanded his people to observe certain holidays and to party!

to do ☑

THROW A CINCO DE MAYO PARTY AND INCLUDE GOD IN YOUR PARTY BY THANKING HIM FOR THE COURAGE AND THE FREEDOM THAT HE GIVES TO YOU.

And Nehemiah continued, "Go and celebrate with a feast of choice foods and sweet drinks, and share gifts of food with people who have nothing prepared. This is a sacred day before our Lord. Don't be dejected and sad, for the joy of the LORD is your strength!" [Nehemiah 8:10]

also on this day

1891

Carnegie Hall opens in New York City with Tchaikovsky as the guest conductor.

Jim Bailey became the first U.S. runner to break the four-minute mile. He was clocked at 3:58.5.

1956

Alan Shepard piloted Freedom 7 to become the first American in space.

1961

In 1840 Britain issued the very first postage stamp. It bore the profile of Queen Victoria and was known as the Penny Black because it was printed in black and cost a penny. Before the advent of the postage stamp, the person receiving the letter was the one who had to pay for the delivery costs. Since the rates were so high, many people refused to accept the letters. In fact some people developed secret codes that they put on the outside of the letter to get around the high costs of postal service. The intended receiver could look at the code, get the message, and refuse delivery of the letter.

Because of this the British post office decided that postage had to be paid *before* the letter was delivered. The payment was marked by a small piece of colored paper on the outside of the letter—the stamp! The idea was so popular that the United States adopted the same system, and in 1847 the U.S. Post Office printed its first stamps, a 5-cent stamp picturing Benjamin Franklin and a 10-cent stamp picturing George Washington.

Did you know that you have been stamped? It's true. The Bible tells us that the Holy Spirit is our guarantee, our stamp, that we belong to God, and that we will receive all his benefits (Ephesians 1:13, 14). Because we bear the stamp of the Holy Spirit, we know that salvation is ours and that we will live forever with Jesus in Heaven.

The best news, though, is that the Holy Spirit's stamp is not only the prepayment of all that is promised to those who believe in Jesus. Right now, Christians have the power and the comfort of the Holy Spirit living in them. We can depend on the Spirit to guide us and enable us to live as God wants us to while we wait for Jesus' return.

Today is the anniversary of the first postage stamp.

By his Spirit he has stamped us with his eternal pledge—a sure beginning of what he is destined to complete. [2 Corinthians 1:22, The Message]

to do ☑

CREATE YOUR OWN PERSONAL STAMP THAT REFLECTS WHAT YOUR FAITH IN JESUS MEANS TO YOU.

also on this day

1915 Babe Ruth hit his first major league home run while playing for the Boston Red Sox.

The Chunnel officially opened. The tunnel under the English Channel links England and France. 1994

stamp of approval

the mark of a great teacher

Today is National Teacher Day.

What difference can a teacher make in someone's life? Well, according to a study undertaken by Johns Hopkins University researchers, all the difference in the world. Several years ago, graduate students at the university interviewed 200 young men, ages 12 to 16. The assignment was to predict the young men's future.

The students went into the inner city of Baltimore to find the boys. Based on their research, they concluded that 90 percent of those boys interviewed would spend time in jail. Some 25 years later, the researchers were sent back to the inner city to discover how close their predictions were. They found 180 of the original 200 young men. And what they discovered amazed them: only four had *ever* been to jail. When asked what changed their lives, the researchers began to get the same answer, "Well, there was this teacher . . ."

So the researchers tracked down the teacher, now living in a retirement home, and asked her about her remarkable influence over these young men. She really could not think of any reason why she would have this kind of influence, except that "I truly loved my students."

What is the difference between a good teacher and great teacher? One word: Love!

Among the many titles given to Jesus is teacher. He is our *rabboni,* meaning "my lord, my master," the most elevated title given to a teacher. And as our lord, Jesus instructs us out of his great love for us and the example that he has given to us: "So now I am giving you a new commandment: Love each other. Just as I have loved you, you should love each other" (John 13:34).

Knowing Jesus and learning from him can make all the difference in your life.

Late one night he visited Jesus and said, "Rabbi, we all know you're a teacher straight from God. No one could do all the God-pointing, God-revealing acts you do if God weren't in on it." [John 3:2, The Message]

also on this day

1789
The first Presidential Inaugural Ball was held in New York City.

1840
Russian composer Tchaikovsky was born.

1934
The world's largest pearl (6.4 kg.) was discovered in the Philippines.

to do ☑

WRITE A NOTE TO YOUR FAVORITE TEACHER TODAY. SHARE WITH THAT TEACHER HOW HE OR SHE HAS MADE A DIFFERENCE IN YOUR LIFE.

the real thing

In 1886, the first Coca Cola® was sold.

The very first Coca-Cola® was sold this day at the soda fountain in Jacob's Pharmacy in Atlanta. Dr. John Pemberton, a pharmacist and Civil War veteran, concocted a fragrant, caramel-colored liquid in a brass kettle in his backyard. Intrigued, he took the liquid down the street to Jacob's Pharmacy. There the mixture was combined with carbonated water and sampled by several customers. All who tasted it agreed that this new drink was something special. Pemberton's book-keeper, Frank Robinson, named the mixture Coca-Cola and wrote out the name in his distinct flowing script—which has become the world's most recognizable logo.

Over the years the company has employed numerous slogans in advertising to communicate in a simple, direct way what the brand is all about. The most repeated theme in the 100-plus years of advertising Coke is reflected in the popular campaign of 1969: "It's the Real Thing." The idea has been reflected in slogans from "Coke Is It!" (1982), "America's Real Choice" (1985), "You Can't Beat the Real Thing" (1990), and the newest slogan, "Coca-Cola . . . Real" (2003). People are drawn to products that are genuine, authentic, and true.

The same can be said about Jesus. He is the real thing, the real choice. He is *it*, genuine, authentic, true. Consider what John wrote about him: "This Jesus is both True God and Real Life" (1 John 5:20, The Message). Jesus said about himself, "I am the way and the truth and the life" and he called himself "the true vine" without whom we can do nothing.

So don't be fooled by the claims of this world that there is a better way or that you don't need Jesus in your life. Jesus is the real thing. Make Jesus your real choice.

to do ☑

COME UP WITH YOUR OWN SLOGAN THAT REFLECTS WHAT JESUS MEANS TO YOU.

And we know that the Son of God has come, and he has given us understanding so that we can know the true God. And now we are in God because we are in his Son, Jesus Christ. He is the only true God, and he is eternal life. [1 John 5:20]

also on this day

1794
The U.S. Post Office was established.

Today is No Socks Day!

Germany officially surrendered, ending World War II.

1945

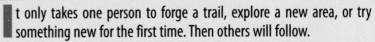

First!

On this day in 1929, Americans Richard Byrd and Floyd Bennett became the first to fly over the North Pole.

I t only takes one person to forge a trail, explore a new area, or try something new for the first time. Then others will follow.

This was certainly true when Richard Evelyn Byrd and his copilot, Floyd Bennett, became the first people to fly over the North Pole. A member of the U.S. Navy, Byrd learned to fly during World War I. He subsequently became a flying instructor for the U.S. Navy and was interested in experimenting with new ways of flying over water out of sight of land—a definite necessity in flying over the pole. Using equipment and techniques that he developed, Byrd and Bennett successfully navigated the North Pole flyover on this day in 1929.

What was most significant about Byrd's successful flight, however, is what happened afterward. Upon Byrd's return to New York, he was asked what his next plans would be. His response? To fly over the South Pole! It was this answer that spurred 11 different expeditions of Americans to explore the South Pole.

When it comes to firsts and leading the way, there is only one first— Jesus. He was God's firstborn from the very beginning (Hebrews 1:6). He was the first in the royal line, the king of all kings (Psalm 89:27). Jesus is the first to rise from the dead and ascend into Heaven to show us the way (Revelation 1:5). He is the very first "in the line of humanity" so that we can see from Jesus' example how we should live and how we should act (Romans 8:29).

So it makes sense that we should follow the first and go where Jesus goes. And if you are the first of your family or your friends at school to follow Jesus, be like Byrd and encourage others to follow your lead.

to do ☑

WITH THE HELP OF A PARENT, RECORD A LIST OF "FIRSTS" IN YOUR LIFE. WHICH "FIRST" DID OTHERS IN YOUR FAMILY FOLLOW? WHICH OF THE "FIRSTS" IN YOUR PARENTS' LIVES HAVE YOU FOLLOWED?

God knew what he was doing from the very beginning. He decided from the outset to shape the lives of those who love him along the same lines as the life of his Son. The Son stands first in the line of humanity he restored. We see the original and intended shape of our lives there in him.
[Romans 8:29, The Message]

also on this day

Today is National Butterscotch Brownie Day.

The lawn mower was patented.
1899

2002

In Bahrain, people were allowed to vote for representatives for the first time in nearly 30 years. Women were allowed to vote for the first time in the country's history.

Today is every parent's dream—a day devoted to cleaning up your room! So on a scale of 1 to 10—with 1 being neat as a pin and 10 being clutter beyond control, how would you rate your room right now? Here are some questions to help you determine the state of your room:

→ Is it impossible to see the floor?

→ Are the clothes you wore from last week still in the same place where you had dropped them?

→ Are there CDs (not in cases) in sight?

→ Are the dust bunnies taking over underneath your bed?

→ Do you have to move things in order to walk from one side of the room to the other?

If you have answered yes to four or more questions, put this book down right now and clean your room! No, wait until you finish reading.

You've probably heard the expression "cleanliness is next to godliness," and while that sounds like it came right out of the Bible, it didn't. But the Bible does tell us that God likes order. Look around the world he created. Everything has its proper place and function. God wants his people to be that way too. In today's verse, Paul is speaking about worship and God's desire that it be done in a certain orderly way. Where there is order, there is God's peace. But when there is disorder and chaos, God cannot work.

The same principle applies to us. When you are disorganized, when you can't find anything because of all the clutter in your room, you will not be able to get things done. Cleaning your room is just one way to bring the order that God desires into your life. And it for sure will lead to a more peaceful family.

to do ☑

SO YOUR ROOM'S COMPLETELY CLEAN? IF NOT, GRAB A GARBAGE BAG AND A DUST CLOTH AND GET TO WORK!

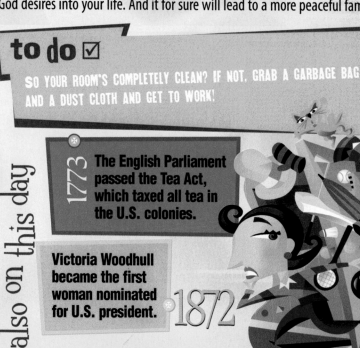

1773 The English Parliament passed the Tea Act, which taxed all tea in the U.S. colonies.

Victoria Woodhull became the first woman nominated for U.S. president. 1872

also on this day

For God is not a God of disorder but of peace, as in all the other churches. [1 Corinthians 14:33]

Today is National Clean Up Your Room Day.

cleanup time

the gift of song

The popular composer Irving Berlin was born on this day in 1888.

Irving Berlin was born Israel Isadore Baline in Russia. During his lifetime, this popular composer wrote such memorable tunes as "White Christmas," "Puttin' on the Ritz," "God Bless America," and "There's No Business Like Show Business." But did you know that Berlin, who wrote the lyrics and music to about 1,500 songs, never had any formal musical training or education?

A self-taught piano player, Berlin played by ear and only knew one key—F-sharp. Later he had a special piano made for him on which he could shift into different keys simply by turning a gear on the piano. During his long career Berlin never learned to read music or write music; instead he relied on a musical secretary to transcribe the songs he wrote.

Berlin had an extraordinary gift of music. Despite having never learned formal composition or music theory, Berlin was able to delight his many fans with wonderful songs that remain popular today.

Do you know who else Berlin delighted by using the gifts and talents given to him? God. It's true. God is delighted when we use the different talents and abilities that he has given to us. Just as he gave Berlin the gift of music, he may have given you the gift of being a good soccer player. Or maybe you are good at math, or you can play the trumpet like no one else can. There are as many combinations of talents and abilities as there are people in the world. And each one brings pleasure to God when it is being used.

So what gifts and talents do you have? What can you do to use your gifts and abilities in a way that will please God?

to do ☑

IF YOU'RE NOT SURE WHAT YOUR PARTICULAR TALENTS AND ABILITIES ARE, THINK ABOUT WHAT YOU LIKE TO DO AND WHAT YOU DO WELL. ASK THOSE WHO KNOW YOU WELL WHAT THEY THINK ARE YOUR TALENTS.

The **steps** of the **godly** are directed by the **LORD**. He **delights** in **every detail** of their **lives**. [Psalm 37:23]

also on this day

1812

The waltz was introduced into English ballrooms.

Today is Eat-What-You-Want Day.

The first tubeless tire was manufactured by B.F. Goodrich.

1947

lady with a lamp

Florence Nightingale was born this day in 1820.

Florence Nightingale was the daughter of a well-to-do family in England. Her family wanted Florence to live the life of a society girl—giving big parties, going to tea, and other activities fitting a wealthy lifestyle. But early on Florence was determined to do something worthwhile with her life—despite her parents' objections.

At age 16 she was certain that God was calling her to serve others. So she secretly began to collect books about nursing. She visited hospitals in London and in the surrounding area to learn more. Her parents tried to discourage Florence, but she was determined. Finally they agreed to send Florence to a hospital in Germany to study nursing. That way, they thought, they could avoid having their daughter "embarrass" the family.

After graduation Florence returned to London to work at a hospital. But it was during the Crimean War that Florence made her mark. She went to the battlefield with 38 other nurses and began setting up a hospital for the wounded soldiers. Each night she would walk the hallways of the hospital with a lamp, and so she became known as "the lady with a lamp."

Florence Nightingale's life was a light for others. She helped save thousands of lives by establishing cleanliness standards for health workers and training other nurses. She established the model for military hospitals and for modern nursing. Despite the many obstacles she encountered, Florence devoted her entire life to serving and helping others.

That's exactly what Jesus wants us to do as well. We are called to help each other and share each other's problems. When we see someone who needs help, our first thought should be, "What can I do?" When a friend calls and says, "I've got a problem," we are called to listen and offer encouragement. And when we are faithful in obeying this command, we shine Jesus' light and love with all we meet.

Share each other's **troubles** and **problems**, and in this way **obey** the **law** of **Christ**.

[Galatians 6:2]

also on this day

Today is National Limerick Day. Recite a favorite limerick to your friend!

Today also is International Migratory Bird Day.

to do ☑

DO YOU KNOW SOMEONE WHO NEEDS HELP? THINK OF WHAT YOU CAN DO TO REACH OUT TO THAT PERSON WITH JESUS' LOVE.

On this day in 1940, Winston Churchill said, "I have nothing to offer but blood, toil, tears, and sweat."

Waging War

These were Winston Churchill's memorable words to his fellow country-men as he took power as Great Britain's new prime minister. It probably was one of the darkest moments in Great Britain's long history. With the threat of war with Germany at their doorstep, Churchill promised to give his all—his blood, toil, tears, and sweat—in fighting their enemy.

Churchill vowed that his new policy in fighting Adolph Hitler would consist of nothing less than "to wage war, by sea, land, and air, with all our might and with all the strength that God can give us; to wage war against a monstrous tyranny, never surpassed in the dark, lamentable catalogue of human crime."

Churchill recognized that his country was facing a foe that would require all the resources that the people of Great Britain had. Anything less would mean certain defeat for their country. Within weeks of this speech, Churchill placed all "people, their services, and their property" into the hands of the government to use for the war effort.

While we do not use the same weapons or methods in fighting our foe, the devil, we certainly need to have the same attitude as Churchill. We are in an all-out daily struggle against Satan that will continue until Jesus returns. But we are not without resources to fight that battle.

At our disposal we have "God's mighty weapons, not merely worldly weapons, to knock down the Devil's strongholds" (2 Corinthians 10:3, 4). And what are those weapons? Prayer, faith, hope, love, God's Word, and the Holy Spirit. By using all these powerful resources that God graciously gives to us, we will be able to defeat Satan and break down the walls he builds up to keep people from God.

to do ☑

THINK OF WHAT MIGHT BE "THE DEVIL'S STRONGHOLDS" IN YOUR LIFE. THEN PRAY SPECIFICALLY FOR GOD'S HELP IN THOSE AREAS.

We are human, but we don't wage war with human plans and methods. We use God's mighty weapons, not mere worldly weapons, to knock down the Devil's strongholds.

[2 Corinthians 10:3, 4]

also on this day

Today is National Apple Pie Day.

Today is also Jumping Frog Jubilee in Angels Camp, California.

1637

Cardinal Richelieu of France created the table knife.

Across the country people who have never looked through a telescope are getting their chance today to gaze at the heavens. The day was first proclaimed in 1973 by Doug Berger, president of the Astronomical Association of Northern California, with the idea of sharing the joy of astronomy with everyone. Berger's idea was to take "astronomy to the people" and set up telescopes where the people were—shopping malls, street corners in the city, parks, and other public places.

It was an instant success. The public was hooked on stargazing. Once people got a glimpse of the stars through the portable telescopes, they wanted more. So when the local observatories held open houses, hundreds flocked to see more through larger and more sophisticated telescopes.

Throughout the centuries humankind has been fascinated by the stars and the planets. From the time that God promised Abraham that he would have as many descendants as stars in the sky, we have fixed our eyes on the skies. Ancient stargazers thought they could foretell the future by looking into the skies, much like today's astrologers. But God warned his people back in Bible times (and us) not to be "seduced by [the stars] and worship them. The LORD your God designated these heavenly bodies for all the peoples of the earth" (Deuteronomy 4:19).

Rather, when we gaze into the night sky, we should remember the one who named and placed each star there. Such heavenly contemplation should instill in us wonder at God's awesome handiwork and his regard for us. Upon such reflection, the psalm-writer concluded: "When I look at the night sky and see the work of your fingers—the moon and the stars you have set in place—what are mortals that you should think of us, mere humans that you should care for us?" (Psalm 8:3, 4).

He counts the stars and calls them all by name. [Psalm 147:4]

Today is Astronomy Day.

stargazing

to do ☑

FIND A TELESCOPE SO YOU CAN DO A LITTLE STARGAZING TONIGHT.

also on this day

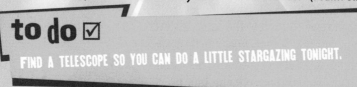

1607 Jamestown was established by English settlers, led by Captain John Smith.

1804 Lewis and Clark left St. Louis for their trek to the Pacific Coast.

'fess up!

Today is True Confession Day.

When some people think about "true confessions," they think of the outrageous headlines of the supermarket tabloids: "I was a teenage werewolf," or "I weighed 500 pounds and never left my house" or "I was raised in the forest by a pack of wild dogs."

For a Christian, "True Confession Day" is every day. When we confess our sins, we are in essence telling Jesus that we know what we've done is wrong and that we are willing to turn from it. We are recognizing that we have this problem called sin and that we need Jesus' help in overcoming it. Through confession we are making sure that we don't try to hide our wrongdoings from God.

And confession is not just for "sensational" sins. It includes the most basic of wrongs we've done ("I called my brother stupid"). True confession for a follower of Jesus is all about reconnecting with God, because we understand that our sin separates us from him. We not only admit our past sins, but we commit ourselves to try not to sin again in the future.

So what happens as a result of confession? That's the wonderful part. When we confess our sins, the Bible tells us that God "is faithful and just to forgive us and to cleanse us from every wrong." We are restored into fellowship with him again. It means we don't have to confess the same sin over and over again. It also means that we don't need to be perfect before God in order for him to accept us. He knows we can't do that. It isn't humanly possible. That's why he sent his Son to die on the cross for us.

True confession brings true forgiveness and restores true fellowship with God.

But if we confess our sins to him, he is faithful and just to forgive us and to cleanse us from every wrong.

[1 John 1:9]

also on this day

Today is National Hug Your Cat Day (if he or she will let you!).

1602

Cape Cod, Massachusetts, was discovered by Bartholomew Gosnold.

1940

Nylon stockings hit the market for the first time.

to do ☑

TAKE A FEW MINUTES RIGHT NOW TO THINK ABOUT WHAT YOU NEED TO CONFESS BEFORE GOD. DON'T WORRY—HE'S LISTENING AND WANTS TO FORGIVE YOU!

let them eat cake

On this day in 1770, Louis married Marie Antoinette.

When Louis, the French heir to the throne, married Marie Antoinette, the daughter of the Austrian Archduchess Maria Theresa and Holy Roman Emperor Francis I, he hoped the union would strengthen France. Four years later, following the death of King Louis XV, those plans took a step forward as the two were crowned king and queen of France.

The plan, however, was doomed to failure. Louis was unable to deal with the severe financial problems his country faced. Even worse, his wife had adopted an extravagant lifestyle that was greatly criticized by the French people. Under Marie's influence, the two became dangerously indifferent to the plight of the people, many of whom were struggling to feed their families from day to day. In what has become a legendary episode, Marie reportedly responded to news that the French people had no bread to eat by declaring, "Let them eat cake." The king and queen of France paid for their arrogance and indifference to the poor people in their country with their lives.

It was this same attitude that God condemned through the prophet Amos: "Listen to me, you 'fat cows' of Samaria, you women who oppress the poor and crush the needy . . ." (Amos 4:1). God's heart has always been for the downtrodden, the oppressed, the poor, and the needy. Consider what God told his people: "There will always be some among you who are poor. That is why I am commanding you to share your resources freely with the poor and with other Israelites in need" (Deuteronomy 15:11).

If we love Jesus, we need to obey God's commands to share what we have and help those less fortunate than we are. What can you do today to reach out to those who need your help?

to do ☑

COLLECT SOME CANNED FOOD AND OTHER ITEMS FROM YOUR FAMILY AND NEIGHBORS. TAKE SEVERAL BAGS OF FOOD TO THE NEAREST FOOD BANK.

Whoever gives to the **poor** will lack **nothing**. But a **curse** will **come** upon those who **close** their **eyes** to **poverty**.

[Proverbs 28:27]

also on this day

1866
Charles Elmer Hires invented root beer.

Spaghetti-O's® went on sale. **1965**

Today is National Bike to Work Day.

Are You a Pack Rat?

Today is Pack Rat Day.

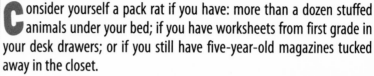

onsider yourself a pack rat if you have: more than a dozen stuffed animals under your bed; if you have worksheets from first grade in your desk drawers; or if you still have five-year-old magazines tucked away in the closet.

By definition, a pack rat is a person who can't bear to throw away *anything*. Now, we all have our pack rat tendencies—some items that we just can't part with. You may have the box of swim team ribbons that you hold on to long after you have quit the team or the Pokémon cards you're saving . . . just in case they make a comeback.

Did you know that a person can be a spiritual pack rat? Take the Pharisees, for example. These were a group of religious leaders during Jesus' time who were the keepers of the rules. They strictly followed the Ten Commandments, but then they had also added *hundreds* of their own rules, traditions, and teachings to God's law. And they believed that their rules were just as important as God's rules. Like pack rats, they had collected all these rules over the years and then tried to force others to follow and live by their rules.

By Jesus' day, the people were under a terrible burden trying their best to keep all those rules. Jesus said, "[The religious leaders] crush you with impossible religious demands and never lift a finger to help ease the burden" (Matthew 23:4). Thankfully for the people then (and for us today), Jesus came to take that burden away.

No amount of rules—no matter how many you accumulate or follow—will earn your way into Heaven. Believing in Jesus is what connects us to God. It's all you need to have eternal life.

to do ☑

TAKE A LOOK IN YOUR CLOSET, OR UNDER YOUR BED, OR IN YOUR DESK. THROW OUT ANYTHING YOU HAVEN'T USED IN A LONG TIME!

For **my yoke** fits **perfectly**, and the **burden** I give you is **light**.

[Matthew 11:30]

also on this day

1804 Napoleon became the Emperor of France.

1989 The longest cab ride ever was recorded at 14,000 miles and cost $16,000.

The first Kentucky Derby was held at Churchill Downs. **1875**

family time

This is National Visit Your Relatives Day.

What's your first reaction to the news that you will be spending the weekend with your relatives? Do you immediately want to jump in the car and say, "Let's go!"? Or are you desperately thinking of any reason as to why you just can't make it?

Maybe you are fortunate to have "relatively" (pardon the pun!) normal aunts, uncles, and grandparents. But if you are like most people, you probably have one or two relatives that are challenging to be with. You know the type: the aunt who insists on sending you the Christmas sweater with Santa on it and wonders why you're not wearing it. Or the uncle who tells the same jokes over and over and over. Or the great-aunt who can't help but pinch your cheek and say, "My, how you have grown!"

The good news is that families—and that includes all your relatives—are one of God's greatest resources! From the very beginning, God made us to live in families (Genesis 1:27, 28). God commanded that our families help teach us about him (Deuteronomy 4:10). We worship with our families (1 Corinthians 16:19) and celebrate with them (Deuteronomy 14:26). Families are where we go for acceptance, encouragement, guidance, and advice. When everyone else disappears, our families are there for us.

So when you think about it, our families are a wonderful gift from God. Celebrate your family—and the relatives too—by giving them the honor and respect they deserve.

Everyone will live quietly in their own homes in peace and prosperity, for there will be nothing to fear. The LORD Almighty has promised this! [Micah 4:4]

also on this day

Today is Armed Forces Day.

1642

The Canadian city of Montreal was founded.

1986

David Goch finished swimming 55,682 miles in a 25-yard pool.

to do ☑

WRITE LETTERS TO (OR E-MAIL) A COUPLE OF YOUR RELATIVES. ASK THEM TO SHARE A STORY ABOUT THEIR FAMILIES WHEN THEY WERE YOUR AGE.

the day of darkness

About midday on this day in 1780, near-total darkness descended on much of New England. The cause is still unexplained.

The days preceding May 19, 1780, in the New England region had featured unusually colored skies—a dirty yellow tinge with a reddish-brown hue. But no one was prepared for what was to take place on this particular day. During the morning hours, the region became unusually dark.

By noon, complete darkness had taken hold. The birds began their evening songs and then stopped singing completely and disappeared. The frogs began to croak. Chickens returned to their roosts, and the cows began their slow walk back to the barns from the pasture. Travel became nearly impossible. Professor Daggett of New Haven, Connecticut, reported: "The greatest darkness at least equal to what was commonly called candlelighting in the evening. The appearance was indeed uncommon, and the cause unknown."

On three different occasions, the Bible refers to the conditions of complete darkness: during creation when the earth was empty and "cloaked in darkness" (Genesis 1:2, 4); during the ninth plague when God brought upon the Egyptians a "deep and terrifying darkness" (Exodus 10:21); and when Jesus hung on the cross, from "noon, darkness fell across the whole land until three o'clock" (Matthew 27:45).

In the Bible darkness has always been associated with judgment of God and with evil. In fact, during the darkness that fell upon New England that day, many people thought it was the final judgment day and attended hastily assembled church services.

The Bible also warns us to not only stay away from the "works of darkness" but to expose them. How do we do that? By remaining connected and by being willing to speak out against what we know is wrong. To do otherwise is to remain in the dark.

Take no part in the worthless deeds of evil and darkness; instead, rebuke and expose them. [Ephesians 5:11]

to do ☑

SIT FOR ABOUT FIVE MINUTES IN TOTAL DARKNESS. AFTERWARD, REFLECT ON HOW THAT FELT BEING IN DARKNESS. HOW DID IT FEEL TO COME BACK INTO THE LIGHT?

also on this day

1995 The world's youngest doctor, Balamurali Ambati, 17, graduated from Mount Sinai Medical School.

Ringling Brothers opened its first circus. 1884

Unrealized Dreams

On this day in 1506, Christopher Columbus died.

to do ☑

READ HEBREWS 11. THEN COMPOSE AN ACROSTIC FOR F-A-I-T-H THAT HELPS YOU UNDERSTAND WHAT IT MEANS TO LIVE BY FAITH. FOR EXAMPLE, **F** COULD STAND FOR FUTURE DREAMS; **A** FOR ALWAYS BELIEVE, AND SO ON.

Christopher Columbus, the great Italian explorer, was the first European to explore the Americas since the Vikings in the 10th century. But it was not an easy undertaking. Columbus' bid to explore the New World was rejected once by the king of Portugal and at least twice by the Spanish King Ferdinand and Queen Isabella before he found support for his journey.

In all, Columbus made four voyages to the New World. On his last voyage in 1502, he sailed for what is now Central America, searching for gold and a strait to connect him to the East Indies. But his ship was in such poor condition that Columbus and his crew were marooned on Jamaica for a year before a rescue ship arrived. He returned to Spain to discover that Queen Isabella had died three weeks earlier and that the king would no longer see him. Columbus died two years later a disappointed man, without fully realizing the scope of his achievement and how it had changed the world.

In Hebrews chapter 11, we discover that many of God's people died without fully realizing the promises that God had given to them (v.13). Abraham died without seeing the nation that his descendants would one day become. The prophets died without seeing the Messiah, whose birth they had predicted. But what they did have was faith—"The confident assurance that what we hope for is going to happen" (v.1). They did not die disappointed, because they had a vision of Heaven, "a better place, a heavenly homeland" (v.16).

It's easy to get discouraged when circumstances get tough or when our plans don't work out. That's when we need to take courage from such heroes of the faith as Noah, Abraham, Moses, and the prophets, and to live in faith as they did.

All of these **people** we have mentioned **received** God's **approval** because of their **faith**, yet **none** of them **received all** that God had **promised**.

[Hebrews 11:39]

also on this day

1837 **Levi Strauss and his partner patented jeans.**

Charles Lindbergh flew his historic solo nonstop transatlantic flight. 1927

1932
Amelia Earhart made her solo flight across the Atlantic Ocean.

first aid

On this day in 1881, the American Red Cross was founded.

For more than 100 years, the American Red Cross has donated blood, time, money, food, medicine, and other forms of relief to people in need. Clara Barton, a Civil War nurse, helped found the organization after hearing about the Swiss-inspired International Red Cross movement while visiting Europe. She returned home to campaign for the formation of a group that would provide lifesaving services and relief during times of war and in times of disasters.

For 23 years Barton headed up the Red Cross. During that time, the organization conducted its first domestic and overseas disaster relief efforts, providing aid to the U.S. military during the Spanish-American War. Since then the Red Cross has added first aid, water safety, and public health nursing programs. In World War II alone, the Red Cross recruited 104,000 nurses, shipped over 300,000 tons of supplies, and initiated a national blood program that collected 13.3 million pints of blood for use by the armed forces.

Organizations like the Red Cross provide vital services for people in need on a large-scale basis. They provide welcome care and relief for those who are hurting, hungry, or homeless because of war or a disaster. The kind of help they offer is basic and essential.

Jesus loved and cared for the poor and the sick, and his followers should also. We may not be able to travel across the country or to other parts of the world to help people in need like those in the Red Cross. But it won't take too much time to find someone who has fundamental needs—food, clothing, medical help, or a place to stay—in your own community.

When we care for those in need around us, no matter how small or simple an act, it is as if we have given it directly to Jesus himself.

to do ☑

COME UP WITH A LIST OF IDEAS OF HOW YOU CAN BECOME MORE INVOLVED IN CARING FOR OTHERS.

Then the **King** will say, "I'm **telling** the solemn **truth**: **Whenever you** did **one** of these things to someone **overlooked** or **ignored**, that was **me**— **you** did it to **me**."

[Matthew 25:40, The Message]

also on this day

1819

The first bicycles in the United States were introduced in New York City.

The first nuclear-powered lighthouse began operations at Chesapeake Bay.

1964

Today is National Waiter/Waitress Day.

At this time in your life, you probably know many things you can't do yet because you are not old enough—like drive a car or vote for a president. Life often is restricted by our ages—we're either too young or too old to do certain things. And it's true that as people age certain more vigorous activities become more and more difficult.

But just when you start to think about age as a limitation, you read about someone like Yuichiro Miura. This 70-year-old school headmaster and former professional skier from Japan became the oldest person to reach the summit of Mount Everest—the world's highest peak! Mr. Miura said climbing the mountain was a dream come true for him. And in accomplishing that feat, the Japanese climber shattered the record previously held by another Japanese man, Tomiyasu Ishikawa, who was 65 when he reached the top of Mt. Everest.

Old age is never a restriction in God's eyes. Think about Noah. He was 600 years old when he first stepped foot on the ark and the flood began! Abraham became a father at age 100. And Moses was over 80 when he returned to Egypt to confront Pharaoh and rescue God's people from slavery. The Bible describes Joshua as "old and well advanced in years" when God commanded him to finish conquering the promised land (Joshua 13:1, NIV). No matter how old a person is, God still can use that person to carry out his work. The psalm-writer put it this way: "Even in old age they will still produce fruit."

Think about the older people you know at your church or in your neighborhood. You can learn much from their experiences and their walk with God. Just ask them!

Even in old age they will still produce fruit; they will remain vital and green. [Psalm 92:14]

On this day in 2003, a 70-year-old man from Japan became the oldest man to climb to the top of Mount Everest.

never too old

to do ☑

RECORD AN ORAL HISTORY OF AN OLDER PERSON FROM YOUR CHURCH. ASK HOW THAT PERSON HAS SERVED GOD AT DIFFERENT STAGES OF HIS OR HER LIFE. SHARE WHAT YOU DISCOVER WITH OTHERS.

also on this day

1933 This was the first reported sighting of the Loch Ness Monster.

Mister Roger's Neighborhood **made its debut on TV.** 1967

**Today is
Penny Day.**

A Penny Saved

Let's be honest. If you saw a penny on the ground, would you bother to stop and pick it up? Most people would probably step right over it and not give it another thought. After all, it's only worth a cent! But on this day that honors the very first currency of any type authorized by the United States, here are a few, well, pennies for your thoughts:

▸ The word *penny* was derived from the British coin pence.

▸ Over 300 billion one-cent coins, with 11 different designs, have been minted since 1787. Lined up edge to edge, these pennies would circle the earth 137 times!

▸ More pennies are produced than any other denomination.

▸ The Lincoln penny was the first U.S. coin to feature a historic figure and was the first coin on which the words "In God We Trust" appeared.

But perhaps the most amazing fact is that one of the most important sources of giving to local charity groups is the penny! Through the power of the penny, charities are able to raise millions of dollars annually for great causes. For example, groups such as Ronald McDonald Children's Charities, UNICEF, and the Salvation Army all rely in great part upon the collection of pennies to fund their organizations.

A penny saved becomes one cent added to another added to another, and before you know it, you soon will have one million pennies! When it comes to giving, the Bible is clear that the amount doesn't matter as much as your willingness to give. So don't think that the pennies you have saved up in your piggy bank are insignificant or that it doesn't "pay" to pick up a lost penny. Even the smallest amount given in the spirit of love can amount to a *big* deal.

to do ☑

START YOUR OWN PENNY HARVEST FOR A MISSION ORGANIZA- TION OR A MINISTRY AT YOUR CHURCH. YOU'LL BE SURPRISED AT HOW QUICKLY THE PENNIES ADD UP!

If **you** are **really eager** to **give**, it isn't **important how much** you are able to **give**. **God wants** you to give what you **have**, **not** what you **don't** have. [2 Corinthians 8:12]

also on this day

Today is National Turtle Day.

Postal cards were sold in San Francisco for the first time. 1873

1827
The first nursery school in the United States was established in New York City.

mary's little lamb

On this day in 1830, Sarah Hale wrote the familiar children's song, "Mary Had a Little Lamb."

For many, this is the first nursery rhyme that they can remember from their childhood. And for countless others, it's the first simple tune played when learning a new instrument. Hundreds upon thousands of school-age children can repeat the familiar lines, but does anyone know anything about the author?

Sarah Josepha Buell was born October 24, 1788, in Newport, New Hampshire. Self-educated, at age 18 she became a teacher in Newport and worked there until 1813, when she married David Hale, a lawyer. When he died nine years later, she was a 34-year-old pregnant mother of four who rose to become one of America's most successful women writers and editors.

Despite her many accomplishments (including successfully lobbying for the establishment of Thanksgiving on the final Thursday of November), Sarah Hale is least known as author of the rhyme "Mary's Lamb." In 1830 American composer Lowell Mason, who had introduced music into American schools' curriculum, asked her to write lyrics for him. He chose eight of her poems to include in his songbook, one of which was "Mary's Lamb." The popular rhyme was then published for decades in McGuffey's readers, the most important schoolbook of the century.

A simple verse, based supposedly on a real Mary who brought her lamb to school, has had an amazing and long-lasting impact on children since its first publication. Likewise, other things that seem small and insignificant have made a huge impact in the world.

Jesus used the image of a mustard seed—the smallest seed a farmer used at that time—to illustrate how God's kingdom grows. God takes faith that may seem small and insignificant and gives it eternal importance.

When you feel that your faith is small or that what you are doing is of little importance, remember Mary's little lamb and the mustard seed. It doesn't take much to make a big impression.

"The Kingdom of Heaven is like a mustard seed planted in a field. It is the smallest of all seeds, but it becomes the largest of garden plants and grows into a tree where birds can come and find shelter in its branches." [Matthew 13:31, 33]

also on this day

1543

Nicolaus Copernicus published proof of a sun-centered solar system.

1983

The Brooklyn Bridge's 100th birthday was celebrated.

to do ☑

THE NEXT TIME YOU SING OR HEAR "MARY HAD A LITTLE LAMB," THINK OF ANOTHER MARY AND HER LITTLE LAMB, JESUS, THE LAMB OF GOD.

daring to be different

On this day in 1981, daredevil Daniel Goodwin scaled Chicago's Sears Tower in 7½ hours wearing a Spider-Man costume.

Wearing a Spider-Man outfit and equipped with three suction cups, Daniel "Spider Dan" Goodwin of Las Vegas began climbing what was then the world's tallest building, the Sears Tower in Chicago. Goodwin climbed for six hours while Chicago city police watched the perilous climb. When Goodwin reached the 50th floor of the skyscraper, he stopped a moment to chat with police, assuring them of his safety. The police agreed to allow Goodwin to continue his climb for another hour until he reached the top, whereupon they promptly arrested him for trespassing!

While the Sears Tower was the first skyscraper that Goodwin scaled as "Spider Dan," it was certainly not the last. He also scaled the John Hancock Building in Chicago and the two towers of the former World Trade Center. Goodwin remarked about his feats, "When I walk through a city and see skyscrapers, the only thing I can think about is climbing them."

You may wonder why anyone would take such a dangerous risk like that. Often that answer lies in a person's desire to achieve fame or notoriety. Sometimes it's because they dare to be different.

As Christians we are challenged to be different from the rest of the world (Romans 12:1, 2). But that doesn't mean that we need to don a costume and attempt some incredibly risky stunt. Followers of Christ dare to be different in the way they act toward others, specifically in loving others with the same kind of sacrificial love that Jesus showed us. That means loving the kid at school who calls you names, loving the teacher who piles on the homework, and even loving your brother when he picks on you.

Now that's *really* daring to be different!

to do ☑

DARE TO BE DIFFERENT TODAY! SHOW JESUS' RADICAL LOVE TO THAT HARD-TO-LOVE PERSON IN YOUR LIFE.

"So now I am giving you a new commandment: Love each other. Just as I have loved you, you should love each other. Your love for one another will prove to the world that you are my disciples." [John 13:34, 35]

also on this day

585 BC
The first known prediction of a solar eclipse was made in Greece.

Approximately 7 million Americans participated in "Hands Across America."
1986

Today is National Tap Dance Day.

Real Heroes

On this day in 1907, John Wayne was born.

One of the most popular actors of all time, John Wayne, was born Marion Michael Morrison in Winterset, Iowa. Wayne planned to attend the U.S. Naval Academy after high school, but he was rejected. So he accepted a football scholarship to the University of Southern California.

While at USC, Wayne's football coach found him a job as an assistant prop man on the set of a movie directed by John Ford. Ford used Wayne as an extra and eventually began to trust the youth with some larger roles. In 1930 Ford recommended Wayne for Fox's epic Western, *The Big Trail*. Wayne won the part, but the movie did poorly.

During the next 10 years, Wayne worked in countless low-budget western films, developing a distinct personality for his cowboy characters. Finally his old mentor John Ford gave Wayne his big break, casting him in the 1939 western, *Stagecoach*. Wayne was Ringo Kid, and he played the role with the essential traits of the characters he used in nearly all of his other movies: a tough and clear-eyed honesty, unquestioning valor, and an almost plodding manner.

The Duke, as he was called, became known for these heroic characters—men of decency, honesty, and integrity. He built his acting career portraying men who did the right thing.

When it comes to *real* heroes, one of the defining characters in the Bible is David. You can almost envision David riding across the Wild West, battling outlaws instead of the Philistines. King David was known for his honesty, his integrity, and his decency. He was given one of the highest honors: in the Bible he was called "a man after [God's] own heart."

You don't have to fight battles to be considered a "kid after God's own heart." Read Acts 13:22 and you'll discover what it takes to be a real hero in God's eyes.

to do ☑

WHO DO YOU CON-SIDER YOUR HEROES? WRITE DOWN ONE OR TWO CHARACTERISTICS OF THOSE PEOPLE YOU ADMIRE THE MOST.

After removing Saul, he made David their king. He testified concerning him: "I have found David son of Jesse a man after my own heart; he will do everything I want him to do."

[Acts 13:22, NIV]

also on this day

Today is National Blueberry Cheesecake Day.

Lewis & Clark first saw the Rocky Mountains. **1805**

1959
The word *Frisbee* became a registered trademark of Wham-O.

The first *Star Wars* movie debuted. **1977**

Disney's dream world

On this day in 1969, construction began on Walt Disney World in Florida.

Walt Disney's Disneyland was created as a place where families could go and lose themselves in a dream world of magic, make-believe, and fun. After its success, Walt had visions for another park, but on a much larger scale. He realized that he had not purchased enough land to do all he had wanted to do at the California site. The real world, he said, was still too close to his land of make-believe.

"I don't want the public to see the world they live in while they're in the park," Disney said. "I want them to feel they're in another world."

Even though Walt Disney never lived to see the opening of Walt Disney World, his vision was fulfilled. From the moment you enter the park, there is a sense of wonder, excitement, and fantasy. At any given moment, you may see Mickey Mouse, Donald Duck, or any number of Disney characters strolling along the grounds. You can cruise through a jungle, ride in a giant teacup, or blast through space.

The real world is nothing like Disney's creation. All you have to do is listen to the news to discover a world filled with conflicts, crime, and tragedy. Jesus told his disciples upfront that their lives would not be trouble-free: "Here on earth you will have many trials and sorrows" (John 16:33). But Jesus gives us a way to cope that is infinitely better than the fleeting fantasy escape of Walt Disney World. Jesus promises the Holy Spirit, our guide and comforter, to help us deal with our troubled world.

to do ☑

FIND OUT MORE ABOUT THE HOLY SPIRIT. READ JOHN 14:15–26 AND JOHN 16:5–15. WRITE DOWN EVERYTHING THAT THE HOLY SPIRIT WILL DO FOR YOU.

also on this day

1937

In California, the Golden Gate Bridge was opened to the public. The bridge connects San Francisco and Marin County.

Today is National Grape Popsicle Day.

"And I will ask the Father, and he will give you another Counselor, who will never leave you." [John 14:16]

the prize that never fades

Jim Thorpe was born on this day in 1888.

Considered by many to be the greatest athlete of his time, Jim Thorpe was born in a one-room cabin in what's now Oklahoma. Thorpe was the great-great-grandson of an Indian warrior and athlete, Chief Black Hawk. Thorpe excelled at every sport he ever played.

Thorpe played football, baseball, and basketball, *and* he trained for the 1912 Olympics in track. He won gold medals in both the decathlon and pentathlon events at the Stockholm Olympics, but he was stripped of those medals when a sports reporter revealed that Thorpe had played semi-professional baseball as a youth. It wasn't until after his death that Thorpe's amateur status as an athlete was restored and his name reentered in the Olympic record book.

Earthly prizes are like that. Someone can take them away if the rules aren't followed or if a mistake is made. They can get lost or stolen. They can collect dust on your shelf or get shuffled into a corner in the back of your closet. Sometimes we win a prize that we want to hold on to, but those trophies and ribbons we've won for swim team, soccer, and other sports soon fade away.

Thankfully, those aren't the only types of prizes that we will receive. As a follower of Jesus, one day when you are in Heaven, you will receive an eternal prize. That's right—a prize that will never fade, collect dust, or get lost, given to us by Jesus himself. And how do we win that prize? Not by running the fastest or scoring the most points or even doing the most good deeds. It's a prize that goes to all who train themselves daily to walk in faith through prayer, Bible reading, and obedience to God.

How's your training going?

to do ☑

MAKE A DAILY "TRAINING" SCHEDULE FOR YOURSELF OF WHAT YOU WILL DO TO KEEP YOUR FAITH IN SHAPE. INCLUDE TIME FOR PRAYER, BIBLE READING, AND PRAISING GOD.

All athletes practice **strict self-control**. They do it to **win** a **prize** that will **fade** away, but **we** do it for an **eternal prize**.

[1 Corinthians 9:25]

also on this day

1805
Napoleon was crowned in Milan, Italy.

1929
Warner Brothers debuted "On with the Show" in New York City. It was the first all-color talking picture.

1934
The Dionne quintuplets were born near Callender, Ontario, to Olivia and Elzire Dionne. The babies were the first quintuplets to survive infancy.

passing the test

On this day in 1953, Sir Edmund Hillary became the first person to climb to the top of Mount Everest.

The North Pole had been reached in 1909, the South Pole two years later. In 1953, the one remaining "frontier" for humans to conquer was Everest, the tallest mountain in the world, standing at an impressive and imposing 29,028 feet. At that time 15 expeditions had attempted to reach the top but had failed. It took a beekeeper from Auckland, New Zealand, and his Sherpa guide Tensing Norgay to accomplish that feat.

Edmund Hillary had devoted years of training to prepare for this attempt. He climbed the Southern Alps in summer and winter to practice both rock climbing and ice pick work and also took up wrestling. In 1951 Hillary made his first trip to the Himalayas, and the following year he joined a British Everest Committee training team.

Even with all these preparations, Hillary faced incredible obstacles. No one really knew the effects of high altitude and thin air on the body. It was an incredible test of strength, stamina, and courage. "We didn't know if it was humanly possible to reach the top of Mt. Everest. And even using oxygen as we were, if we did get to the top, we weren't at all sure whether we wouldn't drop dead or something of that nature," he said.

Hillary endured the test, and for his efforts, he was knighted by Queen Elizabeth and became an internationally known celebrity.

We all have times of testing in our lives. It may be a math class that is particularly challenging or dealing with a person at school who is unpleasant to you. Whatever the test you face, we are instructed to "patiently endure testing" (James 1:12). In addition, "when your endurance is fully developed, you will be strong in character and ready for anything" (James 1:4).

also on this day

1848
Wisconsin became America's 30th state.

1911
The first Indianapolis 500 took place.

1917
John F. Kennedy, the 35th president, was born.

God blesses the people who patiently endure testing. Afterward they will receive the crown of life that God has promised to those who love him.

[James 1:12]

to do ☑

THINK OF A "TEST" THAT YOU ARE FACING RIGHT NOW. ASK GOD TO HELP YOU ENDURE THE TEST.

The saying goes that every dog has its day. Well, each May, dogs, cats, rabbits, fish, birds, and any other kind of animal you can name, have an entire month devoted especially to them. Be Kind to Animals Month is a great reminder of how we should treat our furry, feathered, finned, and scaly friends throughout the year.

The Be Kind to Animals movement was started in 1915 by the American Humane Society as a celebration of animals—both wild and tame. Whether it's taking your dog out for a walk, spreading some bird feed outside, or making sure your pet has a clean, safe place to sleep, caring for animals is our responsibility. From the very beginning, God gave humans authority over the earth and its inhabitants: "Be masters over the fish and birds and all the animals" (Genesis 1:28). That doesn't mean we can do anything we want to God's creatures. Rather, it means that we should care for God's creation as he cares for us.

Here are 10 ways you can get involved in being kind to the animals in your life:

▸▸ Speak out for animals.
▸▸ Report animal cruelty whenever you see it.
▸▸ Adopt a pet from a shelter.
▸▸ Identify your pets with tags.
▸▸ Appreciate wildlife.
▸▸ Leave room in your yard for habitats for wildlife.
▸▸ Make a bird or bat house.
▸▸ Be a good role model for your friends in treating all animals with care.
▸▸ Volunteer at your local animal shelter.
▸▸ Keep on the lookout for stray or injured animals.

Remember, whenever you show kindness to the critters God created, you also are pleasing him.

to do ☑

SPEND AN EXTRA FEW MINUTES PLAYING WITH YOUR PET TODAY. OR IF YOU DON'T OWN ONE, HELP A FRIEND WHO DOES.

Good people take care of their animals, but wicked people are cruel to theirs. [Proverbs 12:10, GNT]

also on this day

1783 **The first daily newspaper was published in America.**

W. G. Young **patented the ice-cream freezer.** 1848

This is Be Kind to Animals month.

animal care

Always Remember

Memorial Day is the last Monday of May.

The first official Memorial Day was declared on May 5, 1868, by General John Logan, the national commander of the Grand Army of the Republic, as a tribute to the soldiers who had sacrificed their lives during the Civil War. The first observation of Memorial Day occurred on May 30, 1868, when flowers were placed on the graves of Union and Confederate soldiers at Arlington National Cemetery in Washington, D.C.

By 1890, the day was recognized by all the northern states. The South had its own Memorial Day until after World War I when the day was changed from honoring just the Civil War dead to include all Americans who had died fighting in any war.

We continue to observe Memorial Day as an important reminder of the many men and women who died serving our country. Remembering the past and honoring the people who have gone before us is important in understanding our history and what makes us Americans. It is also important in understanding our faith.

When Joshua and the Israelites crossed the Jordan River to enter the promised land, they had an important job to do before they began conquering the land. God commanded the people to stop and build a memorial using 12 stones—one for each tribe of Israel. Why did God want them to spend the time doing that? Because he wanted the people to remember who was guiding them and who had brought them into the land. It was important for the people to *remember*.

We too need to remember God throughout the day. You can build memorials to God in your day by taking time to pause and thank God for what he has done for you this day.

to do ☑

REMEMBER YOUR RELATIONSHIP WITH GOD. USE A DRAWING, A BIBLE VERSE, OR A VISUAL CUE (SUCH AS A CERTAIN TREE OR BUILDING THAT YOU SEE FREQUENTLY) AS A REMINDER TO SPEND TIME WITH HIM.

Always remember that it is the LORD your God who gives you power to become rich, and he does it to fulfill the covenant he made with your ancestor.

[Deuteronomy 8:18]

also on this day

1884
Dr. John Harvey Kellogg patented "flaked" cereal.

•1907
The first taxis arrived in New York City.

don't give up the ship

In 1813, Captain James Lawrence, the commander of the USS Chesapeake, exclaimed "Don't give up the ship!"

During the War of 1812, James Lawrence was promoted to captain and was given command of the *Chesapeake* at Boston. On his way out of Boston harbor, he fought the British frigate *Shannon*. In the battle the captain was mortally wounded. As he was being carried from the deck, he shouted, "Tell the men to fire faster and not to give up the ship." That phrase "Don't give up the ship!" became the Americans' battle cry.

Giving up sounds good when life gets tough. Athletes know this. Getting outscored early in the game, they can think, "What's the use. We're gonna get slaughtered!" Or a long-distance runner may fall behind and consider quitting. But then the coach yells, "Don't give up! Keep going! Be strong—you can do it!" And the inspired team or runner works even harder, and, sometimes, even comes from behind to win.

Refusing to give up means doing what we know is right even when we don't feel like it or the odds are stacked against us. We can feel like quitting in a lot of places: in school, doing work, in a relationship, even with our faith.

The early Christians knew that feeling. They lost jobs and friends for following Christ. Eventually the government branded them criminals, jailed them, and treated them terribly. They were told, "Turn your back on Jesus, and we'll let you go." But the believers hung tough because they knew the truth and that God was real.

In today's verse the apostle Paul encourages believers to persevere, to endure. In fact, he said they should be happy because those tough times would make them stronger. Paul knew that—he had endured terrible punishments and abuse for following Christ.

So whatever you face, remember, "Don't give up the ship!" and persevere.

We can rejoice, too, when we run into problems and trials, for we know that they are good for us—they help us learn to endure. And endurance develops strength of character in us, and character strengthens our confident expectation of salvation. [Romans 5:3, 4]

also on this day

1938
The first Superman comic was published.

1938
Baseball helmets were worn for the first time—ouch!

1944
The government of Mexico abolished the "siesta" (naptime).

to do ☑

READ A STORY OF A CHRISTIAN WHO WAS PERSECUTED FOR HIS OR HER FAITH. YOUR PASTOR OR PARENT PROBABLY WILL KNOW WHERE TO FIND ONE. IF NOT, CHECK OUT WWW.PERSECUTION.COM, THE WEB SITE OF VOICE OF THE MARTYRS.

Crown Him!

On this day in 1953, Queen Elizabeth II of England was crowned in Westminster Abbey.

The coronation of a king or queen is magnificent, with grand and colorful ceremonies and pageantry. Thousands of people line the streets as the procession moves slowly to the site. Then, with costumed men trumpeting their arrival, the new king or queen walks up the carpet to the church. At the appropriate time, the climax of the ceremony, the crown is placed on the royal head and he or she is declared to be the king or queen. It's quite an event.

The Bible calls Jesus, "King of kings and Lord of lords." In other words, of all the kings, queens, presidents, prime ministers, and other national leaders who have ever lived, Jesus, our Lord, rules. He doesn't await a coronation—he already is king. He is above all, and, eventually, "at the name of Jesus every knee will bow, in heaven and on earth and under the earth, and every tongue will confess that Jesus Christ is Lord, to the glory of God the Father" (Philippians 2:10–11).

In 1851 Matthew Bridges wrote the hymn, "Crown Him with Many Crowns." Based on Revelation 19:12, it celebrates the truth that Christ truly is our king and that we should honor him as such. You probably remember the song. It begins, "Crown Him with many crowns, the Lamb upon His throne; Hark! how the heavenly anthem drowns all music but its own! Awake, my soul, and sing of Him who died for thee; and hail Him as thy matchless King thro' all eternity."

To have Christ as king, however, means more than saying he is or than singing songs about him. It means honoring him and obeying him. He needs to rule, now, in our hearts. Eventually we will see him in person, in Heaven, and we'll be able to lay all our "crowns" before him.

to do ☑

FIND "CROWN HIM WITH MANY CROWNS" IN A HYMNAL. THEN, PLAY IT ON THE PIANO, SING IT, OR JUST READ THE WORDS. THANK GOD FOR HIS SON, JESUS, KING OF KINGS AND LORD OF LORDS.

The twenty-four elders fall down and worship the one who lives forever and ever. And they lay their crowns before the throne and say, "You are worthy, O Lord our God, to receive glory and honor and power. For you created everything, and it is for your pleasure that they exist and were created." [Revelation 4:10, 11]

also on this day

1883
The first night baseball game was held under the lights in Ft. Wayne, Indiana.

President Franklin D. Roosevelt had the first swimming pool built inside the White House.
1933

President Grover Cleveland got married while serving his term.
1886

Today, most people know the name *Lou Gehrig* only because of a disease named after him—the disease, ALS (Amyotrophic Lateral Sclerosis), that took his life in 1941. But Gehrig was an amazing baseball player, hitting for power and batting average. And for many years he held the record for playing in consecutive games—2,130. During that streak, he played with broken bones (at least 17) and back spasms. No wonder he was called "the Iron Horse."

Eventually, in 1995, Cal Ripken Jr. broke that record. Ripken ended up playing in 2,632 consecutive games. Both of those streaks are amazing. Imagine everything that might keep someone out of a game. In addition to injury, there's sickness, family issues (births, deaths, etc.), and, of course, exhaustion. One thing's for sure—every day, every game, the manager knew that Lou or Cal would be ready to play.

That's faithfulness—being the kind of person who can be counted on, no matter what. You know people like that, don't you? Maybe a teacher, coach, or pastor. Certainly your mom and dad. Hopefully even a friend or two.

God is faithful. Check out Lamentations 3:23: "Great is his faithfulness; his mercies begin afresh each day." We know we can count on God to be with us, everywhere, all the time.

But God wants us to be faithful as well. That's the point of today's verse. Paul was telling the Thessalonian believers he was proud that they had remained strong and faithful, through all kinds of trouble. He knew he could count on them to live for Christ.

How about you? If asked to describe you, would friends and others who know you say "faithful"? Determine to be someone that people, and especially God, can count on. Start a faithfulness streak today.

to do ☑

THINK OF SOMEONE WHO HAS BEEN FAITHFUL TO YOU (A FRIEND, A TEACHER, AND SO FORTH). TAKE A FEW MINUTES AND WRITE THAT PERSON A NOTE, ACKNOWLEDGING HIS OR HER FAITHFULNESS AND THANKING HIM OR HER FOR IT.

We proudly tell God's other churches about your endurance and faithfulness in all the persecutions and hardships you are suffering. [2 Thessalonians 1:4]

he keeps going and going and going

On this day in 1932, Lou Gehrig set a major league baseball record when he hit four consecutive home runs.

also on this day

1800 John Adams moved to Washington, D.C. He was the first president to live in what later became the capital of the United States.

1851 The New York Knickerbockers became the first baseball team to wear uniforms.

it's the truth!

On this day in 620 BC, Aesop was born.

You've probably heard of Aesop (pronounced "ee-sop") because of *Aesop's Fables*. According to one historian, Aesop was a slave who lived in Samos (a Greek island) in the sixth century BC and eventually was freed by his master. We don't know much more. But a bunch of fables carry his name as author: "The Tortoise and the Hare," "The Ant and the Grasshopper," "The Lion and the Mouse," and "The Wolf in Sheep's Clothing" to name a few.

A fable is a made-up story that teaches a lesson. In a fable, we look for the moral to the story. Also, fables often feature talking animals (that's one way to know that they're totally fiction). So fables themselves are not true, but they can convey truths.

Some people say the Bible is a collection of "fables." In other words, they think the stories are interesting and can even teach valuable lessons, but they're not strictly true. Some people might say, for example, that the Israelites didn't really cross the Red Sea on dry ground, that the walls of Jericho didn't really fall down when the trumpets blew, that Jonah wasn't really swallowed by a great fish, and that Jesus didn't really heal people and rise from the dead. Some people take it a step further and choose some stories to believe and some to not believe.

That's wrong.

The Bible is God's Word. It claims to be truth and has proven to be factual and truthful in everything it states. And Jesus said he is *the* Truth (see John 14:6). In today's verses for example, Jesus says that he is telling the truth.

Here's the point—you can believe the Bible, all of it. It's not a fable—it's true. Don't be fooled by anyone who tells you otherwise.

"So when I tell the truth, you just naturally don't believe me! Which of you can truthfully accuse me of sin? And since I am telling you the truth, why don't you believe me?" [John 8:45, 46]

also on this day

1896

Henry Ford made a successful test drive of his new car in Detroit, Michigan. He called the vehicle a "quadricycle."

1919

The U.S. Senate passed the women's suffrage bill, allowing women to vote.

1939

In Oklahoma City, Oklahoma, Sylvan Goldman introduced the first shopping cart—a folding chair mounted on wheels.

to do ☑

GET A CONCORDANCE (SOMETIMES ONE IS IN THE BACK OF YOUR BIBLE). LOOK UNDER THE WORD TRUTH; THEN LOOK UP A BUNCH OF THE VERSES LISTED.

hunger pains

This is National Hunger Awareness Day.

"I'm starving!" When's the last time you said that to a friend or parent? Probably not too long ago. What you really meant was that you hadn't eaten for a couple of hours and would appreciate a snack or an early meal.

But have you ever had excruciating hunger pains? Probably not. Yet every night, millions of people—men, women, and *children*—go to bed hungry, even in the United States, the land of plenty. And in some countries, torn apart by war, devastated by hurricanes or earthquakes, or wiped out by famine, thousands are truly starving—starving to death.

That seems almost hard to believe in a land with restaurants on just about every corner and strip mall and grocery stores with millions of food options. Just think of the food available to you right now and what you have already eaten today. Then think of a small boy or girl living in a sheet metal shack, digging for roots of plants or hunting for insects to eat. That's sure different than a Big Mac®, fries, and a Coke®!

Some people are trying to make a difference, to take food to starving families. You've probably heard of World Vision, Compassion™, Samaritan's Purse, Bread for the World, World Relief, mission agencies, and other similar organizations. And your church and other ministries in the community work hard to assist poor people.

So the next time you're tempted to say "I'm starving," remember what that truly means and think of what you can do to help.

to do ☑

FIND OUT THE LOCATION OF A LOCAL FOOD PANTRY. THEN TAKE A BAG OF CANNED GOODS THERE AS A GIFT FROM YOUR FAMILY, TO HELP FEED THE HUNGRY PEOPLE IN THE COMMUNITY.

Feed the **hungry** and **help** those in **trouble**. Then your **light** will **shine** out from the **darkness**, and the **darkness** around you will be as **bright** as **day**. [Isaiah 58:10]

also on this day

1968

During his campaign for the presidency, Robert F. Kennedy was assassinated in Los Angeles, California.

Apple II, the first personal computer, went on sale.

1977

This is World Environment Day.

This was D-day in 1944.

PURPLE HEART

Beachhead

D-day refers to the beginning of a vitally important battle in World War II, in which the Allies (armed forces from America, England, Canada, and other countries) invaded France along the Normandy coast to fight the German Nazi army. The invasion was *huge*, involving more than 5,000 ships, from battleships to landing craft, that deposited about 130,000 troops on five beaches along 50 miles of coast. Early in the invasion, more than 1,000 transport planes dropped paratroopers as well. The cost of this invasion was also enormous, with total Allied casualties on this one day alone estimated at 10,000, including 2,500 dead. But this was the first step toward victory in Europe.

The Allied commanders chose this invasion strategy because they needed to establish a "beachhead," a place in enemy territory where the army could begin their move to victory. Having gained this beachhead, they could continue to bring in fresh troops who could move deeper into the countryside with their supply lines nearby.

This is often the way wars are won. A beachhead is established, often after a fierce battle. Then the rest of the territory is taken, one day and one battle at a time.

"Beachhead" is a good picture of what God wants to do in our lives. In many ways, we are enemy territory—sinful, selfishly living apart from God and for his enemy (Satan). But when we, by faith, open our lives to God, he comes in and begins to work, changing us on the inside, one day and one battle at a time. His goal? To make us like Christ (see Romans 8:29).

Have you taken that first step? Have you given your life to Jesus? When God invades your life, you'll never be the same. He will gain the victory!

to do ☑

IF YOU'VE NEVER GIVEN YOUR LIFE TO CHRIST, DO IT NOW. FIND A CHRISTIAN ADULT TO HELP AND TO ANSWER ANY QUESTIONS. ALSO, GO ON THE INTERNET AND READ ABOUT D-DAY AND THE BATTLE OF NORMANDY.

For if you **confess** with your **mouth** that **Jesus is Lord** and **believe** in your **heart** that **God raised** him from the **dead**, you **will** be **saved**.

[Romans 10:9]

also on this day

1816 — Ten inches of snow fell in New England. This was known as "the year without a summer."

1933

In Camden, New Jersey, the first drive-in movie theater opened.

What's your favorite ice-cream flavor? strawberry? cookies and cream? pistachio? Probably the all-time favorite is chocolate. In fact, even if that's not your favorite, you probably like it a lot.

Imagine that you're talking to a person your age who has just moved to town. As you talk about family, interests, and likes and dislikes, you discover that your new neighbor has never tasted chocolate ice cream or anything chocolate. You love chocolate, especially chocolate ice cream, and eagerly gobble it up in a cone or bowl, whatever, especially on a hot summer day. So you try to describe the taste and your feelings to your new friend. What would you say? It wouldn't be easy! You might say that it's sweet and then try to find something else that has a similar taste (whatever that might be) and then explain that chocolate is sort of like that but different.

Eventually you'd say, "Hey, you'll never know till you have some. Once you taste it, you'll see what I mean!"

Now imagine that you're trying to tell someone about God and what he means to you. If the person has never met God and knows nothing about him, you'd probably have just about as much trouble as when you tried to describe chocolate ice cream. You could share verses and stories, and those would help, but eventually you'd probably have to say, "Taste and see!"

That's what King David wrote in Psalm 34:8, our verse for today. And it's so true. Anyone who encounters God finds that he is good and that he brings joy.

How does someone "taste" God? By reading his Word, praying, worshiping, and, most of all, by giving his or her life to him. Let everyone know!

to do ☑

READ ALL OF PSALM 34 AND THANK GOD FOR HIS GOODNESS AND JOY YOU'VE EXPERIENCED.

Taste and see that the LORD is good. Oh, the joys of those who trust in him! [Psalm 34:8]

This is National Chocolate Ice-Cream Day.

taste and see

also on this day

1769 Daniel Boone explored the heart of Kentucky. This is Daniel Boone Day.

1776 The United Colonies made a name change and became the United States.

best friends

This is Best Friends Day.

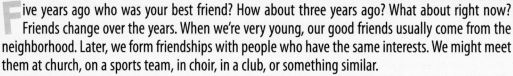

Five years ago who was your best friend? How about three years ago? What about right now? Friends change over the years. When we're very young, our good friends usually come from the neighborhood. Later, we form friendships with people who have the same interests. We might meet them at church, on a sports team, in choir, in a club, or something similar.

Maybe you're the kind of person who has several very good friends and not one *best* friend. Either way, having good friends is important. Everyone wants and needs someone to be close to, to care, to listen, to counsel, and to help.

So how are those friendships formed? And what makes a good friend anyway? Many factors can cause a friendship to begin. Two, as already mentioned, are living near each other and sharing interests and activities. Regardless of how a friendship begins, however, something else has to happen to make it go deeper.

For example, a good friend listens to you, without interrupting. A good friend cares about you, genuinely wanting the best for you. A good friend is honest with you, telling you the truth, even if it hurts. A good friend offers to help when you're in trouble or have a need. And a good friend sticks by you, even if everyone else seems to be deserting. Check our first verse for today. It highlights the last two of those characteristics.

Now that you know what a good friend is, apply those same statements to your friendship performance. In other words, what kind of friend are you? If your friends were interviewed about you, would they say that you listen, care, are honest, help, and are loyal?

If you want to have good friends, you'll have to be one yourself.

to do ☑

WRITE A NOTE TO YOUR "BEST FRIEND" OR ONE OF YOUR VERY GOOD FRIENDS, AND THANK THIS PERSON FOR HIS OR HER FRIENDSHIP. BE SPECIFIC. AND SPEND A FEW MOMENTS PRAYING FOR THIS FRIEND.

A friend is always loyal, and a brother is born to help in time of need. [Proverbs 17:17]

As iron sharpens iron, a friend sharpens a friend.
[Proverbs 27:17]

also on this day

This is National Jelly-Filled Doughnut Day (diet anyone?).

In New York City commercial ice cream was manufactured for the first time. 1786

Barbara Bush, wife of President George H. W. Bush, was born. 1925

Respect

This is Senior Citizens Day.

Have you heard any old people jokes lately? How about negative comments about an old person or old age? You know, statements like, "What are you, old? Move it!" or "Boy, has she aged!" or "She's so wrinkled, she has to screw her hat on!" And what do you think when you see an elderly person moving slowly? Or asking you to repeat your message because he couldn't hear you?

What is old age? Not long ago, it was someone in his or her 40s or 50s. Today, it's probably someone age 70 or above. Whatever the age, if we stay healthy, we'll be there before we know it!

It's easy to make fun of senior citizens. But that's wrong. In fact, the Bible tells us to do just the opposite. Today's verse says to show special "respect for the aged."

We should respect old people because, first of all, they're *people*. Second, we should respect them because of Jesus' Golden Rule, treating others the way we want to be treated. Third, we should respect our elders because they are experienced and wise—they have much to offer in advice, insight, and counsel. Finally, the most important reason for treating our elders with respect is because God tells us to.

Besides not making fun of old people, we respect them by considering their needs. If they can't hear well, we should speak up and talk slower. If they have something to say, we should listen carefully and thank them. If we know of an elderly person in the neighborhood who is struggling physically, we should help with housecleaning, yard work, and so forth. And we should heed the wise counsel of our godly elders and follow their examples.

It's spelled R-E-S-P-E-C-T—the best way to celebrate Senior Citizens Day.

> "**Show** your **fear** of **God** by standing up in the **presence** of **elderly** people and showing **respect** for the **aged**. **I am** the **LORD**." [Leviticus 19:32]

also on this day

Charles Graham received the first patent for false teeth. 1822

1934 Donald Duck made his debut (he still quacks us up).

to do ☑

DO SOMETHING KIND FOR AN ELDERLY PERSON YOU KNOW.

Over the Rainbow

On this day in 1922, Judy Garland was born.

Judy Garland was a movie star and singer who made 32 feature films, did voice-over work, and appeared in at least half a dozen short subjects. She even received a special Academy Award and was nominated for two others. She also starred in 30 TV shows (10 Emmy Award nominations). She won a Tony Award and 5 Grammys, including Album of the Year in 1962. Her real name was Frances Gumm, and she died in 1969.

Most people remember Judy as Dorothy in *The Wizard of Oz*—now you know who she is! When that movie was made in 1939, Judy was only 16 years old. The film has many interesting scenes and characters: munchkins, Tin Man, Scarecrow, Cowardly Lion, Wicked Witch of the West. Perhaps the most memorable is the song, "Somewhere Over the Rainbow." With Dorothy (Judy) singing so sweetly, it has remained popular till this day.

We may think that rainbows have been around forever (or a least as long as we've had rain and sun), but the first rainbow appeared after the great flood. Noah had obeyed God and had built an ark to save his family and the animals. When the waters receded, God promised to never destroy the earth with a flood again. Then he said he would give the rainbow as a sign of his covenant.

So, more than a pretty song in a classic film and more than a pretty splash of colors across the sky, a rainbow reminds us that God loves us and has promised to be with us. With him it's true, as Dorothy sang, "the dreams that you dare to dream really do come true."

to do ☑

EVERY TIME YOU SEE A RAINBOW, THANK GOD FOR HIS GREAT PROMISES AND THE FACT THAT THEY "REALLY DO COME TRUE."

"**When** I **see** the **rainbow** in the clouds, I will **remember** the eternal **covenant** between **God** and **every** living **creature** on earth."

[Genesis 9:16]

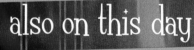

also on this day

1892 — This is National Black Cow Day.

1752 — Ben Franklin flew a kite and discovered electricity in lightning.

Dutch colonists settled on Manhattan Island. 1610

E.T. was one of the most popular movies ever produced, setting box office records in 1982 and continuing to gain viewers and fans ever since.

E.T. stands for "extraterrestrial"—a being from outside the Earth, an "alien." In the movie, a group of these aliens visit Earth but have to leave quickly, leaving one of them behind. A 10-year-old boy, Elliot, finds the alien. The two begin to communicate and soon become friends. E.T learns about life on Earth, and Elliot learns about the true meaning of friendship. E.T. wants to go home, but Elliot knows that if he helps E.T., he'll lose a friend. And the adventure continues.

For many years people have wondered about life on other planets and possible alien visits. Occasionally someone will report seeing a "flying saucer" (possible spaceship). And science fiction shows and books with stories of martians and other visitors have millions of fans.

Some of these stories, like *E.T.*, picture the alien as friendly. But most depict aggressive and hostile figures. All are fiction.

The *real* visitor to Earth from the outside came about 2,000 years ago. We know tons about him, even his name—Jesus. And he didn't come from another planet or galaxy; he came from Heaven, from his Father.

Jesus not only visited Earth, he actually became an "earthling," a human being. Fully God, he became fully man and was born as a baby, in a manger. After living a perfect life, Jesus died on the cross for our sins. Then he rose from death and returned to his heavenly home.

Jesus wants to be your friend. Even more important, he wants to be your Savior! And he wants you, eventually, to come to live with him.

He made himself nothing; he took the humble position of a slave and appeared in human form. [Philippians 2:7]

On this day in 1982, the movie E.T. The Extra-Terrestrial opened in theaters.

to do ☑

REREAD THE CHRISTMAS STORY—LUKE 1 & 2.

also on this day

1910 Jacques-Yves Cousteau was born. He was the famous French underwater explorer who invented the aqua-lung.

1912 Silas Christoferson became the first pilot to take off from the roof of a hotel (but why?).

extraterrestrial

tacos anyone?

This is National Taco Day.

Tacos are a favorite fast food. Tacos probably came to the States from Mexico and, at first, were only available in California or the Southwest. Now we can get them anywhere. And we have all kinds of tacos, even taco salad.

The basic taco has ground beef, cheese, lettuce, tomato, sour cream, and salsa (sometimes other ingredients too) packed in a tortilla shell. So in each bite, you get an explosion of flavors. No wonder they're popular—easy to eat and so tasty!

Can you imagine a taco with only salsa or only lettuce or only sour cream? Of course not. It would be something but certainly not a taco. The mixture and blend of ingredients give it flavor and interest.

The same is true with believers in Christ. The church is a wonderful mixture of personalities, cultures, histories, ages, races, gifts, and talents. This variety flavors the church and makes it effective.

In 1 Corinthians, Paul wrote about this, using the body (not a taco) as his example. Paul said that every person in the church, "the body of Christ," is an important part, even though each person is unique. If everyone had the gift of preaching and no one had the gift of administration, imagine the chaos. It would be like a body with several noses and no arms or legs. A body needs a wide variety of parts, working together.

He also wrote that we shouldn't be jealous of others' gifts. Instead, we should determine *our* gifts and then use them to God's glory.

Think about your church, your part of the body of Christ on earth. What differences in talents, spiritual gifts, experience, and wisdom do you see? Thank God for the variety. And think about your special contribution. What can you do in your church?

also on this day

1880

John Lee Richmond pitched baseball's first "perfect game." He played for the Worchester, Massachusetts, Worcesters.

1929

Anne Frank was born.

Now you are the **body** of **Christ,** and **each one** of you is a **part** of it. [1 Corinthians 12:27, NIV]

to do ☑

INTERVIEW FOUR OR FIVE ADULTS IN YOUR CHURCH, ASKING WHAT THEY THINK ARE THEIR SPIRITUAL GIFTS. THEN ASK A COUPLE OF ADULTS WHO KNOW YOU WELL TO SUGGEST POSSIBILITIES FOR YOUR SPIRITUAL GIFTS.

partial post

In 1920, the U.S. Post Office Department ruled that children may not be sent by parcel post.

OK—now you know, so you have no excuse. You may *not* mail your little brother or sister to anyone, no matter how irritating he or she becomes. (Admit it—you've had that thought.) Someone must have tried it; otherwise, why would we have a rule against it?

Usually we think of mail as a way of sending messages (and packages), of communicating with others. And we love getting letters (and packages) from friends and loved ones. Especially birthday cards with checks enclosed! These days we can communicate almost instantly with cell phones and e-mail.

Communication is at the heart of any relationship. We need to talk, to express, to share, to explain, to clarify, to ask for help, and to receive counsel and encouragement. Think about your best friend at school. Even if you spent most of the day together in classes, in the halls, and riding the bus, you probably talked or e-mailed that evening too, right? And when you're totally out of touch with this person, you can't wait to fill him or her in on your experiences and to catch up. Friends communicate.

You have a relationship with God, right? So how much do you talk? Communication is vital to that relationship too. So how much do you listen?

We talk to God through prayer. Paul wrote, "Pray at all times and on every occasion in the power of the Holy Spirit. Stay alert and be persistent in your prayers for all Christians everywhere" (Ephesians 6:18).

God talks to us through his Word, the Bible. Check out 2 Timothy 3:16.

No one, not even the government or the Postal Service, can keep you from communicating with God. So what's stopping you?

to do ☑

TAKE A FEW MINUTES AND WRITE A LETTER TO GOD, THANKING HIM FOR ALL HE HAS DONE FOR YOU, CONFESSING WHERE YOU'VE LET HIM DOWN AND ASKING FOR HIS HELP. BE SPECIFIC. PUT THE LETTER IN YOUR BIBLE AS A REMINDER OF THE IMPORTANCE OF COMMUNICATING WITH GOD.

Don't **worry** about **anything**; instead, **pray** about **everything**. Tell **God** what you **need**, and **thank** him for **all** he has **done**. [Philippians 4:6]

also on this day 1986

Mary-Kate and Ashley Olson were born.

This is Lobster Day.

This is Race Unity Day.

Under God

In 1954, the phrase "under God" was added to the Pledge of Allegiance.

D STATES O

N GOD WE TRUST

to do ☑

AT YOUR NEXT MEAL WITH YOUR FAMILY, SUGGEST THAT YOU SAY THE PLEDGE OF ALLEGIANCE TOGETHER. AFTERWARDS EXPLAIN TO EVERYONE WHAT "UNDER GOD" MEANS. THEN PRAY TOGETHER, THANKING GOD FOR THIS NATION AND FOR HIS LOVE AND GOODNESS.

Some schools begin the day with everyone reciting the Pledge of Allegiance together. It's a way of honoring the nation and of showing unity. When we say, "I pledge allegiance to the flag of the United States of America and to the republic for which it stands," we are saying that we will be loyal to our "one nation." Then we add, "under God, indivisible, with liberty and justice for all."

Added in 1954, the phrase *under God* is more than a nod God's way—sort of like saying, "God's OK, or "See, we're religious." *Under* means submission, obedience. If a soldier, for example, says that he serves under a certain army officer, he is saying that the officer is his commander and leader. What the officer says, he does, no questions asked.

When we say "under God," we are promising to listen to God and to obey him because he is our leader, our commander.

God is also acknowledged on our coins. Check out one and you'll see the phrase, "In God we trust." This means, simply, that we rely on him, not on money, government, or anything else to satisfy us.

Most Americans say the phrase in the pledge (and spend the money) so quickly that they don't even know what they're saying. When we say the Pledge, we're pledging allegiance to much more than a flag or a country—we are pledging loyalty to God.

So why don't we live like it?

When you **bow down** before the **Lord** and **admit** your **dependence** on **him**, he will **lift** you up and **give** you **honor**.

[James 4:10]

also on this day

This is Flag Day.

This is Family History Day.

⁂ **1775**

The U.S. Army was formed.

upside-down frown

This is Smile Power Day

OK, let's say you're heading for school, and you're running late. The weather's gloomy, matching your mood. You almost trip near the door and splatter yourself and your books on the sidewalk. Out of breath, you rush into class and plop into your seat. Expecting the worst, you look up and see your teacher . . . smiling! Now how do you feel?

Smiles say a bunch. They welcome and invite us, letting us in on the fun. They brighten a room. We *love* seeing smiles from a coach, the principal, our parents, and a friend.

Frowns seem to come more easily, especially when we hear bad news or think about our problems and troubles.

Smiles only come when we're having fun or focusing on what's good in our lives. Here's a short list.

- ▸▸ God created you in his image, loves you, and wants nothing but the best for you.
- ▸▸ God sent Jesus to die on the cross for your sins, so you could live with him forever.
- ▸▸ God has given you life and surrounded you with family, friends, teachers, and others who care about you.
- ▸▸ You can think, talk, see, walk, eat, smell, hear, taste, cry, and laugh (or, at least, most of those).
- ▸▸ You have a great sense of humor.

Think about whose day you can brighten. Be a positive person. Lighten up! Smile! Pass the joy!

Let the words of Christ, in all their richness, live in your hearts and make you wise. Use his words to teach and counsel each other. Sing psalms and hymns and spiritual songs to God with thankful hearts.

[Colossians 3:16]

also on this day

1775

George Washington was appointed head of the Continental Army by the Second Continental Congress.

1836

Arkansas became the 25th U.S. state.

to do ☑

FOR A COUPLE OF HOURS TODAY, TRY SMILING AT EACH PERSON YOU SEE, EVEN TOTAL STRANGERS. WATCH THEIR REACTIONS. MOST WILL PROBABLY SMILE BACK!

On this day in 1858, Abraham Lincoln said, "A house divided against itself cannot stand."

More than 1,000 Republican delegates met at the statehouse in Springfield, Illinois, for their state convention. At 5 PM they chose Abraham Lincoln to run against Democrat Stephen A. Douglas. Three hours later Lincoln delivered his acceptance speech, highlighting the terrible problem of slavery.

He said, "A house divided against itself cannot stand. I believe this government cannot endure permanently half *slave* and half *free*. I do not expect the Union to be *dissolved*—I do not expect the house to *fall*—but I *do* expect it will cease to be divided. It will become *all* one thing or *all* the other."

Some have called this "the speech that changed the world" because it pushed the movement against slavery leading, eventually, to the Civil War.

The phrase, "A house divided against itself cannot stand," quotes the Bible, paraphrasing Matthew 12:25, where Jesus was talking to the Pharisees. Politicians, especially presidential candidates, often quote Scripture. Sometimes the phrase is a correct interpretation and application. At times, however, the person is just trying to sound religious, trying to get support from Bible-believing people.

The real test of whether someone believes what the Bible teaches is how that person lives, not just that he or she mentions a verse or two. That certainly was the case with Lincoln. Because of his deep commitment to God and to God's Word, Lincoln fought to put an end to slavery, for the equality of all human beings.

You probably know many Bible verses, and hopefully you read your Bible often. But make sure that the verses are more than sound bytes or mottoes. Do what the Bible says—live it!

And don't assume someone knows God just because he or she quotes him. Watch the person's life. Then you'll know how he or she really believes.

to do ☑

LOOK UP THE "HOUSE DIVIDED AGAINST ITSELF" SPEECH ON THE INTERNET AND READ THE WHOLE THING. IT WON'T TAKE LONG.

And Jesus knew their thoughts, and said unto them, Every kingdom divided against itself is brought to desolation; and every city or house divided against itself shall not stand. [Matthew 12:25, KJV]

also on this day

1963 Valentina Tereshkova of the Soviet Union became the first woman in space.

This is National Fudge Day.

CHOCOLATE VANILLA FUDGE

True Freedom

june **17**

On this day in 1215, King John of England signed the Magna Carta.

The Magna Carta ("great charter or contract") is thought to be the foundation of liberty for England because it sets out principles of freedom for all the citizens. This official document established for the first time that the power of the king could be limited.

A few hundred years later, the leaders of the American colonies wrote their own charters of liberty: the Declaration of Independence (1776) and the Constitution (1787). These documents helped us gain and then keep our freedom.

But many Americans take their freedoms for granted. They love living in a country where we elect our leaders, instead of living under a dictator, yet they don't vote. They enjoy all the services that the government provides but complain about taxes and may even cheat on them. They appreciate being able to say whatever they like but may try to keep others from speaking different opinions. And they know that freedom of religion is important yet sleep in on Sundays.

All these freedoms are key, but more important is being free on the *inside*. When Jesus lived on earth, Palestine was far from free. The powerful and cruel Roman Emperor ruled the land. Yet Jesus spoke to his followers and the crowds about being "truly free." He wasn't talking about throwing off the Romans or any other earthly ruler. He meant being free from the slavery of sin and death. And he promised that all who believed in him would be released from the worst kind of oppression.

Today, in our country as we enjoy all the freedoms guaranteed by our Constitution's Bill of Rights, we can still be enslaved and oppressed. We need the freedom that only comes through Christ—forgiveness, eternal life, and the ability to live God's way.

Celebrate freedom—your "Magna Carta" in Christ.

to do ☑

TAKE OUT A SHEET OF PAPER. ON ONE SIDE, LIST THE FREEDOMS YOU ENJOY BECAUSE YOU LIVE IN THIS COUNTRY. ON THE OTHER SIDE, LIST THE FREEDOMS YOU ENJOY AS ONE OF GOD'S PEOPLE. THEN SPEND TIME THANKING GOD FOR ALL YOUR FREE-DOMS, ONE BY ONE.

"So **if** the **Son** sets you **free**, you will **indeed** be **free**."
[John 8:36]

also on this day

This is Independence Day in Iceland.

John Wesley was born. **1703**

1885 Speaking of liberty, the Statue of Liberty arrived in New York.

getting antsy

This is National Picnic Day.

The sun shines bright as a gentle breeze rustles the leaves overhead. You spread the blanket on the soft grass and place the basket in the middle. Moments later, with paper plate in hand and seated on the blanket's edge, you reach for Mom's famous fried chicken. But suddenly your leg begins to tickle, so you stop and glance down. There they are—two ants crawling up your calf. Yuck!

Picnics and ants seem to go together. They come with the territory, literally. If we want to enjoy being outside, in nature, then we have to expect nature's visitors and pests.

Some folks might remind us that the ants were there first and that they have a right to a picnic, too (even on your leg). But crawling and buzzing (and biting) creatures usually don't fit into our picture of an ideal event.

Actually, in this world nothing's perfect. Stuff breaks, mosquitoes bite, clothes wear out, hurricanes hit, people let us down, sickness comes, and ants interrupt picnics. And all that imperfection can be frustrating. But that's a reality we have to live with.

At the beginning, the world *was* perfect—God created it that way. But when Adam and Eve disobeyed God, sin entered the world, and everything changed. So everyone since then entered a "fallen" world. Today's verse tells about the terrible effects of sin. It's not a pretty picture.

Eventually, the Bible tells us, God will remake the world, and it will be perfect again (2 Peter 3:13). Won't that be great!

Until then, we'll have to deal with sin and faults and mistakes in ourselves and others and with splinters, blisters, insect bites, weeds, spoiled milk, broken toys, ...

But the future is bright! And every day can be a "picnic day."

to do ☑

TAKE SOME TIME OFF AND GO ON A PICNIC WITH A FRIEND. WHEN YOU SEE AN ANT, THANK GOD FOR HIS BEAUTIFUL CREATION AND FOR HIS PROMISE OF A NEW HEAVEN AND NEW EARTH WITH NO SIN OR DECAY.

When **Adam sinned**, **sin** entered the **entire** human race. **Adam's sin** brought **death**, so **death** spread to **everyone**, for everyone **sinned**. [Romans 5:12]

also on this day

1873 Susan B. Anthony was fined $100 for attempting to vote for a U.S. President.

1942 Paul McCartney of the Beatles was born.

1983 Dr. Sally Ride became the first American woman in space as she traveled aboard the space shuttle Challenger.

W hat comes to mind when you hear the word, "Father"? Some kids have great relationships with their dads. For others, the relationship isn't very strong. And some don't even know who their father is.

The Bible says lots about fathers and children. You've probably heard, "Children, obey your parents" (Ephesians 6:1). That's clear but not always easy to do. As long as we are underage and live under their authority, however, we're supposed to do what our parents tell us to.

Another verse takes a little different slant. Jesus says, "Honor your father and mother" (Mark 7:10). Honoring is different than obeying. To honor someone means to respect that person. And honoring doesn't stop when we grow up and leave home. Adults don't have to "obey" their parents, but they still need to "honor" them.

The way people see their earthly fathers can determine how they see the heavenly Father. That can be good or bad. A child with a wonderful, loving father will tend to see God as wonderful and loving. On the other hand, a child with an abusive father will have a much more difficult time drawing close to a heavenly Father.

It's better to think of it the other way around. That is, we should know that God is a Father in the perfect sense—he's what every father should try to be like. He loves; he disciplines; he cares; he guides; he's with us and for us. Isn't that great! That's why Paul could write, "So you should not be like cowering, fearful slaves. You should behave instead like God's very own children, adopted into his family—calling him 'Father, dear Father'" (Romans 8:15).

No matter what your earthly father is like, you can run to your Father in Heaven.

Thanks God for both dads.

to do ☑

WRITE TWO FATHER'S DAY NOTES. ONE FOR YOUR EARTHLY FATHER AND ONE FOR YOUR HEAVENLY FATHER. SAY THANK-YOU FOR ALL THAT EACH DADDY HAS MEANT TO YOU—BE SPECIFIC. GIVE THE ONE NOTE TO YOUR EARTHLY FATHER, AND PUT THE OTHER NOTE IN YOUR BIBLE AS A REMINDER OF WHAT GOD MEANS TO YOU.

He will turn the hearts of the fathers to their children, and the hearts of the children to their fathers. [Malachi 4:6, NIV]

On this day in 1910, Father's Day was celebrated for the first time—in Spokane, Washington.

also on this day

This is Juneteenth, the oldest known celebration commemorating the ending of slavery in the United States.

After an 83-day filibuster, the Civil Rights Act was approved in Congress.

1964

daddy!

Don't Drop It

See if you can find three Ping-Pong® balls or Nerf® balls (if not, crumple up three sheets of paper). Then see if you can juggle them. After all, it's World Juggling Day.

That's not easy, is it? Your timing and hand movements have to be just right. And that's just tossing and catching three items. Some jugglers can keep five things in the air, juggling everything from flaming sticks to buzzing chain saws!

Even if you can't juggle balls, you probably feel like a juggler at times, as you try to find time for all the activities and demands in your life. You have friends, family, school, church, sports, clubs, and hobbies demanding time and attention, not to mention watching TV, reading books, working on the computer, and playing video games.

So how do you juggle it all? How do you find time for *everything*? Probably not very well, usually dropping a thing or two. That's why we need to set priorities—to decide on the most important activities and do those things first.

Jesus said that the greatest commandment was to "love the Lord your God with all your heart, all your soul, all your mind, and all your strength" (Mark 12:30). At another time, he said we should, "make the Kingdom of God [our] primary concern" (Matthew 6:33). Clearly, then, we know what should be No. 1 on the list of priorities.

Next should come family (remember yesterday's lesson?). And certainly Mom and Dad will help determine other important activities (like school and homework, perhaps).

Keeping all those balls in the air isn't easy. Instead of trying to do everything, make sure you do what's most important.

to do ☑

TAKE AN INDEX CARD AND MAKE A "TO DO" LIST, JOT-TING DOWN EVERYTHING THAT YOU HAVE TO DO IN THE NEXT DAY OR TWO. THEN WRITE "A" BESIDE EACH ITEM THAT IS VERY IMPORTANT. DO THOSE TASKS FIRST! THEN YOU CAN FOLLOW WITH THE "B" AND "C" ITEMS IF YOU HAVE TIME.

"Store your treasures in heaven, where they will never become moth-eaten or rusty and where they will be safe from thieves. Wherever your treasure is, there you heart and thoughts will also be."

[Matthew 6:20, 21]

also on this day

1819 The 320-ton *Savannah* became the first steamship to cross the Atlantic.

West Virginia became the 35th state to join the United States. **1863**

1782 The United States Congress approved the Great Seal of the U.S. and the bald eagle as the nation's symbols.

making summer count

This is the first day of summer.

Summer has arrived—yea! Just about all kids love this time of year. It means a break from school, lazy and sunny days, and, usually, a special family trip or vacation. And the warm weather allows for some great outdoors activities: baseball (playing and watching), picnics (remember the ants!), sailing, swimming, hiking, walking, working in the garden and yard (hey—how'd that one get in there?). You get the picture.

With all the relaxing and playing, however, a person can see the days and weeks fly by until suddenly school's back in session. So now is the perfect time to decide to make summer count—to get some other stuff accomplished, in addition to all the fun.

Here are some suggestions.

You could read a great book, go on a family mission trip, spend a few hours each week helping at a nursing home, compose a song, take music lessons, start a collection, write a letter a week to a missionary or soldier, read a book of the Bible (or more than one), write a short story, bake cookies, grow a garden, and so forth. You get the idea.

It's not that you shouldn't have fun or take a break from "juggling" and doing all the usual work. Have a great time relaxing and playing with friends and family.

Just be sure not to take a vacation from doing good and from God.

Time is short. Make every moment count.

Make the **most** of **every** opportunity for doing **good** in these **evil days**.

[Ephesians 5:16]

also on this day

1731
Martha Washington was born.

1859
Andrew Lanergan received the first rocket patent.

1913
Georgia Broadwick became the first woman to jump from an airplane.

to do ☑

CHOOSE AT LEAST TWO OF THE ACTIVITIES SUGGESTED AND DO THEM. IF YOU DON'T LIKE ANY OF THOSE SUGGESTIONS, ASK MOM OR DAD—THEY'LL HAVE IDEAS.

what a privilege!

On this day in 1970, United States President Richard Nixon signed the 26th amendment, lowering the voting age to 18.

When Congress was debating about whether or not to lower the voting age, many people expressed fear that all the new young voters would change the elections. The reasoning was that young people could be easily influenced by the politicians and then would come out in droves and vote, even if they didn't really understand the issues.

They didn't have to worry. No group of Americans sends a high percentage to the polls. And the youngest voters, 18 to 21, consistently vote in lower numbers than any other group.

What a shame. Voting is such a privilege and honor. Just look at how people turn out for elections in nations that have just won freedom. Huge numbers of people vote. They know the value and importance of free elections.

The Bible tells us, in several places, to be good citizens and to respect those in authority over us. This includes obeying the laws, unless those laws would have us violate God's laws.

You can't vote right now, but you can still be involved in the process. When the next election rolls around, read up on the candidates and their positions. Encourage the voters in your family (mother, father, older brother or sister, aunt, uncle, grandparent) to get out and cast their votes.

Today's verse encourages us to "accept" those in authority over us "for the Lord's sake." This seems to indicate that God has allowed these men and women to be in their government positions for a purpose. So respecting them means much more than being a good citizen; it honors God. And that's most important.

to do ☑

PUT THE PRESIDENT, YOUR SENATORS, YOUR CONGRESSIONAL REPRESENTATIVE, YOUR MAYOR, AND OTHER GOVERNMENT OFFICIALS ON YOUR PRAYER LIST AND PRAY FOR THEM EVERY DAY.

For the Lord's sake, accept all authority—the king as head of state, and the officials he has appointed. For the king has sent them to punish all who do wrong and to honor those who do right. [1 Peter 2:13, 14]

also on this day

1909
The first transcontinental (all the way across America) auto race ended in Seattle, Washington.

The 75th National Marbles Tournament began in Wildwood, New Jersey.

Doughnuts were created—yum!
1863

1998

Spies Are Us

In 1860, the Secret Service was created.

Spy stories are exciting to read or watch. Sometimes the tension comes from worrying that the agent might be discovered. Sometimes we're not sure who the agent is or who he or she is working for.

The main duty of the Secret Service is to protect the president, the vice president, their families, and other dignitaries. In wartime, these agents aid in securing information concerning the enemy's movements—thus the word "secret" in the title.

Being a spy can be dangerous. Secret Service agents have even thrown themselves between assailants and the president, taking the bullet instead of him.

The Bible has a story about 12 spies. Remember? If not, here's a summary.

The Israelites had escaped Egypt and were moving toward the promised land. At the border, before taking the next huge step of fighting the enemy, Moses chose 12 men, one from each tribe, to sneak into the land and check it out. When these spies returned, two of them were excited about the prospects. Knowing that God was with them, they encouraged the nation to move ahead. But the rest of the group gave a different report. Thinking only of the huge enemy soldiers, they were afraid. Unfortunately, those 10 persuaded the people not to trust God and go where he told them. As a result, the Israelites wandered 40 more years in the wilderness.

The two courageous spies, Joshua and Caleb, had it right. They trusted God and not in their strength. They were spies, all right, and *heroes*. In fact, later Joshua ended up being the No. 1 Israelite.

You may not be a spy, but you probably have a good idea of some actions that God wants you to take. Remember Joshua and Caleb, and take your promised land.

to do ☑

READ THE WHOLE STORY OF JOSHUA, CALEB, AND THE REST OF THE SPIES IN NUMBERS 13.

But **Caleb** tried to **encourage** the **people** as they stood before **Moses**. "Let's **go** at **once** to **take** the land," he said. "We can **certainly conquer** it!"

[Numbers 13:30]

also on this day

This is Take Your Dog to Work Day—woof!

Apple Computer unveiled the new Power Mac desktop computer. **2003**

1926

The first lipreading tournament in America was held in Philadelphia, Pennsylvania.

So this is National Forgiveness Day. What does that mean to you? Forgiveness can mean telling someone who owes us money that they don't have to pay—we "forgive" the debt. It may involve accepting someone's apology for hurting us—we say, "I forgive you." Forgiveness may even mean overlooking an insult or wrong by someone, even when that person doesn't know what he or she has done or isn't sorry.

Forgiving someone often is difficult because forgiveness always costs: money (in the case of the debt), revenge (so we can't "get even"), and pride.

But Jesus tells us to forgive others (Matthew 6:14, 15). And what an example Jesus gave us when on the cross he prayed, "Father, forgive these people, because they don't know what they are doing" (Luke 23:34). And whenever we pray the Lord's Prayer, we ask God to forgive us in the same way that we forgive others. Now that's a scary thought!

So who owes you? Maybe a brother, sister, or friend has borrowed something and hasn't returned it. Who has wronged you? Perhaps you felt put down by someone in your neighborhood or school or were treated unfairly by a teacher or coach, or maybe even a parent. Forgiving those people, with no strings attached, will cost you, but it's what Jesus wants. And there's no better time than today and right now.

Forgive and forget.

to do ☑

LET'S TURN THE SITUATION AROUND. WHO HAVE YOU WRONGED? FROM WHOM DO YOU NEED TO ASK FORGIVENESS? GIVE A CALL TO SAY YOU'RE SORRY. DROP A NOTE. DO IT TODAY.

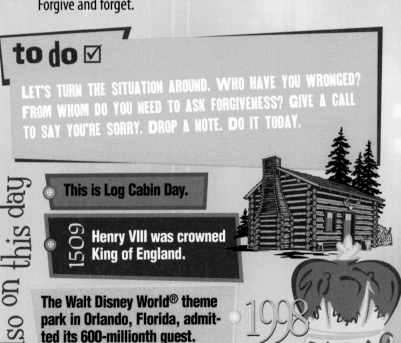

also on this day

This is Log Cabin Day.

1509 Henry VIII was crowned King of England.

The Walt Disney World® theme park in Orlando, Florida, admitted its 600-millionth guest. 1998

it costs **This is National Forgiveness Day.**

82039248584038

"And forgive us our sins, just as we have forgiven those who have sinned against us." [Matthew 6:12]

blinded by pride

In 1876, the Sioux and Cheyenne Indians wiped out Lt. Colonel George Custer and the 7th Cavalry at the Battle of Little Big Horn.

Lt. Colonel Custer was known as a prideful man. Some have written that in addition to being conceited, he also found it difficult to take anyone's advice. His way was always best, so he thought. Thus, as he and his troops were pursuing the Indians, he advanced much more quickly than he had been ordered and neared what he thought was a large Indian village. On the verge of what he thought would be a certain and glorious victory for both the United States and himself, Custer ordered an immediate attack on the village. Thinking that the Indians wouldn't be much of a threat, he split his forces into three parts to ensure that fewer Indians would escape. The attack was one the greatest fiascos of the United States Army, as thousands of Lakota, Cheyenne, and Arapaho warriors forced Custer's unit back onto a long, dusty ridge, surrounded them, and killed all 210 of them. He and his entire force died that day because of his pride.

Today's verse says that "pride goes before destruction." That's true in all areas of life, not just war. For example, take the student who thinks he or she knows it all and doesn't study for the big test; the athlete who thinks that he or she is better than anyone else and doesn't work out; or the business owner who believes customers will keep coming to the store no matter how they are treated. You can imagine the failures, the destructions, that will come to each one.

How's your pride these days? Romans 12:3 says "Do not think of yourself more highly than you ought, but rather think of yourself with sober judgment" (NIV). Having self-confidence is one thing. But thinking you know it all is quite another. We need to be humble, listening carefully to others' suggestions and advice.

Don't let pride trip you up.

to do ☑

TODAY, ASK GOD TO SHOW YOU WHERE YOU HAVE BEEN PRIDE-FUL. AND DO YOUR BEST TO LISTEN CAREFULLY TO OTHERS. YOU DON'T HAVE TO TAKE ALL THEIR ADVICE, BUT YOU CAN ACCEPT IT WITH RESPECT.

also on this day

This is Strawberry Parfait Day (do you know what a "parfait" is?).

The first color TV transmissions were presented on CBS, even though the public did not own color TVs at the time.

The Korean War began.

1950   1951

Pride goes before **destruction**, and **haughtiness** before a **fall**.

[Proverbs 16:18]

keep your balance

In 1819, W. K. Clarkson Jr. patented the bicycle.

You've ridden a bike most of your life, starting with a tricycle. What kind do you ride now? A mountain bike? A many-speed racing bike? Whatever, you'd have to agree that W. K. Clarkson Jr.'s marvelous invention sure beats walking everywhere.

What's the most important part of a bike? We need just about every part to ride safely and comfortably—handlebars, seat, gears, brakes, etc.—but we could still get around without one of those. But imagine trying to ride without wheels—that would be impossible. And for the *best* ride, the wheels should be balanced, with the spokes tight and the tires inflated with the correct air pressure.

A bicycle wheel provides a good illustration for today's lesson. Compare your life to a wheel, and you'll get the idea. A good bicycle wheel needs a solid hub with strong spokes going out to the rim. For balance and strength the spokes should be evenly spaced. The same is true with life. The hub must be solid, able to hold the wheel (life) together and keep it rolling. Our "hub" should be Christ—everything should center on him. Then the spokes represent various areas of life: physical, social, mental, emotional, spiritual, and others. These should go out from the center and be balanced.

Today's verse says Jesus grew in all areas of life, not just one or two. We should do the same. If all we think about is the physical area, we'll be unbalanced and wobble along. The same is true with being all-social, and so forth. And if we are flat on one side, we'll really have a bumpy ride through life.

Every time you see a bicycle, remember the hub and the spokes. Keep Christ at the center and develop *all* the areas.

Have a great ride!

So **Jesus** grew both in **height** and in **wisdom**, and he was **loved** by **God** and by **all** who **knew** him.

[Luke 2:52]

also on this day

1959

The St. Lawrence Seaway was opened.

1981

KEEP THIS COUPON

948046

In Mountain Home, Idaho, Virginia Campbell took the coupons and rebates she had collected and bought $26,460 worth of groceries. After all the discounts, she paid only 67 cents for everything.

to do ☑

TAKE A BIKE RIDE. AS YOU RIDE, PRAY FOR NEEDS AS YOU SEE THEM. AND THINK ABOUT WHAT YOU NEED TO DO TO HAVE A MORE BALANCED LIFE.

Helen Keller was born as a normal baby. But in February of 1882, at 19 months old, she became very sick. No one knew what was wrong, and, for a while, everyone expected her to die. When the fever went down, the family and the doctor thought Helen would be fine. They soon learned, however, that the sickness had left their precious baby blind and deaf.

How terrible that must have been! Then Helen's parents had to care for her, and that became almost impossible. She became a very difficult child, smashing dishes and lamps, screaming, and throwing temper tantrums. Relatives thought Helen should be put into an institution.

When Helen was 6, her family had become desperate. After a visit to a specialist, they were told she would never see or hear again but were told not to give up hope. The doctor believed Helen could be taught, and he advised them to visit a local expert on the problems of deaf children. This expert was Alexander Graham Bell, the inventor of the telephone.

Eventually, they were put in touch with Anne Sullivan, who, through a long and difficult process, taught Helen how to communicate. Read more of this amazing story online or watch the award-winning film, "The Miracle Worker."

Helen Keller proves that every life is valuable, even those who we think have no possible use in society. How much hope, for example, could anyone have for a baby who couldn't see or hear? Yet Helen Keller went on to write, teach, and inspire millions with her story.

So don't give up on anyone. See each person as a valuable creation of God and treat him or her as such. And who knows, God may surprise you with what he will do with that life.

Instead, God deliberately chose things the world considers foolish in order to shame those who think they are wise. And he chose those who are powerless to shame those who are powerful. [1 Corinthians 1:27]

In 1880 Helen Keller was born.

to do ☑

THINK OF THE PEOPLE YOU KNOW WHO ARE PHYSICALLY CHALLENGED: A KID WITH MUSCULAR DYSTROPHY, A MAN WITH A HEARING PROBLEM, A NEIGHBOR WHO CAN'T SEE VERY WELL, AND SO FORTH. TAKE TIME THIS WEEK TO HAVE A GOOD CONVERSATION WITH ONE OF THEM.

also on this day

1829 Mildred J. Hill composed the "Happy Birthday to You" melody.

The state of Illinois enacted the first automobile seat belt legislation. 1955

choose life

From Bad to Good

Tomatoes have become a regular item in our diets, especially in salads. We also eat them fried or baked or right off the vine. And ketchup is loaded with tomatoes, and then there's spaghetti sauce and tomato juice and . . .

With all those tomato uses and products, it's hard to believe that people used to think tomatoes were poisonous. Now we only hear how good they are for us.

Poisonous to nutritious, bad to good—that's a big turnaround!

The Bible has stories like that. At one time, Paul hated Jesus and his followers. Paul definitely was not good. But God turned him around, and he became one of the great evangelists and writers of most of the New Testament. He wrote, "And we know that God causes everything to work together for the good of those who love God and are called according to his purpose for them" (Romans 8:28). The point? Even something that stays bad can be used for good by God.

That's what happened to Joseph. He had a colorful coat and a mess of envious brothers. His brothers were so annoyed by Joseph that they sold him as a slave and then told their dad he had been killed by wild animals. Later, they meet Joseph in Egypt. But this time Joseph is in charge, as Pharaoh's right-hand man. The big brothers fear what Joseph might do to them to get revenge. Instead, Joseph forgives them and points out that what they meant for evil, God turned into good.

The lessons? First, we shouldn't be so quick to call someone bad or "poisonous"—he or she may turn out to be a wonderful person. Second, we should trust that God can take *any* circumstance, no matter how bad, and use it for good.

to do ☑

AT YOUR NEXT FAMILY MEAL WHEN TOMATOES ARE INCLUDED, EXPLAIN TO YOUR FAMILY THAT TOMATOES WERE THOUGHT TO BE POISONOUS AT ONE TIME. THEN SHARE THE TRUTH OF TODAY'S LESSON.

"As far as I am concerned, God turned into good what you meant for evil. He brought me to the high position I have today so I could save the lives of many people." [Genesis 50:20]

also on this day

This is World War I Day.

This is Paul Bunyan Day.

1919

The Treaty of Versailles was signed to end World War I.

take the freeway

In 1953, the Federal Highway Act authorized the construction of 422,500 miles of freeways from coast to coast.

Having national freeways was a great idea. And now the entire country is linked through the interstate system. If you've traveled much with your family, you've probably driven over many of those highways—four lanes or more, cutting through pastures and forests, over mountains and rivers, and around cities, from coast to coast.

Of course, you've also probably seen that some of those *free*ways are now *toll*ways and that, in many areas, they're packed with vehicles. (These days, travelers often look for the old, back roads to avoid the freeways.)

The name *freeway* combines "free" and "highway." The idea was to provide quick and easy routes for cars and trucks.

Our Bible passage for today highlights another freeway, the free highway to Heaven. And it's a route that's open to anyone who believes in Christ.

Notice the words *special favor* and *gift*. They show that salvation (being forgiven for our sins and headed for Heaven) is *free* as far as we're concerned. Did it cost anything? Certainly—this freeway cost Jesus his life on the cross, where he died in our place, to pay the penalty for our sins. But we don't have to earn God's favor. He freely gives us eternal life. That's called grace, and it's amazing!

Some people think they have to work hard to gain forgiveness of sins and salvation—sort of like paying the tolls to be able to use the road. But we could never be good enough to fit into Heaven—we'd have to be perfect. The Bible tells us that, "all have sinned; all fall short of God's glorious standard" (Romans 3:23). But God also promises that, "the free gift of God is eternal life through Christ Jesus our Lord" (Romans 6:23).

So get on God's freeway . . . and spread the good news!

God saved you by his special favor when you believed. And you can't take credit for this; it is a gift from God. Salvation is not a reward for the good things we have done, so none of us can boast about it. [Ephesians 2:8, 9]

also on this day

1735

This is Flower and Camera Day.

1897

The Chicago Cubs scored 36 runs in a game against Louisville, setting a record for runs scored by a team in a single game.

to do ☑

THE NEXT TIME YOU'RE ON A FREEWAY, REMEMBER GOD'S FREEWAY TO HEAVEN AND THANK HIM FOR HIS LOVE AND GRACE.

do you really believe?

On this day in 1859, the French acrobat Charles Blondin walked across Niagara Falls on a tightrope.

Blondin's walk across Niagara Falls was dramatic. On that day, 100,000 people watched him walk on a single 3-inch hemp cord, 1,100 feet long and 160 feet above the falls on one side and 270 feet on the other.

Every day, thousands would gather to see him perform this amazing feat, suspended above the roaring waterfall below. One day Blondin asked the crowd if they thought he could carry a person with him on his tightrope walk. The crowd roared, "Yes," hoping to see an even more amazing event.

He said it again: "Do you really believe I can do it?"

"Yes," they shouted back.

"Then who will come with me? Which one of you will volunteer?" he asked. And the crowd became silent—no one stepped forward.

Finally his manager, Harry Colcord, agreed. So Colcord climbed on Blondin's back, and the two of them walked slowly across.

This true story has been used as an example of faith ever since.

You see, just saying we believe in someone or something is easy. Talk is cheap. But our actions show whether or not we really believe. Hundreds of people *said* they believed Blondin could carry someone with him across the falls. But only one person *truly* believed.

In the same way, many people *say* they believe in God and even in Jesus as Savior. (You'll hear that a lot in an election year.) But they don't want to live the way the Bible says to live; they don't want to *obey* God. Our verse for today says that kind of faith isn't faith at all.

So if you profess to be a believer in God and a follower of Christ, are you really? If so, can people tell by how you live?

to do ☑

MAKE A SHORT LIST OF ACTIONS YOU SHOULD TAKE OR CHANGES YOU SHOULD MAKE IN HOW YOU LIVE TO BETTER DEMONSTRATE YOUR FAITH IN CHRIST. ASK GOD TO HELP YOU DO THESE ACTIONS AND MAKE THESE CHANGES.

So you see, it isn't enough just to have faith. Faith that doesn't show itself by good deeds is no faith at all—it is dead and useless. [James 2:17]

also on this day 1953

The first Chevrolet Corvette rolled off the assembly line in Flint, Michigan. It sold for $3,250 (a lot of money back then).

This is Ice-Cream Soda Day.

The 26th Amendment to the U.S. Constitution, which lowered the voting age to 18, was ratified. **1971**

In 1945, New York became the first state in the country to establish an agency that would assist people who had been treated unfairly because of race, creed, or ethnic background. The State Commission Against Discrimination was given a mission to prevent and eliminate discrimination on the job, to investigate and solve fairly complaints of illegal discrimination, and to develop a human rights legislation and policy for the state. Since it began, the Commission has handled thousands of complaints charging discrimination in employment, public accommodations, and housing.

It's unfortunate that people treat others unfairly. Sometimes people slight others just because they are different and give people like themselves preferential treatment. But in God's family playing favorites is not allowed. God tells us that all people are created in *his* image—that means we all are worthy in his sight. There are no differences between groups of people or individuals in God's eyes. (See Genesis 1:26, 27.)

When Paul wrote to the believers in Colosse, he reminded them that it didn't matter if a person was Jewish or Greek, a slave or free, male or female. Everyone was the same in Jesus. That same truth applies to us today. If we belong to Jesus, there should not be barriers between people based on nationality, education, race, wealth, or power. As members of Jesus' family, we should be about the business of building bridges between people, not walls. Whether we're at church, at school, or in our neighborhood, we should see people the way Jesus sees them.

In this new life, it doesn't matter if you are a Jew or a Gentile, circumcised or uncircumcised, barbaric, uncivilized, slave, or free. Christ is all that matters, and he lives in all of us. [Colossians 3:11]

In 1945, the New York State Commission Against Discrimination was established.

in all fairness

to do ☑

TAKE TIME THIS WEEK TO INTENTIONALLY REACH OUT TO SOMEONE OF A DIFFERENT NATIONALITY, RACE, OR ETHNIC BACKGROUND.

also on this day

Today is Canada Day.

1863 **The Battle of Gettysburg began.**

Zip codes were used for the first time. 1963

aliens!

In 1947, an object crashed near Roswell, New Mexico. Eyewitness accounts led to speculation that it might have been an alien spacecraft.

Mr. and Mrs. Dan Wilmot were sitting on their front porch enjoying the summer evening when they spotted a large glowing object that zoomed through the sky. The object moved so fast that they ran into the yard for a better look. Mr. Wilmot described what he saw as "oval in shape like two inverted saucers." He said that "the entire body glowed as though light were showing through from inside." He estimated that it was about 1,500 feet up in the sky and going at a rate of 400 to 500 miles per hour.

At first Wilmot, a respected and reliable citizen in town, kept the story to himself hoping that others would come forward with the same story. When he finally disclosed what he and his wife had seen, the Roswell Army Air Field announced that it, in fact, had possession of a flying disk. However, a day later the RAAF announced that the object was actually a harmless high-altitude weather balloon. Mystery solved. Or was it?

Speculation continues even today about what actually landed that night on July 2. Many believe that it was a UFO and that there are aliens living somewhere in space.

Whether you believe that or not, the truth is that there *are* aliens living on this planet. In fact, there probably are aliens living in your neighborhood or attending your school. God's Word tells us that an alien is anyone who doesn't know Jesus. At one time, we were all aliens until we learned about Jesus. That's important to remember. We shouldn't treat those who don't know Jesus like they came from another planet, but we should care enough about them to help them know him too!

Remember that you were at **that** time **without Christ**, being **aliens** from the **commonwealth** of **Israel**, and **strangers** to the **covenants** of **promise**, having **no hope** and **without God** in the **world**.

[Ephesians 2:12, NRSV]

also on this day

1937

Aviator Amelia Earhart disappeared while flying over the Pacific Ocean.

1986

Actress and singer Lindsay Lohan was born.

to do ☑

THINK ABOUT THE ALIENS THAT YOU KNOW. HOW CAN YOU HELP THEM MEET JESUS?

over there!

On this day in 1878, George M. Cohan was born.

George M. Cohan, a successful actor, singer, dancer, playwright, composer, director, and producer, was probably America's first superstar. He was, as one of his plays put it, "The Man Who Owned Broadway." Yet aside from his success on the stage, George Cohan is perhaps best known for his greatest hit, "Over There," a patriotic tribute to the men who had enlisted to fight in World War I.

The story goes that Cohan composed the song while traveling on a train from New Rochelle, N.Y., into New York City. It was 1917, and the headlines of the newspapers were filled with stories about the war and America's involvement. Cohan said, "I read those war headlines, and I got to thinking and humming to myself, and for a minute, I thought I was going to dance. I was all finished with both the chorus and the verse by the time I got to town, and I also had a title."

The song became an instant hit with its inspiring, encouraging message:

So prepare, say a pray'r,
Send the word, send the word to beware.
We'll be over, we're coming over,
And we won't come back till it's over
Over there.

These simple verses of encouragement became a powerful tool for the U.S. Army in recruiting men to enlist. For these words and his contribution to the war effort, Cohan was awarded the Congressional Medal of Honor in 1940.

George Cohan's stirring song is a great reminder that we should never underestimate the power of an encouraging word. The Bible tells us in 1 Thessalonians 5:11 that we are to encourage each other. A word of encouragement at the right time can make a huge difference. Try it some time. See how you can change your home, your classroom, or your Sunday school with just a few positive words of encouragement!

to do ☑

DECIDE TO ENCOURAGE ONE PERSON—A FRIEND, FAMILY MEMBER, OR TEACHER—DURING THE ENTIRE DAY. WRITE NOTES, IM, OR SEND E-MAILS THROUGHOUT THE DAY.

also on this day

1878
John Wise flew the first inflatable airship in Lancaster, Pennsylvania.

Jackie Robinson became the first African-American to be inducted into the National Baseball Hall of Fame.
1962

Idaho became America's 43rd state.
1850

Worry weighs a person **down**; an **encouraging word** cheers a person **up**.

[Proverbs 12:25]

Today is Independence Day!

Real Freedom!

The story of America's birthday is a familiar one. After a two-year struggle to work out their differences with England without going to war, representatives from the 13 colonies had gathered in Philadelphia to compose a formal declaration of independence. The first draft, written by Thomas Jefferson, was presented to the Continental Congress on June 28. After numerous changes, a vote was taken late on the afternoon of July 4. Of the 13 colonies, nine voted to adopt it, two voted no (Pennsylvania and South Carolina), and New York abstained. With a decided majority, the document was adopted as an official communication to King George that freedom from British rule had been declared throughout the land.

The principles of freedom that we have come to enjoy as Americans were set forth in this document with these stirring words: "We hold these Truths to be self-evident, that all Men are created equal, that they are endowed by their Creator with certain unalienable Rights, that among these are Life, Liberty, and the Pursuit of Happiness." Because of the vision of our founding fathers we enjoy many freedoms: freedom of speech, freedom of religion, freedom of the press.

As Christians, we also have been called to live in freedom. But just as our freedom to live in this country comes with responsibilities, so too does our freedom in Jesus. Being free doesn't mean that we can do whatever we wish whenever we want. That would make us slaves to sin and making wrong choices. Rather, we are free to do right and to honor God by serving others. We can express our freedom in Jesus by loving and serving others daily.

to do ☑

AS YOU ENJOY THE DAY'S FIREWORKS AND FESTIVITIES, THINK OF ALL THE MANY FREEDOMS YOU ENJOY.

For you have been called to live in freedom—not freedom to satisfy your sinful nature, but freedom to serve one another in love.

[Galatians 5:13]

also on this day

1802 — The U.S. Military Academy officially opened at West Point, New York.

Construction began on the Erie Canal to connect Lake Erie and the Hudson River. 1817

1872 — Calvin Coolidge, the 30th president of the United States, was born in Plymouth, Vermont.

Two years after the French had enjoyed liberation from the Nazi Occupation, they experienced another kind of liberation that took place along the sunny beaches of the Mediterranean. A few daring women decided to wear a new type of bathing suit that showed more than ever had been seen before in public! The tiny two-piece suit was named the bikini, in honor of the tiny Pacific island where the United States was testing the atom bomb. The skimpy new suit caused its own *explosions*, which are still being felt today.

Initially, Americans rejected the bikini outright, preferring the one-piece bathing suit popularized in movies of the early 1950s. But gradually the suit became more accepted by the American culture, and it became popular in the 1960s as a series of *beach movies* made it standard attire. Songs like "Itsy Bitsy Teeny Weeny Yellow Polka Dot Bikini" no doubt helped the skimpy suits become more acceptable. Today the bikini is as popular as ever, but that doesn't mean that the debate about its appropriateness has ended. (Perhaps it goes on in your house as well!)

While such matters are often a matter of personal taste, Paul had a few things to say about what we should think about when it comes to what we wear and how we look. Rather than letting the latest fads dictate what we wear, Paul said we should be more concerned about our inner character. We are more attractive showing kindness, gentleness, and self-control than when we're showing off our bodies with revealing clothing.

Clothes styles come and go. A beautiful character lasts forever.

And I want women to be modest in their appearance. They should wear decent and appropriate clothing and not draw attention to themselves by the way they fix their hair or by wearing gold or pearls or expensive clothes. [1 Timothy 2:9]

In 1946, the bikini made its debut at a Paris fashion show.

to do ☑

TAKE A LOOK AT YOUR CLOSET. WHAT CLOTHES DO YOU HAVE THAT YOU MIGHT NOT WEAR WHEN CONSIDERING PAUL'S WORDS?

also on this day

1865 William Booth founded the Salvation Army in London.

Adelina and August Van Buren started on the first successful transcontinental motorcycle tour to be attempted by two women. **1916**

modesty

"I have not yet begun to fight."

John Paul Jones was born on this day in 1747.

Born in Scotland, John Paul Jones devoted his life to the sea and became known as the "father of the American Navy." At age 13 Jones was apprenticed as a sailor. At 21 he received his first command of a ship. When the Revolutionary War broke out, Jones was in Virginia and joined the colonists. He was commissioned as a first lieutenant in the Continental Navy and made his mark in American naval history attacking British ships.

During one particularly bloody battle, Jones's ship, the *Bon Homme Richard,* had attacked the British ship the *HMS Serapis* in the North Sea off the coast of England. The *Richard* had been blasted in the side and began to lose much of her firepower and her crew. When the captain of the *Serapis* called out to Jones to ask if he was ready to surrender, Jones' stirring reply echoed over the battle: "I have not yet begun to fight." Despite the overwhelming odds, Jones and his crew fought on, even as their ship was sinking beneath them. Eventually it was the *Serapis* that surrendered.

It was in this same spirit that young David approached Goliath, the famous Philistine warrior who stood over nine feet tall! Despite the incredible odds against him, David did not wave the white flag and give up. No, even as Goliath taunted him, David approached his opponent knowing full well whose battle it was—the Lord's! "Everyone will know that the LORD does not need weapons to rescue his people," David declared. "It is his battle, not ours." (See 1 Samuel 17.)

That's good for us to remember as well. Next time you face overpowering odds or difficult circumstances, don't wave the white flag. Instead, turn your battle over to the Lord to win.

to do ☑

COME UP WITH A SLOGAN THAT YOU CAN USE TO REMEMBER TO GIVE YOUR BATTLES TO THE LORD.

No, despite all these things, **overwhelming victory** is ours through **Christ**, who **loved** us. [Romans 8:37]

also on this day

1946

George W. Bush, the 43rd president of the United States, was born.

The Beatles' first film, *A Hard Day's Night,* premiered in London.

This is National Be Nice to New Jersey Week.

1964

kid ambassador

In 1983, 11-year-old Samantha Smith of Manchester, Maine, visited the Soviet Union at the personal invitation of Soviet leader, Yuri B. Andropov.

Ten-year-old Samantha Smith knew that relations between the United States and Russia (then called the Soviet Union) were not good. She knew that both countries promised not to start a nuclear war. But what the youngster couldn't understand was why the two nations continued to make nuclear weapons. Samantha wanted her mother to write a letter to the newly elected Soviet President Yuri Andropov. Her mother said, "Why don't you?" So Samantha did:

> *Dear Mr. Andropov: My name is Samantha Smith. I am ten years old. . . . I have been worrying about Russia and the United States getting into a nuclear war. Are you going to have a war or not? If you aren't please tell me how you are going to not have a war. . . . God made the world for us to live together in peace and not fight.*

When Samantha mailed the letter, little did she know that it would lead to her being invited to the Soviet Union as President Andropov's guest! During her visit, Samantha met and talked with many children her age. She realized that the children in Russia were not so different from her own friends—and that they were as concerned about peace as she was!

Following her visit, Samantha became recognized as a worldwide representative for peace. Tragically, Samantha and her father died in a plane crash two years later. Yet Samantha's work continues through "The Samantha Smith Foundation," which promotes friendship between children of all countries.

You may never get a chance to visit a world leader like Samantha did. You may never even travel to another country. Yet you can be Jesus' ambassador to the world—every time you tell others about him, befriend another person, and share with others what God has given you.

We are Christ's ambassadors, and God is using us to speak to you. We urge you, as though Christ himself were here pleading with you, "Be reconciled to God!" [2 Corinthians 5:20]

also on this day

1940
Ringo Starr of the Beatles was born today.

1980
Olympic champion figure skater Michelle Kwan was born today.

to do ☑

THINK ABOUT WHAT YOU CAN DO TODAY TO BE JESUS' AMBASSADOR FOR PEACE AND FRIENDSHIP IN YOUR NEIGHBORHOOD.

All Tied Up

It began as a sales promotion for a shoe polish company in Wisconsin. Creator Reyn Guyer was toying with the idea of offering color patches that went on kids' feet along with a corresponding walk-around color grid. Then the idea struck Guyer—why not a giant board game with people as the game pieces who had to touch, bend, twist, and otherwise contort themselves to reach the round circles of color?

Guyer called it *Pretzel*, and the idea attracted game giant Milton Bradley. They bought the game, renaming it *Twister*®. Toy stores, however, didn't quite get the concept and company officials felt they had a sure flop on their hands. That is, until the game was played on the *Tonight Show*. The audience was in hysterics as they watched host Johnny Carson try to climb over and around his guest Eva Gabor. *Twister* became an immediate hit, and more than three million games were sold that first year.

If you ever have played the game, you know how difficult it is to remain standing as your opponents stretch underneath you or entwine themselves around your legs. The last person standing wins, but often everyone ends up in a heap!

In a way, sin is like a game of *Twister*. Before you know it, your pride trips you up. Or your anger bends you backwards. Then there's that temptation to tell a small lie, and you are tied up in knots! The writer of Hebrews warned us about "the sin that so easily entangles" and threatens to knock us off our feet.

In order to keep going, we need to avoid getting twisted up in sinful behaviors or attitudes. And how can we do that? By keeping our focus on Jesus—the one who can keep us on our feet.

to do

IF YOU HAVE THE GAME, GET OUT TWISTER AND CHALLENGE YOUR FRIENDS.

Therefore, since we are surrounded by such a great cloud of witnesses, let us throw off everything that hinders and the sin that so easily entangles, and let us run with perseverance the race marked out for us.

[Hebrews 12:1, NIV]

also on this day

1881 Edward Berner, a druggist in Wisconsin, poured chocolate syrup on ice cream in a dish, thus creating the first ice-cream sundae.

1796 The U.S. State Department issued the first passport.

1630 The Massachusetts Bay Colony celebrated the first Thanksgiving.

He's been called "America's oldest living teenager," even though Richard Wagstaff Clark was born on November 30, 1929. (You do the math!) Dick Clark made his breakthrough back in 1956 when he took over as host for a local dance show called *Bandstand*. He convinced ABC to make it a national broadcast, changing the name to *American Bandstand*. The program, with Clark as its clean-cut, well-dressed, well-spoken host, went on to become television's longest-running music-variety show.

Through his show and the many bands he introduced to the public, Dick Clark was a major influence in spreading rock and roll and making it acceptable to the majority of Americans. Even as the music scene and style changed, Clark had the ability to maintain his popularity. He still hosts radio shows and is a familiar face on December 31 as he rings in the New Year on *Dick Clark's Rockin' New Year's Eve*. Moreover, Clark remains as youthful as ever with his boyish good looks and charm.

While hanging onto youth works for Dick Clark, it probably isn't the wisest way to face the future. The truth is that all of God's creation is under the curse that was ushered into the world when Adam and Eve first disobeyed God in the Garden. We know that because of sin all creation is decaying and that we all will face aging and weakening bodies . . . and death.

OK, that's the bad news. The good news is that one day we will be with Jesus in Heaven and we will receive new bodies that will be made to live forever. We won't need to pretend to still be young because we will have a beautiful, resurrected body that will be strong, powerful, and made to last.

to do ☑

IF YOU COULD SELECT YOUR BODY, WHAT QUALITIES WOULD YOU CHOOSE? READ I CORINTHIANS 15:35–44 TO FIND OUT MORE ABOUT THE NEW BODIES WE WILL RECEIVE ONE DAY.

Our bodies now disappoint us, but when they are raised, they will be full of glory. They are weak now, but when they are raised, they will be full of power. [1 Corinthians 15:43]

In 1956, Dick Clark hosted American Bandstand for the first time.

forever young?

also on this day

1850 President Zachary Taylor died in office at age 55 after serving only 16 months.

Tom Hanks was born. 1956

a lasting mark

In 1866, Edison P. Clark patented his indelible pencil.

Back in 1866, inventor Edison P. Clark came up with a mixture of silver nitrate, gypsum, and black lead to devise a pencil that left marks that were nearly impossible to erase. Dubbed the indelible pencil, Clark's invention was the predecessor to today's ballpoint pen. As opposed to dipping a fountain pen into a bottle of ink, Clark's pencils were convenient, less messy, provided a firm, even pressure, and left markings that were relatively permanent.

The indelible pencils, or copying pencils as they were called, were an immediate success. The pencils were widely used whenever there was a need for writing that could not be easily erased, such as in legal documents and other important papers. During World War I copying pencils were used by the thousands each week in completing the vast paperwork associated with the war effort.

Even today with all our technology and array of pens available to us, the indelible pencil still has its uses, primarily during elections where indelible pencils are frequently used to record votes. (Ask your parents if they have used an indelible pencil in this way.)

When God records something permanent, he doesn't use an indelible pencil and paper. God writes on our hearts! In promising his people a new relationship with him, God said he would not write his laws on stone as he did with the Ten Commandments, but on our very hearts. And he does. When we believe in Jesus, we receive the Holy Spirit who helps us desire to know God's laws and obey them. And you can bet that God's laws and Spirit will never fade away.

> "But this is the new covenant I will make with the people of Israel on that day," says the LORD. "I will put my laws in their minds, and I will write them on their hearts. I will be their God, and they will be my people." [Jeremiah 31:33]

also on this day

1890
Wyoming became America's 44th state.

1913
The highest temperature ever recorded in the United States was 134 degrees in Death Valley, California.

1980
Jessica Simpson was born.

to do ☑
CAREFULLY USE AN INDELIBLE PENCIL, IF YOU HAVE ONE, OR A PERMANENT MARKER TO WRITE TODAY'S BIBLE VERSE (OR ANOTHER MEANINGFUL ONE) ON A PIECE OF PAPER OR CLOTH.

the real deal

On this day in 1899, E. B. White, author of the children's classic Charlotte's Web, was born.

E.B. White was the author of more than 20 books of prose and poetry. White made his career at *The New Yorker* magazine, but in 1938 he decided to move to the country. He moved to Maine where he lived on a farm and kept animals—some of whom ended up in his children's books.

Before writing his classic tale *Charlotte's Web*, in which a spider saves a pig from being killed, White wrote about caring for a dying pig at the farm: "One day when I was on my way to feed the pig, I began to feel sorry for the pig because, like most pigs, he was doomed. This made me sad. So I started thinking of ways to save a pig's life." And thus the story of Wilbur was born.

At the heart of the story is the spider, Charlotte, who befriends Wilbur and cleverly comes up with a way to save the pig's life by weaving slogans about Wilbur in her web. Charlotte uses up every bit of her strength to weave one last fantastic message about Wilbur. She dies, knowing she has given her life saving her friend.

That's the kind of love Jesus says we should have for our friends. Now that doesn't mean that you have to die for someone. But it does mean we need to practice the type of love that is willing to give up everything for others. You may show sacrificial love by giving up an afternoon to play with your younger brother, or giving all your allowance to a missionary, or supporting your friend on the soccer team when you didn't make it.

Loving like Jesus will cost you something, but it's worth the sacrifice.

to do ☑

IF YOU HAVE NEVER READ CHARLOTTE'S WEB, CHECK IT OUT OF THE LIBRARY TODAY. AND IF YOU HAVE, TAKE SOME TIME TO REREAD THIS CLASSIC TALE OF FRIENDSHIP AND DELIVERANCE.

And **here** is **how** to measure it— the **greatest** love is shown when people **lay down** their **lives** for their **friends**.

[John 15:13]

also on this day

1767 John Quincy Adams, the sixth president of the United States, was born in Braintree (now Quincy), Massachusetts.

The Air Force Academy was dedicated in Colorado Springs, Colorado, at Lowry Air Base. 1955

Fred Baldasare was the first to swim the English Channel underwater using scuba gear. **1962**

In 1960, the first Etch-a-Sketch® went on sale.

Clean Slate

For more than 40 years, this popular toy with its bright red frame and silver-gray drawing surface has been a childhood classic. Generations of kids have spent countless enjoyable hours twisting and turning the two knobs to create scenes, designs, and words.

Etch-A-Sketch® was developed in the late 1950s by Frenchman Arthur Granjean in his garage. Calling it the *L'Ecran Magique*, the magic screen, toy companies initially ignored Granjean's product. Then in 1960 Ohio Art Company decided to take a chance on the product. They renamed it Etch-A-Sketch, and it became an instant success as the most popular drawing toy in the business.

What makes the toy so popular? Some users must enjoy being able to draw, write, and create thousands of pictures without having to sharpen a pencil or find a piece of paper. Etch-A-Sketch is versatile, no doubt about it. And every kid knows how wonderful it is to be able to start over with a clean slate. A simple shake of the toy, flip it over, and presto! The image is erased and you have an empty screen to begin creating afresh.

Wouldn't that be great if we could apply that same technique to our lives? If the wrong words come flying out of our mouths, simply shake our heads and the words are gone. Make a mistake? Call a do-over, and it's as if it never happened.

Life doesn't quite work that way, does it? But when we do make those mistakes, say the wrong words, or make a bad decision we have the opportunity to have a clean slate when we confess our sins to Jesus. The Bible tells us that when we confess our sins, God is gracious to forgive us and clear our record of sin.

Not a bad deal!

to do ☑

IF YOU HAVEN'T PLAYED WITH YOUR ETCH-A-SKETCH IN A WHILE, TAKE ONE OUT AND SPEND A FEW MINUTES DRAWING. IMAGINE, AS YOU SHAKE THE SURFACE CLEAN, THAT THIS IS WHAT GOD DOES FOR YOU WHEN YOU CONFESS YOUR SINS.

Oh, what joy for those whose rebellion is forgiven, whose sin is put out of sight! Yes, what joy for those whose record the LORD has cleared of sin, whose lives are lived in complete honesty! [Psalm 32:1, 2]

also on this day

100 BC Julius Caesar was born.

E.T. The Extra-Terrestrial broke all box-office records by surpassing 100 million dollars in ticket sales in the first 31 days. **1982**

1984 U.S. Representative Geraldine A. Ferraro of New York became the first woman to be nominated for vice president on a major party ticket.

go to the source

In 1832, Henry Schoolcraft discovered the source of the Mississippi River in Minnesota.

It didn't take the European explorers of the New World long before they stumbled across North America's longest and largest river, the Mississippi. Hernando De Soto and his party were the first European explorers to see the river in 1541. French explorers Marquette, Jolliet, and de La Salle explored the river from the north in 1673. When de La Salle reached the mouth in 1682, he claimed the entire river valley for France.

Discovering the river's source, or headwaters, however, proved a more difficult task. Reluctant to ask the Native Americans for assistance, non-native explorers were unfamiliar with the region of northern Minnesota and often used poorly-drawn maps. It wasn't until 1832, when Henry Rowe Schoolcraft enlisted the help of an Ojibwa guide who led him to Lake Itasca, that the lake was identified as the true headwaters and source of the mighty Mississippi.

Pinpointing the right source is important not only in geography and cartography (the study of making maps), but also in other aspects of life. For example, if you are writing a report for a history class, which source of information would you rather use: what your older sibling remembers about that particular subject or a respected encyclopedia? Or if you wanted information on traveling to a foreign country, would you rely on someone's information who has never been there before or on a reliable travel agent?

The same can be said about our life as well. What is your source of hope? Your comfort? Your faith? Is it based on what someone else has told you or the sentiments of well-wishing friends? When you need a faith that is rock-solid, go to the right source: God, our Father, the source of our comfort, forgiveness, and love.

All praise to the **God** and **Father** of our **Lord Jesus Christ. He** is the **source** of **every mercy** and the **God who comforts** us.

[2 Corinthians 1:3]

also on this day

Today is French Fries Day.

1585
A group of 108 English colonists led by Sir Richard Grenville reached Roanoke Island, North Carolina.

1898
The radio was patented by Guglilmo Marconi.

to do ☑

GET OUT A MAP OF THE UNITED STATES AND TRACE THE PATH OF THE MISSISSIPPI RIVER FROM START (IN MINNESOTA) TO END (IN LOUISIANA).

OK, admit it. If you didn't know that today was Cow Appreciation Day, you probably wouldn't have given a second thought about our bovine buddies. But did you have some cold milk with your cereal for breakfast? Or did you have a slice of cheese on your sandwich at lunch, or enjoy a refreshing bowl of ice cream after supper? You couldn't have done any of those without the help of our friend the cow. Consider the following cow facts:

▸▸ Cows have been used for domestic purposes for more than 5,000 years.
▸▸ Per day, a cow spends 6 hours eating and 8 hours chewing cud.
▸▸ There are an estimated 920 cow breeds in the world!
▸▸ The average cow produces about 10 gallons of milk a day.
▸▸ It takes about 1.5 gallons of milk to make 1 gallon of ice cream.

Now do you feel a greater appreciation for those four-legged creatures that help put milk on your table? Maybe not. We often take for granted what we have in our lives. Sometimes we take for granted even the people in our lives. This is not the attitude that God wants us to have.

In his letter to the people at Ephesus, Paul reminds them that their lives should be marked by an attitude of thankfulness for *everything*—and that includes hard things as well as easy. In all things, Paul said, God is with us, guiding us, helping us, and shaping us. For that we should be extremely thankful!

So take a few moments, not only to appreciate Elsie or Bessie, but also the people God has placed in your life, the place where you live, and the comforts you enjoy each day.

Then tell God thanks.

holy cow!

Today is Cow Appreciation Day!

And you will always give thanks for everything to God the Father in the name of our Lord Jesus Christ. [Ephesians 5:20]

to do ☑

POUR YOURSELF A TALL COLD GLASS OF MILK, GRAB SOME COOKIES, AND START NAMING ALL THE PEOPLE OR ITEMS IN YOUR LIFE THAT YOU HAVE OVERLOOKED. TELL GOD THANKS FOR EACH ONE!

also on this day

1789 The French Revolution began when Parisians stormed the Bastille prison and released the seven prisoners inside.

Alfred Nobel demonstrated dynamite. 1867

The Greatest Outdoor Concert Ever

In 1978, Bob Dylan performed before the largest open-air concert audience for a single artist. Some 200,000 fans turned out to hear Dylan at Blackbushe Airport in England.

Blackbushe Airport, located on the border of Hampshire and Surrey, has long been an aviation hub for the United Kingdom. It was home to squadrons of reconnaissance and fighter operations during World War II and was the welcoming site for notables such as Queen Elizabeth and General Dwight D. Eisenhower.

Despite its long history, nothing could have prepared it for the onslaught of rock music fans that descended upon this airport and its surroundings on July 15, 1978, for "The Picnic at Blackbushe." With special appearances from Eric Clapton and others, Dylan drew more than 200,000 fans to the site for what has gone down in history as the largest open-air concert for a single artist. As one concertgoer remembered it, "It was just one of those special days that happen and you never forget."

Being part of a special celebration or an event like this concert certainly is memorable. But one day we all are going to be part of the biggest, greatest, and largest outdoor celebration ever. Listen to how the apostle John describes that event in the book of Revelation: "Then I looked again, and I heard the singing of thousands and millions of angels around the throne and the living beings and the elders" (5:11).

This will take place in Heaven, before the very throne of God. And not only will a chorus of angels numbering in the millions participate, but John records that people from every nation, tribe, and language will be there along with "every creature in heaven and on earth and under the earth and in the sea" (5:13). And we will all sing the same song: "Worthy is the Lamb."

That will truly be one of "those special days" that you won't want to miss.

to do ☑

READ JOHN'S DESCRIPTION OF THAT INCREDIBLE HEAVENLY CONCERT IN REVELATION 5:1–14.

I **looked** again.
I **heard** a company
of **Angels**
around the **Throne**,
the **Animals**,
and the **Elders**—
ten thousand
times ten thousand
their number,
thousand after
thousand after
thousand.

[Revelation 5:11, The Message]

also on this day

1606 Dutch painter Rembrandt was born.

Today is National Ice-Cream Day. Go enjoy a scoop of your favorite flavor. ✳

1922 The first duck-billed platypus in America arrived from Australia. It was exhibited at the Bronx Zoo in New York City.

time's up!

In 1935, Oklahoma City became the first city in the U.S. to make use of parking meters.

Parking had become a problem in downtown Oklahoma City. The Chamber of Commerce appointed William Magee to come up with a way to discourage people from parking on downtown streets, staying all day, and leaving few spaces for shoppers and others coming downtown.

And so the first parking meters in the United States were installed. The idea was to charge people for the use of the parking space and to limit use of the space. The idea caught on and soon spread to other cities to the point where there are now more than five million parking meters in use throughout the country.

We all are familiar with parking meters. Maybe you even had to race back to the car after an afternoon of shopping before the meter ran out. Maybe your mom or dad has even received a parking ticket because they didn't get back in time. As soon as you drop those quarters in the meter, the clock is running. Your time in that particular parking space is running out!

In a similar way, from the moment we took our first breath as newborns, the clock is ticking for our time on earth. The Bible makes it clear that we each are given a certain number of days to spend on this earth. How we spend our time is entirely up to us. We can either use our time to make sure we're happy and comfortable, or we can use our time to serve and help others.

Paul tells us in his letter to the Colossians that we should "Live wisely among those who are not Christians, and make the most of every opportunity" we have to help others and tell others about Jesus.

So are you merely taking up space, or are you using your time wisely?

The clock is ticking.

to do ☑

GIVE YOURSELF A TIME CHALLENGE TODAY. SET THE KITCHEN TIMER FOR AN HOUR. THEN SEE HOW MANY WAYS YOU CAN SERVE AND HELP OTHERS IN THAT AMOUNT OF TIME.

Live wisely among those who are **not Christians**, and **make** the **most** of **every** opportunity.

[Colossians 4:5]

also on this day

1950

The largest crowd in sporting history was 199,854. They watched Uruguay defeat Brazil in the World Cup soccer finals in Rio de Janeiro, Brazil.

The District of Columbia, or Washington, D.C., was established as the permanent seat of government for the United States.

1790

A year after graduating from Cornell University with a Master's degree in engineering, Willis H. Carrier developed the first air-conditioning system. But the system wasn't designed for home use or personal comfort. Rather, Carrier designed the first system to help a frustrated printer in Brooklyn who couldn't get a decent color image because of changes in the temperature and humidity.

In fact, the widespread use of air-conditioning for homes didn't really catch on until the 1950s. Today, the majority of us couldn't imagine homes, cars, stores, movie theaters, and even schools without the comforts of air-conditioning, especially on days like today!

We all like to feel comfortable. If we're too hot, we look for ways to cool down. If we're hungry, we eat. If we're tired, we take breaks. We want to be comfortable with our friends too. So we hang with friends who have the same interests as we do, who look like us, and who act like we do. New people and new situations can make us feel very uncomfortable—and we don't like getting out of our *comfort zone*.

But the Bible warns us about getting too comfortable. The prophet Amos spoke to the wealthy Israelites, "How terrible it will be for you who lounge in luxury and think you are secure in Jerusalem and Samaria! You are famous and popular in Israel, you to whom the people go for help" (Amos 6:1). We run into trouble when we put our need for comfort before the needs of others or when our comfortable lifestyles make us forget about the people who don't have what we do.

So get out of your comfort zone today. Look for ways you can put others before yourself.

to do ☑

GET OUT OF YOUR COMFORT ZONE TODAY. INVITE SOMEONE NEW OVER OR TAKE TIME TO HELP A NEIGHBOR.

For they are simpletons who turn away from me—to death. They are fools, and their own complacency will destroy them. [Proverbs 1:32]

In 1902, the air conditioner was invented.

creature comforts

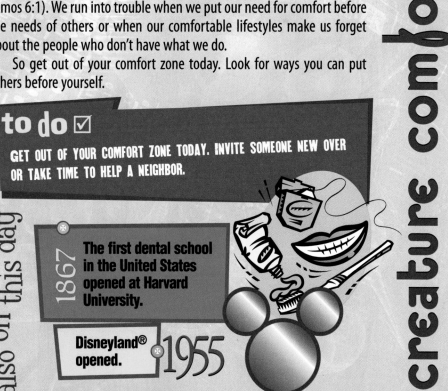

also on this day

1867 The first dental school in the United States opened at Harvard University.

Disneyland® opened. 1955

In 1955, the oldest known musical instrument in the world was found in Slovenia.

Play It Again!

The oldest known musical instrument in the world was found in the Indrijca River Valley in Slovenia. The relic was a bear bone with four artificial holes.

In fact, music has been part of life since the beginning. Check it out. Jubal was named the first musician—inventor of the harp and the flute (Genesis 4:21). Flip a few chapters ahead and we see music mentioned in Laban's interview with Jacob (Genesis 31:27). And what did Moses and the Hebrews do after they safely crossed the Red Sea and escaped from Pharaoh? They sang. (See Exodus 15.)

But undoubtedly the golden age of Hebrew music occurred during the time of David and Solomon. It was an essential part of training in the schools of the prophets (1 Chronicles 25:6). There were professional singers and musicians whose job it was to lead the people in praise songs. In fact, one band mentioned had more than 4,000 musicians (1 Chronicles 23:5). That's a *big* band!

Music was, and still is, an important part of our worship and celebration. Singing is a way of expressing our love and thanks to God. It's a way of sharing our faith with others. As David and the other psalm writers learned from experience, songs can help us express our feelings.

So what are you waiting for? Make a joyful noise. Bang a drum, strum a guitar, hum a tune, play a CD, sing your own song. Do what others have done from the very beginning—let music speak what's in your heart.

to do ☑

PUT ON YOUR FAVORITE CHRISTIAN CD. THEN DO AS THE PSALMIST SUGGESTS: SING A NEW SONG TO GOD, MAKE MUSIC, AND SHOUT FOR JOY!

Sing joyfully to the LORD, you righteous; it is fitting for the upright to praise him. Praise the LORD with the harp; make music to him on the ten-stringed lyre. Sing to him a new song; play skillfully, and shout for joy. [Psalm 33:1-3, NIV]

also on this day

Six planes of the army helped to form an aviation division called the Signal Corps. 1914

•1927

Ty Cobb set a major league baseball record by getting his 4,000th career hit. He hit 4,191 before he retired in 1928.

super-sized!

In 1985, George Bell won first place in a biggest feet contest with a shoe size of 28½. Bell, at age 26, stood 7 feet 10 inches tall.

George Bell is, well, one giant of a man. Even considering NBA standards, George towers over the big guys in the league. Take for example Shaquille O'Neal. He measures a mere 7 feet 1 inch. Even Yao Ming, one of the tallest NBA players, falls a full four inches short of George. And the all-time leading scorer in the NBA, Kareem Abdul-Jabbar? He doesn't measure up either at 7 feet 2 inches.

Super-sized people were a phenomenon even back in Bible times. In Deuteronomy 3:11, Og, one of the Bible giants, is mentioned as having a bed of iron that measured 13 feet long and 6 feet wide. And David's well-known giant opponent, Goliath, was more than 9 feet tall!

When Moses sent out the 12 spies to scout the promised land in Numbers 13:33, 10 of the spies reported seeing giant people so big and tall that "We felt like grasshoppers next to them, and that's what we looked like to them!" Their report, in fact, stopped the Israelites in their tracks, and they refused to enter the promised land. Because of their lack of faith and trust in God, they were sentenced to wandering the desert for another 40 years. And not one of the doubters entered the promised land.

You may know a few tall people but probably no one giant-sized. But that doesn't mean we don't face problems or situations that feel super-sized and overwhelming to us. That's when we need to remember Caleb and Joshua's report to the people. They saw the same giants, but rather than shaking in their decidedly smaller sandals, they were ready to take on their bigger foes. Why? They knew God was on their side and that he was bigger and stronger than any giant, anywhere, anytime.

"Just don't rebel against God! And don't be afraid of those people. Why, we'll have them for lunch! They have no protection and God is on our side. Don't be afraid of them!"

[Numbers 14:9, The Message]

also on this day

1799

The Rosetta Stone, a tablet with hieroglyphic translations into Greek, was found in Egypt.

1940

Winston Churchill used the two-finger V for victory sign for the first time.

to do ☑

JUST FOR FUN, DRAW A CHALK LINE ON YOUR SIDEWALK OR DRIVEWAY THAT MEASURES 7 FEET, 10 INCHES. THEN DRAW ANOTHER LINE THAT REPRESENTS YOUR HEIGHT. IF YOU WANT, ADD A THIRD LINE OF GIANT PROPORTIONS! HOW WOULD YOU FEEL FACING SOMEONE THAT TALL?

check it out!

In 1801, Elisha Brown Jr. presented a 1,235-pound cheese ball to President Thomas Jefferson.

Why would Mr. Brown give the president such an unusual gift? The answer is simple. The 1,235-pound cheese ball was used to feed the White House's giant 500-pound mouse.

Hold on a minute! Before this gets out of hand and you begin telling your friends about this, it's important to know what's true and what's not about this story. It *is* true that President Jefferson received a giant cheese ball, but there was *no* 500-pound mouse living at the White House—then or now.

Whenever you read or hear something, it's always good to check out the facts and make sure you know the truth. In fact, Paul commended the people of Berea because they did just that. When Paul and Silas preached the gospel in their town, the people of Berea diligently searched the Scriptures to check to see if what Paul and Silas said was true. When they decided Paul and Silas spoke the truth, many believed in Jesus.

Determining which teachers spoke the truth and which did not was a big issue back in the days of the early church. That's still the case. Even today a lot of people write or speak with great authority about God, about Jesus, and about the Bible. Some of their messages are true. But sometimes the truth gets lost in the message. Our job is to know what God's Word says and test what is being said.

When you do that, you'll be well-grounded in the truth. And you'll never fall for a story about a 500-pound mouse!

to do ☑

WRITE DOWN THREE WAYS YOU CAN CHECK OUT WHETHER OR NOT SOMETHING IS TRUE.

But **test everything** that is **said**. **Hold on** to what is good.

[1 Thessalonians 5:21]

also on this day

1859 This was the first time that admission was charged to see a ball game. Baseball fans paid 50 cents.

Neil Armstrong took the first steps ever on the moon.

1969

1919 Sir Edmund Hillary, the first man to successfully climb Mt. Everest, was born.

Expect the Unexpected

The first major battle of the Civil War, the Battle of Bull Run at Manassas Junction, Virginia, took place this day in 1861.

For days everyone in Washington and the surrounding area had heard talk of troops gathering outside Manassas Junction 30 miles away. Expectations were high that the Union troops would send the Confederate troops packing, ending the conflict with one fight. So when the word spread that the two armies were going to fight, buggies of spectators traveled to the battleground. Picnic baskets were opened, and the folks waited to watch the show.

No one expected what was to come. Not only were the Union troops soundly defeated, but there were more than 4,000 casualties on both sides. The Battle of Bull Run marked the beginning of a struggle that would last for four long years—and would become America's bloodiest war.

The Jewish people had certain expectations too about the coming Messiah—the one that God promised to send to rescue them. They were expecting a warrior, a king who would conquer the hated Romans and chase them out of their country. They were not expecting Jesus.

The passage in Matthew tells us a lot about the type of king Jesus would be. He would bring justice to the people, but he would not fight or shout or raise his voice in public. Jesus was not the king people expected at all.

Sometimes we too have expectations about Jesus. We expect him to answer our prayers in a certain way or bring us great and wonderful victories. Then when our circumstances don't work out according to our plan, we are disappointed. We may even begin to doubt Jesus' power in our lives.

That's when we need to remember that our expectations may not be accurate. We need to recognize that Jesus acts according to *his* plan and *his* timetable. Not ours.

to do ☑

WHAT IS GOING ON IN YOUR LIFE RIGHT NOW? WHAT ARE YOUR EXPECTATIONS ABOUT THAT SITUATION? IF YOU HAVEN'T ALREADY, TURN THESE CIRCUMSTANCES OVER TO JESUS RIGHT NOW.

"Look at my Servant, whom I have chosen. He is my Beloved, and I am very pleased with him. I will put my Spirit upon him, and he will proclaim justice to the nations. He will not fight or shout; he will not raise his voice in public."

[Matthew 12:18,19]

also on this day

1873 Jesse James and his gang robbed their first train. They stole $3,000.

1931 The first CBS-TV program was aired. The show featured singer Kate Smith, composer George Gershwin, and New York City Mayor Jimmy Walker.

1997

The USS *Constitution*, which defended the United States during the War of 1812, set sail under its own power for the first time in 116 years.

follow the crowd

Legend has it that the German town of Hamelin was overrun with rats. The town council had tried everything to get rid of the rats with no success. Finally the mayor of Hamelin promised to pay 1,000 florins to anyone who could get rid of the rats.

That's when a stranger entered town wearing bright red and yellow clothes, claiming he could rid the town of its rat problem. That night the stranger began playing a soft tune on a flute, drawing out all the rats and leading them to a nearby river where they drowned. When the mayor refused to pay up ("Playing a tune on a flute is not worth 1,000 florins"), the piper returned to town. Playing his flute, the piper enticed the children of Hamelin to follow him. He led them to a cave where they all entered, never to be seen again.

People may argue whether or not this legend is true. But you can't argue with one moral of the story: be careful who you follow!

At times it is easy to follow the crowd. All your friends are watching a TV show that is off-limits to you. Rather than making a scene, you go along with them. Or maybe your friends begin picking on a younger child. You know that's not right, but you go along with it because *everyone else is doing it*.

The people in the early church had to decide who to follow. New teachers and preachers would come into town and speak with great authority about Jesus. Some were false teachers who led people astray, but they attracted a following. Christians may have been tempted to follow the false teachers because they were so popular.

Accepting what's popular can get us into trouble. We need to check what people say and do against what we know is in the Bible. That's the only way we can hold fast to God's truth and protect ourselves from going along with the crowd.

to do ☑

ASK YOUR FRIENDS TO PLAY FOLLOW THE LEADER, BUT ADD A TWIST. LEAD THE GROUP THROUGH YOUR HOUSE OR NEIGHBORHOOD AND DO SOMETHING GOOD ALONG THE WAY. GIVE A FRIENDLY GREETING TO THOSE YOU MEET, CLEAN UP CLUTTER, OR PICK UP TRASH ON THE GROUND.

You seem to believe whatever anyone tells you, even if they preach about a different Jesus than the one we preach, or a different Spirit than the one you received, or a different kind of gospel than the one you believed. [2 Corinthians 11:4]

also on this day

1796 **The city of Cleveland was founded by General Moses Cleveland.**

1926 **Babe Ruth caught a baseball that had been dropped from an airplane flying at 250 feet.**

be a lifelong learner

The first swimming school in the U.S. opened in Boston in 1827.

When the first swimming school in the United States opened in Boston, Massachusetts on July 23, 1827, one of its first pupils was John Quincy Adams. What was most noteworthy about Adams's enrollment was not that he was the president of the United States at the time, but that he was 60 years old and an accomplished swimmer!

While he was president, Adams took a daily swim at 5 AM in the Potomac River. Still he was convinced that he could enhance his swimming skills by enrolling in the newly founded school.

President Adams was a lifelong learner. From his days as a student at Harvard University, Adams was known for his keen mind and wealth of knowledge. In addition to his accomplishments as a lawyer, diplomat, and politician, Adams also had an interest in the arts and sciences. He was instrumental in establishing a national university, financing scientific expeditions, and in building a national observatory. He promoted the Smithsonian Institution.

So it probably should not have been a surprise when Adams showed up that first day of swim classes. Adams was committed to learning—no matter how old he was or how much he already knew. Adams had learned at an early age that there was always something more to learn.

That's not a bad role model to follow. At this stage of your life, while you are forming many of the habits, attitudes, and beliefs that will shape your future, add a love for learning. Be willing to explore new ideas and experiences. Take the time to listen to others who have more knowledge than you. If you do, like President Adams, you will continue to learn and grow throughout your life.

to do ☑

THE OFFICIAL BEGINNING OF SCHOOL IS STILL A FEW WEEKS AWAY. NOW'S A GOOD TIME TO THINK ABOUT FIVE NEW THINGS YOU WOULD LIKE TO LEARN OR TRY IN THE UPCOMING SCHOOL YEAR.

Commit yourself to **instruction**; **attune** your **ears** to **hear** words of **knowledge**.

[Proverbs 23:12]

also on this day

1904

The ice-cream cone was invented by Charles E. Menches during the Louisiana Exposition in St. Louis.

Air Force Colonel Eileen M. Collins became the first woman to command a space shuttle.

1999

Westward Ho!

Today is Pioneer Day.

According to the *American Heritage Dictionary*, a pioneer is anyone who ventures into unknown or unclaimed territory. Between 1839 and 1869, a half-million pioneers ventured westward, following a vision of new opportunities, rich farmland, and wealth.

One of the most popular routes west was the famed Oregon Trail—the only practical way for settlers to cross the Rockies. The journey, however, was exceptionally difficult.

It was a long, hard, often deadly 2,000-mile trek. Many walked the entire way barefoot. One in every 10 pioneers died along the way. Pioneers battled weather, lack of food and unsafe water supplies, disease, and accidental gunshots. But they kept going. Why? They focused on the vision the West promised—plentiful, rich farmland, a new life and opportunities, even the promise of gold.

The pioneers' determination to complete the task in front of them was not unlike those early *pioneers* of Israel who returned to their unclaimed homeland, Jerusalem, after being exiled for 70 years. They returned to a land devastated by war, to a city and temple left in ruins.

Yet, with the leaders such as Ezra and Nehemiah to guide them, the returning Israelites slowly began the difficult process of rebuilding. What kept them going? A vision they had kept alive of Jerusalem's former glory and the knowledge that God himself was with them. When Nehemiah shared this vision with the people, they responded enthusiastically. "Let's get going," they said. "Let's roll up our sleeves and get to work."

When you are facing a large, difficult task, be like Nehemiah and those early pioneers. Don't let the size of the task or the length of the journey deter you. Keep focused on the end result, share that vision with others who can help, and ask God to help you.

Then get to work!

I told them how God was supporting me and how the king was backing me up. They said, "We're with you. Let's get started." They rolled up their sleeves, ready for the good work.

[Nehemiah 2:18, The Message]

also on this day

Today is National Cousins Day.

1897

Famed woman aviator Amelia Earhart was born today.

to do ☑

CHECK OUT A BOOK ABOUT PIONEERS FROM THE LIBRARY. IMAGINE WHAT IT WOULD HAVE BEEN LIKE TO TRAVEL SO LONG AND SO FAR FROM YOUR HOME. WHAT WOULD KEEP YOU GOING?

When the first Europeans from Portugal landed in Japan in 1542, they brought with them two important things—gunpowder and Christianity. At first, the Japanese welcomed the foreign traders, especially because of the new weapons. But as those first missionaries became more and more successful in converting a large number of Japanese to Christianity, the Japanese rulers became alarmed.

In 1587, Toyotomi Hideyoshi issued an edict, throwing out all Christian missionaries from Japan. At first, Hideyoshi's edict was ignored. But he issued a second ban a year later and backed it up by executing 26 Franciscan priests as a warning. The persecution of Christians continued in the years following as more edicts were issued. Finally by 1614, Christianity had been banned throughout all Japan.

This was not the first time Christians faced persecution for their beliefs. Since the days of the early church, believers in Jesus Christ have faced arrests, beatings, and death for their faith. Jesus himself warned his followers that persecution would follow them: "Do you remember what I told you? 'A servant is not greater than the master.' Since they persecuted me, naturally they will persecute you" (John 15:20).

Paul told his followers the same thing: "Everyone who wants to live a godly life in Christ Jesus will suffer persecution" (2 Timothy 3:12). This may not mean that you will be jailed, beaten, or thrown out of town for your faith like Paul and those missionaries in Japan. You may face rejection and mockery as people oppose you because of what you believe and how you live.

What's important is not giving up or giving in. Keep holding on to your faith and living the way God wants you to. He's the only one you need to please!

Anyone who wants to live all out for Christ is in for a lot of trouble; there's no getting around it. [2 Timothy 3:12, The Message]

In 1587, Toyotomi Hideyoshi issued an edict expelling all Christian missionaries from Japan.

banned!

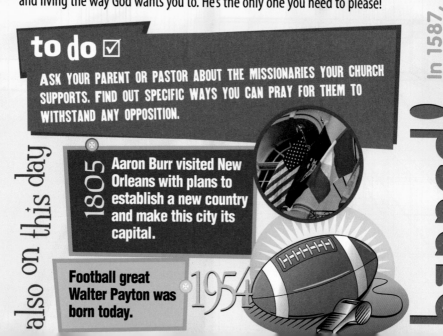

to do ☑

ASK YOUR PARENT OR PASTOR ABOUT THE MISSIONARIES YOUR CHURCH SUPPORTS. FIND OUT SPECIFIC WAYS YOU CAN PRAY FOR THEM TO WITHSTAND ANY OPPOSITION.

also on this day

1805 Aaron Burr visited New Orleans with plans to establish a new country and make this city its capital.

Football great Walter Payton was born today. 1954

Today in 1908, the Federal Bureau of Investigation was founded.

Investigate!

The Federal Bureau of Investigation (FBI) was founded on beliefs held by reformers such as President Theodore Roosevelt that the government should intervene wherever necessary to provide a just society. Further, according to Roosevelt and others, experts in various fields were needed to produce that justice in society.

With this in mind, President Roosevelt instructed Attorney General Charles Bonaparte to create a force of special agents who were well-disciplined and trained to fight corruption and crime at the federal level. On July 26, 1908, 10 former secret service employees and a handful of other investigators became special agents, so the FBI was born. With it was born a strong investigative tradition at the federal government level.

Investigating the facts and evidence is not only useful when trying to solve a crime but also when considering what you believe. Even in King Solomon's day, when TV, newspapers, the Internet, or radio weren't around to broadcast new ideas, there were hundreds of opinions and ideas to study. As Solomon said, "There is no end of opinions ready to be expressed. Studying them can go on forever and become very exhausting!" (Ecclesiastes 12:12).

Investigating other ideas and opinions about how to live is not a bad idea. But, as Solomon warned, it can become a problem if we spend *all* our time pursuing and investigating those ideas and not spending enough time studying God's truth. Our time is better spent investigating what God has to say and making sure we obey his Word. So be wise like Solomon and learn first what God has to say.

to do ☑

SPEND SOME TIME INVESTIGATING GOD'S WORD. PICK A BOOK OF THE BIBLE (MAYBE START WITH MARK), AND MAKE IT A GOAL TO READ ONE CHAPTER EACH NIGHT BEFORE BED.

Those who **obey** him will **not** be **punished**. **Those** who are **wise** will **find** a **time** and a **way** to do what is **right**.

[Ecclesiastes 8:5]

also on this day

1775 Benjamin Franklin became the first Postmaster General.

•1952

Mickey Mantle hit his first grand-slam home run.

are you sure about that?

Today in 2003, the British Broadcasting Corporation reported that there is definitely no monster in Loch Ness.

As early as the 6th century, a monster with a long neck and a huge lumbering body was reported living in Loch Ness. The earliest sighting of the Loch Ness Monster was recorded by St. Columba, according to the writings of Adamnan, in the year AD 565.

But it wasn't until the 1930s, however, that new sightings were reported. At that time, three fishermen reported seeing a disturbance in the water. The men watched as a creature about 20 feet long approached their boat throwing water into the air. Following the story, more people claimed to have seen a strange creature in the Loch.

In 1962, the Loch Ness Investigation Bureau was formed to act as a research organization and clearinghouse for information about the creature. In subsequent years the lake has been scoured, probed, studied, and explored via hot-air balloons, infrared cameras, sonar scanners, and submarines. Finally, in 2003, after an investigation using 600 separate sonar beams and satellite navigation technology did investigators conclude that there was no monster in Loch Ness.

Mythical creatures such as the Loch Ness Monster, Big Foot, and others are amusing to ponder, but when it comes to proving their existence, researchers usually come up empty. There simply is no truth behind the many *sightings*.

Thankfully, our faith is based not on a few *sightings* here or there, but on the witness of thousands, the words passed down directly from Jesus' followers, and the power of the Holy Spirit. We don't need to launch extensive investigations or use the latest in technology to determine the truth of Jesus. Paul reminds us that we have the "full assurance that what we said was true" through the Holy Spirit.

Our faith is sure, certain, and rock solid. Bank on it!

For when we brought you the Good News, it was not only with words but also with power, for the Holy Spirit gave you full assurance that what we said was true. And you know that the way we lived among you was further proof of the truth of our message. [1 Thessalonians 1:5]

also on this day

1909
Orville Wright set a record for the longest airplane flight: 1 hour, 12 minutes, and 40 seconds.

1940
Bugs Bunny made his debut.

1953
The armistice agreement that ended the Korean War was signed.

to do ☑

TAKE A QUICK SURVEY OF YOUR FAMILY AND FRIENDS. FIND OUT HOW MANY OF THEM BELIEVE THAT THERE IS A MONSTER LIVING IN LOCH NESS.

singing telegram

In 1933, the first singing telegram was presented.

When Western Union began its advertising campaign, "Don't Write—Telegraph!" Americans got the message. Beginning in 1935, Western Union offered its first Christmas greeting telegram, complete with a full-color illustration by Norman Rockwell. The greeting could be sent anywhere in the United States for only 25 cents. Soon it was possible to send dozens of special messages, including Santagrams, Bunnygrams, Storkgrams, and Kiddiegrams.

But by far the most popular service Western Union offered was the singing telegram. The very first singing telegram was sent on July 28, 1933, when one of the Western Union operators was asked to sing "Happy Birthday" to movie star Rudy Vallee. Lucille Lips was drafted into service. New York columnist Walter Winchell mentioned the birthday greeting in his column and, by popular demand, the Singing Telegram was born.

It's a tradition that continues today. Dozens of companies offer to send a singing bunny, chicken, dinosaur, or an array of other creatures and characters to serenade the recipient with birthday or anniversary greetings or congratulations.

Maybe you have never received a singing telegram. But believe it or not, someone is singing over you and about you every day! That's right. The prophet Zephaniah describes God in Heaven celebrating over us with song every time we choose to spend time with him, obey him, and follow him.

Think about that for a moment! Every time you pray to God, he sings about it. Every time you choose to help someone, God gives a big high five. Every time you obey your mom and dad, God rejoices.

Since you're reading this devotion right now, God is singing a happy song.

Do you hear it?

to do ☑

CREATE YOUR OWN SINGING TELEGRAM. SING GOOD MORNING TO YOUR MOM OR DAD. TELL YOUR BROTHER OR SISTER WITH A TUNE HOW MUCH YOU APPRECIATE THEM.

For the LORD your God has arrived to live among you. He is a mighty savior. He will rejoice over you with great gladness. With his love, he will calm all your fears. He will exult over you by singing a happy song. [Zephaniah 3:17]

also on this day

1865
The American Dental Association set a code of ethics.

1951
Walt Disney's *Alice in Wonderland* was released.

1939
Judy Garland recorded "Over the Rainbow."

Today is National Parents Day.

F or all the times that your mom bugs you about cleaning your room, or your dad tells you to take out the garbage; for all the times that your parents tell you to eat your veggies and wash your hands—what would we do without our parents?

Who puts food on your table each day and makes sure you have clean clothes to wear? Who takes you to the doctor when you're sick and holds you tight when you are scared? Who loves you no matter how much you mess up and who is always there to cheer you on when you fail? Your mom and dad, of course!

Parents are an important part of God's plan for all his children. God has given them an incredible list of responsibilities: They are to teach their children all about God (Deuteronomy 6:4-7 and Psalm 78:4-7); they are to discipline their children (Proverbs 13:24); and they are to do all of this without aggravating them (Ephesians 6:4 and Colossians 3:21). And this is in addition to all the other ways parents take care and provide for their children. Not an easy task, is it?

So it shouldn't come as a big surprise when God includes in his 10 laws a command to honor and obey our parents. It is the first command that comes with a promise—*if* we honor and obey our parents, *then* we will live in peace. Makes sense, doesn't it?

So what does that mean to *honor and obey* our parents? It means speaking with respect and courtesy to your parents. It means following their teachings and obeying their rules. It means telling your parents thank you for all that they do for you each day.

When we honor and obey our parents, we're really honoring and obeying God. And that pleases God!

"Honor your father and mother. Then you will live a long, full life in the land the Lord your God will give you." [Exodus 20:12]

to do ☑

HONOR YOUR PARENTS TODAY BY DOING SOMETHING SPECIAL FOR THEM. MAKE THEM A PICNIC LUNCH OR DINNER. CLEAN UP YOUR ROOM WITHOUT BEING ASKED. OFFER TO BABYSIT YOUR SIBLINGS SO THEY CAN HAVE A NIGHT OUT.

also on this day

1940 John Sigmound of St. Louis completed a 292-mile swim down the Mississippi River.

The National Aeronautics and Space Administration (NASA) was authorized by Congress. 1958

hooray for parents!

in God we trust

In 1956, the phrase "In God We Trust" was adopted as the U.S. national motto.

In 1864, coins in America began to carry the motto "In God We Trust." Such a motto had been proposed and supported during the Civil War when many Christians urged the country to turn back to God for help during the national crisis. As one minister wrote to the Secretary of the Treasury Salmon P. Chase, such a motto on every coin "would place us openly under the Divine protection we have personally claimed."

In response, Secretary Chase wrote, "No nation can be strong except in the strength of God, or safe except in His defense. The trust of our people in God should be declared on our national coins."

An act to include the phrase "In God We Trust" on two-cent coins was approved by Congress in 1864. Over the years, subsequent laws were passed to include the motto on other coins. The phrase has been in continuous use on one-cent coins since 1909 and on 10-cent coins since 1916. When legislation was passed in 1956 to make "In God We Trust" our national motto, the phrase was then used on paper money. Today it is now included in the background design of all classes and denominations of currency.

Every coin or bill can serve on a daily basis as a wonderful reminder of where we should put our trust. Sometimes when we are faced with an important decision, we feel we can't trust anyone to help us. But wise King Solomon knew that in all matters, big or small, we need to trust God completely and not our own understanding.

That means taking every decision to God and being willing to listen and trust him. As we read God's Word and pray about what's on our mind, God will make his direction clear to us.

Trust him!

Trust in the **LORD** with **all** your **heart**; do **not depend** on your **own understanding**.

(Proverbs 3:5).

also on this day

1863
Henry Ford, inventor of the automobile, was born.

1947
Arnold Schwarzenegger was born.

2003
The last *old-style* Volkswagen Beetle rolled off an assembly line in Mexico.

to do ☑

CARRY AROUND A COIN IN YOUR POCKET OR PURSE AS A DAILY REMINDER OF WHERE YOU SHOULD PUT YOUR TRUST.

in your wildest dreams

J.K. Rowling, author of the popular Harry Potter series,
was born on this day in 1965.

Since she was a little girl, Joanne K. Rowling has been interested in writing. After graduating from college, she first found work as a secretary. Later she spent time teaching English in Portugal before moving to Scotland with her daughter. It was while riding a train back in 1990 that "Harry just strolled into my head fully formed."

It would take another five years, writing while her daughter napped, before Rowling completed the first book, *Harry Potter and the Sorcerer's Stone.* Several publishers turned down the manuscript before one took interest. When the first Harry Potter book was published in 1998, Rowling had no idea of the success her book would have. "I thought I had written something that a handful of people might quite like," Rowling said. "So this has been something of a shock."

When she started out, J.K. Rowling could not have envisioned writing a series that has sold more than a quarter billion books, has been translated into 61 languages, and has been distributed in more than 200 countries worldwide.

Maybe you have dreams of achieving something great, whether it's writing a widely popular series, becoming a great athlete or a famous doctor, or being elected president of the United States! Right now it's hard to imagine what God may have in store for your future.

But Paul assures us in his letter to the Ephesians that we can't even begin to imagine the incredible plans that God has in store for us. Through the Holy Spirit, Paul said, God can accomplish just about anything in our lives—things beyond our wildest dreams.

That's pretty exciting to think about, isn't it? God can do *anything*—there's no limit to what he can achieve through you. So keep dreaming!

to do ☑

WRITE DOWN ON A PIECE OF PAPER SOMETHING THAT YOU WOULD LIKE TO ACCOMPLISH. THEN ASK GOD TO WORK IN YOUR LIFE TO ACHIEVE HIS PURPOSES.

God can do anything, you know—far more than you could ever imagine or guess or request in your wildest dreams! He does it not by pushing us around but by working within us, his Spirit deeply and gently within us. [Ephesians 3:20, The Message]

also on this day

1845

The French Army introduced the saxophone to its military band. The musical instrument was the invention of Adolphe Sax of Belgium.

At age 17, Marilyn Bell of Toronto became the youngest person to swim the English Channel.

1955

On this day in 1790, the first U.S. census was completed.

You Count

I n 1790, 4 million people lived in the United States. The population of the U.S. in the year 2000 was 281,421,906—more than 70 times larger. In fact, the population of New York alone is over 8 million. No wonder traffic is so bad, and we have to wait in all those lines!

With so many people in our states, cities, and schools, it's easy to feel lost in the crowd, like a grain of sand on the beach. A person can even feel small and insignificant at a concert or football game—and, sometimes, even in a large church. We may think, "I'm just one out of so many. No one really sees me or cares about me."

But God considers each person valuable and important. Today's verse says that he created people in his image, and that includes you. Elsewhere in the Bible, God says he gave each person (including you) special talents and abilities. See 1 Corinthians 12. God is always with you, right by your side. Check out Deuteronomy 31:8. And most impressive of all, he sent Jesus to die for you. God loves you that much! Read about it in Romans 5:8.

So whenever you feel lonely or lost—or like a nothing, a nobody, a zero—remember God's truth and promises. With him you count!

to do ☑

THE NEXT TIME YOU'RE IN A CROWD, LOOK AT THE PEOPLE AROUND YOU, ONE PERSON AT A TIME. SAY A SILENT PRAYER FOR EACH ONE. THEN THANK GOD FOR LOVING YOU AND MAKING YOU SPECIAL.

Then God said, "Let us make people in our image, to be like ourselves. They will be masters over all life—the fish in the sea, the birds in the sky, and all the livestock, wild animals, and small animals."

[Genesis 1:26]

also on this day

This is National Inventor's Month.

•1893

Shredded Wheat® cereal was patented by Henry Perky and William Ford.

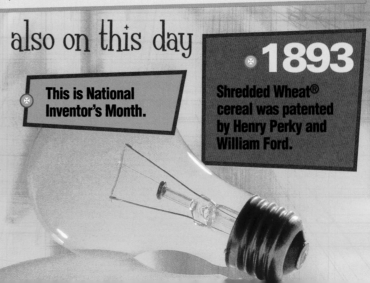

Dave and Jon were the closest of friends. They hit it off right away. You know how sometimes that happens—at a party, in the neighborhood, at church, at school—when you and the other person just click. That's how it was with Dave and Jon, and they became as close as brothers. And that's exactly what they did, even when Jon's powerful father turned violent and tried to keep them apart.

The true story of these true friends is told in the Bible. See the devotion for May 1. Jon—Jonathan—was the son of Saul, Israel's first king. Dave—David—brought down Goliath the giant.

Later, David became very popular throughout the land because of his military victories. King Saul saw him as a threat and even tried to kill David several times. Normally a king's son would be the one to wear the crown, so we might expect Jonathan to be upset with David, just like his father. But none of this came between them. Jonathan accepted the fact that God had chosen David, not him, to be the next king of Israel. David and Jonathan were true friends.

True friends care about us, listen to us, tell us the truth even when it hurts, stick up for us, and stay with us through good times and bad. Everyone needs at least one true friend, but they're rare. Proverbs 20:6 says, "Many will say they are loyal friends, but who can find one who is really faithful?"

If you have that kind of friendship, you are indeed fortunate. If not, remember that friendships go both ways—to have a friend you need to *be* a friend.

And Jonathan made a special vow to be David's friend. [1 Samuel 18:3]

This is National Friendship Day.

to do ☑

WRITE A NOTE OR A LETTER TO A SPECIAL FRIEND. TELL YOUR FRIEND HOW MUCH YOU APPRECIATE HIS OR HER FRIENDSHIP. PRAY FOR YOUR FRIEND TOO.

also on this day

This is Ice-Cream Sandwich Day.

1824 **In New York City, Fifth Avenue was opened.**

Charles A. Wheeler patented the first escalator. 1892

true friends

lurking beneath

On this day in 1958, the Nautilus became the first submarine to cross the North Pole underwater.

Have you ever thought about what it must be like to live on a submarine? Each ship is relatively small for so many sailors, so everything is cramped. For example, 116 men served in the *Nautilus* during the historic trip across the North Pole. The ship was only 319 feet long and 27 feet wide (at the widest place).

It's probably cool, however, to sail unseen beneath everything, and very few people even know you're there. But do you ever wonder what else might be lurking under us or around us?

That's a good question, and the Bible has the answer. Read Ephesians 6:10-18, and you'll discover the real but unseen world of spiritual warfare. Paul tells the believers in Ephesus, and us, that the real opposition to our faith comes from "the evil rulers and authorities of the unseen world, against those mighty powers of darkness who rule this world, and against wicked spirits in the heavenly realms" (v. 12).

That probably sounds scary, but Paul also says that we have armor and weapons (also not visible) that can defeat this enemy. God knows where the enemy lurks, and he will help us fight and win.

So put on your armor and trust your commander!

to do ☑

READ EPHESIANS 6:10-18 AND LIST THE SPIRITUAL ARMOR MENTIONED. USE IT AS A CHECKLIST TO SEE IF YOU'RE READY FOR THE BATTLE.

Use **every** piece of **God's armor** to **resist** the **enemy** in the **time** of **evil**, so that **after** the **battle** you will **still** be **standing firm**.

[Ephesians 6:13]

also on this day

1492

Christopher Columbus left Spain with three ships on a voyage that would lead him to what is now known as the Americas.

Jesse Owens won the first of his four Olympic gold medals. He soon became the first American to win four gold medals at an Olympics.

1936

This is National Watermelon Day.

seed faith

This is National Mustard Day.

What do you like on your hot dog or hamburger or brat? A lot of people prefer mustard, the tangy yellow goo. Actually, mustard comes in three types: yellow, brown, and oriental. Yellow mustard is the most common and is used most often in homes and restaurants as a mild condiment. It is also used in salad dressings, pickles, and some meat products. Brown and oriental mustards are used mainly for hot table mustard, and some for oil and spices. A very popular salad dressing and dipping sauce these days is "honey mustard." That's probably more about mustard than you ever wanted to know.

The Bible records a parable Jesus told about a mustard plant. At that time the mustard seed was the smallest known seed, yet it grew into a huge plant. Jesus compared the disciples' faith to the tiny mustard seed. His point was that their small faith could accomplish much for the kingdom of God.

Sometimes we can think that only "spiritual giants" with vast amounts of faith can do anything for God. This verse says that's not right. Even young and inexperienced Christians can have hope. God will do *huge* things through us, even if we have *tiny* faith.

Faith means trusting in God, relying on him to lead us, to give us what we truly need, and to answer our prayers. Sometimes we can feel like the man who said to Jesus, "I do believe; help me overcome my unbelief" (Mark 9:24, NIV).

So how's your faith these days? How much have you mustered?

"You didn't have enough faith," Jesus told them. "I assure you, even if you had faith as small as a mustard seed you could say to this mountain, 'Move from here to there,' and it would move. Nothing would be impossible." [Matthew 17:20]

also on this day

1956

William Herz became the first person to race a motorcycle over 200 miles per hour when he was clocked at 210.

1966

Many radio stations banned the broadcast of Beatles records because John Lennon had stated that the band was more popular than Jesus Christ.

to do ☑

GET A PACKET OF MUSTARD SEEDS AND PUT THEM WHERE YOU CAN SEE THEM IN YOUR BEDROOM TO REMIND YOU OF FAITH. ASK GOD TO HELP YOU TRUST HIM MORE.

On this day in 1924, the comic strip Little Orphan Annie debuted.

In the Comics

I f you spend much time reading the comics in the newspaper, you may have run across *Little Orphan Annie*. Even if you haven't seen the comic strip, you probably have heard about the musical (and later the movie) *Annie*, based on it. In the musical, Annie sings, "The sun will come out tomorrow!" as she hopefully looks to brighter days ahead. Who would have dreamed that an orphan would become so popular?

Actually, the neediest people in the world are orphans—children with no parents to protect them, care for them, and guide them. Some become orphans when their parents die in war, in famine, or in other disasters. Some children are left as orphans when their parents abandon them. Some countries have huge orphanages.

That's why adoption is such a wonderful gift and act of love. If you were adopted, you know this firsthand. Many couples travel across the world to adopt children, to give them loving homes.

The Bible says a lot about orphans—and widows—with God telling his people to care for these very needy people among them. In today's verse, God is promising to rescue the orphans and widows in Judah.

Today, Christian agencies like Compassion International (www.compassion.net), World Vision (www.wvi.org), and Venture International (www.ventureftf.org) provide opportunities for almost anyone to help. By giving a small amount of money each month, we can sponsor children or families. Besides individuals, often families and youth groups become sponsors. It's a way to show Christ's love "for the least of these" (see Matthew 25:34-40). We can help them know that "the sun *will* come out" and that they can know the Son.

to do ☑

CHECK OUT THE WEB SITES OF THE AGENCIES MENTIONED. TALK WITH YOUR FAMILY ABOUT SPONSORING A CHILD OR FAMILY.

"But I will **preserve** the **orphans** who **remain** among you. Your **widows**, too, will be able to **depend** on **me** for **help**."

[Jeremiah 49:11]

also on this day

1914 **Electric traffic lights were installed in Cleveland, Ohio.**

This is National Sisters Day.

Astronaut Neil A. Armstrong was born. 1930

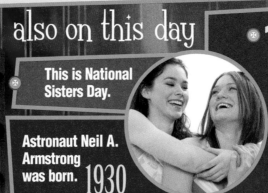

* **1999** First baseman Mark McGuire of the St. Louis Cardinals hit his 500th career home-run.

Located between England and France, the English Channel is 26.69 miles across. Someone swimming it, however, would probably swim an S-shaped route of 30 to 40 miles because of the tides. Add to this the water temperature of 60 degrees Fahrenheit, and you can see why it's such a big deal to successfully make that swim. A swim of 14 hours would probably take 58,800 strokes. Are you tired yet?

In 1952, another famous swimmer, Florence Chadwick, waded into the water off Catalina Island and began to swim the 21 miles to California. She had already been the first woman to swim the English Channel in both directions—amazing!

After more than 15 hours, however, numbed with the cold, she asked to be taken out—she just couldn't go on. Everyone urged her to keep swimming, to not quit. But when she looked toward the California coast, all she could see was dense fog. Later she learned that her goal, her destination, was only a half-mile further. To a reporter she blurted out, "Look, I'm not excusing myself. But if I could have seen land, I might have made it."

That was the only time Florence ever quit. Two months later she swam that same route, and again she swam in fog. But this time she swam with her faith intact. She knew the truth—that somewhere behind that fog was land.

Life can be like that, can't it? Sometimes, when we're in the fog and can't see our goal, we can lose hope and feel like quitting. That's when we need to remember the truths of God's Word. Romans 8:31-38 assures us that God is with us and for us. Have hope, and "keep swimming!"

We work hard and suffer much in order that people will believe the truth, for our hope is in the living God, who is the Savior of all people, and particularly of those who believe. [1 Timothy 4:10]

On this day in 1926, 19-year-old Gertrude Ederle become the first American woman to swim the English Channel.

to do ☑

MAKE A LIST OF TRUTHS ABOUT GOD AND HIS LOVE FOR YOU. WHENEVER YOU FEEL SURROUNDED BY THE FOG OF PROBLEMS, WORRIES, AND QUESTIONS, READ THE LIST AND ASK GOD TO HELP YOU FOCUS ON HIM AND NOT ON THE FOG.

also on this day

1945 The atom bomb was dropped on Hiroshima, Japan.

The first Australian rules football game to be played at night took place at the Melbourne Cricket Ground. The game was to promote the introduction of electricity to the city of Melbourne.

1879

keep swimming

words worth

At about this time every year, the National Scrabble® Championship is held.

Have you every played Scrabble®? It's a word game that has been popular since 1948. Over the years, more than 100 million sets have been sold in 29 different languages. That's a lot of words!

Players in Scrabble form words with the letters they are given and with those already on the board. Each letter has a point value, so the value of a word is the total of the points of all the letters in that word. And the player with the most points wins. In this game, *words count*!

Words matter in life as well. Sometimes we don't think so, and we can be very careless with what we say. For example, sometimes we lie. We may use words like *love* and *friend* when we don't mean them, just to get close to someone. We make promises we don't keep. We can speak harsh words or insults—curse words even. Our words can cost us a ton of "points" in life.

The Bible teaches the importance of being careful with our words. Here are some examples: "The godly speak words that are helpful, but the wicked speak only what is corrupt" (Proverbs 10:32). "From a wise mind comes wise speech; the words of the wise are persuasive" (Proverbs 16:23). "If you claim to be religious but don't control your tongue, you are just fooling yourself, and your religion is worthless" (James 1:26). "And so blessing and cursing come pouring out of the same mouth. Surely, my brothers and sisters, this is not right!" (James 3:10).

How are your words these days? If someone listened carefully to what you say (and how you say it), what would that person conclude about your character?

Make your words count.

May the **words**
of my **mouth**
and the **thoughts** of my **heart**
be **pleasing** to **you**,
O **LORD**, my **rock**
and my **redeemer**. [Psalm 19:14]

also on this day

·782

George Washington created the Order of the Purple Heart to award those who had been wounded in battle.

1888

Theophilus Van Kannel received a patent for the revolving door.

to do ☑

TODAY, WORK HARD AT NOT REACTING WITH HARSH WORDS. INSTEAD, EITHER KEEP QUIET OR SAY SOMETHING POSITIVE AND ENCOURAGING. NOTICE THE EFFECT ON OTHERS.

true north

On this day in 1866, explorer Matthew A. Henson was born.

Matthew Henson, Robert Peary, and their Eskimo guide were the first people ever to reach the North Pole. You may wonder why anyone would want to travel to the North Pole anyway. Perhaps Henson, Peary, and the guide had a spirit of adventure, challenge, and exploration that made the long, cold trip worth it.

Here's an interesting thought. If you were standing on the North Pole, every direction you looked would be south. How about that!

All compasses point to true north. Compass needles point north because of the magnetic pull of the North Pole. When you know where north is, you can find south, east, and west as well. Explorers find north on the compass, get their bearings, and go from there.

Remember when you got lost in the neighborhood as a little kid? You probably didn't have a compass with you, but you looked around for something you recognized. Then you saw a familiar landmark—like a church, school, or store—and you knew how to get home from there. You got your bearings and got going.

People need direction in life too, and they certainly need to know the way to Heaven. They need a "true north," a landmark to show the right route.

Jesus said, "I am the way." In fact, he said he was the only way. To have eternal life in Heaven, we have to go through him. This means trusting in him as Savior and then following where he leads.

If we keep focused on Christ, we'll head in the right direction and never be lost.

to do ☑

MEMORIZE TODAY'S VERSE, JOHN 14:6. IT MAY BE SHORT AND SIMPLE, BUT IT'S THE MOST IMPORTANT TRUTH YOU'LL EVER KNOW.

Jesus told him, "**I am** the **way**, the **truth**, and the **life**. **No one** can come to the **Father** except **through** me."

[John 14:6]

also on this day

1963

The Great Train Robbery took place in Britain. A gang of 15 thieves stole 2.6 million pounds in bank notes (about 5 million dollars).

A. T. Marshall patented the refrigerator.

1899

On this day in 1678, American Indians sold the Bronx to Jonas Bronck for 400 beads.

Such a Deal!

When the Native Americans sold their land for 400 beads, they probably thought they were getting a good deal. A few hundred years later, we look back and say, "Are you kidding? Do you know how many billions of dollars that property in New York City is worth? They were robbed!"

Do you ever wonder why some people make bad deals? Perhaps they are fooled. Maybe they don't know the value of what they are trading away. Or perhaps they are just caught up in the emotion of the moment and don't think. Sometimes we want to scream at them, "What are you doing? That's a *bad* deal!"

Genesis 25 tells us of one of the all-time bad deals in history involving two brothers, Esau and Jacob. Esau, the older brother, stood to gain their father's inheritance—it was his "birthright." But one time, after going all day without much to eat, Esau returned from an unsuccessful hunting trip, and there was Jacob, stirring some stew he had made. Famished, weak, and feeling desperate, Esau begged his brother for food. That's when the deal was struck, with Jacob asking for Esau's birthright. And Esau traded his future in exchange for some stew.

"What a terrible transaction!" we exclaim. "A stupid mistake!" Yet people continue to follow Esau's example today. Kids will trade their future for something that seems to satisfy them right now, like drugs or alcohol. And because of their bad decisions, young people suffer awful consequences.

The lesson is clear. No matter how "hungry" you feel at the time, and regardless of the pressure from others, keep your eyes on God's plan and purpose for you. Don't trade your life for a bowl of soup.

to do ☑

READ THE WHOLE STORY OF ESAU AND JACOB IN GENESIS 25:19–34 AND 27:1–40. THEN WRITE "REMEMBER ESAU" ON A CARD. PUT IT IN A PLACE THAT YOU CAN SEE IT TO REMIND YOU EVERY DAY TO MAKE GOOD DECISIONS.

So **Esau swore** an **oath**, thereby **selling all** his **rights** as the **firstborn** to his younger **brother**. Then **Jacob** gave **Esau** some **bread** and **lentil stew**.

[Genesis 25:33, 34]

also on this day

1974
President Nixon resigned.

The *Columbia* returned to Boston Harbor after a three-year voyage. It was the first ship to carry the American flag around the world. **1790**

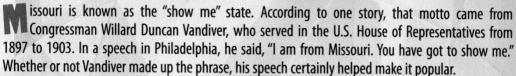

show me

On this day in 1821, Missouri became America's 24th state.

Missouri is known as the "show me" state. According to one story, that motto came from Congressman Willard Duncan Vandiver, who served in the U.S. House of Representatives from 1897 to 1903. In a speech in Philadelphia, he said, "I am from Missouri. You have got to show me." Whether or not Vandiver made up the phrase, his speech certainly helped make it popular.

The saying means that Missourians are not gullible—they can't be easily fooled or taken in. They need to see the proof to make sure. That's not a bad idea. We *should* think things through, check things out, make sure the salesperson is telling the truth before buying.

Thomas, one of the original 12 disciples, was that kind of guy—a "show me" disciple. In fact, he's known as "doubting Thomas" because of this tendency.

After Jesus was crucified, the disciples were together in a room hiding from the authorities. Jesus appeared to them alive. But Thomas wasn't there. Later, when told about Jesus' appearance, Thomas said, "I won't believe it unless I see the nail wounds in his hands, put my fingers into them, and place my hand into the wound in his side" (John 20:25). Thomas had to see to believe—he had to be shown. And when he saw Jesus, he believed.

The disciples didn't make up the story about the resurrection. They all saw Jesus with their own eyes. John would later write, "The one who existed from the beginning is the one we have heard and seen. We saw him with our own eyes and touched him with our own hands. He is Jesus Christ, the Word of life" (1 John 1:1).

God isn't afraid of our questions. He doesn't mind when we say, "show me." So keep asking, keep investigating, and keep trusting.

> Then [Jesus] said to Thomas, "Put your finger here and see my hands. Put your hand into the wound in my side. Don't be faithless any longer. Believe!" [John 20:27]

also on this day

1833
The village of Chicago (population, 250) was incorporated.

1846
The U.S. Congress chartered the Smithsonian Institution. The "Nation's Attic" was made possible by a donation of $500,000 from scientist Joseph Smithson.

to do ☑

THINK OF TWO OR THREE TOUGH QUESTIONS ABOUT GOD OR THE BIBLE. DON'T JUST MAKE THEM UP. THESE SHOULD BE REAL QUESTIONS YOU HAVE. ASK THEM OF A PARENT, AN OLDER BROTHER OR SISTER, OR A SUNDAY SCHOOL TEACHER.

The middle of August—the middle of the summer—usually means *hot*. And on a hot summer day, nothing refreshes more than a cold glass of Kool-Aid®, lemonade, or water. Knowing that, many kids set up stands in front of their homes. And for just a few nickels or dimes, a person can have a cup of refreshment. If you've ever had a lemonade stand like that, you probably didn't make much money, but you sure made some people happy.

When Jesus told his disciples, "I tell you the truth, anyone who gives you a cup of water in my name because you belong to Christ will certainly not lose his reward" (Mark 9:41, NIV), the disciples weren't thinking of setting up a refreshment stand on the front lawn. They knew that Jesus was emphasizing the importance of reaching out in love and kindness to those who are needy, especially his followers. Later Jesus said, "I was hungry, and you fed me. I was thirsty, and you gave me a drink. I was a stranger, and you invited me into your home. . . . I assure you, when you did it to one of the least of these my brothers and sisters, you were doing it to me!" (Matthew 25:35, 40).

The point is that Jesus wants us to help people who need help, offering food, drink, and shelter in his name. And we must go to the needy; we are not to sit and wait for them to come to our "stand." When we give a cup of water in his name, we are doing it for Jesus—wow!

Think of someone who could really use a refreshing word of encouragement, a helping hand, or a meal. What can you do to give that person aid?

Now that would be cool!

to do ☑

TALK TO YOUR PARENTS. BRAINSTORM WAYS YOUR FAMILY CAN WORK TOGETHER TO PREPARE A MEAL FOR SOMEONE IN YOUR NEIGHBORHOOD OR CHURCH WHO NEEDS IT.

kool

This is National Kool-Aid® Day.

also on this day

1860 The first silver mill in America (to be successful) began operation. It was located in Virginia City, Nevada.

In Bloomington, Minnesota, the Mall of America opened. At the time it was the largest shopping mall in the United States. **1992**

"And if you give even a cup of cold water to one of the least of my followers, you will surely be rewarded." [Matthew 10:42]

On this day in 1877, Thomas Edison invented the phonograph and made the first sound recording.

True Tunes

What's your favorite kind of music? rock? rap? country ("I've Been So Lonesome in the Saddle Since My Horse Died")? contemporary Christian?

When do you usually listen to your favorite music? In the car? Over head phones? on the CD player in your room? all of the above?

When Thomas Edison invented the phonograph (later called a "record player"—your parents probably had one), he never dreamed what would follow—records, cassette tapes, CDs, music videos, Internet, MP3s. It's amazing how much music has become part of our lives. We even hear tunes in elevators, stores, restaurants, and at athletic events.

Music touches our emotions, affecting our moods. Think of the songs played at someone's party or before a professional basketball game— exciting and upbeat. Compare that to what you would hear at a funeral— somber and reflective. And, of course, we have rap, protest songs, stirring marches, and all those mushy love songs.

Some tunes will always be connected to certain important events. A song can remind you of a neat vacation, a celebration, or a holiday. Hearing it brings back memories.

In worship services, music is used to set the mood, to stir our emotions, to proclaim great truths, and to praise God. Today's verse encourages God's people to "break out in praise and sing for joy." The verses that follow mention using musical instruments to bring glory to God.

Throughout Scripture you'll find other encouragements to express ourselves with music. These days, we can do that in so many ways, and we have a ton of outstanding Christian artists and songs.

So don't hold back—shout to the Lord!

to do ☑

IF YOU HAVEN'T DONE THIS LATELY, PULL OUT SEVERAL OF YOUR FAVORITE WORSHIP AND PRAISE CDS. LIE ON YOUR BED AND LISTEN TO THEM, SOAKING IN THE GREAT MUSIC AND TRUTHS CONVEYED.

Shout to the **LORD**, all the **earth**; **break** out in **praise** and **sing** for **joy**!

[Psalm 98:4]

also on this day

Disinfectant was used for the first time during surgery by Joseph Lister. ✹ **1865**

✹ **1994**
Major league baseball players went on strike rather than allow team owners to limit their salaries. The strike lasted for 232 days. As a result, the World Series was not played for the first time in 90 years, and interest in baseball went way down for a while.

chaos?

On this day in 1907, the first taxicab traveled the streets of New York City.

New York City's cabs have become legendary. Drivers are known to weave almost recklessly around other cars to deliver their passengers quickly to their destinations. And thousands of taxis fill the city's streets every day.

Imagine climbing in a cab. Suddenly you are rushing through traffic. With the car swerving, horn honking, and tires squealing, you feel unsafe and out of control in chaos and confusion.

But change the scene—you're out of the cab and on the observation deck of the Empire State Building, one of the tallest buildings in New York. The sky is clear, and the sun is shining, and you look down on the traffic below. The streets are packed as usual with cars, and you see all the yellow taxicabs mixed in the traffic. Instead of chaos and confusion, however, everything looks neat and orderly. The cars stop at the red lights and move ahead on green. You don't hear the horns and tires, and the pedestrians seem safe and unconcerned about the cars moving past them.

What a difference!

Sometimes life can seem confusing and terrifying. We can't see where we're going—we certainly don't know the future. And we seem to be pressed in on all sides by problems and concerns.

But if we could change the scene and look at our lives from God's point of view—well above the action—we would see order and purpose.

In today's Bible passage, King David looks at life from God's perspective, and he loves it! Knowing that God could see everything and was totally in control, David could have hope and joy.

How about you? Don't get depressed when life seems chaotic. Trust your mighty God and hope.

to do ☑

TAKE A SHORT FIELD TRIP TO A TALL BUILDING. IF YOU CAN. GO TO THE TOP FLOOR AND LOOK DOWN AND AROUND. NOTE THE DIFFERENCE THAT A POINT OF VIEW MAKES. THEN THANK GOD THAT HE SEES EVERYTHING THAT HAPPENS IN YOUR LIFE AND THAT HE IS IN CONTROL.

You chart the path ahead of me and tell me where to stop and rest. Every moment you know where I am. You know what I am going to say even before I say it, LORD. You both precede and follow me. You place your hand of blessing on my head. Such knowledge is too wonderful for me, too great for me to know! [Psalm 139:3-6]

also on this day 1860

Annie Oakley, sharp-shooter and star of Buffalo Bill's Wild West Show, was born.

This is International Left Hander's Day.

The American flag was raised for the first time in Los Angeles, California.

1846

C an you imagine a building project lasting 632 years? For example, what if your family had hired a company to build an addition to your house and it took that long—you'd get pretty tired waiting. And you'd wonder what was wrong with that contractor!

On the other hand, with projects that we know will take many years to finish, we're a lot more patient. In fact, knowing that progress is being made, even a little, gives us hope.

Take a baby, for example. We don't expect a newborn to get up off the delivery table, walk to the closet, throw on clothes and a coat, and then drive home. We know that the baby needs to be a *baby* for a while and that, with the right food and care, the baby will grow and mature. Then, eventually, after a few years he or she will be able to get dressed, eat solid food, read, shoot hoops, use a TV remote, drive a car, and clean up his or her room (maybe that's asking too much). You get the point.

Spiritual growth works the same way. We start as spiritual babies when we give ourselves to Christ. But then something wonderful happens—we begin to grow. You see, the Holy Spirit starts changing us on the inside, helping us mature in our understanding of who God is and who we are in relation to him.

Just like physical growth, spiritual growth happens gradually—not all at once. Sometimes we wonder if we're growing at all. But today's verse assures us that we are. That's because *God* is doing the work.

Knowing that should give us hope . . . and joy!

And I am sure that God, who began the good work within you, will continue his work until it is finally finished on that day when Christ Jesus comes back again. [Philippians 1:6]

On this day in 1880, the Cologne Cathedral in Cologne, Germany, was completed after 632 years of rebuilding.

to do ☑

FIND A FAMILY PHOTO ALBUM AND CHECK OUT PICTURES OF YOURSELF AS A BABY, A TODDLER, AND LITTLE KID. COMPARED TO HOW YOU ARE TODAY, YOU'VE REALLY GROWN, RIGHT? THEN THINK OF HOW YOU'VE GROWN SPIRITUALLY (WHEN YOU GAVE YOUR LIFE TO CHRIST, WHEN YOU BEGAN READING THE BIBLE FOR YOURSELF, WHEN YOU STARTED PARTICIPATING IN WORSHIP). THANK GOD FOR HIS WORK IN YOU.

also on this day

1936 The first basketball competition was held at the Olympic Games in Berlin, Germany.

The Oregon Territory was established. 1848

under construction

Today is National Relaxation Day.

Relax

Relax. Take it easy. Chill out. "That's easy to say," you respond, "but I have things to do, places to go, and people to meet. I'm just too busy for any downtime."

Most people seem to live that way these days. We pack our schedules with activities and events from morning to night: music lessons, sports practices, parties, classes . . . and every break is filled with phone calls, Internet, and homework. We get up early in the morning and go to bed late at night—even in August, during summer vacation.

But rest and relaxation are important, giving us time to refresh our spirits, to recharge our batteries. God made us that way. In fact, he even included rest in the Ten Commandments. Remember the one about the Sabbath? Check out today's verse. One day in seven was to be set aside for worship and rest. That's why we have a day every week when we go to Sunday school and church. But observing a Sabbath should involve more than that. It should actually be a day of rest, a day when we break out of our regular routine and reflect on God. For some people, that day is more packed and crazy than any other—and they miss the point.

Our weekly rest should be a time for changing the routine and doing activities that refresh us, not tire us out. This means we should have our chores done beforehand and not wait till the last second. And watching TV doesn't count as resting. If you don't do so the other days of the week, the Sabbath provides a good opportunity for doing something with the family, reading the Bible or another uplifting book, taking a long walk, writing letters, and spending time thinking and praying.

At the end of your Sabbath day, you should feel recharged and ready to face the week. Every week you need a National Relaxation Day.

to do ☑

TRY IT. THIS NEXT SUNDAY, SPEND THE WHOLE DAY IN WORSHIP AND REST.

But the seventh day is a day of rest dedicated to the LORD your God. On that day no one in your household may do any kind of work. This includes you, your sons and daughters, your male and female servants, your livestock, and any foreigners living among you. [Exodus 20:10]

also on this day

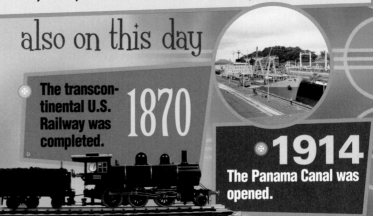

The transcontinental U.S. Railway was completed. **1870**

1914
The Panama Canal was opened.

good as gold

On this day in 1896, gold was discovered in Canada's Yukon Territory.

Thar's gold in them thar hills!" That shout, or one similar, repeated in countless cowboy films, signaled the "gold rush" to California, when thousands of people moved west to seek their fortunes.

Canada also had a gold rush. Within the year after its discovery in the Yukon Territory, more than 30,000 people rushed to the area to look for gold. They searched high and low, digging mines, panning in rivers and streams, and even scraping with their bare hands. The drive for instant wealth became consuming for many—they had caught "gold fever."

Gold remains one of the world's most precious metals. We refer to gold when speaking of almost anything of great value. We might say, for example, "His word is gold" or "It's good as gold," and we give gold medals to Olympic winners and gold records to best-selling artists.

Interestingly, the Bible refers often to gold—315 times, to be exact. Usually, of course, the reference is to the precious metal. Many times, however, gold is used in a comparison, with God saying that his Word or his people are *more precious* than gold or anything like it.

Refining is the process by which gold is purified and all the impurities are burned away. In today's passage, Peter says that believers will be refined—tested, like gold, by the fires of pressure and persecution. Strong faith helps us come through those trials strong and pure.

We can be tested by others pressuring us to do something wrong or to not stand up for what is right. Tests can involve people making fun of us because of our faith. We can also be tested by temptations. But if our faith is truly "gold," we will come through the trials even stronger than before.

So how are you doing in this purification process? Be golden!

These trials are only to test your faith, to show that it is strong and pure. It is being tested as fire tests and purifies gold—and your faith is far more precious to God than mere gold. [1 Peter 1:7]

also on this day

1858
A telegraphed message from Britain's Queen Victoria to U.S. President Buchanan was transmitted over the recently laid trans-Atlantic cable.

1960
Joseph Kittinger set the free fall world record when he fell more than 16 miles (about 84,000 feet) before opening his parachute over New Mexico.

to do ☑

READ THE FOLLOWING VERSES CONCERNING "GOLD" AND "PURIFYING": PSALM 19:9, 10; PSALM 119:127; MARK 9:49; 2 TIMOTHY 2:20, 21; JAMES 5:1–3; 1 PETER 1:18.

pretenders

On this day in 1939, the movie *Wizard of Oz* opened.

You've probably seen the classic film *Wizard of Oz* several times.

Remember the story? Dorothy lives on a farm in Kansas until a tornado picks up her house and deposits it in the land of Oz. Wishing to return home, Dorothy begins to travel to the city of Oz where a great wizard lives. Along the way she meets a Scarecrow who needs a brain, a Tin Man who wants a heart, and a Cowardly Lion who desperately needs courage. They all hope the Wizard of Oz will help them before the Wicked Witch of the West catches them.

And remember what happens when they finally get in to see the wizard? What a shock! The great and mighty Oz turns out to be a frightened little man hiding behind a curtain and using a microphone to amplify his voice. He has no power or authority at all—he is a pretender.

You probably won't ever meet a Tin Man, Scarecrow, and Lion, and hopefully you'll never experience a tornado. But you certainly *will* encounter "pretenders"—people who make grand claims about having inside knowledge and truth that they really don't.

Don't be fooled.

The Bible warns us to watch out for false teachers and to reject their lies. The apostle Paul told the leaders of the church at Ephesus: "I know full well that false teachers, like vicious wolves, will come in among you after I leave, not sparing the flock" (Acts 20:29).

Our source of truth is the Bible, God's Word. So be sure to check the messages you hear with Scripture. Just because someone looks good, sounds good, and has a magnetic personality doesn't mean that he or she is telling God's truth. Look behind the curtain.

to do ☑

CHECK OUT 1 JOHN 2:21, 22 AND 4:1, 2.

When we tell you this, we do not use words of human wisdom. We speak words given to us by the Spirit, using the Spirit's words to explain spiritual truths.

[1 Corinthians 2:13]

also on this day

1790

The capital city of the United States became Philadelphia instead of New York City.

A hot air balloon was used to carry mail for the first time. John Wise left Lafayette, Indiana, for New York City with 100 letters, but he had to land after only 27 miles.

1859

The Visited Planet

On this day in 1966, the first pictures of the Earth taken from moon orbit were sent back to the United States.

For centuries people have gazed on the moon and thought about what it must be like on that cold, pockmarked sphere. Eventually we found out through NASA's Apollo program, with moon orbits and photos sent back to Earth. And on July 20, 1969, Neil Armstrong stepped out of the capsule and onto its surface.

Now imagine that *you* are orbiting the moon, or even standing on it, and looking back to Earth. What do you see? What are you thinking? Most astronauts said that from the moon, Earth looked beautiful—but very small.

Standing on Earth and looking up we can feel pretty big and important. In reality, planet Earth is tiny compared to other planets in our solar system, and it's a mere speck in the universe.

Several years ago a man named J. B. Phillips wrote a short story titled, "The Visited Planet." In it several angels in Heaven discuss the fact that God chose Earth, our tiny and insignificant planet, for his home. They are amazed that Jesus came to Earth, born as a human baby, to be one of us. Like our astronauts, only much further out, they were looking at the world. "Why would the Father choose that place and those creatures?" they wonder.

Good question. But aren't you glad he did? Because we live on the "visited planet," because Jesus became one of us and lived and died for us, we can have eternal life. Then one day we will rise higher than any space explorers have ever gone and meet him face to face in Heaven. Wow!

to do ☑

ON A CLEAR NIGHT, GO OUTSIDE AND LOOK UP AT THE MOON AND STARS. TAKE A GOOD LOOK AT THE MOON AND IMAGINE WHAT IT WOULD BE LIKE TO STAND UP THERE AND TO LOOK BACK AT EARTH. NEXT, COUNT THE STARS. THEN SPEND A COUPLE OF MINUTES THANKING GOD FOR SENDING JESUS TO EARTH AND FOR LOVING YOU.

When I look at the
   night sky and see
   the work of your
   fingers—
the moon and the
   stars you have set
   in place—
what are mortals that
   you should think
   of us,
mere humans that you
   should care for us?
[Psalm 8:3, 4]

also on this day

Virginia Dare became the first child to be born on American soil of English parents. **1587**

•1774
Meriwether Lewis, U.S. explorer, was born. He was the leader of the Lewis and Clark Expedition.

"It'll Never Fly?"

On this day in 1871, Orville Wright was born.

"It'll Never Fly?"

The Wright brothers were right!

You've heard of Orville and Wilbur, right? They were the first people to successfully fly and control an aircraft with a motor. In other words, they invented the airplane.

Ever since the first human beings watched birds flap, rise, glide, and soar, they have yearned to fly. And through the years, many tried in some very unusual ways, usually involving homemade wings strapped to their backs. Those attempts ended in failure, often in disaster. So when Orville and Wilbur mentioned their desire to fly, their friends probably thought, "Yeah right! Like that'll ever happen!" And then, when the brothers built the airplane, the critics must have said, "It'll never fly!"

But it did, and now we have props and jets and supersonics and ultra-lights and rocket ships and space shuttles. Think of the impact that the Wright brothers made on the world.

Maybe you have a dream. It could be an invention, but it might be a vision of your future, career, or calling. Perhaps it's a personal goal or even an idea for changing society. And maybe you've shared your dream with others who have put it down with comments like, "It'll never fly!"

Don't get discouraged and don't give up. God wants us to think big for him. Way back in 1792, William Carey, a great missionary pioneer, said, "Expect great things from God; attempt great things for God." What a *great* philosophy of life!

So keep your vision, trust God, and work hard to make it happen. And maybe some day you'll be famous like the Wrights, and we'll write about you—right?

Where there is no vision, the people perish. [Proverbs 29:18, KJV]

to do ☑

ON A PIECE OF PAPER, FINISH THESE SENTENCES: "IF I COULD BE ANYTHING, I WOULD _____." "IF I COULD DO ANYTHING, I WOULD _____." "IF I COULD CHANGE ANYTHING, I WOULD _____." ASK GOD TO SHOW YOU STEPS TO TAKE TO FULFILL THOSE DREAMS.

also on this day

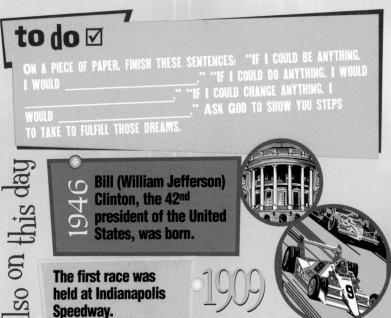

1946 Bill (William Jefferson) Clinton, the 42nd president of the United States, was born.

The first race was held at Indianapolis Speedway. 1909

On this day in 1833, Benjamin Harrison, the 23rd president of the United States, was born.

misty

Be honest—before reading the previous sentence, had you ever heard of Benjamin Harrison? If so, it's probably just a vague memory of something said in a history class. Yet Benjamin Harrison was President of the United States for four years (1889–1893). And he was considered a good president, with a solid foreign policy and no scandals.

This provides a great illustration and learning opportunity.

Check out the verse for today. James is saying that we should realize how quickly time passes and how short our lives really are. Like the morning fog, or as one translation puts it, "a mist," life is fragile and passes quickly.

That's hard to understand when we're young, when a year seems like forever. But the older we get, the faster time flies and the years zoom past us. Ask your grandparents.

When Benjamin Harrison won the presidential election, he reached one of the highest points that any American can ever hope for. Yet, just 115 years later, very few people remember him or anything about his life or administration. How quickly we forget. Think about today's newsmakers—in a year or two we won't remember them.

Life is short, no matter how long we live. There's an old saying that you may have seen on a wall plaque: "Only one life, it will soon be past. Only what's done for Christ will last." We should spend our lives living for God and doing what he wants and not worrying so much about being a big deal in the world.

After all, "this world is fading away, along with everything it craves. But if you do the will of God, you will live forever" (1 John 2:17).

to do ☑

THINK BACK OVER THE LAST YEAR. THINK ABOUT HOW THINGS THAT ONCE SEEMED IMPORTANT HAVE FADED IN TIME. ASK GOD TO HELP YOU CONCENTRATE ON THINGS THAT HAVE ETERNAL VALUE.

How do you **know** what will happen **tomorrow**? For your **life** is like the morning **fog**— it's here a **little** while, then it's **gone**. [James 4:14]

also on this day

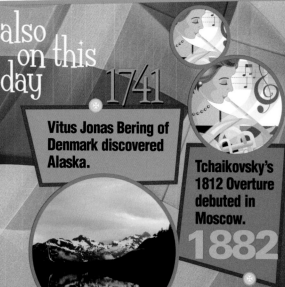

1741
Vitus Jonas Bering of Denmark discovered Alaska.

Tchaikovsky's 1812 Overture debuted in Moscow.
1882

a test of honesty

On this day in 1971, 16-year-old Laura Baugh won the United States Women's Amateur Golf tournament.

When Laura Baugh won, she was the youngest winner in the history of the tournament. Golf is a crazy sport, isn't it? Some people play all their lives, taking lessons, practicing diligently, and buying all the best equipment, but never get very good. Yet along comes someone like Laura who wins a major tournament as a teenager.

Golf, like almost no other sport, tests a person's honesty. That's because golfers (except in big tournaments) keep their own scores. Typically, after everyone putts out at a hole, the person with the scorecard will ask, "What did you get?" And that's the test. Will the golfer honestly admit that he or she shot a 7? Or will he or she conveniently forget a swing and say 6? And what about when a golfer is standing behind some trees, swings hard, and moves the ball ahead just a couple feet. None of his or her fellow golfers sees the swing—nobody knows! So does he or she count that swing? That's the test.

God values honesty. Many times in the Bible we read statements like, "The godly are directed by their honesty" (Proverbs 11:5), and "LORD, you are searching for honesty" (Jeremiah 5:3). So it's no wonder that David asked God to lead him "along the path of honesty."

You may not play golf, but your honesty can be tested in other ways. Someone may, for example, give you too much change after a purchase. Do you give it back? Or you may be caught in doing something wrong. Do you admit your guilt? Or perhaps you find something valuable in the park. Do you try to find the owner?

Make the right choice. Walk along the path of honesty.

also on this day

1912
Arthur R. Eldred became the first American boy to become an Eagle Scout, the highest rank in the Boy Scouts of America.

1959
Hawaii became America's 50th state.

1984
Victoria Roche, a reserve outfielder, became the first girl ever to compete in a Little League World Series game.

> Teach me how to live, O LORD.
> Lead me along the path of honesty.
>
> [Psalm 27:11]

to do ☑

FOR THE NEXT FEW DAYS, BE ALERT FOR TESTS OF YOUR HONESTY. EVERY TIME YOU NOTICE ONE, SAY THIS BRIEF PRAYER: "THANK YOU, GOD, FOR THIS TEST. IT'S AN OPPORTUNITY TO CHOOSE TO DO RIGHT."

Widely regarded as the most famous painting in history, the *Mona Lisa* was painted by Leonardo da Vinci in 1503 to 1506 in Florence, Italy. Featuring the woman with the mysterious smile, the painting is 20 7/8 inches by 30 inches, oil on poplar wood, and resides in The Louvre Museum in Paris, France (unless it has been stolen again). Its value is considered to be *priceless*. No wonder people get upset when the *Mona Lisa* is stolen!

Have you ever wondered why some art is considered valuable while other art is not? What gives something value? The oil, poplar wood, and paint that make up *Mona Lisa* didn't cost much—so the painting is worth much more than the artist's materials and tools. Certainly the quality of the art and the identity of the artist have a lot to do with its price.

Do you know that *you* are priceless too? You are *much* more valuable than the chemicals and other ingredients found in your body. You have value *because of your creator*. That's right. The Bible tells us that God created human beings (including you) in his image (Genesis 1:26, 27), that he formed you and watched you before you were born (Psalm 139:13-16), and he continues to work in you, making you more and more like his Son (Romans 8:29).

Get the point? You are priceless—certainly much more valuable than any work of art, even the *Mona Lisa*. It's as though God has your picture on his refrigerator—he's so proud of you.

So smile, be confident, and celebrate! You're something else!

"Look at the birds. They don't need to plant or harvest or put food in barns because your heavenly Father feeds them. And you are far more valuable to him than they are." [Matthew 6:26]

On this day in 1911, Leonardo da Vinci's **Mona Lisa** was stolen from the Louvre Museum in Paris.

to do ☑

TODAY, LOOK FOR BIRDS. EVERY TIME YOU SEE ONE, REMEMBER GOD'S LOVE AND YOUR VALUE . . . AND THANK HIM.

also on this day

1902
In Hartford, Connecticut, President Theodore Roosevelt became the first president of the United States to ride in an automobile.

The Victor Talking Machine Company began to manufacture the Victrola record player. *1906*

priceless!

Spitballs and Pitfalls

On this day in 1982, Gaylord Perry of the Seattle Mariners was ejected from a game for throwing an illegal spitball.

A spitball is an illegal pitch in baseball. When throwing this pitch, the pitcher will put some kind of substance like spit, petroleum jelly, or something similar, on the ball. This causes the ball to move, making it difficult for a batter to hit.

For many years, spitballs were permitted in baseball's major leagues. But throwing this pitch was outlawed in 1920. Many pitchers still used the illegal pitch, however, working hard to hide their actions. Every now and then, like on this day in 1982, an umpire will catch a pitcher messing with the ball and toss him out of the game.

In baseball and in other sports, players cheat because they want to win and will do most anything to gain the victory. They know cheating is wrong, but they do it anyway, hoping to not get caught. In baseball, a player is permitted to "steal," as in steal a base. In basketball, it's OK, and even encouraged, to "fake" (pretend to do one thing but then do something else). Other games and sports have actions that are wrong *outside the game* but are all right inside the game. But doing something that is not allowed *inside the game*, even if it wouldn't be wrong in the rest of life, is cheating. It's wrong, even if you don't get caught. Sometimes cheaters win games, but actually they're losers.

The heat of competition can make cheating very tempting, especially when others do it and when you think you can get away with it. Don't give in. Instead, be a person who plays the game honestly and fairly, and within the rules. You will be respected, and you will honor God. And if you happen to lose the game, you're still a winner.

to do ☑

IN YOUR NEXT GAME, EVEN IF IT'S JUST IN THE PARK, AT SUMMER CAMP, OR IN YOUR HOME, DETERMINE TO PLAY WITHIN THE RULES.

The LORD hates cheating, but he delights in honesty.

[Proverbs 11:1]

also on this day

1838 Mount Holyoke Female Seminary in South Hadley, Massachusetts, graduated its first class. It was one of the first colleges for women.

1913 Automobiles were legally allowed to enter Yosemite National Park, California, for the first time.

don't waffle

This is National Waffle Day.

A dictionary might define *waffle* as "a crisp cake of batter baked in a waffle iron." You're probably very familiar with that type of waffle. Whether smothered in strawberries and whipped cream or just covered with butter and syrup, a waffle can be a delicious treat. The point of having National Waffle Day is to get people to eat more waffles.

But the word as a verb has another definition: "to avoid committing one's self, to speak both sides of an issue." We hear waffle used this way quite often during elections when candidates accuse each other of "waffling" or "flip-flopping." They certainly aren't talking about eating crisp cakes of batter, but about not taking a stand on the issues.

Waffling isn't limited to politicians. Everyone is susceptible—parents, kids, lawyers, doctors, sales people, police officers, mechanics—even Christians. Someone might ask, for example, "What do you think about Jesus?" A *waffle* answer would sound something like this: "Well, uh, I don't know, uh, I mean I think he is God but, you know, people have a lot of different ideas. . . . I guess I could go either way. . . ."

When it comes to our faith, the Bible tells us to be confident and committed to the truth. Otherwise, we will "waver back and forth" (*waffle*) in everything we do.

When asked about Jesus, we should answer, "He is God and man. He came to earth, lived a perfect life, died on the cross, and rose from the dead. He lives today and is my Savior. I trust in him." No waffling there!

So on this National Waffle Day, go ahead and eat one . . . but don't *be* one.

A doubtful mind is as unsettled as a wave of the sea that is driven and tossed by the wind. People like that should not expect to receive anything from the Lord. They can't make up their minds. They waver back and forth in everything they do. [James 1:6, 8]

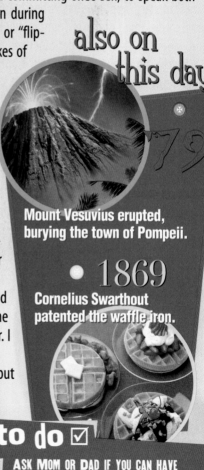

also on this day

'79

Mount Vesuvius erupted, burying the town of Pompeii.

1869

Cornelius Swarthout patented the waffle iron.

to do ☑

ASK MOM OR DAD IF YOU CAN HAVE WAFFLES FOR BREAKFAST SOMETIME THIS WEEK. THEN, AS YOU EAT, TELL YOUR FAMILY ABOUT THE OTHER KIND OF WAFFLING.

I mean it!

This is National Kiss-and-Make Up Day.

The expression, "kiss and make up," usually means that two people who have been arguing have made peace with each other. The argument is over. They're friends again.

As a dispute or conflict is resolved, the two people don't actually have to kiss, although that often happens with a husband and wife. Often the two will shake hands, pat each other on the back, hug, or just say, "Hey, that's OK." The important thing is that they both *mean* it when they admit their wrongs and ask for forgiveness.

As you know, people can pretend to feel bad about something they've done or said. They may even state, "I'm sorry for doing that," when they really mean, "I'm sorry I got caught." Some people are so phony that they can smile and be all friendly, when inside they are very angry and upset. They may even say, "Don't worry about it. It's OK. Let's get together," but they're really thinking, "I never want to see you again!"

Several times over the past few months, we've discussed honesty. Today's topic is another way to be honest—in our relationships. When we say something to someone, especially when we "kiss and make up," we need to be sincere. Otherwise we shouldn't say it. We shouldn't pretend to be sorry when we're not. Instead, we should work to resolve the conflict so we really can heal the relationship.

Today's verse talks about "genuine affection." Notice the emphasis on *genuine*—this means being a true friend, not a phony one.

True friends don't always agree or get along—conflicts arise in any relationship. But true friends say what they mean and mean what they say to each other. They're honest with each other, not phony.

So look for sincere people to be your friends. And be a genuine friend to them.

to do ☑

JOT A QUICK NOTE TO A GOOD FRIEND, EXPRESSING YOUR SINCERE APPRECIATION FOR THE FRIENDSHIP. THEN MAIL IT.

also on this day

Ivan the Terrible, the first tsar of Russia, was born.

1530

This is National Children's Day.

Love each other with **genuine affection**, and take **delight** in **honoring** each other.

[Romans 12:10]

This is Women's Equality Day.

Many years ago in the United States (and even today in many countries), women didn't enjoy many of the rights that men had. They couldn't own property, vote, or have certain jobs. They were almost treated like property. Some couples were sad when their new baby turned out to be a girl. That's hard to believe, but it's true.

That's wrong, of course. Girls and women should have the same rights and opportunities as boys and men, including being paid the same amount for the same kind of work. Because of this, many people protested and worked hard to make the appropriate changes. And, eventually, laws and customs were changed.

Some people seem to think that equality means being the same. But that's not true. Men and women are equally valuable, but they're definitely different. The Bible makes this very clear. God created male and female—two distinctly different types of people. Both were special creations of God, made in his image, but they were different. We're still different.

We can see the obvious physical differences between men and women. Women can have babies and men can't. But through research scientists are finding even more fascinating differences between the genders—the way male and female brains work, for example. God built in differences that aren't easy to see, but are important, and help men and women to complement each other. One sex is not better than the other.

So celebrate the differences and the way God made you. And, while you're at it, respect the opposite sex—they're special to God too.

He created them male and female, and he blessed them and called them "human." [Genesis 5:2]

to do ☑

TAKE SOME TIME AND ANALYZE YOUR MOM AND DAD. WRITE DOWN HOW THEY ARE THE SAME AND HOW THEY'RE DIFFERENT. BE SURE TO NOTE HOW THEY THINK AND FEEL. THEN CONSIDER HOW YOU ARE BECOMING LIKE THEM. HOW DO YOU FEEL ABOUT THAT?

also on this day

1498 Michelangelo was commissioned to sculpt the *Pieta*, his famous statue showing Mary holding Jesus' body after the crucifixion.

The school board of St. Louis, Missouri, authorized the first public kindergarten in the United States. **1873**

equal but different

reach for the stars

On this day in 1984, President Ronald Reagan announced that the first citizen to go into space would be a teacher.

Everyone says that teachers are important. We even have National Teacher Day (May 7). But when President Reagan announced that the first citizen in space would be a teacher, he was showing the nation that teachers really are special.

Eventually, Christa McAuliffe was chosen. Then, tragically, she died when the Challenger exploded on take-off on January 28, 1986.

Not all teachers are like Christa McAuliffe, who was willing to risk her life on an exploration adventure. But all teachers are involved in a daily adventure as they help students explore nature, history, language, government, faith, mathematics, relationships, art, and many other fields of study.

While teachers are important, they may not always feel special. Some teachers feel that they are not paid enough for the work they do and that their students can treat them very poorly. Teachers may feel overworked and taken for granted. They may feel pressure from both the school administration and from the parents of their students.

Teachers aren't perfect, of course, and some teach better than others. But all teachers deserve respect and honor. We honor teachers by paying attention in class, by asking good questions, by having a positive attitude, and trying our best to learn, even when it's hard.

Think where you'd be without teachers and what you've learned in the past. And imagine all the great learning in your future—middle school, high school, college, and graduate school—and the talented teachers who'll guide you.

Thank God for your teachers. Honor them and, like Christa McAuliffe, reach for the stars.

"Oh, **why** didn't I **listen** to my **teachers**? **Why** didn't I pay **attention** to those who gave me **instruction**?"

[Proverbs 5:13]

also on this day

1886

The island volcano of Krakatoa in Indonesia erupted. It was heard over 3,000 miles away and was one of the biggest natural disasters ever.

1908

Lyndon B. Johnson, the 36th president of the United States, was born.

to do ☑

EVEN THOUGH YOU MAY NOT BE IN SCHOOL RIGHT NOW, MAKE A LIST OF YOUR CURRENT TEACHERS. BE SURE TO INCLUDE YOUR SUNDAY SCHOOL TEACHER, MUSIC TEACHER, COACH, AND OTHERS. THIS WEEK, THANK EACH ONE FOR DOING A GREAT JOB.

free at last!

On this day in 1963, Martin Luther King Jr. gave his famous "I Have a Dream" speech.

Martin Luther King Jr. stood on the steps at the Lincoln Memorial in Washington, D.C., and delivered this speech to more than 250,000 people. Dr. King had prepared a short talk and was about to sit down when gospel singer Mahalia Jackson called out, "Tell them about your dream, Martin! Tell them about the dream!" What followed was his amazing speech.

Dr. King spoke with passion and sincerity: "I have a dream that my four little children will one day live in a nation where they will not be judged by the color of their skin but by the content of their character. I have a *dream* today! . . . I have a dream that one day every valley shall be exalted, and every hill and mountain shall be made low, the rough places will be made plain, and the crooked places will be made straight, and the glory of the Lord shall be revealed and all flesh shall see it together. . . . And this will be the day, this will be the day when all of God's children will be able to sing with new meaning, 'My country 'tis of thee, sweet land of liberty, of thee I sing. Land where my fathers died, land of the Pilgrim's pride, from every mountainside, let freedom ring!' And if America is to be a great nation, this must become true."

He ended with this stirring proclamation: "And when this happens, when we allow freedom to ring, when we let it ring from every village and every hamlet, from every state and every city, we will be able to speed up that day when *all* of God's children, black men and white men, Jews and Gentiles, Protestants and Catholics, will be able to join hands and sing in the words of the old Negro spiritual, 'Free at last, free at last. Thank *God* Almighty, we are free at last.'"

Because of Christ, we will be "free at last." Thank God!

to do ☑

GO ON THE INTERNET AND SEARCH FOR THIS FAMOUS SPEECH. YOU'LL FIND IT UNDER "I HAVE A DREAM." THEN LISTEN TO OR READ THE WHOLE SPEECH.

Now that we are **saved**, we **eagerly** look forward to this **freedom**. For if you **already** have something, you **don't** need to **hope** for it. [Romans 8:24]

also on this day 1830

The Tom Thumb was demonstrated in Baltimore, Maryland. It was the first passenger train to be built in America.

Mark Spitz won the first of his seven gold medals at the Summer Olympics in Munich, Germany.

1972

1907 Two teenagers started the American Messenger Company, which later became UPS.

A Spoonful of Sugar

On this day in 1964, the movie Mary Poppins began showing in American theaters.

You've probably seen the movie *Mary Poppins*. If not, you should—it's great fun. The story revolves around a new nanny who arrives to take care of a banker's children. She helps the children magically explore the world around them, and at the same time, she brings the family closer to each other.

In one memorable scene, Mary gets the children to do an unpleasant task by singing, "A Spoonful of Sugar Helps the Medicine Go Down." Her point is that difficult jobs can be made easier when we approach them with a good attitude—the "spoonful of sugar."

It's true, right? Think about the difference an attitude makes. If you're in a bad mood, *everything* is a pain. No matter what we're asked to do, we gripe, complain, whine, and mope. Then the job seems to be twice as difficult and take twice as long as it should.

In contrast, when we're "up," feeling good about life, Mom, Dad, coach, teacher, or even a sibling can ask us to do something, and we'll get right on it—no problem! We have a good feeling of accomplishment when we're finished.

And here's the great part—we can *choose* our attitudes. Even in the worst circumstances, we can choose to look on the bright side, to have a positive spirit. That's like adding our "spoonful of sugar" to the bad-tasting "medicine" in life.

So are you positive? Make that choice.

to do ☑

FOR THE NEXT 24 HOURS, CHOOSE A POSITIVE ATTITUDE, NO MATTER WHAT HAPPENS OR WHAT YOU'RE ASKED TO DO.

Your **attitude** should be the **same** that **Christ Jesus** had.

[Philippians 2:5]

also on this day

1892 Pop (Billy) Shriver of the Chicago Cubs caught a ball that was dropped from the top of the Washington Monument in Washington, D.C.

◆1886 In New York City, Chinese Ambassador Li Hung-chang's chef invented chop suey.

For more than 23 years, David Letterman has hosted his late night television talk show, first on NBC (1982–1993) and then on CBS. Known for his off-the-wall humor, a regular feature has been "stupid human tricks." That's where individuals will display their unique talents or abilities. The tricks aren't really stupid—they're just strange and different, like the rest of the show.

The fact is, all of us humans do "stupid tricks" every day. We take actions and make choices that take us in the wrong direction. Sometimes when we make bad choices, our actions hurt ourselves and others. We may give in to temptation, waste time and money, or disobey our parents . . . not too smart.

The worst trick, however, is to put anyone or anything in God's place in our lives. The Bible calls this idolatry. An idol can be almost anything, even things that aren't usually seen as bad. If it becomes more important to us than God, taking his place, then it's an idol. An idol can be a hobby or sport, a talent or an interest, a person or relationship, a possession or money.

So think about it—do you have any idols? Keep God first in your life. Don't pull a "stupid human trick."

The wisest of people who worship idols are stupid and foolish. The things they worship are made of wood! [Jeremiah 10:8]

to do ☑

TAKE A SHEET OF SCRATCH PAPER AND LIST EVERYTHING IN YOUR LIFE THAT HAS THE POSSIBILITY OF BECOMING AN IDOL. THEN PRAY ABOUT EACH ITEM ON THE LIST, GIVING IT TO GOD.

also on this day

William Penn sailed from England and later established the colony of Pennsylvania in America. **1682**

Thurgood Marshall was confirmed by the Senate as a Supreme Court justice. Marshall was the first black justice to sit on the Supreme Court. **1965**

The space shuttle Discovery lifted off for the first time. 1984

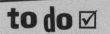

stupid human tricks

On this day in 1993, the Late Show with David Letterman debuted on CBS.

fame!

On this day in 1995, the Rock and Roll Hall of Fame and Museum opened in Cleveland, Ohio.

Having fame means being famous, being known by a lot of people. Some individuals are well-known, not for the good they do, but for their *bad* actions. We call them infamous. Criminals, terrorists, tyrants, and other terrible characters fall in that category.

Most of the time, when we talk about fame, we mean people who have achieved something significant and good. And in America we have carried this to an extreme. We now have halls of fame for rock-and-roll music, baseball, football, radio broadcasting, Italian Americans, and freshwater fishermen—just to name a few. And almost every week seems to feature some sort of special awards show. We certainly seem obsessed with fame.

Actually it starts when we're quite young, and we try hard to be popular in our school, neighborhood, town or even church. Looking back, we can think of how silly it all seems—why did we think being a big deal in elementary school was so important?

Fame at any level in this world really is *no big deal* and shouldn't be so important to us. Instead, we should be concerned with what God thinks of us, not people, and we should be concerned with spreading his fame.

Pharaoh was a big deal in Egypt and in the whole world of his day. But that meant nothing, zero, zilch, zip in the big picture. In fact, God told him (see today's verse) that he had only been allowed to have power and prestige so that *God's fame* would spread.

Here's the point: whether you're a big deal or little deal, famous or unknown, popular or not, what matters most is if you are working to spread God's fame. So what do people know about God from knowing you? Seek heavenly fame.

to do ☑

THINK OF THE CHRISTIANS WHO HAVE INFLUENCED YOU THE MOST (PARENTS, OTHER RELATIVES, SUNDAY SCHOOL TEACHERS, PASTORS). THEY MAY NOT BE FAMOUS IN THE WORLD'S EYES, BUT THEY'RE IN YOUR "HALL OF FAME." THANK GOD FOR INVESTING IN YOUR LIFE THROUGH THOSE OTHER BELIEVERS.

For the Scriptures say that God told Pharaoh, "I have appointed you for the very purpose of displaying my power in you, and so that my fame might spread throughout the earth."

[Romans 9:17]

also on this day

1964
California officially became the most populated state in America.

1887
The kinetoscope was patented by Thomas Edison. The device was used to produce moving pictures.

Titanic became the first movie in North America to earn more than $600 million. **1998**

work hard!

Labor Day is celebrated on the first Monday in September.

Labor Day was created by the labor movement to honor the achievements of American workers. It is a yearly tribute to the contributions workers have made to the strength, prosperity, and well-being of our nation.

The very first Labor Day was celebrated on Tuesday, September 5, 1882, in New York City. Two years later, the first Monday in September was selected as the holiday, and labor officials in New York City urged labor organizations in other cities to follow New York's example and celebrate a "workingman's holiday" on that date.

Finally, in 1894 (an election year), President Grover Cleveland signed into law a bill that would officially make Labor Day a national holiday. He had hoped that in doing so he would gain the support of workers for his reelection. It didn't work, and he lost.

While the holiday has its roots in the political movement of workers, today the holiday is more a tribute to summer's last long weekend. Still, honoring work and those who do it is a good thing to do, and it has a biblical basis. In the Bible we learn that God wants his people to pay workers fairly and promptly (Deuteronomy 24:14, 15 and Malachi 3:5). Hard work is encouraged (Ecclesiastes 5:12), and laziness is criticized (Proverbs 10:4; 10:26; 12:24). And Paul urged believers to follow his example and work hard so that they would not be a burden to anyone (1 Thessalonians 2:9).

In addition, God also honors all those who work for him. Paul reminds us in 1 Corinthians 15:58 that our work is important. Whatever work we do for God—whether it's helping out with Sunday school or volunteering to collect food for the needy—will have eternal results.

So what are you waiting for? Get to work!

So, my dear brothers and sisters, be strong and steady, always enthusiastic about the Lord's work, for you know that nothing you do for the Lord is ever useless.

[1 Corinthians 15:58]

also on this day

Today is Emma M. Nutt Day in honor of the first telephone operator.

1972 America's Bobby Fischer beat Russia's Boris Spassky to become the world chess champion. The chess match took place in Reykjavik, Iceland.

to do ☑

WRITE A NOTE TO ONE OR MORE OF THE WORKERS IN YOUR LIFE—A TEACHER, PASTOR, POLICE OFFICER, DOCTOR—AND THANK THEM FOR THE WORK THEY DO TO HELP MAKE YOUR LIFE BETTER.

In 1985, it was announced that the *Titanic* had been found 560 miles off the Newfoundland coast. It had been missing for 73 years.

Now That's Worth It!

Even though it had been missing for more than 73 years, the search for the *Titanic* had never stopped. The ill-fated luxury liner, billed as the safest ship ever built, left England on April 10, 1912. Her passengers were a mixture of the world's wealthiest along with immigrants seeking their fortune in America. Four days into her journey, she struck an iceberg, and less than three hours later, sank into the frigid waters of the North Atlantic Ocean.

What fascinated people about the tragedy then was that the ship represented the best in technology at the time. It took the very best of technology 73 years later to discover the *Titanic*'s final resting place. Teams of scientists from France and the United States joined efforts using state-of-the art sonar and video camera equipment to locate the ship. The efforts had begun in early 1985, but the first visual contact of the sunken ship did not occur until September 1.

Imagine the countless hours and thousands of dollars that went into finding that one lost ship. Even after it was discovered, researchers kept its exact location a secret for fear that treasure-seekers would try to find the ship and steal items from it.

What treasure do you seek? How long would you search for it? Jesus said that the most valuable treasure is the kingdom of Heaven. A person should be willing to give up everything to have it. In Matthew 13:45, 46, Jesus describes a pearl merchant who discovered the most valuable pearl imaginable. When he found it, the merchant sold everything he had to own that pearl.

That's how we should be when it comes to God's kingdom. Don't let anything distract or prevent you from seeking God's kingdom.

to do ☑

WHAT DOES IT MEAN TO SEEK GOD'S KINGDOM? WRITE DOWN THREE WAYS YOU CAN DO THAT TODAY.

"Again, the Kingdom of Heaven is like a pearl merchant on the lookout for choice pearls. When he discovered a pearl of great value, he sold everything he owned and bought it!" [Matthew 13:45, 46]

also on this day

1666
The Great Fire of London was started. Ten thousand buildings were destroyed, but only six people were killed.

The U.S. Treasury Department was established. **1789**

Out of all 50 states in America, there's one state that comedians seem to enjoy putting down more than any other—New Jersey. So many jokes have been made about the state that a day has been proclaimed "Be Nice to New Jersey Day." Whether it's the funny "Joisey" accent, the famous mosquitoes, the New Jersey Turnpike ("which exit do you live off of?"), or the number of toxic garbage dumps in the state, New Jersey gets a bad rap.

But did you know that two of the nation's oldest universities, Princeton and Rutgers, are located in New Jersey? President Grover Cleveland came from the state, as well as singers Frank Sinatra and Bruce Springsteen. The state ranks in the Top 10 in the nation in the number of manufacturing sites and in payroll. And its nickname is the Garden State.

So why do people like to pick on New Jersey so much? Maybe because it makes them feel better about the place they live knowing that there's a worse place to be. Or they like to think that they're somehow better people because they *don't* live in New Jersey.

Paul warned us about having an attitude like that. In Philippians 2:3, 4, Paul said followers of Christ need to think of others more highly than themselves. That means instead of thinking how great we are at soccer, we should applaud our teammates' efforts. Instead of thinking how smart we are, we should take note of the kid who excels at working with his hands or creating graphics on the computer. Our model should be Jesus who, even though he was God himself, came to earth as a helpless baby and lived his entire life serving others.

So the next time you meet someone from New Jersey, resist the urge to laugh. Instead say, "Hey, what a great state. Tell me about it!"

Don't be selfish; don't live to make a good impression on others. Be humble, thinking of others as better than yourself. Don't think only about your own affairs, but be interested in others, too, and what they are doing. [Philippians 2:3, 4]

to do ☑

SHOW SOMEONE, EITHER THROUGH WORDS OR YOUR ACTIONS, THAT YOU THINK HIGHLY OF THEM.

also on this day

1783 The Revolutionary War ended with the Treaty of Paris.

The first professional football game was played in Latrobe, Pennsylvania. The Latrobe YMCA defeated the Jeannette Athletic Club 12–0. **1895**

hey, you guys! be nice to us!

Today is National Be Nice to New Jersey Day.

american idols

In 2002, singer Kelly Clarkson was voted the first American Idol on the Fox TV series.

Since the show made its debut in 2002, *American Idol* has captured the attention of people throughout the country. Millions of viewers tune in each week to watch the talent show. They vote to determine which of the contestants will remain to sing another week. Eventually contestants are whittled down to a final pair—and in 2002 Kelly Clarkson won the honor of being the first American Idol by beating out Justin Guarini.

Clarkson went from a virtual unknown to an overnight household name. Soon after winning the contest, Clarkson not only received a check for $1 million, but she also signed a recording contract, appeared on numerous TV shows, and has produced several top-selling CDs. In addition, she has become the inspiration of millions of young singers who believe they have what it takes to become the next American Idol.

As *American Idol* entered its fourth season, America's obsession for this talent search remained strong. The *American Idol* Web site was the most-searched site on the Internet. As one entertainment watcher put it, "Americans worship the 'Idol.'"

Whoa! Idols in modern-day America? What's that about? Throughout the Bible, particularly in the Old Testament, God warned his people to stay away from idols—false gods that people made from stone, wood, or metal. But in reality, an idol is anything that takes our attention and our worship away from God. Your idol could be television, video games, sports, or even a person like an American Idol winner.

While none of these things are bad in and of themselves, when we spend too much time and energy devoted to that one thing, we are in danger of making that an idol in our lives.

Is there something in your life that's threatening to become an idol?

Do not put your **trust** in **idols** or make **gods** of **metal** for your-selves. **I**, the **Lord**, am your **God**.

[Leviticus 19:4]

also on this day

1781

Los Angeles was founded by Spanish settlers.

1888

George Eastman registered the name *Kodak* and patented his roll-film camera. The camera took 100 exposures per roll.

to do ☑

SURVEY YOUR FAMILY AND FRIENDS. ASK THEM TO NAME THREE IDOLS THAT COULD COME BETWEEN THEM AND GOD.

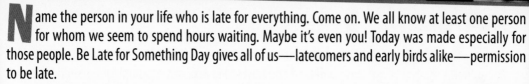

don't be late!

Today is Be Late for Something Day.

Name the person in your life who is late for everything. Come on. We all know at least one person for whom we seem to spend hours waiting. Maybe it's even you! Today was made especially for those people. Be Late for Something Day gives all of us—latecomers and early birds alike—permission to be late.

Now there are times when you don't mind being late—like when there's a family get-together of your least favorite relatives or the dentist appointment that you've been dreading. You don't mind being late for dinner when the menu includes brussel sprouts and liver. But you sure don't want to be late for dessert or going to your friend's house when you are going to try out the latest video game. And you probably don't want to be late for school—because too many tardies may land you in the principal's office!

Definitely you don't want to be late for God. Sometimes, especially when it comes to God, we feel we have all the time in the world. You think, "I'll start having a daily quiet time next month. I'm really busy with _____ (fill in the blank) right now." Or "I'll start a prayer journal next week when school settles down." Or even, "I don't have to start getting serious about God right now. I'm young! I'll think about him later."

It's true that right now is an exciting time for you. Many opportunities are available to you. It seems as if you have your whole life ahead of you. There's plenty of time. But *now* is the time to begin those habits and form that relationship with God while you are young, energetic, and open. Later may be just that—too late.

As Jeremiah says, "Give glory to the Lord your God before it is too late."

to do ☑

COUNT THE TIMES YOU ARE LATE FOR SOMETHING TODAY OR TIMES YOU HAVE TO WAIT FOR OTHER PEOPLE BECAUSE THEY ARE LATE.

Give glory to the LORD your God before it is too late. Acknowledge him before he brings darkness upon you, causing you to stumble and fall on the dark mountains. For then, when you look for light, you will find only terrible darkness. [Jeremiah 13:16]

also on this day

1930
Charles Creighton and James Hagis drove from New York City to Los Angeles and back—all in reverse gear. The trip took 42 days in their 1929 Ford Model A.

Sam Houston was elected as the first president of the Republic of Texas.

1836

1698
Russian Czar Peter the Great imposed a tax on beards.

Marquis de Lafayette was born in 1757.

Never a Rebel

Although Marquis de Lafayette was a member of the wealthy French nobility, he decided at a young age to volunteer his services to the American fight for independence. When he was only 20, Lafayette left his homeland and traveled to America to volunteer his services.

When the Continental Congress met Lafayette and heard of his desire to serve without pay as an officer in the army, they immediately made him a Major General. Later that summer Lafayette met General George Washington, and a friendship developed between the two men that lasted throughout Washington's lifetime.

How strong that bond was between the two men became evident later. In December of 1777, Lafayette had joined Washington at his winter quarters at Valley Forge. At that time, several officers tried to stir up opposition to Washington and have him replaced as commander of the armies. When they approached Lafayette, he not only turned them down, but also wrote a letter to Washington pledging his unfailing loyalty to him. To Lafayette, his friendship with Washington was more important than the possibility of advancing his own career.

Friends do that. They stand by their friends. They don't look for ways to benefit themselves at the expense of a friend. And they don't join with others who are plotting against a friend.

When others try to get you to join them instead of sticking by a friend, be like Lafayette. Refuse to go along with their plans. Then pledge your loyalty to your friend. Your friend won't ever forget it!

to do ☑

WHO HAS BEEN LOYAL TO YOU? TAKE TIME TO THANK THEM FOR STANDING BY YOU WHEN TROUBLES COME.

My **child**, **fear** the LORD and the **king**, and don't **associate** with **rebels**.

[Proverbs 24:21]

also on this day

Jane Addams was born. She was the founder of the Hull House and was the first woman to win the Nobel Peace Prize. ✱ **1860**

✱**1899**
Carnation processed its first can of evaporated milk.

The first Barbie® doll was sold by Mattel Toy Corporation.
1959

inner beauty

In 1921, the first Miss America Beauty Pageant was held in Atlantic City, New Jersey.

When officials introduced the first Miss America Beauty Pageant, they said, "Miss America represents the highest ideals. She is a real combination of beauty, grace, and intelligence, artistic and refined. She is a type which the American girl might well emulate."

In years since then, Miss America winners have been intent on making a difference in people's lives through charitable and community projects. For example, Jean Bartel, Miss America 1943, used her celebrity in the war effort, and she was credited with selling more war bonds than anyone else in the country—$2.5 million worth of them. Kate Shindle, Miss America 1998, spent her year of service talking to groups about the HIV-AIDS cause, attending the 12th World AIDS Conference in Geneva, Switzerland.

Miss America today continues that tradition, traveling more than 20,000 miles a month, promoting her ideals and carrying out her commitment to help others. According to pageant officials, Miss America is more than just a title. Miss America represents a tradition of style, sophistication, and service.

Thousands of years before Miss America ever walked down the runway in Atlantic City, a young Jewish girl won a beauty pageant of her own. For her beauty and grace, Esther earned the title Queen and an honored place in her husband's palace. Yet, when she was faced with a choice of losing all of it, including her life, in order to help save her people, Esther knew she had only one choice. She had to speak up, no matter what the consequences.

Esther's beauty and character won the king's heart and affection. But it was her courage and her willingness to serve others that saved God's people.

Esther was more than just another queen. She was God's woman, ready to answer his call.

When it was Esther's turn to go to the king, she accepted the advice of Hegai, the eunuch in charge of the harem. She asked for nothing except what he suggested, and she was admired by everyone who saw her. [Esther 2:15]

also on this day

1533 Queen Elizabeth I of England was born.

1813 The nickname *Uncle Sam* was first used as a symbolic reference to the United States.

1860 American painter Anna Mary (Robertson) Moses was born in New York. Today is known as "Grandma Moses Day."

to do ☑

MAKE A LIST OF THE CHARACTERISTICS THAT YOU BELIEVE MAKE A PERSON TRULY BEAUTIFUL. WHO BEST FITS THOSE TRAITS?

unconditional pardon

In 1974, President Gerald Ford gave unconditional pardon to Richard Nixon for any crimes committed during the Watergate scandal.

Following the 1972 presidential election, the country was shocked by the growing revelation of a scandal of political sabotage, criminal crimes involving burglary and break-ins, and a massive cover-up operation that crept all the way into the White House and the Oval Office. As a result, President Richard Nixon resigned from the presidency and left the White House.

Vice President Gerald Ford took office and soon after decided, "My conscience tells me clearly and certainly that I cannot prolong the bad dreams that continue to reopen a chapter that is closed. My conscience tells me that only I, as President, have the constitutional power to firmly shut and seal this book." And so, Gerald Ford gave Richard Nixon an absolute and unconditional pardon.

It was a highly unpopular decision, and it probably cost President Ford reelection to office in 1976. Despite that, President Ford has maintained that it was best for the country.

We don't like it when people seem to "get off the hook" and are not punished for their wrongdoings. We want justice. Or do we? What about when it comes to the wrong things we do? Aren't there times when we would really appreciate an "unconditional pardon" when we mess up?

The good news is that because of Jesus and his sacrifice on the cross, we *always* have an unconditional and absolute pardon for our sins. Remember the two thieves who were crucified along with Jesus that Good Friday? One mocked Jesus. The other, realizing who Jesus really was, asked for a pardon. Remember Jesus' words? "I assure you, today you will be with me in paradise."

Pardoned. Forgiven. That's good news for people who mess up, make wrong choices, and do bad things. That's good news for all of us.

And Jesus replied, "I assure you, today you will be with me in paradise."

[Luke 23:43]

to do ☑

WHAT DO YOU NEED AN UNCONDITIONAL PARDON FOR TODAY? ASK JESUS. HE WILL PARDON YOU.

also on this day

Today is National Grandparents Day. Give one of yours a call or a hug today!

Today also is National Iguana Awareness Day. (Don't hug an iguana!)

The Real Marathon

In 490 BC, the Battle of Marathon took place between the invading Persian army and the Athenian army. The marathon race originated from the events surrounding that battle.

to do ☑

CREATE A TRAINING SCHEDULE FOR FOLLOWING GOD'S RULES EACH DAY. YOU MIGHT WANT TO INCLUDE A TIME FOR PRAYER, A TIME TO READ THE BIBLE, AND TIME TO WORSHIP GOD.

The very first marathon, a long-distance footrace then of 25 miles, was held in 1896 at the first modern Olympic Games in Athens, Greece. The race was staged to celebrate the run of messenger Pheidippides from the battlefield at Marathon to Athens in 490 BC.

The story goes that Pheidippides ran the 25 miles to announce the victory of the Athenians over the Persian army. Upon reaching Athens and proclaiming, "Rejoice. We conquer!" he fell down dead. Some 2,000 years later, his countryman, Spiridon Loues, won the 1896 marathon.

Since that time, the marathon has been a staple of every Olympic competition. The race was imported to the United States, when the Boston Athletic Association held its first ever marathon in 1897. The Boston Marathon remains the oldest continuously held marathon.

The distance of the marathon was later established at 26 miles, 385 yards at the 1908 Olympics in London, because that was the distance between the start at Windsor Castle to the finish line at the Olympic stadium.

Running a marathon understandably requires great stamina and a strenuous training regimen. But it also requires that runners follow the rules and finish the course. Running 24 miles won't cut it. Jumping in at the last two miles and crossing the finish line isn't acceptable. Anything less than running the full course is cheating.

It's understood by any athlete participating in any event that in order to qualify for the prize, one has to follow the rules and perform according to the accepted standards. Cheaters are disqualified. The same is true in living the Christian life. Like athletes running a marathon, we have to train hard, follow the rules, and keep to the course that God has set before us. At points along the way, we will grow tired. We may even feel like quitting, or perhaps even cheating, to finish the race. That's when we need to rely on God to help us maintain the course and finish the race.

Only then will we win the prize.

Follow the **Lord's rules** for doing his **work,** just as an **athlete** either **follows** the **rules** or is **disqualified** and wins no **prize.**

[2 Timothy 2:5]

also on this day

Today is Teddy Bear Day.

California became America's 31st state. 1850

1999

The Sega Dreamcast™ game system went on sale. By 1 PM, all Toys "R" Us locations in the United States had sold out.

fast food

In 1953, Swanson began selling its first TV dinner.

What became a basic part of the American diet back in the 1960s (and was the forerunner of today's fast-food culture) was actually a hasty solution to a big problem—what to do with about 270 tons of leftover Thanksgiving turkey! Gerald Thomas, a C. A. Swanson & Sons executive, had 10 refrigerated railcars full of unsold turkeys. So, Thomas decided, why not package the turkey, along with some side dishes, in segmented trays that were used for airline food service?

To market the idea, the Swanson exec named it TV Dinner—the perfect meal to enjoy while watching that new phenomenon, television. Swanson came out with 5,000 TV dinners featuring turkey, corn bread dressing and gravy, buttered peas, and sweet potatoes. It cost 98 cents and came in a box resembling a TV.

The original 5,000 dinners was a gross underestimation. Swanson went on to sell 10,000,000 TV dinners that first year. Of course, not everyone was thrilled with TV dinners. The Swansons received their share of hate mail, mostly from upset husbands who missed their home-cooked meals.

Those early TV dinners were among the first convenience products offered to American households. Convenient and time-saving products have become an essential part of our time-pressured culture. We have convenience stores, drive-through banks, drugstores, cleaners, and fast-food restaurants. Any number of products and services promise us fast, quick, time-saving solutions to our problems.

But there is no such thing as a drive-through church or an instant Christian. The Christian life requires a lifetime investment of daily growth, patience, and perseverance. There are no shortcuts to faith.

to do ☑

THINK BACK ON LAST WEEK. HOW MANY TIMES DID YOU EAT FAST FOOD? USE A DRIVE-THROUGH SERVICE? WHAT CONVE-NIENCE PRODUCTS DO YOU USE EVERY DAY?

also on this day

1913
The Lincoln Highway, the first paved coast-to-coast highway, opened in the U.S.

Elias Howe received a patent for his sewing machine.
1846

I **pray** that your **love** for each other will **overflow more** and **more**, and that you will keep on **growing** in your **knowledge** and **understanding**.

[Philippians 1:9]

Stephen Foster, who became the first composer of distinctly American popular songs, got his start in the business in a most unusual way. The youngest of nine children, Foster taught himself to play and write music because his parents did not approve of his interest.

Foster's big break in composing came when he was 18. At the time, Foster was a bookkeeper, working for his brother. He had written a song, "Oh Susannah," that was performed for the first time in public. Legend has it that Foster sold the rights to the song for a bottle of whiskey. The song went on to become the most popular tune in the country, adopted as the theme song of the California Gold Rush. Now some say Foster received $100 for the song. Either way, Foster had sold himself short.

Esau, twin brother of Jacob, did something similar. You remember the story. Tired and hungry, Esau had returned from hunting looking for something to eat. For the price of a bowl of stew, Esau sold his birthright to his younger twin. Esau gave up his inheritance because he was "starving."

At that moment, Esau was only concerned with satisfying his hunger. He lost sight of the "big picture" and sold something of great value for mere stew. Foster too might have felt pressured to do whatever he could to sell his first song.

Maybe we feel pressured to get good grades, so we cheat on the test. Or we feel pressured to be popular, so we do something we know is not right to fit in. We sell ourselves short because we have lost sight of what's really important. Keep your focus on God and what pleases him. That way you will always come out ahead.

In 1847, "Oh Susannah" was sung in public for the first time. Stephen Foster sold the rights to the song for a bottle of whiskey.

Make sure that no one is immoral or godless like Esau. He traded his birthright as the oldest son for a single meal. [Hebrews 12:16]

to do ☑

FIND A RECORDING OF STEPHEN FOSTER'S SONGS. LISTEN TO THE SONGS THAT WERE POPULAR BACK IN THE LATE 1800S.

also on this day

1936 Boulder Dam (now called Hoover Dam) was dedicated by Franklin D. Roosevelt.

Terrorists attacked the World Trade Centers in New York City and the Pentagon in Washington, D. C..

2001

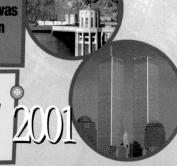

don't sell yourself short

In 1984, Michael Jordan signed a seven year contract to play basketball with the Chicago Bulls.

Never Say Never

No one could have foreseen the impact that Michael Jordan would have on the game of basketball when he signed his name to that first contract with the Chicago Bulls. Just consider a *few* of his accomplishments during his career:

- ➤ Ten-time All-NBA First Team selection (1986–87 to 1992–93, 1995–96 to 1997–98)
- ➤ Selected in 1996 as one of the "50 Greatest Players in NBA History"
- ➤ A member of six Chicago Bulls NBA championship teams (1990–91, 1991–92, 1992–93, 1995–96, 1996–97 and 1997–98)
- ➤ Six-time NBA Finals Most Valuable Player

The list of Michael Jordan's accomplishments goes on and on. But did you know that, while growing up, Michael Jordan was continually beaten by his older brother, Larry, in one-on-one pickup games? Or that he was cut from the high school varsity basketball team as a sophomore? Yet, instead of giving up, Jordan used these failures to motivate him to greater achievements, practicing hour after hour on the court. "Whenever I was working out and got tired and figured I ought to stop, I'd close my eyes and see that list in the locker room without my name on it," Jordan said. He eventually made the team and led it to the state championship.

We all have dreams and plans for our future. And we all can work hard to make those dreams come true. But unless we include God's plan for us in our endeavors, we are going to miss out on a lot. God alone knows what is best for us. He alone can fulfill his purposes for us. We need to entrust our goals, our plans, and our dreams with him.

What are your dreams? What are your goals and plans for the future? Tell God about them, and as the psalm-writer says, let God "work out his plans for my life."

to do ☑

WRITE DOWN THREE GOALS YOU HAVE FOR THE FUTURE. NOW WRITE TODAY'S BIBLE VERSE UNDERNEATH THOSE GOALS. TALK ABOUT YOUR PLANS WITH GOD.

The **LORD** will **work out** his **plans** for my **life**— for your faithful **love**, O **LORD**, endures **forever**. [Psalm 138:8]

also on this day

✱ Today is Video Games Day. Play one of your favorite games!

English explorer Henry Hudson sailed down what is now the ✱ **Hudson River.** 1609

✱**1873**
The first practical typewriter was sold to customers.

what really matters

Today is Commodore John Barry Day.

Name some heroes from the American Revolutionary War, and men like George Washington, Thomas Jefferson, John Adams, Patrick Henry, John Hancock, and Paul Revere come to mind. But what about John Barry?

Did you know that Commodore John Barry was also a hero of the American Revolution and the holder of the first commission in the United States Navy? Most likely not. But in 1981, President Ronald Reagan designated September 13 as "Commodore John Barry Day." In his proclamation, President Reagan noted that Barry became a national hero after capturing the British warship *Edward* on April 7, 1776. He further distinguished himself as a fighter and a seaman.

But according to President Reagan, Barry's greatest contribution went beyond his heroics and patriotism. He was a "man of great insight who perceived very early the need for American power on the sea." Barry had the ability to see the bigger picture and what was truly important for this young nation.

The ability to discern—to tell the difference between right and wrong, between what's important and what's not—is valuable not only in founding a nation, but also in daily living. In Philippians, Paul urged young believers to understand what is truly important. Why? So that they would be able to live according to Jesus' standards and values.

There are many voices telling you how to live and what's really important. Judging from society's messages, you may be tempted to think that what's important is to drive the right car, wear the right clothes, and hang out with the cool people. A better place to discern what's important is in God's Word and what Jesus has to say.

Be like Commodore Barry today and look for what's really important.

For I want you to understand what really matters, so that you may live pure and blameless lives until Christ returns. [Philippians 1:10]

also on this day

1788

New York City became the capital of the United States.

1916

Author Roald Dahl was born today.

to do ☑

STUMP YOUR FRIENDS AND FAMILY TODAY. ASK THEM IF THEY KNOW ABOUT COMMODORE BARRY. TELL THEM WHY HE IS IMPORTANT TO REMEMBER.

hallelujah!

In 1741, George Handel completed Messiah in time for an orphans' charity concert.

At age 56 George Handel had given what he had considered his farewell concert. Discouraged and dejected, Handel felt a failure. That's when a wealthy friend, Charles Jensen, gave Handel a libretto based on the life of Christ, taken right from the Bible. At the same time, Handel received a commission from a Dublin charity to compose a work for a benefit performance.

With the libretto in hand, Handel set to work on August 22, 1741. He became so absorbed in his work that he never left the room of his small London house, rarely stopping to eat. Within six days, he had completed part one. In nine more days, he had finished part two, and in another six, part three. The entire orchestration was completed in another two days. In all, 260 pages of manuscript were filled in 24 short days. Handel's title for the commissioned work was simply *Messiah*.

With tears running down his face, Handel recounted that while writing what has become the hallmark of that work, the "Hallelujah Chorus", "I did think I did see all heaven before me, and the great God himself."

Handel's awe-inspiring composition, with its inspiring lyrics and stirring sounds, may be the closest we come on this side of Heaven to experiencing what John—and indeed Handel himself—saw when the doors of Heaven were opened to them:

"Then I heard again what sounded like the shout of a huge crowd, or the roar of mighty ocean waves, or the crash of loud thunder: 'Hallelujah! For the Lord our God, the Almighty, reigns' (Revelation 19:6).

It is the victory song that resounds in Heaven when Jesus comes to judge the wicked and joins with his bride—the faithful believers from all time.

You won't want to miss that!

to do ☑

SPEND SOME TIME TODAY LISTENING TO GEORGE HANDEL'S MESSIAH.

Then I heard again what sounded like the shout of a huge crowd, or the roar of mighty ocean waves, or the crash of loud thunder: "Hallelujah! For the Lord our God, the Almighty, reigns." [Revelation 19:6]

also on this day

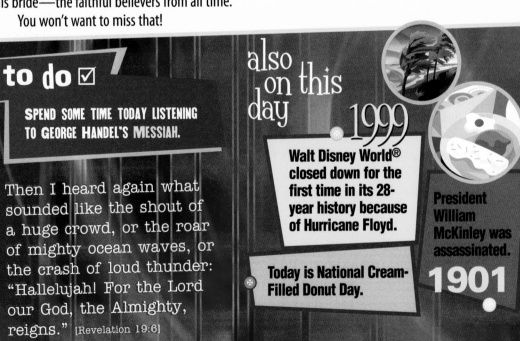

1999 Walt Disney World® closed down for the first time in its 28-year history because of Hurricane Floyd.

President William McKinley was assassinated. **1901**

Today is National Cream-Filled Donut Day.

Born to Be Wild!

Today is Born to Be Wild Day!

Since today is Born to Be Wild Day, let's take a look at the Bible's "wild boy". Remember him, the prodigal son in Luke 15:11-32? According to Webster's Dictionary, *prodigal* means reckless, extravagant . . . in a word, wild.

So here's the situation. A father had two sons. One day the younger son asked the father for his inheritance right away. The father agreed, and the son took off. The son spent all his money on wild living. Soon his money ran out and he had nothing to eat.

The son was so desperate that he begged a local pig farmer to hire him to feed the pigs. But no one gave the son anything. Soon the pig's food even looked good to him. The son, with all his wild living, had hit rock bottom.

Finally the son came to his senses. He decided that even his father's hired men were better off than he was. Maybe if he begged his father for forgiveness, his father might hire him. So he headed for home. When the boy was still a way off, the father saw him coming. Filled with love and compassion, he ran to hug his son. The story ends with the father holding a huge party to celebrate his son's return.

Even though the son had messed up big time, the father still loved him and welcomed him back. That's good news because we all have our "wild" days—those times when we do what we want to do and forget about God. When we do, the best thing to do is remember that God is always waiting with open arms for us to return.

to do ☑

READ THE STORY OF THE PRODIGAL SON IN LUKE 15:11-32. IMAGINE THAT YOU ARE ONE OF THE CHARACTERS IN THE STORY (THE YOUNGER BROTHER, THE FATHER, THE OLDER BROTHER). HOW WOULD YOU HAVE REACTED?

"We must **celebrate** with a **feast**, for this son of mine was **dead** and has now **returned** to **life**. He was **lost**, but now he is **found**." So the **party** began.

[Luke 15:23, 24]

also on this day

1984 Prince Harry of Wales was born.

·1928
Alexander Fleming discovered the antibiotic penicillin in a mold.

William H. Taft, the 27th president of the United States, was born today. **·** **1857**

free to worship

We typically think about the Pilgrims once a year when Thanksgiving rolls around. And then it's usually about the great feast they had with the Indians. End of story. But did you realize that the story—and the importance—of the Pilgrims is more than that? The Pilgrims left us a legacy not just of turkey, stuffing, and pumpkin pie, but of the freedom to worship as we please each and every Sunday.

In 1608, it was apparent to this group that they could no longer live in England and worship as they were told. They wanted to worship in a church that placed its authority solely in the Bible. They longed for the opportunity to choose their own church leaders by a common vote. So they left for Holland in order to live by the principles expressed in 2 Corinthians 6:17: "Therefore, come out from them and separate yourselves from them, says the Lord."

After 12 years, the group decided they had to move again because of the hard life and discouragement that they had found in Holland. Even in Holland, the Pilgrims discovered that they were losing the simplicity and purity of lifestyle and worship that they wanted. So they returned to England, and on this day in 1620, 102 Pilgrims set out for America in search for a better life for their children and for the freedom to worship as they pleased.

Because of the Pilgrims' determination to worship and live as they deemed right in God's eyes, we now enjoy the freedom of religion. America's founding fathers saw the importance of religious freedom and made sure that was preserved in the Constitution. We can worship how we please, in whatever church we deem appropriate, without any thought of persecution or danger.

You can thank the Pilgrims for being willing to "earnestly search" for God.

O God, you are my God; I earnestly search for you. My soul thirsts for you; my whole body longs for you in this parched and weary land where there is no water. [Psalm 63:1]

to do ☑

IF YOU CAN, READ MORE ABOUT THE PILGRIMS. WRITE DOWN THREE THINGS THAT YOU APPRECIATED MOST ABOUT THIS GROUP OF PEOPLE.

also on this day

1782 The Great Seal of the United States was impressed on a document to negotiate a prisoner-of-war agreement with the British. It was the first official use of the impression.

Today is Collect Rocks Day!

where's your citizenship?

Today is Citizenship Day.

This day honoring all U.S. citizens, whether native-born or foreign-born, was originally celebrated on the third Sunday in May as "I Am an American Day." But in 1952, President Harry Truman signed a bill establishing today as the Citizenship Day, moving the celebration to the day on which the U.S. Constitution was signed in 1787.

The intent of the day is to recognize all those who have become American citizens during the preceding year. The day typically is marked with pageantry and speeches to impress upon these new citizens the privileges and the responsibilities of being a U.S. citizen.

To become a U.S. citizen, you must have lived in the United States for five years. You must be a person of good character, have a basic knowledge of U.S. history and government, and can read, write, and speak basic English. You must be 18 years old, legally competent, and express your allegiance to the United States. You must fill out the proper forms and pass a citizenships test.

It can be a long, hard process, and not everybody who wants to become an American citizen is accepted. That's why this day is so meaningful to the hundreds of thousands who do become citizens during the year.

But did you know that if you are a follower of Christ, then you are a citizen of a kingdom far greater than America? The Bible tells us that when we believe in Jesus we join the kingdom of God, and we will someday live forever in Heaven. We don't have to live there a certain number of years, be a certain age, pass a test, or fill out any forms. Our citizenship in Heaven becomes official the very moment that we confess our faith in Jesus Christ.

For that privilege, you receive God's love and forgiveness, his guidance and protection, and life with him forever. Not a bad deal.

to do ☑

WRITE DOWN THREE THINGS YOU ENJOY BECAUSE YOU ARE AN AMERICAN CITIZEN. NOW WRITE DOWN THREE THINGS YOU ENJOY BECAUSE YOU ARE A CITIZEN OF HEAVEN.

But **we are citizens** of **heaven**, where the **Lord Jesus Christ** lives. And we are **eagerly** waiting for him to **return** as our **Savior**. [Philippians 3:20]

also on this day

1796
President George Washington's Farewell Address was read before the Congress.

Phillip W. Pratt patented a version of the sprinkler system.

1872

fun with modeling dough

Today is National Play-Doh® Day.

How long has it been since you've dug your hands into a great big glob of blue, red, or yellow Play-Doh®? Remember how much fun it was to craft a whole host of creations by squeezing, rolling, and molding the colorful substance in the bright yellow containers? Maybe you even had a Fun Factory, where you inserted the modeling dough into molds and then squeezed out the fun shapes.

Play-Doh brand modeling dough has been around since 1956 when brothers Noah and Joseph McVicker invented the compound. Originally it was designed to be a wallpaper cleaner (don't try that at home!), but its similarity to modeling clay, without the toxicity or mess, made it a better toy. In fact, Joseph McVicker became a millionaire before his 27th birthday after re-releasing the product as a toy. Since that time, more than 700 million pounds of the modeling dough have been sold.

Over the years, sparkling, scented, and glow-in-the-dark versions of this product have been produced. But the real attraction is how easy it is to sculpt and fashion any number of creations using this soft, malleable dough. Then when you're done, you simply squish your creation into one large lump and stuff it back into its can to use for another day.

Imagine how much fun God had in shaping us. He had all the colors, the variety, and the shapes imaginable at his fingertips to mold each one of us. Isaiah writes that God is the potter and we are the clay. God forms us and shapes us not only in the way he created us, but also through our experiences and the circumstances in which he has placed us.

He *is* the sculptor. We are his modeling dough.

And yet, **LORD**,
  you are our **Father**.
We are the **clay**,
    and you are the **potter**.
We are all **formed** by your hand.

[Isaiah 64:8]

also on this day

1709

Samuel Johnson, the creator of the first dictionary of the English language, was born.

1947

The U.S. Air Force was established.

to do ☑

HAVE SOME FUN WITH MODELING DOUGH TODAY! YOU CAN EVEN MAKE YOUR OWN BY USING A RECIPE FROM WWW.KINDERPLANET.COM/PLAYDO.HTM.

Shivers me timbers! Today be the day that all landlubbers and me hearties join in and talk like pirates. A few pointers are all that's needed before you be talking like a swashbucklin' jack. So here you be:

First off, double up on all your adjectives. Pirates never speak of a big ship— it's always a "great, grand ship." It's not a pretty girl—it's a fine beauty of a lass. And remember, a pirate is never content to just say never. No, it's "no nay ne'er!"

Next, all me hearties have to drop their *g*'s when speakin'. Now you'll get words like *rowin'*, *sailin'*, *fightin'*. Drop your *v*'s (as in *ne'er*, *e'er* and *o'er*). Final lesson. No nay ne'er say, "I am" or "You are." Any sailor worth his or her weight in doubloons of gold says "I be" or "you be." Now put it all together, and mateys, you be fine swashbucklin', dashin' buccaneers. No swabbies around here, no nay ne'er!

Now there's not much use for talking like a pirate (other than to impress your mateys!), but if you want to communicate with others who are different from you, it does help to speak *their* language. That doesn't just mean knowing how they talk, but also what their interests are and what they like.

The apostle Paul discovered this as he traveled to different places to share the gospel. Wherever he went he did his best to fit in with those around him and speak their language.

That meant that Paul did what was best for those around him, not just what pleased him. That's a good lesson to follow when we want to talk to our friends at school about Jesus. Are they into music? Then invite them to a Christian rock concert. They like sports? Speak their language, get on the team, and show them what Jesus is all about.

Arrrrrr!

That is the plan I follow, too. I try to please everyone in everything I do. I don't just do what I like or what is best for me, but what is best for them so they may be saved. [1 Corinthians 10:33]

Today is National Talk Like a Pirate Day.

to do ☑

GO AHEAD. TALK LIKE A PIRATE TODAY. HERE'S SOME WORDS YOU MAY NEED TO KNOW: AHOY (HEY!); AYE (YES); MATEY (FRIEND OR SHIPMATE); YO-HO-HO (A GOOD PIRATE LAUGH).

also on this day

1881 James A. Garfield died of wounds from an assassin. The 20th president had lived for 11 weeks after being shot.

1982 Scott Fahlman became the first person to use : -) in an online message.

ahoy mateys! arrrr!

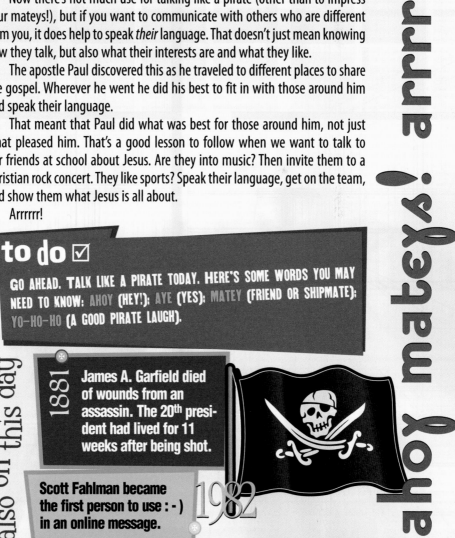

Today is National Student Day.

Be a Student of Life

What kind of student are you? When you come home from school, do you: (a) immediately crack the books; (b) grab a snack, watch a few TV shows, and then hit the books; or (c) What? Do we have homework tonight?

When you are given a chance to do extra credit assignments, do you: (a) thank the teacher and immediately get to work; (b) consider how much time is involved and how much you really want to raise your grade before tackling extra credit; or (c) figure anything that has the word *extra* in it means just that—extra work. No thank you.

When there is something you don't understand in school, do you: (a) ask questions until you do understand; (b) wait until you see if it's going to be on test and then ask your best friend to explain it; or (c) figure that eventually you'll understand it by the time you graduate from high school.

If you answered mostly *a*'s, then good for you! You are a true student. But really, anyone can be a student—no matter how old. The dictionary describes a student as one who is an attentive learner and sharp observer. You can study anything—from bugs to rap, from computers to the arts. You also can be a student of God's Word. Psalm 119—the longest psalm ever written—is all about the benefits of studying God's Word every day.

Here are just a few of those benefits—we'll be happy (v. 2); we'll stay pure (v. 9); we will have understanding (v. 34); we will find comfort (v. 50); and we will find guidance (v. 105) and great peace (v. 165). Because of that we should, like the psalm-writer says, delight in God's Word, meditate on it daily, put it into practice and live by it daily, and hide God's Word in our hearts.

What kind of student are you of God's Word?

to do ☑

TAKE THE CHALLENGE AND READ PSALM 119. YOU MAY WANT TO READ IT OVER SEVERAL DAYS. OR READ IT ALOUD WITH ANOTHER FRIEND OR FAMILY MEMBER. UNDERLINE THE VERSES THAT MEAN THE MOST TO YOU.

How can a **young person** live a **clean life**? By **carefully reading** the **map** of your **Word**.

[Psalm 119:9, The Message]

also on this day

1921 KDKA in Pittsburgh, Pennsylvania, became one of the first radio stations to offer a daily newscast.

Chester A. Arthur became the 21st president. President James A. Garfield had died the day before. **1881**

1952 James Meredith, an African-American student, was blocked from enrolling at the University of Mississippi by Governor Ross R. Barnett. Meredith was later admitted.

give peace a chance

Today is the International Day of Peace.

The International Day of Peace was established in 1982 through the United Nations as a day set aside for the entire world to observe nonviolence and peace. Since 9/11, the world's attention has been focused on terror, fear, and war. But behind the scenes, a worldwide movement for peace has been growing.

Organizers try to involve as many people as possible in observing the day. Videoconferences have been set up with children in countries that have experienced war. The World Peace Flag is raised during a ceremony at UN headquarters. An International Day of Peace Vigil, a 24-hour observance for peace and nonviolence, has been organized in places of worship, in neighborhoods, and communities.

People have worked tirelessly to have the entire world observe a Global Day of Ceasefire on this day. The UN has set a goal to involve as many as one billion people worldwide in peace activities. Their hope is that if "we can create one day of peace, we will realize that we can work together to create a culture of peace, one day at a time."

Too often we think of peace as merely the absence of any conflict. We think about peacemakers as passive and nonaggressive. But peace does not just happen. We have to *work* at creating peace. In the Bible, Peter urged believers to "work hard" at living in peace with each other. That means being active in forming good relationships, in resolving problems before they arise, and working with others to ensure a peaceful home, church, or community.

So what can you do today to make peace where you are? It starts one day at a time, one person at a time. Let peace begin with you.

Turn **away** from **evil**
and do **good**.
Work **hard** at living
in **peace** with **others**.

[1 Peter 3:11]

also on this day

Today is World Gratitude Day.

This is Deaf Awareness Week.

1937
J.R.R. Tolkien's *The Hobbit* was first published.

to do ☑

MAKE A SIMPLE PEACE PLEDGE. HOW CAN YOU WORK AT PEACE WITHIN YOUR FAMILY OR AMONG YOUR FRIENDS TODAY?

be a good neighbor

Today is Good Neighbor Day.

In the early 1970s, Becky Mattson from Lakeside, Montana, recognized the importance of having and being good neighbors. So she started an effort to make this a national day. Three presidents (Richard Nixon, Gerald Ford, and Jimmy Carter) along with many state governors all issued proclamations calling for a Good Neighbor Day.

Finally in 2003 the U.S. Senate passed a resolution to make September 22 National Good Neighbor Day. Here are some ideas for observing it: Bake some cookies and take them over to your next-door neighbor. Smile and wave hello to your neighbors when you see them outside. Do a chore secretly for your neighbors—rake their lawns, sweep their driveways, bring in the trash cans.

Even though this day has been set aside as Good Neighbor Day, the writer in Proverbs makes it clear that we should not ignore an opportunity to help our neighbor. In other words, we don't need a Good Neighbor Day to help someone out. Whenever the opportunity arises, we should be ready to lend a hand, pitch in, and help out.

And since Jesus pointed out that our "neighbor" is anybody with whom we come in contact (see Luke 10:25-37), then that means we need to extend help to our classmates, the kids on the bus, and even people we don't know. That means taking the time to explain a homework assignment, bringing home books to a sick classmate, or helping clean up after a project.

Think about it. We are to treat our neighbors as we would like them to treat us. Makes sense, doesn't it?

to do ☑

READ THE STORY OF THE GOOD SAMARITAN AGAIN IN LUKE 10:25-37. THINK ABOUT THESE QUESTIONS: WHO ARE MY NEIGHBORS? HOW CAN I BE A GOOD NEIGHBOR?

If you **can** help your **neighbor now**, **don't** say, "Come back **tomorrow**, and **then** I'll **help** you."

[Proverbs 3:28]

also on this day

1999

The record for drinking ketchup was set by Dustin Phillips on this day. He drank a 14-ounce bottle of ketchup through a straw in 33 seconds.

Today is Elephant Appreciation Day.

1952

Caesar Augustus, or Gaius Julius Caesar Octavianus as he was known earlier in his life, was the very first Roman emperor. Generally considered the greatest of all the Roman emperors, Caesar Augustus ruled for more than 40 years and ushered in an era of peace, prosperity, and greatness. During his reign, Augustus ended a century of civil wars.

Augustus, a title he was given in 27 BC that means "revered one," created Rome's first permanent army and navy. He rebuilt Rome from brick into marble, building the Senate a home and constructing numerous temples to Roman gods. But despite all these accomplishments that are credited to Augustus, his greatest contribution to all human history came as a result of his effort to reform Rome's finance and tax system.

For as Luke records it, "About that time Caesar Augustus ordered a census to be taken throughout the Empire." What Augustus had intended as a means to tax the people to support his military operations, God used for a much different purpose. Augustus's decree set in motion the events that were prophesied hundreds of years earlier concerning the birth of God's own Son, Jesus Christ. Mary and Joseph had to travel to Bethlehem. There Mary gave birth to her firstborn Son, Jesus, just as the prophet Micah had written in Micah 5:2.

Augustus's decree went out according to God's perfect timing and according to God's perfect plan for bringing his Son into the world. Augustus, who was considered to be god-like by the Roman citizens, was really just a role player in the real drama of God coming to earth.

to do ☑

READ MICAH 5:2, WHICH WAS WRITTEN HUNDREDS OF YEARS BEFORE CAESAR AUGUSTUS EVEN THOUGHT ABOUT ISSUING HIS DECREE.

About that time Caesar Augustus ordered a census to be taken throughout the Empire. [Luke 2:1, The Message]

Today in 63 BC, Augustus Caesar was born.

a greater purpose

also on this day

1838
Victoria Chaflin Woodhull was born. She became the first female candidate for the U.S. president.

The planet Neptune was discovered by German astronomer Johann Gottfried Galle.
 1846

no time to panic

On this day in 1869, thousands of businessmen were financially ruined after a panic on Wall Street.

This day in 1869 is popularly referred to as Black Friday—a dark financial day in which a small group of businessmen tried to control the gold market by selling gold for a much higher price than it was worth. The men connived to hike the price of gold more than $20 per share in just a day. When the government released more than $4 million worth of gold on the market, the price dropped dramatically.

Within 15 minutes, the price of gold had dropped from $162 per share to $133. Thousands of investors were ruined. Fortunes were lost. Many Wall Street businesses were ruined. The nation's business community was paralyzed. That's what happens in a panic. One action sets in motion another action—and soon thousands of people are unable to do anything.

When have you panicked? Maybe it was the night before a big test. You have studied as much as you can when panic sets in. You begin to worry you won't remember what you have studied. You are so worried that you can't sleep, and you start worrying about not being able to sleep and how that will affect your test-taking . . . you can see what happens when panic hits.

How can you stop from panicking? Well, first take a deep breath. Then (you know what's coming next), pray! That's what Daniel did when faced with the impossible task of not only interpreting the king's dream but also telling the king what his dream was! (Read about it in Daniel 2.) Daniel could have panicked. He could have run around wringing his hands and crying, "Oh no! What am I going to do?" Instead, Daniel enlisted the help of his friends and asked them to pray!

There's no need to panic when God is on your side. Prayer beats panic any day.

> But I keep right on praying to you, Lord, hoping this is the time you will show me favor. In your unfailing love, O God, answer my prayer with your sure salvation. [Psalm 69:13]

also on this day

1664
New Jersey, named after the Isle of Jersey, was founded.

1947
Kenneth Arnold reported seeing flying saucers over Mt. Rainier, Washington.

to do ☑

READ DANIEL 2. LOOK FOR ALL THE WAYS THAT DANIEL BEAT A POSSIBLE PANIC ATTACK.

got it covered!

Today is Yom Kippur.

Yom Kippur, or the Day of Atonement, remains one of the most holy religious holidays in the Jewish faith. Since Old Testament days, the Day of Atonement is the day to ask God's forgiveness for the people's sins as a nation. The Hebrew word for *atone* means "to cover." Since Old Testament sacrifices could not actually remove sins, the sacrifices made could only cover the sins.

Today, people of the Jewish faith observe Yom Kippur through confessing their sins together at the synagogue. Yom Kippur is also a day of *not* doing. The people may not eat, drink, wash, or wear leather shoes.

In Bible times on this day, the people would confess their sins as a nation and the high priest would enter the Most Holy Place to make atonement for those sins. One of the events connected with the Day of Atonement was the presentation of two goats before God. One goat was chosen to be sacrificed as a sin offering; the other goat was chosen to be the scapegoat. In essence, all the people's sins were placed on the scapegoat and then the goat was sent away into the wilderness.

The two goats represented how God was dealing with the people's sins. God forgave the people's sins through the sacrifice of the first goat. Through the second goat, God was removing their sins. This ritual had to be repeated every year. But for those who believe and follow Jesus Christ, his death on the cross replaced this system once and for all.

The moment we turn to Jesus, confess our sins, and ask for forgiveness, we are forgiven. Because of Jesus' blood shed on the cross, our sins not only are covered, but are removed forever.

to do ☑

DO SOME RESEARCH AND FIND OUT MORE ABOUT HOW JEWISH PEOPLE CELEBRATE YOM KIPPUR TODAY.

also on this day

1981

Sandra Day O'Conner became the first female Supreme Court Justice.

The first newspaper was published in America.

1690

On this day,
atonement will be
made for **you**,
and you will be **cleansed**
from all your **sins**
in the **LORD's** presence.

[Leviticus 16:30]

Planting Seeds

In 1774, John Chapman was born. He is better known as Johnny Appleseed.

John Chapman was born on this day in Massachusetts in 1774. Johnny Appleseed, as he became known, spent 49 years of his life walking the American wilderness planting apple seeds.

Johnny was a kind and gentle man—liked by everyone who met him. Even animals seemed drawn to his gentle ways. His clothes were made from sackcloth, and his hat was a tin pot that he also used for cooking! His favorite book? The Bible!

Many stories grew around this man who walked around the country barefoot, planting seeds wherever he went. The stories surrounding this man are legendary. It was said that he made his drinking water from snow by melting it with his feet. Another story had it that Johnny fell asleep and a rattlesnake tried to bite him, but the snake's fangs couldn't penetrate the tough soles of his feet.

Johnny Appleseed's dream was for a land where blossoming apple trees were everywhere and no one was hungry. It is said that more than 200 years later, orchards in Illinois, Indiana, Kentucky, Pennsylvania, and Ohio still have trees bearing apples resulting from the seeds Johnny planted.

The apostle Paul was also a planter of seeds. The seeds that Paul planted, however, bore a fruit of a different kind. Paul planted the seed of the gospel wherever he went. He told whoever would listen the good news of Jesus Christ and the promise of eternal life.

Think about it. You are reading this book today because of the seeds that Paul planted years and years ago! Someone heard about Jesus from Paul and told someone else, who told someone else . . .

Now it's your turn to go and plant seeds for Jesus!

to do ☑

ENJOY AN APPLE TODAY IN HONOR OF JOHNNY APPLESEED. AS YOU DO, THINK ABOUT SEEDS YOU CAN PLANT FOR JESUS AT SCHOOL AND IN YOUR NEIGHBORHOOD.

My job was to **plant** the **seed** in your **hearts**, and **Apollos watered** it, but it was **God**, not **we**, who made it **grow**.

[1 Corinthians 3:6]

also on this day

1789 The U.S. Postal Service was founded.

John Philip Sousa, the "King of Marches," performed his first concert. 1892

⋇**1985**
Shamu was born today at Sea World in Orlando, Florida. Shamu was the first killer whale to survive being born in captivity.

I t's fun visiting new places—new sights to see, new foods to taste, new people to meet, and wonderful memories to take home with you. Each time you visit another new city, state, or country, you broaden your horizons and become more of a world-class citizen. In fact, since 1979 the United Nations has worked to promote tourism by declaring this day World Tourism Day (WTD).

The idea behind WTD is to make the public more aware of the value of travel and tourism on all levels—locally, nationally, and internationally. To help achieve this goal, the UN suggests that countries around the world join this effort by declaring World Tourism Day as a "special day for the entire national territory." Activities such as free entry for tourists and citizens to museums, national parks, and other sites of interest are suggested to promote the day. Special transportation, commemorative postage stamps and medals, Miss (or Mister) WTD competitions, and tourism fairs are all part of the ongoing celebration of this worldwide tourism effort.

While it's fun to visit new places, it's always good to come back home. The comforts of home await you—your own bed, familiar faces and foods, the freedom to kick back and just do nothing, and maybe the warm reception of the family pet. Coming home is always a welcome end to the traveler.

The writer of Hebrews says that the day that we arrive in Heaven will be our last and best homecoming. This world is not our home. Really, we are just tourists on this earth, visiting for a while, seeing the sights, meeting new people, having all sorts of different experiences. We will not feel completely comfortable and at home until we are with Jesus in the city of Heaven.

So while we're on this earth, take advantage of all the world has to offer. But remember not to get too attached because it is only temporary.

One day we'll be home. And it will be good.

For this world is not our home; we are looking forward to our city in heaven, which is yet to come. [Hebrews 13:14]

to do ☑

VISIT YOUR LOCAL TRAVEL AGENCY (OR THE LIBRARY) AND COLLECT SOME BROCHURES FOR PLACES THAT YOU WOULD LIKE TO VISIT SOME DAY.

also on this day

1954 The *Tonight Show* made its debut on NBC-TV with Steve Allen as host.

1989 Two men in a barrel went over the 176-foot high Niagara Falls. Jeffery Petkovich and Peter Dernardi were the first ever to survive the Horseshoe Falls.

there's no place like home

a good teacher

In 551 BC, teacher and philosopher Confucius was born.

According to Chinese tradition, Confucius was a thinker, political figure, educator, and founder of the *Ru* School of Chinese thought. His teachings, preserved in the *Analects,* form the foundation of much of Chinese thought on the education and behavior of the ideal man.

During his lifetime Confucius is credited with having taught 3,000 students, although tradition has it that only 70 were said to have truly mastered the arts that he cherished. Confucius was willing to teach anyone, no matter what their social standing, as long as they were eager and tireless. His curriculum included morality, proper speech, government, and the refined arts, which included ritual, music, archery, chariot-riding, calligraphy, and computation.

Confucius never lectured at length on any one subject. Instead, he posed questions and used stories or analogies until his students arrived at the right answers. But the hallmark of Confucius's thought was his emphasis on education and study. Confucius believed that the only path to true understanding was through long and careful study. To Confucius that meant finding a good teacher and imitating his words and deeds.

Nearly 500 years later, a teacher of a different sort came upon the scene. Like Confucius, he taught through stories and questions, but he taught lessons of eternal significance: love, mercy, forgiveness, obedience, faithfulness. What's more, his teachings were the ultimate authority because they came straight from his Father in Heaven. The teacher? Jesus Christ, the Son of God.

Since Jesus' time on earth, hundreds of millions have followed his teachings and imitated his life. While Confucius' claimed his teachings led to true understanding, accepting Jesus as Savior and following his teachings leads to eternal life.

Jesus is the greatest teacher of all time. Imitate his words and deeds. That is the way to life.

to do ☑

WRITE DOWN THREE THINGS THAT YOU HAVE LEARNED FROM JESUS' TEACHINGS AND HIS LIFE.

Don't **ever** let **anyone** call you '**Rabbi**,' for you have only **one teacher**, and **all** of you are on the **same** level as **brothers** and **sisters**. [Matthew 23:8]

also on this day

1892

The first nighttime football game took place under electric lights. The game was between Mansfield State Normal School and the Wyoming Seminary.

The first around-the-world flight was completed when two U.S. Army planes landed in Seattle, Washington. The trip took 175 days.

1924

undeserved favor

In 1989, Bruce Springsteen overheard a woman talking about her financial problems and medical bills. A week later the woman received a check from Springsteen for $100,000.

It was totally unexpected. Rock star Bruce Springsteen stopped in a small salon in Prescott, Arizona, and played a few songs with the band there. That alone must have been a treat for the unsuspecting patrons who happened to be in the salon at the time. But the story doesn't end here.

While sitting around after playing with the band, Springsteen overheard a woman talking about her financial problems that stemmed from some very large medical bills. A week later, the woman received a check in the mail from Springsteen for $100,000.

Imagine how that woman must have felt, opening the letter and seeing this totally unexpected check: amazed, shocked, surprised? And likely she felt deep gratitude for the generous nature of this gift. The woman did nothing to earn that check. She was merely the recipient of Springsteen's generosity and compassion. It was a gift.

Imagine. We are the recipients of God's undeserved favor and grace, on a daily basis. We do nothing to deserve it. In fact, in some instances, we have even turned away from God and are actively disobedient to him. We can do nothing to earn God's grace, love, or forgiveness. It is a gift.

God's gift of grace doesn't depend on how good we are (we aren't), or on how much time we have spent in study and prayer (although that's good). It is not given to us because we deserve it. God's gift is freely given out of the abundance of his love, kindness, and compassion toward *all* his creatures.

The only thing left for us to do is accept it with thankfulness and praise.

And if they are saved by God's kindness, then it is not by their good works. For in that case, God's wonderful kindness would not be what it really is—free and undeserved. [Romans 11:6]

also on this day

Today is National Goose Day and National Pumpkin Day.

1951

The first network football game was televised in color by CBS-TV. The game was between the University of California and the University of Pennsylvania.

1983

A Chorus Line became the longest-running show on Broadway.

to do ☑

THINK ABOUT IT. HOW HAS GOD SHOWN HIS UNDESERVED KINDNESS AND LOVE TO YOU TODAY? TAKE TIME TO THANK HIM RIGHT NOW.

Today in 1902, rayon was patented.

Man-Made

Rayon was the first man-made manufactured fiber. Developed in France in the 1890s, it was originally called "artificial silk." Although it was patented on this day in 1902, it wasn't until 1924 that the term *rayon* was officially adopted by the textile industry.

Unlike most man-made fibers, rayon is not synthetic (that is, made up of chemical compounds like nylon.) Instead, rayon is made from wood pulp, a natural material. For that reason, rayon's properties come closer to those of other natural fibers such as cotton or linen than those of synthetic fibers such as nylon and polyester.

At first, rayon was manufactured for decorative uses. But as its properties and relatively inexpensive cost became more desirable, clothes manufacturers began to blend rayon with other fabrics such as cotton and wool. Today, rayon's many desirable properties make it a popular choice among some designers, and it appears in more high-end apparel than before.

As good a fiber as rayon has become, it still pales in comparison to natural fibers, such as silk, wool, linen, and cotton. These remain the most reliable and most used fibers in high-end clothing because natural fibers last longer, and the fabrics breathe and are more comfortable to wear than man-made.

When it comes to man-made versus God-made, nothing truly beats God's natural creation. And no one on this earth can add an ounce of creativity or wisdom to what God already possesses. God is the source of all wisdom (Proverbs 2:6). He makes the smartest, most intelligent humans seem foolish when compared to him (1 Corinthians 1:20). God does not rely on us to help him run the world (thankfully!). We are nothing compared to his greatness (Psalm 8).

While it is good for man to use the creativity and intelligence to create, invent, and design new things, we need to remember the source of all wisdom, creativity, and intelligence—our creator God.

Everything else pales beside him.

to do ☑

READ PSALM 8 ALOUD. REFLECT ON GOD'S GREATNESS AND OUR POSITION BEFORE HIM. THANK HIM THAT HE HAS "CROWNED US WITH GLORY AND HONOR."

Can a **person's** actions be of **benefit** to **God**? Can even a **wise** person be **helpful** to **him**?

[Job 22:2]

also on this day

1787
The ship *Columbia* left Boston and began the trip that would make it the first American vessel to sail around the world.

1947
The World Series was televised for the first time.

Chewing gum tycoon William Wrigley Jr. was born. 1861

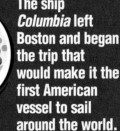

You may have heard of this popular television show. Each week, Ralph Edwards, the host, would walk in carrying a large book and say to a shocked person: "_____ (person's name), this is your life." Then for the next half hour, significant people from the past would be ushered in one at a time, much to the surprise and delight of the guest. Edwards might say, for example, "This person was your closest companion for three years . . . your babysitter!" Then the former babysitter would walk in and the two would hug, and the babysitter would tell something about the honored person. That may sound boring, but it could be a very emotional show, especially when family and old friends would be reunited.

How would that show play out for you if it were held today? Who would you like to see from your past—people with whom you were close or who played important roles in your life? They could include a friend from your old neighborhood, a favorite teacher, your former piano teacher, a distant relative, or even a babysitter.

Now think of those who should have you on their shows. Have you been that close to anyone in the past? Have you made a significant impact on anyone's life?

It's always good to think about this as we live each day because the days pass so quickly, and, before we know it, the years fly by too. Think back to the wall plaque we talked about in August that said "Only one life, it will soon be past. Only what's done for Christ will last." It's true.

That means we should be living each day as though it counts for eternity. So think about it: If God were to surprise you with "This is your life," what important events would he highlight?

"For I was hungry, and you fed me. I was thirsty, and you gave me a drink. I was a stranger, and you invited me into your home. I was naked, and you gave me clothing. I was sick, and you cared for me. I was in prison, and you visited me." [Matthew 25:35, 36]

On this day in 1952, the show This Is Your Life began airing on NPC TV.

to do ☑

GET THE ADDRESSES FROM YOUR PARENTS FOR A FEW OF THE SIGNIFICANT PEOPLE IN YOUR PAST. THEN WRITE EACH ONE A THANK-YOU NOTE.

also on this day

This is National Heart Magic Day.

This is International Day of Older Persons.

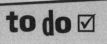

Walt Disney World® opened in Orlando, Florida. *1971*

this is your life

flying pigs

This is World Farm Animals Day.

That'll happen when pigs fly!" You've probably heard that expression and may even have used it a time or two. It means, "It will never happen!" Just think how thrilled all those chickens, cows, goats, sheep, and pigs are! You could check every farm, all over the world, and you'd never find that a pig has ever sprouted wings and then flown across the barnyard. If it ever happens . . . now that would be news!

Tons of things can seem impossible, almost as far-fetched as a flying pig. That's what the disciples thought after hearing Jesus one day. Jesus had said that a camel could go through the eye of a needle easier than a rich man could get into Heaven. As you might imagine, the disciples exclaimed, "Then who in the world can be saved?" (Mark 10:26).

That's when Jesus said, "Everything is possible with God."

Does that mean we should be on the lookout for flying pigs? No. But God *could* give them wings if he wanted to—he can do *anything* and *everything*. What it means is that we should never give up on people or situations that seem impossible to us.

God tells us to pray, to bring all our requests to him (Mark 11:24; Ephesians 6:18; 1 John 5:14, 15). So we should be talking with him about everything, even impossibilities: a relationship that has soured, a sick friend, an unbelieving friend who seems so far from the Lord—all our fears, hopes, and dreams. God specializes in the impossible.

Jesus looked
   at them **intently** and said,
"**Humanly** speaking, it is
           impossible.
But **not** with **God**.
   Everything is **possible**
with **God**." [Mark 10:27]

also on this day

1869

Mahatma Gandhi was born.

1950

The *Peanuts* comic strip by Charles Schultz first appeared in newspapers.

to do ☑

WHAT SEEMINGLY "IMPOSSIBLE" SITUATION DO YOU FACE AT HOME, AT SCHOOL, WITH FRIENDS, OR SOME OTHER SITUATION? SPEND TIME, RIGHT NOW, PRAYING ABOUT IT. THEN THANK GOD FOR HIS ANSWER AND BE READY TO ACCEPT IT.

mind matters

This is Techies Day.

The nickname *techie* implies someone who knows how things work—especially computers, cell phones, PDAs, and other technical devices. We tend to think of such a person as intelligent, though maybe weak in social skills or relationships. That's because many techies wrap their lives in technology just about every minute. So they don't have time for playing sports, singing, or messing around with friends.

While there's no doubt that our lives ought to be balanced, we need to be careful about pre-judging others. Remember that God created each person, including you, with unique characteristics, abilities, and potential in *every* area of life. Every individual is strong in some area and weak in another. We need to celebrate each other's strengths and accommodate each other's weaknesses.

Several years ago the United Negro College Fund began using the slogan, "A mind is a terrible thing to waste" as they raised money for their cause. It's true! God gave us our brains, our minds, and he wants us to use them, not waste or abuse them.

Jesus told his followers that they were to love God, "with all your heart, all your soul, and all your mind" (Matthew 22:37). Using our minds the way God intended involves thinking (what we dwell on, daydream about, and focus on), studying (learning about ourselves, the world, and God), and doing (putting into practice what we learn). Our minds control just about everything else that we do—no wonder they're so important. Want proof? Check out today's verse.

You can be smart, intelligent, and use your brain without becoming a techie. Love the "Lord your God . . . with all your mind."

to do ☑

IN HONOR OF **TECHIES DAY**, SPEND TIME WITH A TECHIE TODAY. YOU MAY WANT TO GRAB A SNACK AFTER SCHOOL WITH HIM OR HER. ASK WHAT HE OR SHE HAS BEEN WORKING ON LATELY. PROBABLY YOU'LL LEARN SOMETHING. OH YEAH—ASK GOD TO HELP YOU USE YOUR MIND FOR HIS GLORY.

If your sinful nature controls your mind, there is death. But if the Holy Spirit controls your mind, there is life and peace. [Romans 8:6]

also on this day

This is National Carmel Custard Day (sounds yummy).

The Mickey Mouse Club premiered on ABC-TV.

1955

Toot Your Flute?

You've probably never celebrated Toot Your Flute Day, or even heard of it. This sounds a lot like "blow your own horn," an old expression that means bragging or boasting about yourself and your accomplishments. Neither of these sayings is about music—just talking. The basic idea is that we ought to broadcast our accomplishments and let people know what we've done.

That may sound tempting to do when no one seems to notice our victories or good deeds and others seem to get all the credit and recognition. We can feel like screaming, "Hey! Look at me! Here's what I did!" And having an International Day like this one seems to give us permission to let everyone know how good we are.

The Bible has another idea, wrapped up in the word *humility*.

As you read Scripture, you will come upon this word and idea quite often—everything from "The LORD . . . shows favor to the humble" (Proverbs 3:34) to "Anyone who becomes as humble as this little child is the greatest in the Kingdom of Heaven" (Matthew 18:4).

Being humble means doing what we know is right and not caring who gets the credit. It means working on the fringes, outside the spotlight. It involves serving faithfully.

Having humility is difficult in a world where pride rules, where people trash talk, flaunt their accomplishments, parade their trophies, and strive to be No.1. It doesn't seem fair that no one notices or appears to care about us or what we do.

But God sees . . . and he cares.

Today's verse provides a powerful reminder—God is "mighty" and "in his good time" he will honor us. And his honor is the only one that really matters anyway.

to do ☑

TODAY, PURPOSELY DO SOMETHING FOR SOMEONE ANONYMOUSLY. IN OTHER WORDS, DO A GOOD DEED WITHOUT EVER LETTING THE PERSON KNOW THAT YOU WERE THE ONE WHO DID IT. YOU COULD GIVE A GIFT, CLEAN A SIBLING'S ROOM, PICK UP TRASH IN THE PARK—BE CREATIVE. REMEMBER, NO MATTER HOW TEMPTING, NEVER TELL ANYONE WHAT YOU DID. THE POINT IS NOT TO GET CREDIT BUT TO KNOW THE PURE JOY OF HUMBLE SERVICE.

So **humble** yourselves under the mighty **power** of **God**, and in his **good time** he will **honor** you.

[1 Peter 5:6]

also on this day

This is National Denim Day. Can you say *jeans*?

The first volunteer fire department was established in New York City by Peter Stuyvesant. **1648**

1957
The Soviet Union launched *Sputnik I* into orbit around the Earth. It was the first human-made satellite to enter space.

be contagious
This is World Smile Day.

Have you ever had one of those days when everyone seems to be in a bad mood? When that happens, we feel yucky—the bad mood seems to spread from person to person. Smiles are rare on days like that.

On the other hand, think of the difference a smile makes. Imagine you're walking home from school after a hard day. Head down, you're shuffling along. Coming toward you is someone you haven't seen for a couple of days. This person greets you by name and with a huge smile. Immediately you feel better, and you may even smile back.

If a bad mood is contagious, smiles are even more so. When you smile at someone, that person probably will return the smile. And the smiling will help raise your mood, even if it's just a tiny bit.

"Isn't that phony?" you ask. "Should I smile even when I don't feel like it?"

That's a good question. The secret is to think of a reason to smile. You will feel like smiling when you remember everything good that God is doing in your life.

You're reading this, so God must have given you sight. He gave you the ability to learn to read. And where did you get this book? If it was a gift, God gave you someone who thought enough of you to buy something for you. If you bought it yourself, then God gave you the money and the time and the opportunity.

Those reasons for smiling may seem small, but they're important. Add to that list your other physical and mental abilities, family members and friends, and church, school, special groups, clothes, food, entertainment, and transportation. Don't forget love, peace, freedom, and friendship.

But the best gift of all is Jesus. He left Heaven to live and die to pay for you, so you could have forgiveness and eternal life. Even on the worst day, that's a reason for joy, and a reason to smile!

For sure God has smiled on you—pass it on.

also on this day

This is National Come and Take It Day. (I hope "it" is free!)

1921 The World Series was broadcast on radio for the first time.

May the **LORD** **smile** on **you** and be **gracious** to you. [Numbers 6:25]

to do ☑
THIS IS AN EASY ONE. FOR THE NEXT 24 HOURS, TRY SMILING AT EVERYONE YOU MEET. WATCH HOW THEY REACT. THEN THANK GOD FOR ONE OF HIS AMAZING GIFTS TO YOU.

D o you know what *frugal* means? You should, because this is Frugal Fun Day, and you'll want to celebrate in the right way, don't you? Anyway, *frugal* means "thrifty, careful with money". Frugal people do more with less and are wise with how they spend their money.

Being frugal isn't easy. Advertising calls us to splurge and buy a lot of stuff for ourselves, especially whatever is "new," "improved," "state of the art," "the latest," and what everyone else seems to have. Somehow we think that if we have that game or outfit we'll be happy. But we soon tire of it (or it breaks), and we have to get the next "latest" one.

It's a trap—money and possessions will never satisfy us. That's the point of today's Bible passage. Solomon wrote it, and he was one of the richest people who ever lived.

And to top it off, remember that the Bible also talks about stewardship. That means using wisely the resources that God has entrusted to us: using and investing them for good purposes, not misusing or wasting them. This applies to our talents and abilities, our time, and, of course, our money.

So having a day to emphasize "frugal fun" is probably good. In fact, every day ought to be a "frugal fun day." We can enjoy ourselves and others without spending much money: hanging out and talking, playing ball in the park, making up new games with stuff we already have, getting out some of the really old games the family hasn't played in years, making up and telling jokes—use your imagination.

Celebrating God's goodness is easy . . . and cheap!

to do ☑

TAKE ONE OF THE SUGGESTIONS ABOVE. LIKE GETTING OUT AN OLD GAME AND PLAYING IT WITH YOUR FAMILY. IT'LL BE FUN AND FRUGAL.

simply living

This is International Frugal Fun Day.

also on this day

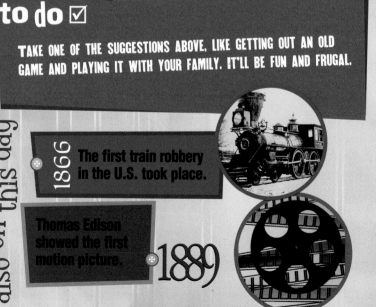

1866 The first train robbery in the U.S. took place.

Thomas Edison showed the first motion picture. **1889**

Those who love money will never have enough. How absurd to think that wealth brings true happiness! The more you have, the more people come to help you spend it. So what is the advantage of wealth—except perhaps to watch it run through your fingers! [Ecclesiastes 5:10, 11]

Little Ones

This is Child Health Day.

Remember singing "Jesus Loves Me" when you were small? Just about every child who has ever been to church knows that song. The verse goes (sing along if you want to): "Jesus loves me this I know, for the Bible tells me so. Little ones to him belong. They are weak, but he is strong."

Jesus had been busy teaching, healing, and answering difficult questions—pretty much adult stuff. So when parents brought their children to Jesus for his prayers, the disciples tried to shoo them away, thinking Jesus was too busy to mess with kids.

Not only did Jesus tell the disciples to let the children come, he also explained that children were very important to him and his kingdom. Thus the phrase, "Little ones to him belong."

Children are "little" and "weak," especially babies and toddlers. In fact, they depend on moms and dads and big brothers and sisters for *everything*. They own nothing and have no power. They're helpless—the opposite of what the world counts as important. We tend to value people based on their abilities, possessions, and positions in society. Yet Jesus says people need to become like little children if they want to be his followers. Luke reports that after calling for the children, Jesus said, "I assure you, anyone who doesn't have their kind of faith will never get into the Kingdom of God" (Luke 18:17).

So how do you get along with little kids, especially when they're crying? How about when Mom or Dad asks you to pick up after them, change a diaper, or babysit? Are they annoying, a pain, an inconvenience?

Whenever you have those feelings, remember Jesus' words and thank God for all his children, especially the little ones.

to do ☑

IF YOU HAVE A LITTLE BROTHER OR SISTER, TODAY OFFER TO HELP TAKE CARE OF HIM OR HER BEFORE BEING ASKED. AND BE ESPECIALLY KIND TO ALL THE LITTLE ONES IN YOUR LIFE.

But **Jesus** said, "**Let** the **children** come to me. Don't **stop** them! For the **Kingdom** of **God belongs** to such as **these**."

[Matthew 19:14]

also on this day

This is World Habitat Day.

1968
The Motion Picture Association of America adopted the film-rating system that ranged from *G* to *X*.

october **08**

fluffernutter

This is National Fluffernutter Day.

I n case you don't know, a *fluffernutter* is a sandwich made with lightly toasted white bread, peanut butter, marshmallow cream, and chocolate topping. Sounds rich and delicious, but oh so fatty.

What a combination! How do cooks and chefs think up recipes like that? Do you suppose they suddenly think "Hey, I'll mix peanut butter and marshmallow cream" or do they have a more scientific approach? Maybe it's just trial and error. First they try peanut butter and mustard (yuck!), then peanut butter and barbeque sauce (no!), then cabbage, then . . . How'd you like to taste-test those combinations?

Some food combinations sound weird but taste great. A fluffernutter is one of those.

Here's another unusual combination—faith and works. How is it unusual? You see, some people think a person can get right with God by doing good works, and that if a person's good acts outweigh the bad ones, he or she will get into Heaven. The Bible clearly teaches, however, that people are saved by grace through faith (see Ephesians 2:8, 9). But then in James (today's verse), we see faith and works together. It seems to say that faith and works *have to* be combined. Are you confused?

James is not saying that we do good deeds *in order to* be saved. Instead, he is saying that faith in Christ *results* in good deeds. That is, we do what is right *because* we know God—not to make us right with him.

Talk is cheap. But works show whether or not a person truly has faith. A person becomes a Christian by trusting in Christ—that's it. But then he or she lives differently, reading God's Word and doing what it says.

Faith and works—they really *do* go together.

to do ☑

ASK YOUR MOM TO MAKE A FLUFFERNUTTER SANDWICH FOR YOU. WHEN SHE ASKS WHAT IT IS, EXPLAIN THAT IT'S A LOT LIKE FAITH AND WORKS—AN UNUSUAL COMBINATION—BUT IT TASTES YUMMY. THEN MAKE ONE FOR HER!

also on this day

This is National Children's Day. Give yourself a present!

The Great Fire of Chicago started, eventually destroying about 17,450 buildings. **1871**

So you **see**, it isn't **enough just** to have **faith. Faith** that **doesn't show** itself by **good deeds** is **no** faith at all—it is **dead** and **useless**.

[James 2:17]

At 555 feet high, the Washington Monument is one of the tallest masonry structures in the world, towering over everything in Washington, D.C. From the top you can see the Lincoln Memorial, the White House, the Thomas Jefferson Memorial, and the Capitol building.

Washington, D.C., is filled with monuments, but just about every city and town has them. Some are huge, like the U.S.S. *Arizona* Memorial in Pearl Harbor in Hawaii, and some small, like roadside plaques.

Monuments and memorials remind us of important events and people. (We talked about this on Memorial Day.) At this stage in your life, memorials probably don't mean as much as they will when you get older, but your parents may find some of them very moving. Monuments and memorials were important to God's people in the Old Testament as well. After a great victory (or great tragedy), they would erect one so that the Israelites would never forget the event and the lessons learned. Today's verse is a good example. These remembrances usually marked a *spiritual* occasion, helping everyone remember God and his great work among them.

We've gotten away from building spiritual memorials, so we find it easy to forget those times when God acted in a mighty way on our behalf. Maybe we ought to start that tradition again. For example, you may have a rock or shell from a camp, retreat, or vacation where you made an important decision. It sits on your shelf, reminding you of that special time. Photographs are great for this, as long as we have them out where we can see them. Keeping a journal or diary is another way of remembering what God has done. You can go back and read what you were feeling at a tough time in your life, and then weeks or months later see how God used that time for your growth.

Make a point of remembering God's goodness and your special moments with him.

to do ☑

THINK OF A FITTING MEMORIAL FOR WHEN YOU ACCEPTED CHRIST AS SAVIOR. YOU MIGHT WANT TO WRITE THE DATE, TIME, AND PLACE ON A CLEAN SHEET OF PAPER, DECORATE IT, AND PUT IN ON A BEDROOM WALL.

"Then you can tell them, 'They remind us that the Jordan River stopped flowing when the Ark of the LORD's covenant went across.' These stones will stand as a permanent memorial among the people of Israel." [Joshua 4:7]

On this day in 1888, the public was admitted to the Washington Monument for the first time.

remembering

also on this day

1002
This is Leif Erikson Day. On this day in 1002, Leif Erikson landed on North America.

Helen Moss joined the Brownies at the age of 83. She became the oldest person to become a member.
1983

All Dressed Up

On this day in 1886, the first dinner jacket was worn to the autumn ball at Tuxedo Park, New York.

Now you know where the name *tuxedo* came from. And ever since that fateful day in New York, men have been wearing tuxes at special occasions.

Actually getting dressed up can be fun, especially when we're looking forward to the event—a concert, a dinner, a party, a wedding. But have you ever heard the expression, "All dressed up, but no place to go"? That paints a very sad picture. It implies that the person either missed the party or didn't get invited.

Jesus once described the kingdom of God as a party, a banquet, a wedding feast (see Matthew 22:1-14). And he talked about the necessity of wearing "the proper clothes" (v. 11). He was illustrating the truth that everyone who enters Heaven must be clothed in Christ's righteousness. God provides the "formal attire" for the occasion.

Today, many people think God will allow them to party at his banquet because they are decent people—they haven't done anything really terrible, or they have done a bunch of good deeds. Those "clothes" might look OK here on earth, but they won't make it there. The Bible is very clear that only by putting our trust in Jesus—believing in him as God's Son and that he died on the cross for our sins, admitting our sinfulness, and asking him to take over—can we be saved.

And you know what's really sad? These *right* clothes are available to anyone who believes, yet so many refuse. They'd rather wear their rags than God's "tuxedo."

There's another event where a person wears fancy clothes—for his or her funeral. Everyone goes there sooner or later. Sadly, many will be all dressed up with no good place to go.

to do ☑

STOP AND PRAY RIGHT NOW FOR YOUR RELATIVES, FRIENDS, AND NEIGHBORS WHO DO NOT KNOW CHRIST. ASK GOD TO OPEN THEIR HEARTS TO HIM AND HIS FREE GIFT OF FORGIVE-NESS AND SALVATION.

And just as it is destined that each person dies only once and after that comes judgment, so also Christ died only once as a sacrifice to take away the sins of many people. He will come again . . . he will bring salvation to all those who are eagerly waiting for him."

[Hebrews 9:27, 28]

also on this day

This is Bring Your Teddy to Work Day. (Can you bear it?)

The United States Naval Academy opened in Annapolis, Maryland. **1845**

⊛ **1969**
Pro football quarterback Brett Favre was born.

truth or consequences

On this day in 1759, Parson Mason Weems was born.

Who on earth was Parson Mason Weems? you're probably wondering. Well, in his book, *The Life and Memorable Actions of George Washington*, he wrote about young George cutting down the cherry tree. When confronted by his father, George supposedly said, "I cannot tell a lie," and then he admitted his guilt.

That's an interesting story, and it's usually presented as historical fact. But no one has been able to verify that the event actually occurred. Evidently Mr. Weems invented the story to create a better image of George Washington for the American people.

These days stories, especially ones about famous people, spread quickly. Many people believe the stories just because they're in print. Urban legends are that way. And some phony stories are hoaxes—started by someone trying to fool others.

These tales may cause people to respond foolishly. Some damage reputations. So be careful what you believe when you read or hear something. Always try to find out the truth.

In many of the early churches, false stories—rumors and teaching—were being spread. Unfortunately some of the new believers were being fooled and led astray. So the apostle Paul wrote them to bring them back to the truth of God's Word.

Today's Bible selection is one of those occasions. Paul was shocked that the Galatians were "being fooled by those who twist and change the truth concerning Christ."

That's a good lesson for us, especially with so many false stories flying around these days. We should *always* check with the Bible to see if a statement or story is true. That goes for what we see on TV and in movies, what we read in books and on the Internet, and what we hear. The *truth* is way more important than an interesting story.

Don't be fooled!

also on this day

This is National Sausage Pizza Day.

1984
Space shuttle *Challenger* astronaut Kathryn Sullivan became the first American woman to walk in space.

I am shocked that you are turning away so soon from God, who in his love and mercy called you to share the eternal life he gives through Christ. You are already following a different way that pretends to be the Good News but is not the Good News at all. You are being fooled by those who twist and change the truth concerning Christ. [Galatians 1:6, 7]

to do ☑

ASK YOUR PARENTS TO TELL YOU ABOUT THE URBAN LEGENDS THEY ONCE BELIEVED WERE TRUE. HAVE THEM TELL YOU HOW THEY DISCOVERED THAT THE STORIES WEREN'T TRUE. THEN ASK ABOUT SOMETHING THEY'VE HEARD ABOUT GOD THAT ISN'T TRUE AND WHAT THE TRUTH IS.

october **12**

rain reign

On this day in 1823, Charles Macintosh of Scotland began selling raincoats.

Rain can be a pain, especially on the plain, especially when you have to work or play in it. And rain in October can really make life miserable in the colder parts of the country. Of course, marvelous inventions such as the umbrella and raincoat make it easier to venture out into the storm.

Weather is interesting. We're all affected by it but can do very little about it, except, of course, prepare, choose a good attitude, and respond. For example, you've made plans, but now it's pouring—your plans and hopes are dashed. How will you react? Many mope and complain and whine. That self-centered approach helps no one and just gets on everyone's nerves. A better response is to thank God for the rain, smile, and adjust the schedule.

Some people pray for good weather when they're worried about an important outside event. They don't want it to rain on their parade, picnic, or ball game.

Others, especially farmers, pray *for* rain—at the right time and in the right amount—because their lives depend on having crops to harvest and sell.

So would it be fair to the farmer who desperately needs rain for us to ask God to withhold it so we can get in nine innings or have a day at the beach?

It's a balance. We want rain because we want green lawns, healthy trees, beautiful flowers, and delicious veggies and bread and corn-fed cattle and chickens. But at times we *don't want* rain because we don't want activities rained out and because we're already soaked.

So what are we to do? Well, we can *pray*— talking to God about how we feel. We can remember the farmers and thank God for his provision. We can *plan*—adjusting our attitude and schedule. And we can *prepare*—keeping the umbrella and raincoat handy, just in case.

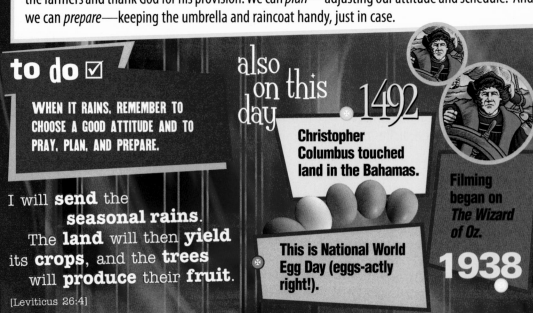

to do ☑

WHEN IT RAINS, REMEMBER TO CHOOSE A GOOD ATTITUDE AND TO PRAY, PLAN, AND PREPARE.

I will **send** the **seasonal rains**. The **land** will then **yield** its **crops**, and the **trees** will **produce** their **fruit**.

[Leviticus 26:4]

also on this day

1492

Christopher Columbus touched land in the Bahamas.

This is National World Egg Day (eggs-actly right!).

Filming began on *The Wizard of Oz.*

1938

Cornerstone

On this day in 1792, the cornerstone of the Executive Mansion was laid in Washington, D. C. The building became known as the White House in 1818.

In ancient times, a cornerstone was the most important building block for any structure. It's placement and shape determined the form of the whole building. It still usually refers to the first stone of a new building, laid at a corner where two walls begin. Because of this role, the word became associated with something or someone very important. So you might hear that an athlete is the cornerstone of the team.

These days, as in 1792, the cornerstone will often be laid with great fanfare and ceremony for a noteworthy construction project.

In today's Bible passage, cornerstone is used as a symbol, and Jesus quoted this verse to refer to himself. When questioned by the religious leaders, he replied, "Didn't you ever read this in the Scriptures? 'The stone rejected by the builders has now become the cornerstone. This is the Lord's doing, and it is marvelous to see'" (Matthew 21:42).

Acts 4:11, Ephesians 2:20, and 1 Peter 2:4-7 also refer to Jesus as the cornerstone, emphasizing that our salvation—in fact, our very lives—must be built on Christ. Otherwise, like a poorly constructed building, everything will crumble.

Peter wrote: "As the Scriptures express it, 'I am placing a stone in Jerusalem, a chosen cornerstone, and anyone who believes in him will never be disappointed'" (1 Peter 2:6). That's great news!

You will hear about many options for building your life. You might be tempted, for example, to build on money and possessions and worldly success. Or you might find that special person and try building your life on him or her—on love. Education, talent, and power are other popular options. But none of those will work as a sufficient cornerstone. Only Christ will do. And those who believe in him will never be disappointed.

to do ☑

GO TO A LARGE, OLD CHURCH, THE LIBRARY, CITY HALL, OR ANOTHER IMPORTANT BUILDING IN TOWN. FIND THE CORNERSTONE AND NOTE WHAT IT SAYS. THEN, RIGHT THERE, THANK JESUS FOR BEING YOUR CORNERSTONE.

The **stone rejected** by the **builders** has now **become** the **cornerstone**.

[Psalm 118:22]

also on this day

This is U.S. Navy Day.

The U.S. Continental Congress ordered the construction of a naval fleet. 1775

1995 Walt Disney World® in Orlando, Florida, admitted its 500-millionth guest.

What the big deal about hair, anyway? We cut it, comb and brush it, color it, wash it, spray it, and style it—no wonder people worry about losing their hair! It's a big part of life.

Most bald people (usually men) got that way because of heredity. Scientists say that the mother's side of the family is the source of genetic baldness. If a man's mother's father was bald, the man has a higher chance of going bald himself.

Some people have lost their hair through illness or medical treatments. Others shave their heads to make a statement or to be free of all the mess and work of hair care.

Be Bald and Be Free Day was probably started by men who had lost their hair and had dealt with it. It's as if they wanted to shout, "Hey, I'm hairless—bald—and it's OK! In fact, I like it."

In the Bible, you'll find people with a wide variety of hair lengths. Samson, for example, had extra long hair—the secret to his strength (Judges 16:17-19). Elisha became angry when a crowd of youths mocked him by calling him "baldhead" (2 Kings 2:23-25). Absalom had long luxurious hair that weighed five pounds when he cut it (2 Samuel 14:26).

Undoubtedly the most startling statement in the Bible about hair is in today's passage. Jesus was speaking to the crowd and his closest followers, telling them that they shouldn't worry because they were valuable to God. So valuable in fact, that God even knew all the details of their lives—even the number of hairs on their heads.

Some bald people joke that God doesn't have to work very hard counting their strands of hair. But Jesus' wasn't really talking about our scalps and follicles. He was making the point that each person is valuable to God, including *you*. How great is that?

So every time you comb or brush your hair, say thanks to God for his love and care. Hey! That rhymes!

to do ☑

TYPE OUT THE PHRASE "I'M A BIG, HAIRY DEAL TO GOD." CUT IT OUT, AND TAPE IT TO YOUR COMB OR BRUSH. IT WILL REMIND YOU OF YOUR VALUE TO GOD.

also on this day

1926 The book *Winnie-the-Pooh* by A. A. Milne was published.

Martin Luther King Jr. received the Nobel Peace Prize. *1964*

hairy deal

This is National Be Bald and Be Free Day.

8203908858840398

"And the very hairs of your head are all numbered. So don't be afraid; you are more valuable to [God] than a whole flock of sparrows." [Luke 12:7]

poetic justice

This is National Poetry Day.

"**R**oses are red, violets are blue; some poems rhyme, but this one doesn't."
Since it's National Poetry Day, it was only right to begin with a poem—well, sort of a poem. Speaking of that, how do you feel about poetry and poems? It's a style of writing that has been around for many years. And, like it or not, when you get to high school, you'll read a ton of poems in literature classes.

In giving us his Word, God used a variety of authors and writing styles and types. The Bible has historical books (such as Genesis and Acts), prophetic books (such as Isaiah and Amos), letters (such as Galatians and 1 John), gospels (such as Matthew and Luke), and apocalyptic books (such as Revelation). In fact, one whole section in the Old Testament is labeled as poetry. This section has Job, Psalms, Proverbs, Ecclesiastes, and Song of Songs.

You can find poems in other parts of the Bible, but Psalms has some amazing ones. Check out Psalm 127, for example. It begins, "Unless the LORD builds a house, the work of the builders is useless. Unless the LORD protects a city, guarding it with sentries will do no good" (v. 1). And a little later, you'll find: "Children are a gift from the LORD; they are a reward from him" (v. 3). That's talking about *you*, so now you like poetry, right?

to do ☑

TRY READING A PSALM A DAY FOR THE NEXT WEEK OR SO. LET GOD'S WORD PRESENTED THROUGH POETRY SINK IN. AND TRY YOUR HAND AT EXPRESSING YOURSELF THROUGH A POEM.

Restore our fortunes, LORD,
    as streams renew the desert.
Those who plant in tears
    will harvest with shouts of joy.
They weep as they go to plant
    their seed,
    but they sing as they return
        with the harvest.

[Psalm 126:4-6]

also on this day

1860

In her letter to presidential candidate Abraham Lincoln, Grace Bedell, age 11, said he would look better if he grew a beard.

I Love Lucy premiered on television.

1951

This is National Grouch Day.

get your **words** worth

This is National Dictionary Day.

You probably think this special day was begun by publishers to sell more dictionaries. Perhaps, but it also honors Noah Webster. He was born on this day in 1758 and is famous for writing *Webster's Dictionary*.

After graduating from college, Noah Webster taught school but became very dissatisfied with the American school system. Often as many as 70 children of all ages would be jammed into one room, with poorly-written books, no desks, and untrained teachers. How'd you like to try learning there? In 1783, he wrote his own textbook: *A Grammatical Institute of the English Language*. A few years later, at age 43, Noah started writing the first American dictionary. He thought Americans should spell, pronounce, and use words the same way. A dictionary helps do just that because it explains the correct meaning, spelling, and pronunciation of each word.

It's important for words to have exact meanings; otherwise everyone would get confused. We know that the word *groceries*, for example, refers to food and related items, not plumbing supplies. And when we order a glass of milk at a restaurant, we would be shocked if the server were to bring a hammer. Saying what we mean and meaning what we say is important for good communication.

In our verse for today James points out the importance of being known as people who clearly state what they mean. You don't have to be a walking dictionary, but you should mean what you say.

Don't you just hate it when someone told you yes and then later said, "I really didn't mean that—I meant 'maybe'"? *Yes* should mean "positively, for sure, certainly."

> Above all, my brothers,
>   do not swear—not by heaven
> or by earth or by anything else.
> Let your "Yes" be yes, and your
> "No," no, or you will be con-
> demned. [James 5:12, NIV]

also on this day

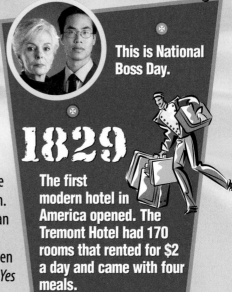

This is National Boss Day.

1829

The first modern hotel in America opened. The Tremont Hotel had 170 rooms that rented for $2 a day and came with four meals.

to do ☑

FOR THE NEXT WEEK OR SO, CHOOSE A WORD EACH DAY FROM THE DICTIONARY (SUCH AS TRANSIENT, UBIQUITOUS, EVOCATIVE, OR PROFOUND). LEARN ITS MEANING AND SPELLING, AND THEN USE IT IN A SENTENCE WHEN TALKING WITH YOUR PARENTS OR ANOTHER ADULT. THEY'LL BE AMAZED!

Flip through the pages of a *National Geographic Magazine,* and you'll quickly be amazed at the great photography. Their writers and photographers literally travel to the ends of the earth, from Alaska to Afghanistan and from mountaintops to ocean depths, to get interesting stories. And they always capture human emotions, fascinating culture, and natural beauty in their pictures.

If you read more than one issue, you'll be struck with the differences in cultures, yet the similarities among people. All people have the same basic needs—food, water, shelter—and they experience the same emotions, including love, hate, fear, longing, grief, and joy. Every people group has mothers and fathers struggling to raise their families, workers trying to make a living, and children looking for fun. Everyone also has a spiritual side, expressed in a wide variety of ways.

When Jesus told his disciples to take the gospel message "to the ends of the earth," they didn't know about people living on the other side of the world. Unlike you, they didn't have TV, the Internet, and *National Geographic.* And those disciples certainly had no idea of modern America with almost 300 million people. But Jesus knew. And he was serious about his command to make disciples of *all* the nations (Matthew 28:19). That's because all people have something else in common—they all need Christ. And ever since then, groups of believers have spread the Word through conversations, meetings, events, missionaries, and media.

You can be part of this process. You can pray; you can give money to help support ministries and missionaries; you can share the good news with a friend. In so doing, you will be part of the team to take Christ to the ends of the earth.

to do ☑

THE NEXT TIME YOU SEE A PICTURE OF SOMEONE LIVING AT "THE ENDS OF THE EARTH," PRAY THAT HE OR SHE WILL HEAR THE GOSPEL, RESPOND IN FAITH, AND FIND NEW LIFE IN **C**HRIST.

"But when the Holy Spirit has come upon you, you will receive power and will tell people about me everywhere—in Jerusalem, throughout Judea, in Samaria, and to the ends of the earth." [Acts 1:8]

On this day in 1888, the first issue of **National Geographic Magazine** was released at newsstands.

to the ends of the earth

also on this day

1979 Mother Teresa of India was awarded the Nobel Peace Prize.

This is National Pasta Day.

Upside Down

On this day in 1961, Henri Matisse's painting, Le Bateau, went on display at New York's Museum of Modern Art.

to do ☑

GO ON-LINE AND TRY TO FIND LE BATEAU. LOOK AT IT UPSIDE DOWN AND, THEN, RIGHT SIDE UP. SEE IF YOU CAN FIGURE OUT WHAT IT IS SUPPOSED TO MEAN.

When you read the fact for today, you probably thought, "What's the big deal about that?" Good question. But get this: It was discovered 46 days later that the painting had been hanging upside down! That means hundreds, maybe thousands, of people had passed by, viewing the painting and making comments such as, "Beautiful," "Interesting," "I see what Matisse was doing . . ." when they didn't have a clue. They weren't looking from the artist's point of view, so they didn't really know how to view it.

How would you like to be an artist and have *your* paintings hung upside down and interpreted that way?

This may sound strange, but listen carefully: Followers of Jesus can be easily misunderstood. People look at their lives and think they have Christians figured out, but they're looking "upside down." They just don't get it.

This has been going on for 2,000 years. Today's passage explains that, according to the people of Thessalonica, Paul and Silas had turned the world "upside down." The people were afraid of the two because their message was so different and hard to understand. You see, Jesus' values are the opposite of the world's. His followers live differently. The lives of those who follow Jesus are changed dramatically.

If the Thessalonians had looked at Paul and Silas from the artist's (God's) point of view, they would have seen the truth—the gospel message was actually turning the world *right side up.*

So don't be surprised if people misunderstand you, your lifestyle, and your message. They don't know the artist. Ask God for ways to introduce them, to open their eyes to the truth.

Not finding them there, they dragged out Jason and some of the other believers instead and took them before the city council. "Paul and Silas have turned the rest of the world upside down, and now they are here disturbing our city," they shouted. [Acts 17:6]

also on this day

This is National Chocolate Cupcake Day.

Inventor Thomas Edison died. 1931

1958
The first computer-arranged marriage took place on Art Linkletter's television show.

full surrender

On this day in 1781, the American Revolutionary War ended.

A war ending is a big deal. One side has to admit defeat and then surrender. Imagine how humbling that must be for the king, generals, or other losing leaders! Then the defeated armies and people must submit to the power and authority of the conquerors.

Wars are ugly. Combatants and innocent civilians get hurt and killed, and cities and villages get destroyed. Even the victorious army suffers great losses. No wonder we want to avoid war if at all possible.

Regardless of how you feel about fighting and war, you're in one. The Bible explains that spiritual warfare is going on all around us. It's a war between God and Satan for control of the universe and for people's hearts.

The Bible also says God will win. Check out the book of Revelation for all the details. But every day brings battles. Satan works hard at trying to prevent people from hearing God's truth and joining him. He also tries to keep Christ's followers from living right and joining the battle. So God tells us about armor to wear and weapons to use (see Ephesians 6:10-18).

What God wants is total surrender. That's right. The first step to winning in life is to give up, stop resisting God, and give ourselves totally to him—no strings attached.

This is tough because we don't like the idea of giving up control of our lives. We think we know best and that we need to be strong and do things ourselves. Wrong. Remember, Jesus said that the person who seeks to save his life will lose it (Matthew 16:25).

So if you want to win the battle *and* the war, give up and surrender totally to God.

Submit to God's royal son,
    or he will become angry,
   and you will be destroyed in the
midst of your pursuits—
for his anger can flare up in an instant.
   But what joy for all who find
protection in him! [Psalm 2:12]

also on this day

1849

Elizabeth Blackwell became the first woman in the United States to receive a medical degree.

1914

The U.S. Post Office first used an automobile to collect and deliver mail.

to do ☑

IN WHAT AREAS OF LIFE HAVE YOU BEEN RESISTING GOD? TAKE TIME, RIGHT NOW, TO TALK WITH HIM ABOUT THOSE THINGS. SURRENDER FULLY TO YOUR KING.

appreciation

This is Sunday School Teacher Appreciation Day.

When you hear the word *school,* what comes to your mind? "Yuck!"? A building? A difficult teacher? You and a bunch of friends on the playground?

School can bring many mental pictures, not all of them positive. Maybe that's why some kids find it hard to like the idea of "Sunday *school.*" They've already had five days of lessons and lectures, teachers and tests, and desks and detentions, and now another one!

Actually Sunday school was begun in England many years ago to be a place where poor children could learn. Instruction in the Christian faith was just one part of what they were taught. These days the teaching in Sunday School classes almost totally focuses on Bible lessons and faith.

To appreciate your teachers, first you have to appreciate Sunday school. That can happen if you stop thinking of it as the same as other schools. You could, for example, call it "Sunday Surprise," "Bible Adventure," "Church Challenge," or something similar. This might help you look forward to the time more.

Next, consider the leader—your teacher. This person has worked hard preparing for his or her time with you, going over lesson plans, looking up Bible verses, gathering props, materials, and refreshments. He or she has been praying—for you and the others in your group. This person is a *volunteer*—he or she doesn't get paid for spending time with you every week.

Finally, remember the reason for having Sunday school—to teach kids about God. You're not against that, are you? Approaching each class with a positive attitude probably will help you get closer to your teacher and closer to God.

OK, so are you ready to "appreciate" now? Get to it!

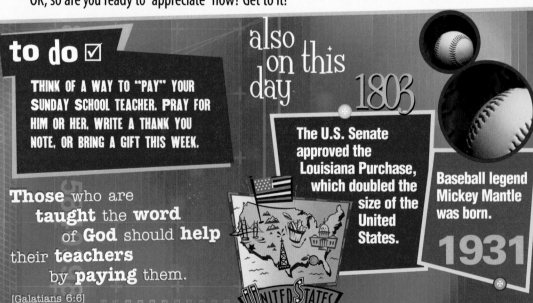

to do ☑

THINK OF A WAY TO "PAY" YOUR SUNDAY SCHOOL TEACHER. PRAY FOR HIM OR HER, WRITE A THANK YOU NOTE, OR BRING A GIFT THIS WEEK.

Those who are **taught** the **word** of **God** should **help** their **teachers** by **paying** them.

[Galatians 6:6]

also on this day

1803

The U.S. Senate approved the Louisiana Purchase, which doubled the size of the United States.

UNITED STATES

Baseball legend Mickey Mantle was born.

1931

You may remember back in January we highlighted the patenting of the lightbulb. So why talk about this again? Let's shed a little light on the topic.

Imagine life without lightbulbs. Consider how many you use every day. Start in your room and think about all the lights in your house. At school, you'll find lots—in hallways, classrooms, locker room, gymnasium, cafeteria. Don't forget those in your school bus and cars. And what about streetlights, traffic lights, and warning lights? Oh yeah, you also have flashlights, reading lights, spotlights, strobe lights, lasers, neons, blacklights, LCDs, refrigerator lights, clock lights . . . you probably can think of even more.

Without lights your world would be dark, especially at night. You could use candles, kerosene, or torches, of course, but that would be very inconvenient. So, thanks again, Thomas Edison.

But also remember: having lights is not enough; you need to *use* them.

Makes sense, right? Otherwise, you'd spend a lot of time in the dark—getting lost, bumping into things, and losing stuff.

Jesus said, "I am the light of the world" (John 8:12; 9:5). He said his followers should be light to a dark world (Matthew 5:14-16). Today's verse tells us to "walk in the light." This means following close to Christ and obeying him.

Look closely at the world and you'll find darkness—millions of lost people searching for the way. Their light has come, but they keep struggling in the dark. Would you rather stumble in darkness? Hit the switch and then walk in the light.

But if we walk in the light, as he is in the light, we have fellowship with one another, and the blood of Jesus, his Son, purifies us from all sin. [1 John 1:7, NIV]

On this day in 1879, Thomas Edison invented the lightbulb.

to do ☑

FOR THE NEXT HOUR OR TWO, SAY A SHORT PRAYER EVERY TIME YOU SEE A LIGHTBULB. IF THE LIGHT IS TURNED ON, THANK GOD FOR HIS LIGHT AND ASK FOR HIS GUIDANCE. IF THE LIGHT IS OFF, THANK GOD FOR HIS LIGHT AND CONFESS THOSE TIMES WHEN YOU'VE "WALKED IN DARKNESS."

also on this day

1956 ✴ **Actress Carrie Fisher was born. She played the part of Princess Leia in the *Star Wars* films.**

✴ **This is National Reptile Day.**

in the light

clonely you

On this day in 1938, the first copy was made on a Xerox® machine.

That first copy must not have been very good, because copiers weren't used much until about 40 years later. Then for many years Xerox was the only company known for copiers. That's why people will often say, "I'll make a Xerox" when talking about making a photocopy of something. These days many companies make great copiers of all types. In fact, copiers have become so common that we can't remember life without them.

Others have been talking about copies—scientists. You've probably heard of cloning. That's the process of making an exact copy of a plant or animal. Some of these scientists are even talking about cloning humans. So far that's illegal. Hopefully it'll stay that way.

Even if scientists could "copy" human beings, however, no one could make another *you*. When God made you, he made a one-of-a-kind, unique model. No one else, not even an identical twin, has your exact combination of physical characteristics, personality, talents, likes and dislikes, abilities, personal history, and so forth. No one else has the same future either.

And here's the best news of all: God loves you just as you are—the way he made you. In other words, you don't have to change your looks, your personality, or anything else about yourself to please him. It doesn't mean everything you *think* and *do* is OK. God wants us to have the right attitudes and actions to obey him. But you're not a clone; you're a "masterpiece" (see today's verse). Remember that when you're feeling lost in the crowd.

God has a great future in store for you. And there will never be another you!

For **we** are **God's masterpiece**.
He has **created** us anew
in **Christ Jesus**, so that
we can do the **good things**
he planned for us **long ago**.

[Ephesians 2:10]

also on this day

This is National **Color Day.**

This is National **Nut Day.**

1746
Princeton University was founded.

to do ☑

ASK YOUR MOM OR DAD HOW HE OR SHE HAS SEEN YOU CHANGE FOR THE BETTER AS YOU HAVE GROWN OLDER. THEN THANK GOD FOR MAKING YOU UNIQUE AND FOR HIS CONTINUING WORK IN YOU.

Q & A

This is National TV Talk Show Host Day.

Television talk shows have multiplied like rabbits. You can find one on the air at virtually any time, day or night. Who would ever have guessed that Americans would have so much to talk about?

If you watch for very long, you'll soon realize that one of the keys to a show's success is the host's ability to ask good questions—thoughtful questions that draw out interesting answers. Imagine a guest hearing a series of questions like, "How are you?" or "Do you think it'll rain?" Now that would get old real quick!

If you want good answers, you have to ask good questions.

So here's a question for you: Imagine you're a talk show host and *God* is your guest. If you could ask God one question, what would you ask?

Habakkuk had that opportunity. As a prophet his job was to give God's message to the people. The problem, however, was that Habakkuk had more questions than he had answers. What did he do? He took his questions directly to God. You can find his questions and God's answers in the little book of the Bible that bears the prophet's name. In fact, today's verse contains Habakkuk's first question.

We can learn much from Habakkuk. Perhaps the most important lesson is that we can ask God any question—nothing is too difficult or boring or outrageous. He can handle all our questions. Check out God's response to Habakkuk. God didn't zap him or put him down; he took the questions seriously and gave serious answers.

So what about your nagging doubts and serious issues? Bring them to God—he can take it. And he'll point you to the answers.

to do ☑

READ THE WHOLE BOOK OF
HABAKKUK (IT WON'T TAKE LONG).
NOTE HABAKKUK'S QUESTIONS
AND GOD'S ANSWERS.

How **long**, O **LORD**,
    must I **call** for **help**?
But **you** do **not listen!**
    "**Violence!**" I **cry**,
        but you do **not**
come to **save**. [Habakkuk 1:2]

also on this day

1992

Japanese Emperor Akihito became the first Japanese emperor to stand on Chinese soil.

Song parodist "Weird Al" Yankovick was born.

1959

This is National Mole Day (Can you dig it?)

This is United Nations Day.

United?

On this day in 1945, the United Nations came into existence. As the name indicates, the goal is for the nations of the earth to be "united." According to the preamble of the U.N. charter, "We the peoples of the United Nations determined . . . to combine our efforts to accomplish these aims."

Being united is a wonderful ideal. Too often the nations of the world are terribly divided. Every day we hear of wars and other international conflicts. Because we desire unity and dislike conflict, however, we can get the idea that being unified or united is more important than anything else. Sometimes to keep the peace in a relationship, we might hide our real feelings. Or we may keep our thoughts to ourselves in a class even though we disagree with what's being taught. Certainly peace and unity are important, but truth is more important.

Jesus warned his followers that their beliefs and allegiance to him would cause problems. In today's verse, he says that instead of peace on earth, he brings "a sword." Jesus wasn't telling his disciples to be disagreeable. He was simply explaining that they shouldn't expect to be welcomed by everyone.

Jesus claimed to be the only way to God. This truth challenges people who think that all religions lead to God. Jesus wants our complete allegiance. That doesn't sit well in countries run by dictators or dominated by another religion. Jesus tells his followers to live right and to stand for what's right. That doesn't win many friends with those pressuring us to do wrong.

Better to be united with Christ and his people than to be the friend of the world.

to do ☑

THINK OF PEOPLE WHO HAVE GIVEN YOU A HARD TIME BECAUSE OF YOUR FAITH IN CHRIST. SPEND SOME TIME PRAYING FOR THEM RIGHT NOW.

also on this day

This is National Bologna Day (no matter how you slice it).

*1901

Anna Taylor was the first person to survive going over Niagara Falls in a barrel.

"Don't **imagine** that I came to bring **peace** to the **earth**! **No**, I came to bring a **sword**."

[Matthew 10:34]

What a fantastic invention! Before microwaves, cooking meals took a while. Now we can warm up leftovers or cook a TV dinner in minutes. It's also great for heating drinks, popping popcorn, thawing meat, and dozens of other tasks.

Although we can eat sooner than before, we often wish the process were even faster. It's the same with computers. Not very long ago, personal computers were rare, expensive, and slow. But now we can't seem to get them to go fast enough. And what about the Internet? Only recently has it exploded into our lives as a great tool for communication and information, but we have come to expect it to serve us faster and faster. Dial-up seems almost prehistoric, and e-mail has morphed to instant messaging.

The inventions and technological advances are great, but often they raise our expectations for speed. We live in the instant society. We want everything *now*!

Some things *can't* be rushed. Physical growth takes time. You may want to be taller right now, but you'll have to wait. Other things *shouldn't* be rushed—like education. Learning through books, classes, and experience takes years. At other times conditions *force* life to slow down—such as traffic on roads and airports during bad weather.

You've probably heard, "Patience is a virtue." It's true! And it's listed in the fruit of the spirit (Galatians 5:22, 23). God knows that at times we will need to wait—for answers to prayer, for help in trouble, for relief from pain, for his kingdom to come. So he wants us to develop patience, to learn to wait and to depend on him in the meantime.

So the next time you're standing at the microwave, sitting at the computer, or standing in line, take a deep breath, relax, and learn a lesson in patience.

to do ☑

TODAY TRY TO TAKE EVERYTHING A BIT SLOWER. INSTEAD OF RUSHING AROUND, TRY RELAXING. AND AS YOU WAIT FOR THE COMPUTER TO CONNECT, THE PHONE TO RING, OR YOUR FAVORITE TV SHOW TO BEGIN, REMEMBER THE IMPORTANCE OF PATIENCE.

We also pray that you will be strengthened with his glorious power so that you will have all the patience and endurance you need. May you be filled with joy. [Colossians 1:11]

On this day in 1955, the Tappan Company introduced the microwave oven.

also on this day

1964 The Rolling Stones first appeared on the *Ed Sullivan Show.*

Painter Pablo Picasso was born. 1881

instant?

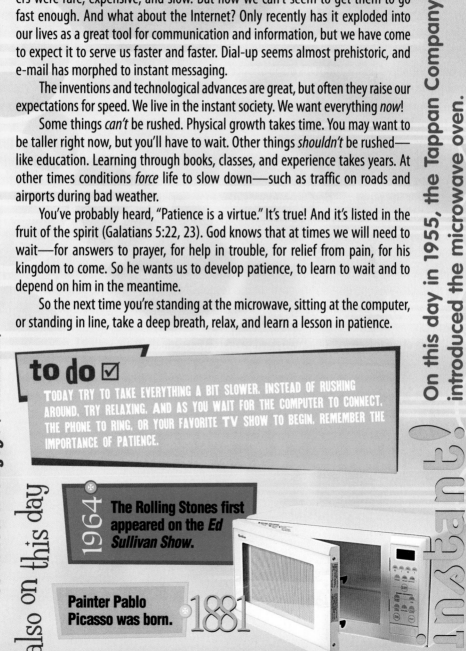

october **26**

the buck stops here

On this day in 1949, President Harry Truman
raised the minimum wage from 40 to 75 cents an hour.

One of President Truman's most famous sayings is "The buck stops here." That sign sat on his desk for all to see. Even though he raised the minimum wage, the saying didn't refer to money. It meant that the President was taking responsibility for his actions.

"Passing the buck" (blaming someone else) is easy and comes naturally. This practice began in Eden when God confronted Adam about his disobedience. Adam answered, "It was the woman you gave me who brought me the fruit, and I ate it" (Genesis 3:12).

Whenever we do something wrong, we tend to make excuses or to blame someone else. "It wasn't my fault!" "The sun got in my eyes." "She made me do it." "I couldn't help it."

That happened in ancient Israel too. Saul, Israel's first king, grew impatient waiting for the prophet Samuel and decided to make a sacrifice to God. The problem was, according to God's law, only a priest should offer sacrifices. When confronted by Samuel with his sinful actions, Saul made excuses, saying that he "felt obliged to offer the burnt offering" (see today's passage). Because of Saul's sin and his refusal to accept responsibility for what he had done, he lost the kingdom.

The lesson is clear: when we mess up, on purpose or accidentally, we need to admit our wrong and take responsibility.

"The buck stops here" means making decisions and doing the work that we are expected to do without pushing it off on someone else. Every position has responsibilities. Think about your parents. They provide for the family—food, clothes, housing, and protection. That comes with being a parent. And they don't pass the buck.

That's the other lesson for today: we need to do our jobs and do them well.

to do ☑

MAKE A SMALL SIGN WITH THE SAYING "THE BUCK STOPS HERE" AND PUT IT ON YOUR DESK. USE IT TO REMIND YOU TO TAKE RESPONSIBILITY FOR YOUR ACTIONS AND TO DO YOUR ASSIGNMENTS.

"So I said, 'The Philistines are ready to march against us, and I haven't even asked for the LORD's help!' So I felt obliged to offer the burnt offering myself before you came."
"How foolish!" Samuel exclaimed. "You have disobeyed the command of the LORD your God. Had you obeyed, the LORD would have established your kingdom over Israel forever." [1 Samuel 13:12, 13]

also on this day 1881

The famous shootout at the OK Corral occurred in Tombstone, Arizona.

Two whales, trapped for nearly three weeks in an arctic ice pack, were freed by Soviet and American ice-breakers. 1988

go M.A.D.

This is National Make a Difference Day.

Several years ago, Ron Hutchcraft, nationally known youth worker and speaker, held large "Go M.A.D.!" rallies. He wasn't encouraging kids to be angry or act crazy. He was urging Christian teenagers to Make A Difference in the world for Christ.

Young people often feel as though they can't do much in the world. After all, they don't have power, position, or prestige (or much money). Even adults can feel this way when they consider the enormous problems in the world and think about being just one person out of millions.

But every person, young or old, can make a difference for good.

That's certainly what happened hundreds of years ago in the hills by the Sea of Galilee. Remember the story? A huge crowd had followed Jesus to hear him teach. It was getting to be mealtime, but they were far from town. Jesus asked Philip, one of the disciples, where they could buy food. Philip answered that he didn't know; besides, they didn't have enough money to feed so many people.

Then Andrew mentioned that a boy had a small lunch, then added, "But what good is that with this huge crowd?"

Remember what happened next? Jesus took the few loaves and fish and used them to provide food for everyone, with 12 baskets leftover.

That day the disciples learned that Jesus could use every person (no matter how young) and every contribution (no matter how small) to make a difference. What's important is not the giver or the size of the gift but the Savior who takes it and uses it for his glory.

You *can* make a difference—in your family, neighborhood, school, church, and the world. It starts with giving your resources, your talents, your time, and most important, yourself to Christ.

"There's a young boy here with five barley loaves and two fish. But what good is that with this huge crowd?"

[John 6:9]

also on this day

1858
Roland Macy opened Macy's Department Store in New York City.

1858
Theodore Roosevelt, 26th president of the United States, was born.

1925
Fred Waller received a patent for water skis.

to do ☑

GET A SMALL PACKET OF STICKY NOTES AND PRINT "M.A.D." ON A BUNCH OF THEM. THEN POST THEM INSIDE THE FRONT COVERS OF YOUR BOOKS AND NOTEBOOKS TO REMIND YOU OF TODAY'S LESSON.

october **28**

On this day in 1886, France presented the United States with the Statue of Liberty.

Breathing Free

Standing on Liberty Island in New York Harbor, the Statue of Liberty is one of the most recognized symbols of political freedom and democracy in the world. Dedicated on this day in 1886, the statue was designated a National Monument on October 15, 1924.

"Lady Liberty" has become the great symbol of freedom, especially for immigrants entering America. The inscription at the base of the statue states, "Give me your tired, your poor, your huddled masses yearning to breathe free . . ." and many thousands have passed her on their journey to citizenship.

Yet there is a symbol far greater than the Statue of Liberty. And the freedom it represents is eternal. This symbol is a cross.

Actually a cross is kind of a strange symbol when you think about it. Crosses were used for executions. To think of a cross is sort of like thinking of an electric chair or a gallows—not a pretty thought. But God has turned what was evil and ugly into what is good and beautiful.

The Bible teaches that the penalty for sin is eternal death. When Jesus was crucified he paid the penalty for the sins of all humanity. Sin also enslaves us while we are alive. But because of the cross, we can be free from both the penalty and power of sin. By believing in Jesus and trusting in him alone, we can be totally forgiven and have new life! Now that's *real* freedom.

Thank God for the cross of Christ and breathe free.

to do ☑

TODAY, LOOK FOR CROSSES. YOU'LL SEE THEM IN VERY UNUSUAL PLACES. FOR EXAMPLE, EACH TELEPHONE POLE FORMS A CROSS. EVERY TIME YOU SEE ONE, THANK GOD FOR SENDING JESUS TO DIE FOR YOU IN YOUR PLACE.

Finally, they came to a place called The **Skull**. All three were **crucified** there— **Jesus** on the **center cross**, and the two **criminals** on either side.

[Luke 23:33]

also on this day

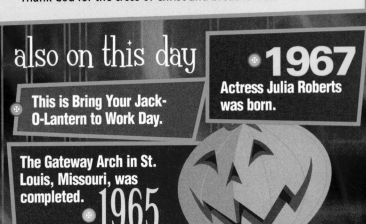

This is Bring Your Jack-O-Lantern to Work Day.

The Gateway Arch in St. Louis, Missouri, was completed. **1965**

1967
Actress Julia Roberts was born.

This day was known as Black Tuesday, and it began the Great Depression, the worst economic slump in U.S. history. And this slump spread to virtually the entire industrialized world.

During the first part of this decade, the Roaring Twenties, everyone was doing very well, or so it seemed. Salaries were up and people were buying lots of stuff, especially cars. The twenties also saw a stock market boom. People were investing a lot of money, and the stock values kept increasing. Life was good until Black Tuesday.

People began to panic and banks started to fail. Some people lost all their investments and savings. Many felt desperate, and quite a few committed suicide.

Can you imagine losing *everything*? What a terrible feeling!

At one time in his life, the apostle Paul had a lot going for him. He was well educated, a respected member of the community, and one of the elite—the "in crowd." And to top it off, he was seen as a very religious person. From almost any angle he looked good.

But then he met Jesus and began to see life differently. What he once thought was important, now he considered "worthless." He willingly gave it up to follow Christ. Check out today's passage and the surrounding verses.

It's easy to become confused and think that money, possessions, and popularity are all important. And when we don't get them, or worse yet we lose them, we can feel devastated. But that's the world's lie. Far more important are heavenly treasures and what God thinks of you. Keep your focus on Christ and his kingdom, and life will make sense.

to do ☑

GET A COPY OF TODAY'S NEWSPAPER OR A RECENT MAGAZINE. FLIP THROUGH IT AND LOOK FOR EVIDENCES OF WHAT THE WORLD SAYS IS VALUABLE. CONSIDER THE CONTRAST TO WHAT GOD SAYS IS REALLY IMPORTANT.

also on this day

1863 The International Committee of the Red Cross was founded.

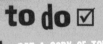

This is Oatmeal Day. Have a bowl!

I once thought all these things were so very important, but now I consider them worthless because of what Christ has done. Yes, everything else is worthless when compared with the priceless gain of knowing Christ Jesus my Lord. I have discarded everything else, counting it all as garbage, so that I may have Christ. [Philippians 3:7, 8]

On this day in 1929, the stock market crashed.

lost and found

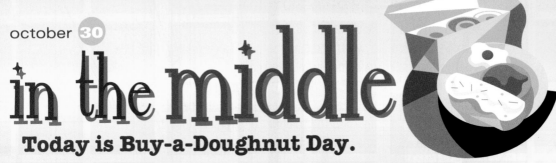

in the middle

Today is Buy-a-Doughnut Day.

Ah, doughnuts—those sticky, sweet, tasty treats. What's your favorite—glazed? chocolate? sprinkled?

You may have wondered who invented the doughnut. According to one story, in 1847 a New England sea captain, Hanson Gregory, punched holes in dough because his mother's doughnuts were not cooked in the center. Whether or not that's true, the hole means that the baker uses fewer ingredients in each doughnut, and they are easy to stack on a stick (or a finger).

Some people say that doughnuts aren't good for us because they're fattening. But they sure can't say that about the hole—it has *zero* calories.

In many ways doughnuts are like life apart from God—appealing and tasty on the outside, but empty in the middle. Solomon wrote about the emptiness of life in Ecclesiastes. Look at today's verse where he says that life is meaningless.

Some people seem to spend their lives trying to live on doughnut holes. Solomon was that way for much of his life. He tasted it all: money, power, possessions, fun, and romance. We've already discussed Solomon several times in this book. But with every bite of life, Solomon wanted more. And when he got to the center, it was empty!

A better approach would be to see life as a nutritious meal; you know, one with the necessary fruits and vegetables to help you grow strong. Add meat, bread, and other essential foods, and you'll do well. Then you can have the doughnut for dessert.

Real life begins with God in the center. Leave him out, and existence is as empty as a doughnut hole.

also on this day

This is Haunted Refrigerator Day. (Leftovers, anyone?)

1735 John Adams, the second president of the United States, was born.

1990 Tunnelers met under the English Channel and connected England to France.

"**Everything** is **meaningless,**" says the **Teacher,** "utterly **meaningless!**"

[Ecclesiastes 1:2]

to do ☑

GET A COUPLE OF DOUGHNUTS AND CHALLENGE A SIBLING OR A PARENT TO AN EATING CONTEST. EACH PERSON SHOULD PUT THE DOUGHNUT ON A FINGER AND THEN EAT AS MUCH AS POSSIBLE WHILE KEEPING A CIRCLE OF DOUGH AROUND THE FINGER. THEN YOU CAN EXPLAIN HOW DONUTS ARE A LOT LIKE LIFE.

BOO!
This is Halloween.

Halloween has grown to be a huge holiday in the U.S. People decorate their homes and dress up in costumes at parties. Children go door-to-door begging for candies with the familiar phrase, "Trick or treat."

Originally this was sort of a religious day, as it preceded All Saints Day. But it has become anything *but* religious these days. Many of the decorations feature hideous, frightening creatures. Images of violence and death abound. "Haunted" houses draw people who pay for the privilege of screaming in terror. Everywhere, there is an atmosphere of darkness, evil, and fear.

What scares you—really frightens you, and not just like a silly Halloween party?

Some people are afraid of heights; others fear being in crowds. Some people run from clowns, while others hate being up high. One of the biggest fears, believe it or not, is speaking in front of a group. And if people are honest, just about everyone admits to fearing death.

If you read the Bible for very long, you'll read, "Fear not" or "Don't be afraid." In Deuteronomy 31:8, Moses told Joshua, "Do not be afraid or discouraged, for the LORD is the one who goes before you. He will be with you; he will neither fail you nor forsake you." What a great promise!

And look at the verse for today in which John explains why we don't have to fear: because God loves us.

So whenever you feel afraid, remember God is with you. Most of all, remember that he loves you!

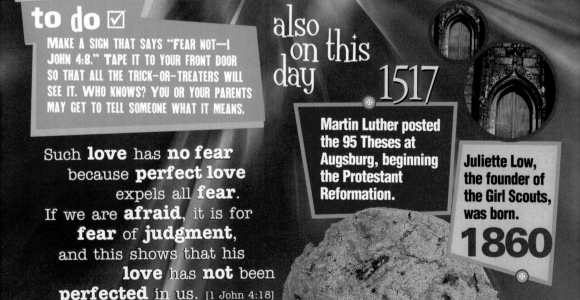

to do ☑

MAKE A SIGN THAT SAYS "FEAR NOT—1 JOHN 4:8." TAPE IT TO YOUR FRONT DOOR SO THAT ALL THE TRICK-OR-TREATERS WILL SEE IT. WHO KNOWS? YOU OR YOUR PARENTS MAY GET TO TELL SOMEONE WHAT IT MEANS.

also on this day

1517

Martin Luther posted the 95 Theses at Augsburg, beginning the Protestant Reformation.

Juliette Low, the founder of the Girl Scouts, was born.

1860

Such **love** has **no fear** because **perfect love** expels all **fear**. If we are **afraid**, it is for **fear** of **judgment**, and this shows that his **love** has **not** been **perfected** in us. [1 John 4:18]

november **01**

Today is Men Make Dinner Day.

Dinner's Ready?

It's official! Today women across the country have permission to hang up their aprons and hand over the whisk and the spatula to the men. It's time for Men Make Dinner Day!

So what feelings does the thought of your dad making dinner bring? Maybe fear, if Dad's last creation was inedible and ended up in the garbage disposal. Amusement, if your dad hasn't mastered the art of microwaving. Joy, if you know that Dad cooking dinner means you get your choice of carryout.

To be fair, many men know their way around the kitchen. Some of the world's greatest chefs are men. Not all men panic when they are faced with preparing a meal. But one time, Jesus' friends were anxious when they were given the task of feeding a crowd.

A huge crowd of people had been sitting all day listening to Jesus speak. At first the disciples had suggested that the crowd leave and find their own food. But Jesus told them, "You feed them." That's when they panicked! How were they going to find—never mind pay for—enough food to feed all those people? After all, there were no fast-food joints to zip into and pick up cheeseburgers for five thousand.

Yet when the disciples listened and followed Jesus' instructions to gather all the available food and arrange the people in groups, they witnessed a miracle meal. You know the story. Jesus took two fish and five loaves of bread, prayed for God's blessing, and then fed *everyone*.

So the next time you are given an "impossible" assignment—whether it's cooking a meal for your family or working on a difficult project—don't panic. Let Jesus in on it. Do all you can, and then ask God to do the rest!

to do ☑

TEAM UP WITH YOUR DAD TO PREPARE DINNER FOR THE FAMILY TONIGHT.

If you will only **obey me** and **let** me **help** you, then you will have **plenty** to eat.
[Isaiah 1:19]

also on this day

Today is All Saints Day.

President John Adams became the first president to live in the White House. **1800**

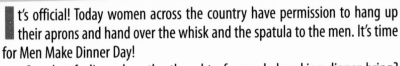

1512 Michelangelo's paintings on the ceiling of the Sistine Chapel were first exhibited to the public.

the wilderness man

Daniel Boone, the American frontiersman, was born on this day in 1734.

Even as a boy, Daniel Boone was training for his future as a man of the wild. Growing up in the Pennsylvania countryside, the young boy made friends with the Indians living nearby and learned the habits of the wildlife. At age 19, Boone fought in the French and Indian War, where he met John Finley—a hunter who had explored some of the western wilds and who filled the young man with dreams of exploring the land for himself.

It wasn't until 1767, when Daniel was 33 and married, that he set out to explore the uncharted territory that is now Kentucky. It took Daniel and his companions two years to travel and explore one end of Kentucky. On later trips Boone worked to clear the Wilderness Road and establish a settlement that became known as Boonesborough.

At age 64 Boone set out again—this time for the Missouri region. As he paddled by in his canoe, folks would ask him, "Why are you leaving Kentucky?" to which Boone replied, "Too crowded."

John the Baptist was another man who felt most comfortable in the wilderness. John ate insects and wild honey, dressed in camel hair, and lived alone in the desert. Far from any distractions, John could hear God's instructions. And his unconventional manner certainly caught the people's attention. What better way to point to the coming of the Messiah?

John was confident of what God wanted him to do. He prepared people for the coming of the Lord: "Someone is coming soon who is far greater than I am" (Mark 1:7).

Take a lesson from John. You don't have to eat bugs or live in the desert. But you can reduce the distractions in your life that keep you from hearing God's voice clearly. And you can introduce people to Jesus.

This messenger was John the Baptist. He lived in the wilderness and was preaching that people should be baptized to show that they had turned from their sins and turned to God to be forgiven. [Mark 1:4]

also on this day

1795
James K. Polk, the 11th president of the United States, was born.

1865
Warren G. Harding, the 29th president of the United States, was born.

1989
Carmen Fasanella retired after 68 years and 243 days of taxicab service in Princeton, New Jersey.

to do ☑

GO OUT IN THE BACKYARD OR A NEARBY PARK AND SPEND SOME TIME IN A PLACE WHERE YOU ARE AWAY FROM DISTRACTIONS. LISTEN FOR GOD SPEAKING TO YOU.

bread of life

Today is Sandwich Day.

The sandwich actually goes back as far as the first century BC when the famous rabbi, Hillel the Elder, started the custom of eating a mixture of chopped nuts, apples, and spices between two matzos. In the Middle Ages, thick slices of coarse stale bread called trenchers were used instead of plates. Piles of meats and other foods were placed on top of the bread to be eaten with the fingers.

But it wasn't until the late 1700s that the first written record of *sandwich* appeared in a Londoner's journal. The cooks at London's Beef Steak Club were said to have invented the first sandwich in 1762. John Montague, the Fourth Earl of Sandwich, was a frequent diner at the restaurant and a devoted card player. Reluctant to quit playing, Montague would order his valet to bring his meal to him—a piece of meat tucked between two pieces of bread. Soon others began ordering "the same as Sandwich," and the name stuck!

However you slice it, bread is what makes the sandwich. Without it, what do you have? A slice of ham and cheese. Tuna on a plate. A glob of peanut butter and jelly. Clearly, it's the bread that gives the definition and substance to this lunchtime staple. Throughout all cultures and ages, bread has been an important food source.

Jesus called himself "the living bread that came down out of heaven." Just as we all need bread and food to satisfy our hunger and to help keep us alive, we also need Jesus to keep us going spiritually. And just as we need to eat every day, we need to connect with Jesus on a daily basis. That means spending time praying and reading the Bible to get our daily serving of "living bread."

Have you had your daily bread?

to do ☑

MAKE UP YOUR OWN SANDWICH CREATION TODAY. ENJOY IT. AND THEN EXPLAIN TO SOMEONE ABOUT THE "LIVING BREAD."

also on this day

1957 *Sputnik II* was launched by the Soviet Union. It was the first man-made satellite to put an animal into space, a dog named Laika.

Minnesota elected Jesse "The Body" Ventura, a former pro wrestler, as governor. **1998**

I am the living bread that came down out of heaven. Anyone who eats this bread will live forever; this bread is my flesh, offered so the world may live. [John 6:51]

Overcoming Obstacles

The patent for the artificial leg was granted to Dr. Benjamin Franklin Palmer in 1846.

Dr. Benjamin Franklin Palmer had lost a leg in an accident. Determined not to let this tragedy hinder him from living a full life, Palmer looked for solutions. Failing to find any type of device that would help him walk as normally as possible, Palmer did the next best thing—he invented an artificial leg.

Palmer's design included springs and hidden joints that gave the appearance of natural movement. For his efforts Palmer received an award at the first World's Fair at the Crystal Palace in London in 1851.

Palmer's response to his situation was different from the man in the Bible who spent his days lying by the pool of Bethesda. You can read about him in John 5:1-14. Although the man had been lying there for 38 years, no one was able to help him . . . until Jesus came upon the scene.

Jesus took one look at the man and asked him, "Would you like to get well?" The man replied, "I can't, sir." Then after the man had explained all the problems he faced, Jesus simply told him, "Stand up, pick up your sleeping mat, and walk." And the man did so.

We have a choice when facing difficult and hopeless situations. We can give up, feeling hopeless and trapped like the man at the pool before he met Jesus. Or we can respond like Palmer and look for solutions to our problems. A positive attitude is necessary to overcome obstacles.

to do ☑

WHAT DIFFICULTY ARE YOU FACING TODAY? HOW WOULD YOU DESCRIBE YOUR ATTITUDE IN THIS SITUATION? WHAT COULD YOU DO TO TAKE THAT FIRST STEP TOWARD A SOLUTION?

Jesus told him, "**Stand up**, pick up your sleeping mat, and **walk**!"
[John 5:8]

also on this day

Today is National Candy Day.

In Egypt, Howard Carter discovered the way into the lost tomb of Pharaoh Tutankhamen. **1922**

1965
Lee Ann Roberts Breedlove became the first woman to exceed 300 mph in a jet-powered car.

celebrate failure?

Today is Guy Fawkes Day.

Today marks the anniversary of the Gunpowder Plot, a conspiracy to blow up the English Parliament and King James I in 1605. On November 5, King James was to open Parliament. But the conspiracy came to light when a mysterious letter was sent to Lord Monteagle, urging him not to attend Parliament on opening day.

When the contents of the letter were brought to the attention of others in Parliament, an extensive search of the House of Lords was conducted. In the cellar underneath the building, 36 barrels of gunpowder that were overlaid with iron bars and firewood were discovered. Guy Fawkes, one of the conspirators, was arrested when he entered the cellar.

Guy Fawkes Day—the remembrance of the failure to blow up Parliament—is still celebrated in Britain today with fireworks and bonfires on which effigies of the conspirators are burned.

Seems strange doesn't it, to have a holiday marking the failure of something? Usually we celebrate victories like the Fourth of July.

When the Roman and Jewish leaders nailed Jesus to the cross, they thought they had gotten rid of Jesus and his radical ideas for good. Little did they expect what was to happen three days later when Jesus left the tomb. Not only was Jesus alive, but his followers were energized and empowered to spread the gospel.

Easter marks the failure of men to defeat Jesus—and ultimately the failure of Satan to defeat God's plan to offer salvation to all people who accept forgiveness of their sins through Jesus. Satan must have been dancing on that dark Friday afternoon, but it was God who did the ultimate victory dance.

Victory in failure? You bet!

to do ☑

CELEBRATE SATAN'S FAILURE TODAY BY THANKING GOD FOR THE GREAT VICTORY AT THE CROSS WHEN JESUS DEFEATED SIN, GUILT, AND DEATH.

But **now** in a **single victorious stroke** of **Life**, all three—**sin**, **guilt**, **death**—are **gone**, the **gift** of our **Master**, **Jesus Christ**. **Thank God!**

[1 Corinthians 15:57, The Message]

also on this day

1872
Susan B. Anthony was fined $100 for attempting to vote in the presidential election. She never paid the fine.

The game Monopoly® was introduced by Parker Brothers Company.
1935

President Franklin D. Roosevelt won an unprecedented third term in office.
1940

Without a doubt, Abraham Lincoln is counted among America's greatest presidents. His firm belief that the government should be a positive force to serve people guided him through his life and was at the heart of his desire to become president of the United States.

But it was not a goal that Lincoln easily or quickly achieved. His career path was littered with setbacks and failures. In his first attempt at running for political office as a state representative in 1832, Lincoln finished eighth out of 13. So he returned to practicing law. Then he won a seat in the Illinois Legislature in 1834.

Over the next decade, however, Lincoln suffered numerous business and political setbacks. During that time Lincoln's sweetheart died, he suffered a nervous breakdown, and he was defeated for Speaker of the Illinois House. Lincoln was overlooked for the nomination for U.S. Congress in 1843. He was elected three years later, but lost his renomination bid two years after that. In 1854, he was defeated for the U.S. Senate, denied the nomination for Vice President in 1856, and again defeated for U.S. Senate in 1858.

With so many failures in his life no one would have blamed Lincoln for giving up and going back to his law practice. But because he was determined to achieve his political goals and dreams, Lincoln never gave up. Though he was knocked down repeatedly, Lincoln continued to get back up and continue on.

That is the very promise that God gives to us in Psalm 37:24. Read it for yourself. God's promise is that he watches over every step we take. When we stumble, when we fail and suffer setbacks, God is there to help us keep going. He promises to hold on tightly to our hands and lead us on.

So next time you fail at reaching your goal, remember Abe and his persistence. Then remember the one who will hold you up and keep you going!

Though they stumble, they will not fall, for the LORD holds them by the hand. [Psalm 37:24]

On this day in 1860, Abraham Lincoln was elected president.

SUCCESS!

to do ☑

WHAT FAILURE HAVE YOU EXPERIENCED LATELY? THINK ABOUT HOW YOU CAN USE THAT EXPERIENCE TO HELP YOU IN ACHIEVING YOUR GOALS.

also on this day

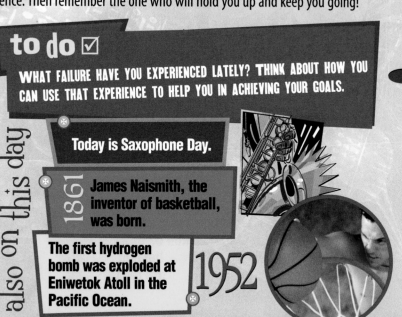

Today is Saxophone Day.

1861 James Naismith, the inventor of basketball, was born.

The first hydrogen bomb was exploded at Eniwetok Atoll in the Pacific Ocean.

1952

Today is Hug a Bear Day.

The Security Blanket

Maybe you don't want to admit it. Maybe you think that you are too old for such things, or maybe you think that you're the only one who still has something soft and cuddly to hold on to during a storm. But let's be honest. If someone were to search underneath your bed or to look under your pillow or hunt through the back corners of your closet, that person might just discover a frayed, torn piece of blanket, or a one-eyed stuffed animal with one of its limbs just barely hanging on.

Like Linus's faithful blanket, this well-worn and well-loved object has been there for you through all sorts of situations. It was "Teddy" that helped you get through those terrible thunderstorms. You clung to "Bunny" when you were traveling to your new home. It was "Blankie" that comforted you on those long afternoons when you were sick and Mom couldn't be by your side.

We all have those moments in our lives when we need to feel secure. We need to know that someone is with us when we feel all alone; that someone is there to comfort us when we are frightened or anxious about facing something new. We want someone there to comfort us when we are feeling down.

The good news is that we have someone like that in our lives 24-7. Jesus is there whenever we need him, wherever we are, in whatever situation we find ourselves. Listen to these words Jesus spoke to his disciples: "And be sure of this: I am with you always, even to the end of the age." *I am with you always.* We need never fear being alone or being scared or being abandoned. Jesus is with us. Always.

That's the best security blanket ever.

to do ☑

GO AHEAD, HUG A BEAR—OR A BLANKIE OR A BUNNY, OR WHATEVER CUDDLY THING YOU CHERISH—TODAY! BUT REMEMBER WHERE YOU FIND YOUR REAL SECURITY.

"And be **sure** of **this**: I am **with you** always, **even** to the **end** of the **age**."

[Matthew 28:20]

also on this day

1893
The state of Colorado granted women the right to vote.

President Franklin D. Roosevelt became the first person to win a fourth term as president. 1944

1965
The Pillsbury Doughboy® debuted in television commercials.

I need more time!

Today is Ample Time Day.

You probably have heard someone complain, "I just don't have enough time!" Maybe it was your mom as she was trying to get dinner on the table while picking you up from soccer practice. Maybe it was your teacher as he pushed to finish the math chapter before the big test. Maybe it was even you as you tried to finish your homework so you could have time to hang out with your friends.

So it probably comes as good news that today is Ample Time Day—it means you have enough time to do whatever you need to get done. Well, not really. Just saying we have ample time doesn't make it so, does it? Yet the truth is God has given each one of us 24 hours every day—ample time to get done everything that *he* wants us to do that day.

So what's the problem? Why is it that we always feel rushed and out of control? Why is it that we usually come to the end of the day and say, "Gee, I wish I had more time to do _____." We either are trying to do too much during one day, or we are wasting our time on unimportant things (like watching TV!).

As Ecclesiastes 3:1 tells us, God has given us time for "every activity under heaven." God has a plan for everything that has already happened, for everything that is happening right now, and for everything that will happen. There is ample time for everything to happen according to God's plan.

That's good news when you do get that "I don't have enough time" feeling. Remember, God is in charge of time. There is always ample time to do what God has planned for you. Just ask him!

And this is his plan: At the right time he will bring everything together under the authority of Christ—everything in heaven and on earth. [Ephesians 1:10]

also on this day

1656

Edmond Halley was born. Halley was the first to calculate the orbit of a comet that was named after him. The comet appears every 76 years.

1793

The Louvre Museum in Paris opened to the public for the first time.

to do ☑

SAY YOU DON'T HAVE ENOUGH TIME? MAKE A CHART OF EVERYTHING YOU HAVE TO DO TODAY AND THEN PLACE THOSE ITEMS IN ORDER OF IMPORTANCE. MAKE SURE TO INCLUDE TIME FOR GOD!

story time

This is Family Stories Month.

The holidays are just around the corner, a time for family get-togethers, lots of good food—and storytelling! Yes, that's right. It's inevitable that when families get together the stories begin flowing. "Remember when we . . . " "When I was your age . . . " "Did I ever tell you about the time . . . ?"

Family stories are important. Some stories may make us laugh, some may encourage us in our tough times, and some may cause us to think. But most important, these stories bond us together as family because these stories form our shared history. It's what makes our family unique. Every family has its own stories to tell.

The same is true with God's family. Just as God was sending Moses to Pharaoh with warnings about the upcoming plagues, he told Moses, "You will be able to tell wonderful stories to your children and grandchildren." Imagine the stories Moses had to tell!

On numerous occasions the Israelites were told to tell stories about God and what he had done for them. Why? Because such stories helped the people remember God's care for them. Remembering God's deeds in the past encouraged the people during the difficult times, helped to strengthen their faith, and built their trust in God.

When we share stories about what God is doing in our lives and what he has done in the past, we also are building our faith and encouraging others. When you tell someone how God has helped you in a particular situation, you challenge that person to trust God. When you share how God encouraged you through a particular Bible verse, someone else may find the same strength.

You're part of God's family. What stories do you have to share?

to do ☑

TELL A STORY TODAY ABOUT WHAT GOD HAS DONE IN YOUR LIFE.

You will be able to tell wonderful stories to your children and grandchildren about the marvelous things I am doing among the Egyptians to prove that I am the LORD. [Exodus 10:2]

also on this day

1906

President Theodore Roosevelt left for Panama to see the progress on the new canal. It was the first foreign trip by a U.S. president.

Giant pandas were discovered in China.

1927

The Berlin Wall was opened by East Germany.

1989

Always Faithful

In 1775, the Continental Congress passed a resolution declaring that "two battalions of Marines be raised" for service as landing forces with the Naval fleet. This formation of the Continental Marines marked the birth of the United States Marine Corps, which was officially commissioned through an act of the new United States Congress in 1798.

Serving on both land and sea, the early Marines supported General George Washington when he crossed the Delaware River to surprise the Hessians in New Jersey. They fought alongside John Paul Jones on his ship. They participated in many operations during the War of 1812, fighting alongside Andrew Jackson in defeating the British at New Orleans. Since their inception, the Marines have served in all the wars of the United States and have carried out more than 300 landings on foreign shores.

One of the defining characteristics of the Marine Corps is its motto, *Semper Fideles*—a constant reminder of the Marines' devotion to the Corps and Country. These two words, meaning "always faithful," describe a Marine's commitment to his or her duty. The Corps proudly points out that Marines throughout their history have lived up to this motto, as proved by the fact that there has never been a mutiny among the Corps.

Faithfulness, staying true to someone or something in thought, word, and action, is part of God's very character (Psalm 89:8). The Bible tells us that God's faithfulness is great (Lamentations 3:23), unfailing (2 Timothy 2:13), and that it will never end (Psalm 146:6). God will do what he says he is going to do—and the proof of that is his Son, Jesus.

Even when our faith is weak and we have trouble staying faithful, God will be there and will take care of us.

He is always faithful.

to do ☑

DO YOU KNOW THE "THE MARINES' HYMN"? FIND A RECORDING TODAY AND LISTEN TO IT. OR FIND A COPY OF IT AND READ IT. THE FIRST TWO LINES REFER TO BATTLES FOUGHT EARLY ON IN THE MARINES' HISTORY.

God will surely do this for you, for he always does just what he says, and he is the one who invited you into this wonderful friendship with his Son, Jesus Christ our Lord.

[1 Corinthians 1:9]

also on this day

1483 **Martin Luther was born.**

***Sesame Street* premiered on PBS.** 1969

1951 Direct dial telephone service was first available coast to coast.

the greatest sacrifice

Today is Veterans Day.

I n 1921, an unknown American soldier was buried in Arlington National Cemetery. Similar ceremonies had occurred earlier in England and France, where an unknown soldier was buried in each nation's highest place of honor (Westminster Abbey in England and the *Arc de Triomphe* in France).

These memorial services all took place on November 11, the anniversary of the end of World War I. In 1926, Armistice Day was recognized as a holiday and 12 years later it became a national holiday. On June 1, 1954, the name was changed to Veterans Day to honor all war veterans.

In issuing his Armistice Day proclamation, President Woodrow Wilson said, "To us in America, the reflections of Armistice Day will be filled with solemn pride in the heroism of those who died in the country's service and with gratitude for the victory, both because of the thing from which it has freed us and because of the opportunity it has given America to show her sympathy with peace and justice in the councils of the nation."

The day is a solemn occasion to honor those who have made the greatest sacrifice—giving up their lives for their country, for peace, for justice, and for the end of tyranny. While the death of any soldier is tragic, we can more readily understand the loss of life when the cause is, as President Wilson said, peace and justice. We would find it harder to accept dying for a cause that is evil or bad.

That's exactly what Jesus did. He didn't die for just people, or even good people. He died for sinners—people who were weak, who ignored God, and who did wrong things. He died for us because he *loved* us.

That is the greatest sacrifice.

But God showed his great love for us by sending Christ to die for us while we were still sinners. [Romans 5:8]

to do ☑

VISIT YOUR LOCAL CEMETERY AND HONOR A WAR VETERAN BY PLACING FLOWERS ON THE GRAVE.

also on this day

1620 The Mayflower Compact was signed by the 41 men on the Mayflower when they landed in what is now Provincetown Harbor. The compact called for "just and equal" laws.

Kate Smith first sang Irving Berlin's "God Bless America" on the radio. 1938

entrance exam

In 1954, Ellis Island closed after processing more than 20 million immigrants since 1892.

During its peak years between 1892 and 1924, Ellis Island received nearly 12 million immigrants hoping to enter America's "front doors to freedom." Thousands of immigrants arrived each day, standing in long lines waiting to be studied for any signs of disability or disease.

From the moment they arrived the immigrants were under inspection. Public Health Service doctors looked for anyone who wheezed, coughed, shuffled, or limped as they climbed the stairs to the great hall of the Registry Room. Following that initial inspection, another group of doctors examined each immigrant, checking for 60 different symptoms.

Passing that inspection, the hopeful immigrant then waited in another line for five hours to reach the next station. Here inspectors verified 29 bits of information, such as age, occupation, marital status, and destination, in order to determine an immigrant's "social, economic, and moral fitness." During the peak years of Ellis Island's operation, nearly 20 percent of all immigrants were detained before being allowed into the country.

Imagine if we had to go through an intense entrance examination before entering Heaven. God could ask such questions as these: Are you healthy enough? Have you helped anyone recently? Do you obey your mom and dad? When was the last time you sinned? Can you name all the books of the Bible?

Thankfully for us, there is only one question that we need to answer when we arrive at Heaven's doors. Is Jesus your Lord and Savior? For, as the Bible tells us, it is by faith in Jesus Christ, in believing that he died for our sins once for all, that we gain entrance into eternal life.

That's it. Test over. How would you do?

to do ☑

NEARLY 100 MILLION AMERICANS TODAY CAN TRACE THEIR ROOTS BACK TO ELLIS ISLAND. CHECK INTO YOUR FAMILY HISTORY TO SEE IF ANY FAMILY MEMBERS PASSED THROUGH ELLIS ISLAND.

For it is by believing in your heart that you are made right with God, and it is by confessing with your mouth that you are saved.

[Romans 10:10]

also on this day

1859

The first flying trapeze act was performed by Jules Leotard at Cirque Napoleon in Paris, France. He was also the designer of the garment that is named after him.

Theodore W. Richards of Harvard University became the first American to be awarded the Nobel Prize in chemistry.

1915

random acts of kindness

Today is National World Kindness Day.

Remember a time when someone acted kindly toward you? Maybe someone stopped to help you pick up your books when you dropped them in the crowded school hallway. Or maybe someone noticed you sitting by yourself in the lunchroom and sat with you. Or maybe someone gave you a cold drink of water while you were outside on a hot summer day.

We rarely forget such acts. A little kindness can get us through a bad day, or help us to finish a task. Kindness by its very definition is doing something that pleases others—not ourselves. When we receive an act of kindness, it means that someone is more concerned about us than they are about themselves. Kindness is treating others with love and respect. Pretty amazing, isn't it?

What's even more amazing is that God acts with kindness toward every one of us. Think about it. What have you done today that makes you deserving of God's kindness? The answer is probably nothing. On a daily basis none of us is deserving of God's unending kindness.

How does God treat us kindly? First, by sending his Son Jesus to die for us and to take the punishment we deserve for our sins. Second, by giving us time to recognize this fact and to turn from our sinful ways. God is infinitely patient, infinitely loving, and infinitely kind.

So next time you have an opportunity to show a little kindness to someone else, remember God's kindness toward you. And take the time to stop and lend a hand, listen to a friend, or befriend someone who is looking a bit down.

Kindness goes a long way.

Don't you realize how kind, tolerant, and patient God is with you? Or don't you care? Can't you see how kind he has been in giving you time to turn from your sin? [Romans 2:4]

also on this day

1789 Benjamin Franklin wrote a letter to a friend in which he said, "In this world nothing can be said to be certain, except for death and taxes."

1805 Johann George Lehner, a Viennese butcher, invented the frankfurter.

1907 The first helicopter flight lasted 20 seconds and took place just a foot off the ground.

to do ☑

GO AHEAD. SHOW GOD'S KINDNESS TO SOMEONE BY CONDUCTING YOUR OWN "KINDNESS RAID." DO SOMETHING NICE FOR SOMEONE ELSE, BUT DON'T TELL!

One of the most successful sports companies ever, Nike® began as a small distributor of Japanese running shoes, operated out of Phil Knight's car. But the founders of Blue Ribbon Sports, Bill Bowerman and Knight, had a greater vision: to design a lighter, more durable racing shoe for runners that would make them go faster.

The two combined marketing strategy and their own design for a "waffle" running shoe that eventually caught on in the running community. The company took off in 1972, when Knight developed the trademark swoosh (which he bought from an art student for $35) and changed the name to Nike. Years later, the company got its biggest boost when they signed NBA rookie Michael Jordan to endorse and launch the new Air Jordan shoes—the longest lasting line in all of shoe history.

Nike began selling running shoes not only to athletes, but to everyone. Its motto, "Just do it," has become one of the most successful ad campaigns ever, lasting more than 12 years. The slogan was Nike's way of telling people, no matter who they are, that if they wear the shoes, they can do it!

It's not a bad slogan for our faith. If you believe in Jesus and have the Holy Spirit, you will be able to "Just do it!" Paul says that to Timothy in his parting words to his young friend. Timothy had been facing opposition to his leadership and his message because of his youth. In what is essentially a fired-up pep talk, Paul urges Timothy to be bold—to go for it, to just do it. Because Timothy had the Holy Spirit, he had a faith based in power, love, and discipline.

If you have the Holy Spirit, you do too. Just do it!

This is why I remind you to fan into flames the spiritual gift God gave you when I laid my hands on you. For God has not given us a spirit of fear and timidity, but of power, love, and self-discipline. [2 Timothy 1:6, 7]

In 1972, Blue Ribbon Sports became Nike®.

to do ☑

ASK THE HOLY SPIRIT TO GIVE YOU THE STRENGTH AND BOLDNESS TO SHARE YOUR FAITH WITH YOUR NON-CHRISTIAN FRIENDS.

also on this day

1889 *New York World* reporter Nellie Bly began an attempt to surpass the fictitious journey of Phileas Fogg in *Around the World in 80 Days* by Jules Verne. Bly succeeded by finishing the journey in 72 days, 6 hours, and 11 minutes.

The first streetcar went into operation. **1832**

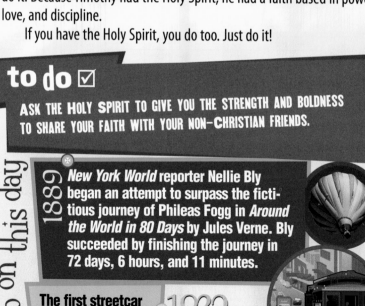

just do it!

Can You Hear Me Now?

In 1901, Miller Reese Hutchinson patented an electrical hearing aid.

Up until the early 1900s, people who suffered a loss in hearing had to rely on ear trumpets and hearing tubes that were designed to amplify sound. Early hearing aids took on many styles. Some were large and cumbersome; others were smaller in an attempt to make them inconspicuous. Some were inexpensive, made from materials like tin, while others were crafted out of silver.

However, all the devices operated on the principle of collecting sound from a relatively large area and funneling it into a smaller space. As the sound moved into a progressively smaller space and into the ear, the sound strengthened. Hearing tubes served to conserve sound energy by restricting it to a smaller space as it moved from a sound source to a person's ear.

In the 1890s, inventors wanted to create a hearing device that would be more powerful than trumpets or tubes. Miller Reese Hutchinson was the first to patent a practical electrical hearing aid in 1901. Hutchinson's hearing aid used carbon to transmit sound. Although it caused a lot of static and sound distortion, the electrical hearing aid indeed provided more powerful amplification. And it was the basis for the modern-day hearing aid.

Although such devices are undeniably helpful in assisting people in hearing, there is no man-made device that aids in *listening*. Jesus made a great distinction between hearing and listening. On several occasions Jesus referred to people as having ears that did not hear (Matthew 13:14, 15). They *heard* what Jesus was saying, but because they had closed their hearts to his message, they didn't obey it.

Jesus talks about a different kind of hearing that requires listening with your mind and your heart. It means taking time to reflect on what God's Word says and then to act on it.

Do you hear Jesus now?

to do ☑

SPEND SOME TIME LISTENING TO JESUS WITH YOUR MIND AND YOUR HEART. WHAT DO YOU HEAR HIM SAYING?

"Anyone who is **willing** to **hear** should **listen** and **understand!"**

[Mark 4:9]

also on this day

Today is America Recycles Day.

The first U.S. poultry show opened in Boston. **1849**

•1806

Explorer Zebulon Pike spotted the mountaintop that became known as Pikes Peak.

trust me!

On this day in 1952, in the **Peanuts** comic strip, Lucy first held a football for Charlie Brown.

Any fan of *Peanuts* knows the scenario: Lucy promises to hold the football for Charlie Brown as he runs up and kicks it. Charlie Brown approaches the ball, and just as he is about to boot it, Lucy pulls the football away. Charlie Brown flies into the air and lands on his backside.

The gag started back in 1952, and it never changed. Lucy would promise, Charlie Brown would trust her, and then BOOM! He was back on the ground. When you see Charlie Brown hand his football to Lucy you want to shout, "Don't do it, Charlie Brown! She hasn't kept her promise yet! Don't trust her!"

You probably can think of a time when someone broke a promise to you. Maybe a friend promised to come to your volleyball game and never showed up. Or your parent promised to take you to the movies and then didn't. Whenever a promise is broken, it feels as if someone has just pulled the football out from under us. We're disappointed, hurt, and we're a little reluctant to trust that person again.

That's why we need to be good promise-keepers, so we don't pull a Lucy on someone else. Our words are important.

When Moses gave God's laws to the Israelites, he made sure they understood that the promises they made were binding. No one was going to force them to fulfill their vows, but a broken promise meant a broken trust and a broken relationship.

If you want others to consider you a trustworthy person, make sure you keep your promises. Do exactly as you say you are going to do.

A **man** who makes
a **vow** to the **LORD**
or makes a **pledge** under **oath**
must **never break it**.
He must **do exactly**
what he **said** he would **do**.

[Numbers 30:2]

also on this day

Today is National Moms and Dads Day.

This is Life Writing Month.

1864
Union General William T. Sherman and his troops began their famous March to the Sea during the Civil War.

to do ☑

SO HOW ARE YOU DOING IN THE PROMISE-KEEPING DEPARTMENT? RATE YOURSELF ON A SCALE OF 1 TO 10, WITH 10 BEING THE HIGHEST PROMISE-KEEPER EVER. WHAT CAN YOU DO TO IMPROVE YOUR RATINGS?

dancing fool

In 1913, Kaiser Wilhelm banned the German armed forces from dancing the tango.

The tango was born in the back streets of Buenos Aires among the hundreds of thousands of Europeans who emigrated to South America looking for a new life. The dance was a combination of the many different cultures and dance styles represented in that mix of backgrounds.

Despite its humble beginnings, the dance was quickly adopted by the high-class Parisian dance salons and took Europe by storm. It became fashionable to throw tango parties and tango tea dances. By the early 1900s, the dance had become so popular that it attracted the attention of many church and government leaders.

Because of its daring character, Cardinal Amette in Paris declared that "Christians should not in good conscience take part in it." Then Kaiser Wilhelm II of Germany forbade his officers to dance the tango while in uniform, describing the dance as "an affront to common decency."

Despite these bans the tango survived, particularly through the First World War, as people sought distractions from the horror of war. Today the tango is part of any ballroom dancing repertoire, and its effects on "common decency" are no longer feared.

Dancing, in all its various forms and styles, has frequently been a source of controversy. King David came under scrutiny by his wife Michal when he danced with abandon before the Ark of the Lord. As Michal watched her husband (and king) leaping and twirling with joy, she had nothing but contempt for him. In her eyes David was making a complete fool of himself, and yes, was even "an affront to common decency."

But David saw it differently. How else could he express his irrepressible joy before God? After all, he had much to celebrate. As he told Michal, he had been chosen over her father Saul to be the next king of Israel. It was worth acting like a fool to David in order to show his joy in the Lord.

How can you show your joy to God today?

to do ☑

CLOSE THE DOOR TO YOUR ROOM, PUT ON YOUR FAVORITE PRAISE SONG CD, AND DANCE BEFORE THE LORD TO SHOW HIM YOUR JOY.

I was dancing before the LORD, who chose me above your father and his family! He appointed me as the leader of Israel, the people of the LORD. So I am willing to act like a fool in order to show my joy in the Lord. [2 Samuel 6:21]

also on this day

1869

The Suez Canal opened in Egypt, linking the Mediterranean and the Red Sea.

Today is National Remembrance Day.

U.S. President Richard Nixon told the national press, "people got to know whether or not their president is a crook. Well, I'm not a crook."

1973

In 2001, Nintendo launched the sales of its latest video game console—the GameCube®. Unlike the flat reception the video game console received in Japan, the U.S. launch smashed all previous sales records. GameCube became the fastest-selling console of all time.

Video games can be fun and exciting. With the help of state-of-the-art graphics and special effects, players can jump into the cockpit of a space ship or explore an ancient fantasy world on horseback. And no matter what happens during the course of the game, if you need to stop, you simply hit the pause button, save your game, and pick it up again on another day.

And here's the beauty of video games—there are no consequences. Or at least no *real* consequences. Sure, you might lose points for not hitting enough targets. Or you might not make it to the next level. But you get as many chances as you want to go back and replay the game.

Real life is nothing like the video games we play. When you make a choice or decide to take a certain action, there are consequences. For example, maybe you choose not to study for the math test. Possible consequence? A failed test. Or maybe you decide you don't have time to help your friend. Consequence? A hurt relationship that needs fixing.

Sometimes we get a retest, or our friend forgives us and gives us another chance. But as the writer of Proverbs advises, it is wiser to consider the consequences of a particular action or decision beforehand.

A prudent person foresees the danger ahead and takes precautions. The simpleton goes blindly on and suffers the consequences. [Proverbs 27:12]

On this day in 2001, the GameCube® home video game console was released in the United States.

to do ☑

IT'S TIME FOR "DECISIONS AND CONSEQUENCES." THINK OF THE DECISIONS YOU MADE TODAY. WHAT WERE THE CONSEQUENCES? WHAT MIGHT BE SOME POSSIBLE FUTURE CONSEQUENCES?

also on this day

1820 Captain Nathaniel Palmer became the first American to sight the continent of Antarctica.

Mickey Mouse made his debut in *Steamboat Willie*. **1928**

face the consequences

have a no-good absolutely horrible day

We all have had our share of bad days. You remember—like the day when you got up late for school, you couldn't find a pair of socks that matched, your hair wouldn't lie down straight, and then you discovered that your dog really had eaten your homework.

And that's before you even walked out the door! It got worse. You ran into your first class only to hear your teacher say, "Put your books away. We're having a pop quiz." Then you discovered at lunch that you picked up your brother's lunch instead of yours. And he likes sardines with peanut butter! Do you need to hear more?

The apostle Paul had a couple of very bad, no-good, horrible days. In fact, he probably could claim he had some bad, no-good, horrible weeks, months, even years. Listen to some of what Paul experienced as he carried the gospel of Jesus Christ from place to place: "Five different times the Jews gave me thirty-nine lashes. Three times I was beaten with rods. Once I was stoned. Three times I was shipwrecked . . . " (2 Corinthians 11:24-25). Paul lived with weariness, pain, sleepless nights. He went without food, clothing, or water.

Talk about your bad days! And what was Paul's reaction to all that he experienced? He was glad. Why? Because Paul had learned that through his weaknesses, through his very worst moments, Jesus' strength and power were demonstrated. At his very lowest, Paul was able to have confidence and courage because of Jesus' words: "My power works best in your weaknesses."

The same is true for you. Jesus promises to be there when all else is falling apart in your life. So bring it on. Have a Bad Day Day—and don't sweat it.

Each time he said, "My gracious favor is all you need. My power works best in your weakness." So now I am glad to boast about my weaknesses, so that the power of Christ may work through me. [2 Corinthians 12:9]

also on this day

1863
Abraham Lincoln delivered the Gettysburg Address.

1895
The "paper pencil" was patented by Frederick E. Blaisdell.

1954
Two automatic toll collectors were placed in service on the Garden State Parkway in New Jersey.

to do ☑

ASK SOMEONE IN YOUR FAMILY TO TELL YOU ABOUT THEIR "VERY BAD, NO-GOOD" DAY. THEN TELL THEM WHY IT REALLY WASN'T SO BAD, AFTER ALL.

a whale of a tale

In 1820, an American ship sank after being attacked by a whale.

The story goes, there was this great big fish that weighed over 80 tons. A whale actually, and it attacked this ship off the coast of South America and sank it!

You're probably saying, "Oh yeah, sure. What a fish story." But this one is true. The 283-ton *Essex* was a whaling ship that hailed from Nantucket, Massachusetts. It was out at sea in pursuit of sperm whales, which were hunted for their bone and oil. When the crew went after a bull whale, it rammed the ship twice. The 80-ton whale was able to capsize the ship. The 20 crew members were able to flee the ship in three open boats, but only five of the men survived to tell the tale.

If this story sounds somewhat familiar, it's because the incident became the plot for another famous whale of a tale, Herman Melville's *Moby Dick*.

The Bible has its own fish story. A wayward prophet named Jonah once had a very close encounter with a large fish of his own. You remember—God told Jonah to go one way, but Jonah got on a ship and went off in the opposite direction. Then God sent a tremendous storm and the sailors, frightened for their lives, threw Jonah overboard to stop the storm.

God calmed the waters and then sent a huge fish to swallow Jonah to save him from drowning. Talk about your fish tales!

Some people think that the story of Jonah and the whale is just that—a fish story. But if we believe that God is who he said he is, then we need to trust everything about him. Jesus himself used the story of Jonah living in the belly of a fish for three days as an illustration of his death and resurrection (Matthew 12:39, 40).

And that's no fish story!

to do ☑

READ THE BOOK OF JONAH, ALL FOUR CHAPTERS. WHAT DO YOU THINK IS THE MOST AMAZING PART OF THAT STORY? SHARE IT WITH SOMEONE IN YOUR FAMILY.

also on this day

1941

The U.S. State Department started requiring photographs for passports.

The United Nations adopted the Declaration of Children's Rights.

1959

Today is National Peanut Butter Fudge Day.

For as Jonah was in the belly of the great fish for three days and three nights, so I, the Son of Man, will be in the heart of the earth for three days and three nights.

[Matthew 12:40]

Today is World Hello Day.

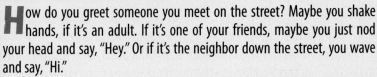

Hello!

How do you greet someone you meet on the street? Maybe you shake hands, if it's an adult. If it's one of your friends, maybe you just nod your head and say, "Hey." Or if it's the neighbor down the street, you wave and say, "Hi."

We probably wouldn't greet another person by rubbing noses with them, as they do among the Maori people in New Zealand. And we most likely wouldn't greet another person by giving them a kiss on each check, as some European cultures do.

The way we greet others really depends on our cultural habits and behaviors. A common hand gesture that we often use—the "thumbs up"—is interpreted in a completely different way in another part of the world. It helps to know something about different cultures so that we don't make people feel uncomfortable or offended.

For example, we are taught that when you talk to someone, you should look that person in the eye. In many Asian cultures, looking a person in the eye is considered disrespectful. Many consider a light touch on the arm as acceptable when talking with another person. In some Middle Eastern cultures, touching another person is highly offensive.

There is one surefire way to greet another person that is always appropriate—as Paul puts it, to "Greet each other in Christian love." When we reach out to others as Jesus did, we will be concerned about that person and what makes him or her comfortable. We will make every effort to make the person feel welcomed and loved—no matter whether that person lives next door, around the block, or across the globe.

That kind of hello goes beyond all cultural and ethnic barriers.

to do ☑

TALK TO SOME OF YOUR FRIENDS WHO HAVE DIFFERENT CULTURAL BACKGROUNDS FROM YOU. FIND OUT HOW THEY GREET ONE ANOTHER IN THEIR CULTURE.

Greet each other in **Christian love**. **Peace** be to **all** of **you** who are in **Christ**.

[1 Peter 5:14]

also on this day

1877 Thomas A. Edison announced the invention of his phonograph.

1922 Rebecca L. Felton of Georgia was sworn in as the first woman to serve as a member of the U.S. Senate.

The Alaska highway across Canada was formally opened. **1942**

Morse code, the language developed by Samuel Morse and Alfred Vail to be used over the telegraph, is a series of dots and dashes that form each letter of the alphabet. The code was the only way to effectively and rapidly communicate over long distances before telephones and two-way radios were available.

One of the most famous words in the Morse code is SOS—the international distress signal. The series of letters was chosen not because it stood for Save Our Ship or Save Our Souls, but because the three dots for S and the three dashes for O made a clear and distinct signal.

Other combinations were initially suggested, but those were abandoned either because the signal got lost in the static or could not be sent as rapidly as SOS. So the International Radio Telegraphic Convention in Berlin adopted the SOS distress signal in 1906. The U.S. did not adopt it until after the sinking of the *Titanic* in 1912.

Over the years, the public has associated SOS with Save Our Ship or Save Our Souls because that is what often occurred when the signal was sent out. Once the signal went out over the airwaves, the hope was that someone somewhere would respond and come to the rescue.

Thankfully, we don't need any special code or equipment such as a telegraph to send out a distress signal to Jesus. Jesus is in the business of SOS—saving our souls. And he does so whenever and wherever anyone is ready to call on his name and seek him. All it takes is a prayer that can be said at anytime, and Jesus will respond.

For he wants everyone to be saved and to understand the truth. For there is only one God and one Mediator who can reconcile God and people. He is the man Christ Jesus. [1 Timothy 2:4, 5]

In 1906, the International Radio Telegraphic Convention in Berlin adopted the SOS distress signal.

to do ☑

FIND A COPY OF THE MORSE CODE. LEARN HOW TO TAP OUT "JESUS SAVES."

also on this day

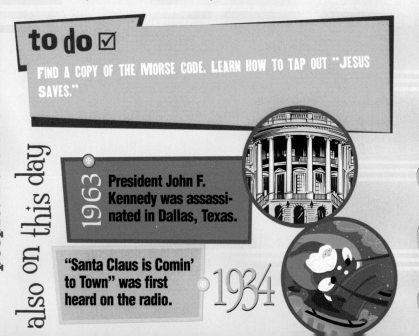

1963 President John F. Kennedy was assassinated in Dallas, Texas.

"Santa Claus is Comin' to Town" was first heard on the radio. **1934**

SOS

keep sharp!

In 1897, the pencil sharpener was patented.

It's the day of the big math test. You have prepared well for this particular test, right down to making sure you have a nicely sharpened pencil with a good eraser. You work your way through the first two pages and are about to tackle the third when the point of your nicely sharpened pencil snaps off.

No reason to panic. You simply ask permission to get up and use the pencil sharpener. Within seconds, your pencil is sharpened to a fine point, and you are ready to work again.

You can thank the work of John Lee Love of Fall River, Massachusetts. The "Love Sharpener," dating back to 1897, sounds much like the sharpeners in use today—gadgets where the pencil is inserted into the opening of the sharpener, the handle is turned, and the shavings stay in the sharpener.

The pencil sharpener is handy if all you are trying to sharpen is a pencil. But what if you are trying to sharpen your wisdom, your ability to make good decisions, or your ability to tell right from wrong? Where do you go for that kind of sharpening and shaping? The writer of Hebrews said that you don't have to look any further than God's Word, the Bible.

You probably never thought of the Bible as a life-skills sharpener, but that's exactly what it is. In the book of Hebrews, the author says that the Word of God is full of "living power." And it is sharper than the sharpest knife. It has the ability to cut through our thoughts, attitudes, and choices and point us to what is right and good. God's Word has the ability to sharpen us for God's purposes and to shape our lives.

So next time you read the Bible, think of the pencil sharpener and allow God's Word to keep you sharp. Get the point?

to do ☑

CONSIDER HOW IN THE LAST WEEK GOD'S WORD HAS SHARPENED YOUR LIFE. WRITE DOWN (PREFERABLY WITH A SHARPENED PENCIL) ONE OR TWO WAYS.

For the word of God is full of living power. It is sharper than the sharpest knife, cutting deep into our innermost thoughts and desires. It exposes us for what we really are. [Hebrews 4:12]

also on this day

1804

Franklin Pierce, the 14th president of the United States, was born.

The first jukebox made its debut in San Francisco.

Today is National Buy Nothing Day.

1889

a thirst quencher

Today is National Espresso Day.

You probably haven't joined the crowd yet, but we have become a nation of coffee drinkers, particularly of specialty coffee drinks such as lattes, frozen coffee drinks, and espressos. Consider the popularity of Starbucks—just one of many coffee companies. The company, which started in 1971 as a coffee roasting facility, has grown to more than 8,000 cafés in more than 30 countries.

The company turned the corner and found success when one of its marketing executives was traveling through Italy. Howard Schulz was inspired by the old Italian coffee bar tradition of serving freshly brewed espresso and cappuccino drinks. Schulz went back to Seattle and convinced his bosses to give his idea a chance. In 1985, the first coffee bar opened in Seattle and the coffee craze was on.

Some people will tell you that they just can't seem to start their day without a mocha latte or a double-shot cappuccino. Without their coffee they can't function. Or if it isn't coffee, maybe it's that morning cup of juice, a nice hot tea, or a frothy glass of cold milk.

Of course people really don't need a double-shot latte to get through the day. Our daily existence doesn't depend on whether or not we have a coffee each morning. But there is one drink that promises to do more than just get us through our day. This particular drink promises to all who drink deeply of it eternal life. And once we drink we will never be thirsty again.

Jesus offers us "living water." The spiritual side of us needs food and water to grow and function. That means we need to nourish ourselves with God's Word on a daily basis. We need to quench our thirst by staying connected to Jesus through prayer and Bible study.

Drink up!

Anyone who drinks the water I give will never thirst—not ever. The water I give will be an artesian spring within, gushing fountains of endless life. [John 4:14, The Message]

also on this day

1615
French King Louis XIII married Ann of Austria. Both were only 14 years old.

1784
Zachary Taylor, the 12th president of the United States, was born.

to do ☑
ENJOY YOUR FAVORITE BEVERAGE. THINK OF ALL THE WAYS THAT KNOWING JESUS IS LIKE HAVING A COLD DRINK OF WATER ON A HOT, HOT DAY.

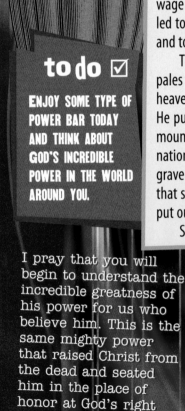

In 1867, Alfred Nobel patented dynamite.

Power Up

Early scientists recognized that they had a powerful explosive source in the compound nitroglycerine. The only problem was that nitroglycerine was extremely sensitive to the slightest shock, so it was very difficult to determine under which conditions it would explode.

Alfred Nobel began to study the problem. He realized that he needed a safe way to transport the nitroglycerine. Nobel's solution was to mix the nitroglycerine (an oily substance) with silica (a ground-up mineral), forming a dough-like paste that could be molded into any shape. He called this compound dynamite, from the Greek *dynamis,* meaning "power."

Soon after Nobel developed a blasting cap that would safely detonate the dynamite. His resulting product is considered as one of humankind's most important inventions. It has changed the way we live, changed the way we wage war, and it also changed the face of the earth. The power of dynamite led to the construction of large buildings, the creation of roads and tunnels, and to the mining of precious natural resources.

Though we marvel at such an explosive resource, the power of dynamite pales in comparison to the power of our God. With a word he created the heavens and earth. At his command the sun and moon came into existence. He put the stars in place and named each one. God has the power to move mountains, part seas, and calm the winds at his command. He controls the nations and all their rulers. It is the same power that raised Jesus from the grave and defeated death and Satan with one blow. The incredible news is that such a power source is available to us every day as we come to God and put our confidence in him.

So power up!

to do ☑

ENJOY SOME TYPE OF POWER BAR TODAY AND THINK ABOUT GOD'S INCREDIBLE POWER IN THE WORLD AROUND YOU.

I pray that you will begin to understand the incredible greatness of his power for us who believe him. This is the same mighty power that raised Christ from the dead and seated him in the place of honor at God's right hand in the heavenly realms. [Ephesians 1:19, 20]

also on this day

Today is National Parfait Day.

Lech Walesa won Poland's first popular election. **1990**

1817 The first sword swallower in the United States performed in New York City.

Imagine hearing about lions, possibly reading about lions, but never actually seeing one. It would be hard to imagine a lion's majestic demeanor or experience its powerful roar from mere words. So it must have caused quite a stir when the first lion was exhibited in the United States.

That milestone event took place on this day in 1716, at the home of Captain Arthur Savage on Brattle Street, Boston. The lion, which had been tamed for exhibition, was advertised in *The Boston News Letter* in the following way: "All persons having the Curiosity of seeing the noble and Royal Beast the Lyon, never one before in America, may see him at the House of Capt. Arthur Savage near Mr. Colman's Church, Boston."

Imagine not only seeing a lion for the first time, but seeing it in someone's home!

Sometimes we need to use more than our eyes to truly see and know something. Sometimes we need our hearts as well. A good example of this is the two blind beggars who sat by the road. They could hear the commotion of Jesus approaching, and so they shouted, "Son of David, have mercy on us!"

These men called Jesus "Son of David," because they knew the Messiah would come from David's family *and* because they knew without a doubt that Jesus was that long-awaited Messiah. They could "see" Jesus was the Messiah with their hearts, while the other religious leaders who saw Jesus' miracles were blind to his true identity.

As you get to know Jesus through God's Word and through others, make sure you are seeing him with both your eyes and your heart.

Two blind men were sitting beside the road. When they heard that Jesus was coming that way, they began shouting, "Lord, Son of David, have mercy on us!" [Matthew 20:30]

In 1716, a lion was exhibited for the first time in America.

heart sight

to do ☑

TRY THIS: DESCRIBE SOMETHING YOU HAVE SEEN TO A FAMILY MEMBER OR FRIEND. BASED ON YOUR DESCRIPTION, ASK THEM TO DRAW IT.

also on this day

1789 President George Washington set aside this day to observe the adoption of the U.S. Constitution.

The state of West Virginia was created (out of Virginia) over a dispute concerning slavery. West Virginia was against slavery. 1861

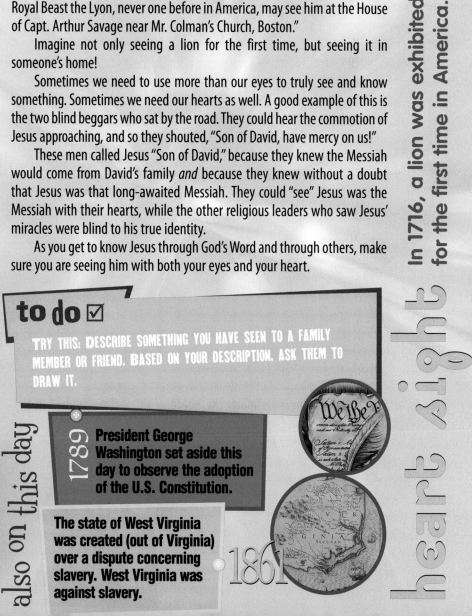

give peace a chance

In 1896, Alfred Nobel established the Nobel Peace Prize.

Several days ago you read about Alfred Nobel, the inventor and developer of dynamite. Twenty-eight years after inventing that useful but destructive product, Nobel stipulated in his will that the fortune he had amassed be used to celebrate and honor achievements in Physics, Chemistry, Physiology or Medicine, Literature, and Peace.

Shortly before his death, Nobel made arrangements for the prizes that bear his name. He did not want to be remembered as the man who developed the most destructive weapon the world had ever seen, but as a man who loved literature and peace. The creation of these awards was Nobel's life dream.

Although there are more than 300 peace prizes given out each year, the Nobel Peace Prize has become the most well known. It is awarded to those who "shall have done the most or the best work for fraternity between nations, for the abolition or reduction of standing armies and for the holding of peace congresses." Since 1901, the prize has been awarded to people such as Nelson Mendela, President Jimmy Carter, and Mother Teresa.

When it comes to true peace, however, there is only one who is worthy of receiving an award for doing the most work for all nations and all people—Jesus Christ. Because of his willingness to go to the cross and take the punishment for sins through his death, we have peace with God. Not the kind of peace that the world thinks about—the absence of war or feelings such as calmness and tranquility. The peace Jesus achieved makes us right with God. We no longer are considered God's enemies, but his friends. Our sin no longer blocks us from a relationship with God.

That's a prize-winning peace, don't you think?

Therefore, since we have been made right in God's sight by faith, we have peace with God because of what Jesus Christ our Lord has done for us. [Romans 5:1]

also on this day

1885
The earliest photograph of a meteor shower was made.

1910
New York's Pennsylvania Station opened.

1940
Martial arts actor Bruce Lee was born.

to do ☑
MAKE UP YOUR OWN PEACE AWARD AND GIVE IT TO SOMEONE YOU KNOW WHO WORKS HARD TO KEEP THE PEACE.

let's give thanks

In 1863, the first Thanksgiving was celebrated as a regular American holiday.

You probably already know that President Abraham Lincoln issued a proclamation in 1863, declaring the fourth Thursday in November as an official day to give thanks to God for his many blessings and provisions throughout the year. But did you ever stop to consider that Lincoln's call for thanksgiving came while the country was involved in the Civil War?

"In the midst of a civil war of unequaled magnitude and severity," President Lincoln found much for which to give thanks to God. Peace had been preserved with other nations, laws had been respected and maintained. The population of the country had continued to increase, farming and industry were thriving, and the country remained strong—all blessings that Lincoln attributed to "the Most High God."

"It has seemed to me fit and proper that they [God's gracious gifts] should be solemnly, reverently and gratefully acknowledged as with one heart and one voice by the whole American People," President Lincoln wrote.

Thousands of years earlier, another ruler had declared a day of thanksgiving and praise to God. King David, having just brought the Ark of God into Jerusalem, led the people in a celebration of thanksgiving with this song, "Give thanks to the LORD and proclaim his greatness. Let the whole world know what he has done. Sing to him; yes, sing his praises. Tell everyone about his miracles" (1 Chronicles 16:8, 9).

In David's song, the people were instructed in how to give true thanksgiving: remembering what God has done; telling others about it; showing God's goodness to others; and offering back to God gifts of service.

What can you do today to remember, tell, show, and serve as thanksgiving to God?

to do ☑

AS PART OF YOUR THANKSGIVING CELEBRATION, READ DAVID'S SONG OF THANKSGIVING IN 1 CHRONICLES 16:7–36.

Give **thanks** to the LORD and **proclaim** his **greatness**. Let the **whole world** know what **he** has **done**.

[1 Chronicles 16:8]

also on this day

1520
Portuguese navigator Ferdinand Magellan reached the Pacific Ocean after passing through the South American strait.

Today is National French Toast Day. Enjoy some!

American-born Lady Astor was elected the first female member of the British Parliament.
1919

On this day in 1898, C. S. Lewis was born.

A Faith Decision

C. S. Lewis, one of the most respected Christian writers, is the author of the beloved children's classic *Narnia* tales. Yet it took Lewis until his adult life before he became a Christian and accepted the truth about God.

As a youngster growing up in Northern Ireland, Lewis was raised as a Christian. He even turned more to the Christian faith after his mother died in 1908. But in his teens Lewis abandoned his faith. He became more interested in German mythology, which led him to see Christianity as "kind of . . . nonsense into which humanity tended to blunder." Lewis became an atheist (one who believes there is no God) while a student at Oxford University and remained one well into his thirties.

After graduating in 1925 with honors, Lewis became an English professor at Magdalen College. During that time he met fellow writers and friends, J. R. R. Tolkien (author of the *Lord of the Rings* trilogy) and Hugo Dyson. Lewis became a Christian after a long discussion with Tolkien and Dyson about the Christian faith. The next day Lewis recalled, "When we set out [by motor-cycle to the Whipsnade Zoo] I did not believe that Jesus Christ was the Son of God, and when we reached the zoo I did."

Lewis went on to become a strong defender of the faith, and no doubt would agree with the psalm writer that "Only fools say in their hearts, 'There is no God.'" The good news for Lewis and anyone with doubts is that God is patient with us and is eager for all to come to the same conclusion of faith as Lewis (2 Peter 3:9).

In *The Case for Christianity* Lewis wrote, "Now is our chance to choose the right side. God is holding back to give us that chance. It won't last forever. We must take it or leave it."

Have you taken it?

to do ☑

IF YOU HAVEN'T ALREADY DONE SO, GET A COPY OF *THE LION, THE WITCH, AND THE WARDROBE* FROM THE LIBRARY AND READ IT.

Only **fools** say in their **hearts**, "There is **no God**." They are **corrupt**, and their **actions** are **evil**; no one does **good**!

[Psalm 14:1]

also on this day

1929
The first airplane flight over the South Pole was made by U.S. Navy Lt. Commander Richard E. Byrd.

1934
The Chicago Bears beat the Detroit Lions in the first NFL game broadcast nationally.

real joy

In 2001, McDonald's teamed up with a popular toy store chain to provide the toys for its Happy Meals®.

It started in 1978 as a promotion at a Kansas City McDonald's, when a toy was offered to kids along with their hamburger, fries, and shakes. The introduction of the Happy Meal® took the country by storm, and, for more than 25 years, young customers have enjoyed getting a fun toy along with their meal.

In fact, these toys have become popular collector's items worldwide. Some people are so obsessed with their toy collection that they go to multiple restaurants and buy (maybe not eat!) as many kids' meals as it takes to complete a portion of their collection.

With such a highly successful marketing concept, other major retailers sought partnerships with the restaurants in order to get their merchandise into children's hands. And it didn't take Hollywood long to catch on, either. Now nearly every major family film release is accompanied by a kids' meal tie-in.

While some might think that collecting toys brings happiness, what brings you happiness? Maybe it's new clothes, or a fun afternoon with your friends. Or maybe it's spending a quiet afternoon reading. Whatever it might be, we need to remember that true happiness comes from only one source—and that's a rock-steady relationship with Jesus Christ. Our joy comes from knowing Jesus and knowing that he is with us always. And what's better, it's this type of joy that helps us through the tough times—when the friends aren't there, the shoes have holes in them, or the toys break down.

Jesus never fails us. He is always with us, and that should bring you real happiness and joy.

So be truly **glad**! There is **wonderful joy** ahead, even though it is **necessary** for **you** to **endure** many **trials** for a while. [1 Peter 1:6]

also on this day

Stay Home Because You're Well Day.

1835 Samuel Clemens (Mark Twain) was born.

1875 A.J. Ehrichson patented the oat-crushing machine.

to do ☑

MAKE A LIST OF WHAT MAKES YOU HAPPY. NOW CROSS OFF ANYTHING THAT IS TEMPORARY OR DEPENDS ON YOUR CIRCUMSTANCES. WHAT'S LEFT ON YOUR LIST?

a good mystery

Sherlock Holmes, a fictional English detective, achieved fame through several novels by Arthur Conan Doyle. In each story Holmes and associates would try to solve an unsolved crime. Eventually, using his incredible observational and deductive skills, Holmes would solve the mystery.

Do you enjoy mysteries? Many books and popular TV shows feature crime-solving detectives, investigators, police officers, district attorneys, and citizens. It's fun to follow the clues and identify the villains.

But some mysteries can't be solved by mere human beings. Today's Scripture, for example, explains "the great mystery of our faith"—the story of God becoming a human being. For 2000 years, people have been trying to answer this one: How could Jesus be fully God and fully human? What does it mean to be the "God-man"? It's a mystery, and it's unsolvable because God is way beyond our ability to think and figure out.

Some people think they have to understand something in order to believe in it. So they only accept what they can touch, taste, see, hear, and feel—like food, snow, toys, friends, school buildings, and homework. Because they can't see God, and certainly can't understand everything about him, they find it difficult to believe in him at all.

That's where faith comes in.

Jesus lived on earth, died, and rose from the dead. That's history. But it's also "mystery" because the Bible says he was *sinless* and lives *now* in Heaven and in us through the Holy Spirit.

Thank God for this "great mystery of our faith." Believe!

Without question, this is the great mystery of our faith: Christ appeared in the flesh and was shown to be righteous by the Spirit. He was seen by angels and was announced to the nations. He was believed on in the world and was taken up into heaven. [1 Timothy 3:16]

to do ☑

TALK TO YOUR MINISTER AND ASK ABOUT THE GREAT "MYSTERIES" OF THE CHRISTIAN FAITH.

also on this day

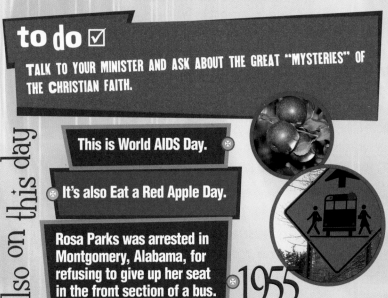

This is World AIDS Day.

It's also Eat a Red Apple Day.

Rosa Parks was arrested in Montgomery, Alabama, for refusing to give up her seat in the front section of a bus. *1955*

A Little Guy

On this day in 1804, Napoleon was crowned Emperor of France.

NAPOLÉON BONAPARTE,
LIEUTENANT COLONEL 1ᵉ Bⁿ DE LA CORSE en 1792.

A masterful general, an amazing military tactician, and a superb administrator, Napoleon Bonaparte was also an utterly ruthless dictator. Later in his career he thought he could do no wrong. So his name is often connected with overreaching military ambition and great pride. Although Napoleon conquered much of Europe, he lost two-thirds of his army in a disastrous invasion of Russia.

Because Napoleon was short (nicknamed "the Little Corporal"), short men who are overly aggressive are said to have a Napoleon complex. They seem to try to act taller and bigger by coming on strong in relationships and business.

The Bible tells about a man who probably had that kind of complex. Zacchaeus was a little guy, and in his job as tax collector he was mean and dishonest. Remember the story? Read it in Luke 19.

One day, as Jesus was making his way through town, Zacchaeus had to climb a tree to see him. Jesus saw him, called him by name, and asked to go to his house. And that's when Zacchaeus's life turned around. Instead of the taxman who got rich by cheating his neighbors and lording it over them, he became an honest man, humbly submitting to the Lord.

What made the difference? He experienced Jesus' love, acceptance, and forgiveness.

Here's the deal. Whether you're short or tall, coordinated or uncoordinated, exceptional or average, Jesus loves you and accepts you as you are. You don't have to pretend to be someone you're not or try to be different to be accepted by God.

So change your Napoleon complex to a Zacchaeus complex. Come down from that tree and meet the Savior.

to do ☑

TAKE OUT A SHEET OF PAPER AND WRITE DOWN ALL THE WAYS THAT YOU FEEL INADEQUATE OR WISH YOU WERE DIFFERENT. INCLUDE PHYSICAL AND PERSONALITY CHARACTERISTICS, NATURAL ABILITIES, AND PAST EXPERIENCES. THEN THANK GOD FOR EACH ONE AND ASK HIM TO SHOW YOU HOW YOU CAN SERVE HIM AS YOURSELF, THE WAY HE MADE YOU.

When Jesus came by, he looked up at Zacchaeus and called him by name. "Zacchaeus!" he said. "Quick, come down! For I must be a guest in your home today."
[Luke 19:5]

also on this day

This is National Fritters Day.

Circus entrepreneur Charles Ringling was born. 1862

1990 The midwest section of the United States prepared for a massive earthquake predicted by Iben Browning. Nothing happened, by the way.

that's a relief!

On this day in 1931, Alka-Seltzer® sold for the first time.

You know how Alka-Seltzer® works, right? Take a couple of the tablets, drop them in water, and watch them fizz and disintegrate. Then drink it up. It's supposed to bring relief to aching stomachs and heads and stuffy noses.

Relief means change, a break in the action, a new approach, and a turn for the better. We have relief pitchers in baseball and relief workers in areas hit by natural disasters. We talk about getting relief from a cold snap in winter, and when we hear good news (like, "No homework today"), we say, "That's a relief!" We usually associate relief with stopping pain and feeling better.

That's the good news. But here's the bad. The Bible says that hell is a place of *"no relief."* Check out today's Bible verse. There, medicine won't help. A new weather front won't change conditions. No one and nothing will be able to relieve the suffering in that terrible place. What an awful prospect!

Heaven, on the other hand, is all about relief from the sin and suffering in life. Instead of pain, we'll have pleasure. Instead of darkness, light. And we'll be reunited with loved ones. Now that's the place to be!

So what makes the difference? How does a person avoid hell and make it to Heaven? Only by grace through faith (see Ephesians 2:8, 9).

When we trust in Christ as Savior, turning over control of our lives to him, we are saved from eternal death. We receive eternal life and become members of God's eternal family.

What a relief!

to do ☑

GET A CONCORDANCE. LOOK UP HEAVEN AND READ ALL THE RELATED VERSES. DO THE SAME FOR HELL.

The smoke of their torment rises forever and ever, and they will have no relief day or night, for they have worshiped the beast and his statue and have accepted the mark of his name. [Revelation 14:11]

also on this day 1833

Oberlin College in Ohio opened as the first truly coeducational (admitting both men and women) school of higher education in the United States.

SALT

This is National Ice Cream Box Day (Cool!).

Mr. Gaillard must have lived in a warm climate; otherwise, how could he test his mower?

Ah, grass—the green stuff that comes after the snow leaves and the ground thaws. You may have had to mow the lawn as one of your chores. If you use a power mower, aren't you glad for Mr. Gaillard's fine invention? But 1812—why did it take so long for power mowers to get to the public? They didn't become popular till the 1960s. Don't ask; just start and push.

You probably have mixed feelings about chores. You know jobs have to be done, but you really don't like doing them. What if no one washed the dishes? Soon the kitchen would be overflowing with plates, silverware, and glasses. And if no one took out the garbage, what a smelly mess you'd have! Your parents could pay an outsider to do those jobs, but that would waste a lot of money. Besides, chores help the family work together, with every person playing an important role—like a team.

The Bible talks about teamwork, especially in the church. Today's verse, for example, says each person should do his or her "own special work." Paul also wrote, "We work together as partners who belong to God" (1 Corinthians 3:9).

Certainly some jobs are more unpleasant or more difficult than others, but someone has to do them. And sometimes we compare our chores to others' and don't think we got a fair deal. Instead, we should do these family jobs with a good attitude. Paul even told slaves, "Work hard and cheerfully at whatever you do, as though you were working for the Lord rather than for people" (Colossians 3:23).

So grab that shovel (or mower) and smile!

to do ☑

TODAY, DO YOUR CHORES BEFORE BEING REMINDED BY YOUR MOTHER OR FATHER. WATCH HOW THEY REACT. CAUTION: THEY MAY BE SHOCKED AT YOUR ACTIONS AND POSITIVE ATTITUDE.

Under [Christ's] direction, the whole body is fitted together perfectly. As each part does its own special work, it helps the other parts grow, so that the whole body is healthy and growing and full of love. [Ephesians 4:16]

On this day in 1812, Peter Gaillard patented the power mower.

power up

also on this day

1619 America celebrated the first Thanksgiving Day in Virginia.

This is National Wear Brown Shoes day.

Clean!

This is National Bathtub Day.

Yucky. Filthy. Dirty. Smelly. Nothing feels worse than being gross all over. Sometimes it's so bad that you don't want to be around yourself.

Then you jump in the shower or tub and scrub all the crud away with hot water, soap, and shampoo. Nothing feels better than being totally clean.

We can be dirty inside, too. Even when we've scrubbed off all the smelly mess on our skin, in our hair, and under our nails, we can feel as though we need to wash our minds and hearts. Dirty thoughts and hateful feelings can mess up our tidy lives. And then there's envy, pride, greed, deceit, anger, and other evil plots and plans. Sin has a way of soaking us through and through.

That's when we need a *real* bath—a cleansing of the soul and spirit.

We don't need a bathtub for this procedure. We just need to place ourselves in the shower of God's grace. He promises that when we confess our sins, he will cleanse us, forgiving us completely. Then, not only will we feel clean, we will actually be clean inside—where it really counts. And once we're clean inside, God can use us to do his work. That's what today's verse is talking about.

Consider a drinking glass. Before drinking out of it you want the glass to be clean. And it's not enough to wipe off the outside—you'll make sure the inside has been thoroughly washed, too.

Your life is like that glass. When God cleans you on the inside he can use you to take his life-giving message to others.

Do you need a "bath," a spiritual cleansing? Let God make you totally clean!

to do ☑

EVERY TIME YOU USE SOAP TODAY, REMEMBER THAT YOU ARE CLEAN IN CHRIST. ASK HIM TO KEEP YOU PURE FOR HIS USE.

If you keep yourself pure, you will be a utensil God can use for his purpose. Your life will be clean, and you will be ready for the Master to use you for every good work.

[2 Timothy 2:21]

also on this day

This is International Day of Disabled Persons.

Christopher Columbus discovered Hispaniola. 1492

1782 Martin Van Buren, the 8th president of the United States, was born.

twice free!

On this day in 1865, the 13th Amendment to the U. S. Constitution was ratified.

The 13th Amendment abolished slavery. This didn't end racism and discrimination in the United States, but at least the terrible act of one human being enslaving another was illegal.

In America we understand and value freedom. Not only do we stand against slavery, but we also guard carefully the other freedoms guaranteed by our Constitution. But here's a startling truth—people, even Americans, are slaves and not truly free at all.

The Bible tells us that every person is born a sinner and is a slave to sin. No matter how nice we are and how hard we try, we cannot go a day without sinning. Those sins separate us from God. He's holy and perfect, and we are very unholy and imperfect. So we have no freedom to come to him and even to do what is right.

That's where Christ comes in. When we trust in him, he frees us from our bondage to sin and from our slave-master, Satan. And he frees us to make the right choices and to follow him. Instead of slaves, we become God's very own children.

We don't need an amendment to the Constitution to make this true. God's Word—his "constitution"—guarantees it. You are free indeed!

So you should not be like cowering, fearful slaves. You should behave instead like God's very own children, adopted into his family— calling him "Father, dear Father."

[Romans 8:15]

also on this day

This is St. Nicholas Day.

1877

Thomas Edison demonstrated the first gramophone, with a recording of "Mary Had a Little Lamb."

1926

In Italy, Benito Mussolini introduced a tax on bachelors.

to do ☑

READ THE BOOK OF PHILEMON. IT'S THE STORY OF A MAN WHO WAS A SLAVE WHO BECAME TWICE FREE.

sneak attack

On this day in 1941, Pearl Harbor was bombed by the Japanese, bringing the U. S. into the World War II.

We weren't prepared. It was a sneak attack.

At about eight o'clock in the morning on Sunday, December 7, 1941, approximately 100 ships of the U.S. Navy lay in the harbor at Oahu, Hawaii. Suddenly Japanese planes burst through the clouds and began raining bombs, eventually destroying 188 planes, damaging or destroying 8 battleships, and leaving 2,403 people dead. The United States was thrust into the Second World War.

This terrible attack was a surprise because the United States was not at war with Japan. In fact, just before the attack Japanese officials had been in Washington discussing peace.

Sneak attacks are effective because the opposition isn't prepared to defend and to fight back. Think of the difference if America had known the Japanese were coming!

Christians are like soldiers, pilots, and sailors. We're in a war. Satan and his forces want to hurt and defeat us. And Satan specializes in sneak attacks. Today's verse describes him as a "roaring lion" prowling for victims.

As you know, lions sneak up on their prey and then pounce. Quickly the unsuspecting victim is toast. It's an accurate picture of how the devil works.

That's why we need to be ready, to be on our guard. Satan doesn't announce, "Hey, here I am, coming to get you!" Instead, he quietly tempts us to do wrong. Often he twists God's words (like he did with Adam and Eve) to get us confused. Sometimes the temptations are big, but often he is content to have us just become bored with our faith.

To be ready, on guard, we need to stay close to God and his Word. And in every temptation we need to rely on God to give us the strength to resist.

to do ☑

GO ONLINE OR CHECK AN ENCYCLOPEDIA AND READ MORE ABOUT PEARL HARBOR AND THE MONUMENT TO THE MEN AND WOMEN WHO DIED THERE.

Be careful! Watch out for attacks from the Devil, your great enemy. He prowls around like a roaring lion, looking for some victim to devour. [1 Peter 5:8]

also on this day

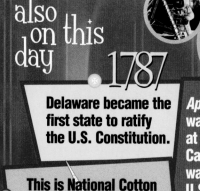

1787

Delaware became the first state to ratify the U.S. Constitution.

This is National Cotton Candy Day.

Apollo 17 was launched at Cape Canaveral. It was the last U.S. moon mission.

1972

For the Birds

On this day in 1909, the Birdbanding Society was founded.

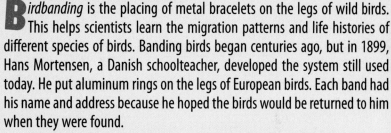

Birdbanding is the placing of metal bracelets on the legs of wild birds. This helps scientists learn the migration patterns and life histories of different species of birds. Banding birds began centuries ago, but in 1899, Hans Mortensen, a Danish schoolteacher, developed the system still used today. He put aluminum rings on the legs of European birds. Each band had his name and address because he hoped the birds would be returned to him when they were found.

Bird migration is fascinating, and scientists still can't figure out how it works. Think about it—birds aren't very strong, yet some travel great distances, flying days without stopping. The blackpoll warbler, a North American bird about the size of a sparrow, for example, flies nonstop almost 2,500 miles to South America where it lives for the winter. God created these birds with the desire, stamina, and navigation system to make that trip.

The Bible mentions at least 24 kinds of birds, beginning with creation (Genesis 1:20-23). You probably remember reading about doves, roosters, and eagles. Often the eagle is used as an example of God's care (see Exodus 19:3, 4). God also says that we can become "like eagles." These magnificent birds soar above the earth riding the wind currents. Vultures (Matthew 24:28) are ugly and feed on dead and decaying animals—yuck!

So which bird would you rather be like? Our verse for today tells how to be an eagle. The secret? "Wait on the Lord." That means trusting in God and relying on him instead of friends, family, money, or government for salvation and security.

You can fly like an eagle. Soar in faith!

to do ☑

MEMORIZE TODAY'S VERSE, ISAIAH 40:31. IT'S A GREAT ONE TO REMEMBER, ESPECIALLY WHEN YOU'RE HAVING A TOUGH DAY.

But those who wait on the LORD will find new strength. They will fly high on wings like eagles. They will run and not grow weary. They will walk and not faint. [Isaiah 40:31]

also on this day

This is National Brownie Day.

The United States entered World War II when it declared war against Japan. **1941**

1998
The first female ice hockey game in Olympic history was played. Finland beat Sweden 6-0.

The *American Minerva* was the first daily newspaper in New York City. From there, newspapers were started all across the country.

Newspapers have become a regular part of daily life in America. Today's papers include not only news, but also opinion columns, features, comics, and advertisements.

These days, most people also get news from TV, radio, and the Internet, all much more immediate than the papers. But before those outlets, newspaper vendors would stand at street corners and yell, "Extra! Extra! Read all about it!" to inform everyone that something important had happened.

When you have news, you want to get out the word. The Bible calls the message of Christ the good news. That's because without Christ, just about everything else is bad news. The worst news of all is that all people are dead in their sins and have no hope for eternal life. Romans 3:23 says, "For all have sinned; all fall short of God's glorious standard." And Romans 6:23 says, "For the wages of sin is death, but the free gift of God is eternal life through Christ Jesus our Lord." Did you get that? The first verse is the *bad* news, but the second gives hope.

No wonder the Bible calls it *good news*.

So here's the question: What are we doing to get the word out? God doesn't tell us to stand on a corner and shout, but we can use other ways to tell our friends and family about Christ. First, we should live out the good news. And then, when God gives us opportunities, we should tell people what Christ has done for us and what he can do for them.

And we can show them the Bible where they can "read all about it."

to do ☑

TAKE A FEW MINUTES AND WRITE A BRIEF NEWSPAPER-STYLE ARTICLE ON THE GOOD NEWS OF JESUS CHRIST. MAKE UP A HEADLINE TO GO WITH YOUR ARTICLE.

On this day in 1793, the American Minerva was published for the first time.

extra! extra! ¡extra!

also on this day

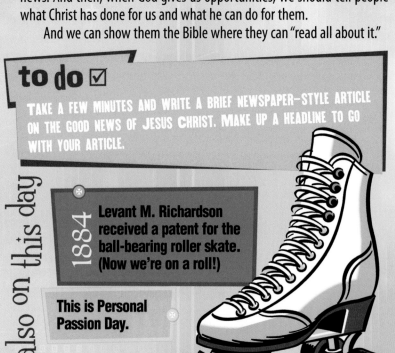

1884 Levant M. Richardson received a patent for the ball-bearing roller skate. (Now we're on a roll!)

This is Personal Passion Day.

Here begins the Good News about Jesus the Messiah, the Son of God.

[Mark 1:1]

any given sunday

On this day in 1939, the National Football League's attendance
exceeded 1 million in a season for the first time.

That's a lot of sports fans, especially in 1939. But these days, with 31 teams and huge stadiums, the NFL's attendance totals about 16 million for a season or about 1 million *each week*. And just think how many people are watching on TV!

As impressive as those numbers are, however, consider this: on any given Sunday, there are more people at church than at NFL games. That's right. According to studies, 44% of adult Americans attend church regularly, so that would make about 65 million every week. How about that, sports fans?

Jesus said, "Upon this rock I will build my church, and all the powers of hell will not conquer it" (see today's verse). He was talking about people, not buildings. Christ's church includes all people who trust in him as Savior, all over the world. So it's HUGE.

Unlike pro football, you won't find vendors, cheerleaders, scoreboards, or referees in a church service, and you won't need a ticket. But you can find excitement. Nothing could be more thrilling, for example, than to hear God speak through his Word and watch the Holy Spirit transform lives. And best of all, everyone wins. The champions in football and other sports are soon forgotten as we look to find new winners and heroes, but what happens in church lasts forever.

Hebrews 10:25 says not to neglect meeting together, "but encourage and warn each other, especially now that the day of [Christ's] coming back again is drawing near." Makes sense.

See you in church!

to do ☑

THIS SUNDAY IN CHURCH LOOK AT PEOPLE, ESPECIALLY THOSE YOU KNOW WELL, IN A DIFFERENT WAY. THINK OF HOW GOD HAS CHANGED THEIR LIVES. THANK GOD FOR HIS GREAT WORK AND FOR HIS CHURCH.

also on this day

This is Human Rights Day.

Poet Emily Dickinson was born.

1830

Now I say to you that you are Peter, and upon this rock I will build my church, and all the powers of hell will not conquer it.

[Matthew 16:18]

the greatest!

On this day in 1981, Muhammed Ali fought his last fight.

In 1960, 18-year-old Cassius Clay won a boxing gold medal at the summer Olympics in Rome, pummeling a Polish opponent in the final. So proud of his medal, Cassius wore it continually for two days.

After the Olympics Cassius Clay turned pro and boasted, "I am the greatest." Then he seemed to back up his claim by winning every fight. Before many fights he predicted the round in which he would win, and his predictions proved to be accurate. In 1962 he proclaimed, "I'm not the greatest; I'm the double greatest. Not only do I knock 'em out, I pick the round." Later Clay changed his name to Muhammad Ali.

Eventually Ali was the three-time world heavyweight champ, defeating Sonny Liston (1964), George Foreman (1974), and Leon Spinks (1978) for the title. He also fought Joe Frazier three times (1971–75), winning twice. Certainly Ali was a great boxer; perhaps even, as he claimed, "the greatest of all time."

But only one person can truly claim the title of "the greatest." That person is Jesus, the King of kings and Lord of lords. Not everyone recognizes that fact these days, but eventually everyone will, even Ali. As today's passage states, "at the name of Jesus every knee will bow, in Heaven and on earth and under the earth, and every tongue will confess that Jesus Christ is Lord."

Did you get that? *Every* knee will bow—on earth (all people), in heaven (including angels), and under the earth (including demons).

Knowing this can give us hope and courage. We are following the right leader, the only one who can give us eternal life. Other people may not understand that Jesus is God and the Messiah, but they will eventually. He truly is *the greatest*.

Because of this, God raised him up to the heights of heaven and gave him a name that is above every other name, so that at the name of Jesus every knee will bow, in heaven and on earth and under the earth, and every tongue will confess that Jesus Christ is Lord, to the glory of God the Father. [Philippians 2:9–11]

also on this day

This is National Noodle Ring Day.

1844

Dr. Horace Wells became the first person to have a tooth extracted after receiving an anesthetic (laughing gas) for the dental procedure.

to do ☑

TODAY, LISTEN AND WATCH CAREFULLY FOR THE WORDS GREAT AND GREATEST. EVERY TIME YOU HEAR OR READ ONE OF THOSE WORDS, THINK OF JESUS AND THANK GOD FOR GIVING US HIS SON, "THE GREATEST OF ALL TIME."

Think back to your last family trip. Did you stay at a motel along the way? Even if you didn't, you probably saw a bunch of them. We've come a long way since the first motel in 1925. Now national motel chains, independent motels, bed and breakfasts, and hotels dot the landscape. So every night millions of travelers must need places to stay.

Way back before motels, like in Bible times, travelers would sleep outside or in the few available inns. Remember when Mary and Joseph traveled to Bethlehem? Mary "gave birth to her first child, a son. She wrapped him snugly in strips of cloth and laid him in a manger, because there was no room for them in the village inn" (Luke 2:7).

Often travelers, even strangers, would be welcomed into homes where they could stay the night for free. The Bible says that Christians are expected to show hospitality toward others. Paul wrote: "When God's children are in need, be the one to help them out. And get into the habit of inviting guests home for dinner or, if they need lodging, for the night" (Romans 12:13).

Showing hospitality means being kind to strangers, helping people in need, and even opening our homes when we can. In fact, our verse for today implies that when we do this we might even be entertaining angels and not even know it.

You don't own a house, and you're probably not going to open a motel any time soon. But still you can be hospitable by being nice to the new kid in the neighborhood, in school, or at church. And you could invite him or her over to your house to hang out and mess around. You would make that "stranger" feel welcome, and you'd be acting like Jesus.

Don't forget to show hospitality to strangers, for some who have done this have entertained angels without realizing it! [Hebrews 13:2]

On this day in 1925, the Motel Inn, the first motel in the world, opened in San Luis Obispo, California.

hospitality rocks

to do ☑

THINK OF SOMEONE NEW TO YOUR SCHOOL, CHURCH, OR NEIGHBORHOOD. GO OUT OF YOUR WAY TO BE FRIENDLY TO HIM OR HER. AND, IF THE TIME IS RIGHT, INVITE HIM OR HER OVER TO YOUR HOUSE.

also on this day

1792 In Vienna, 22-year-old Ludwig van Beethoven received his first lesson in music composition from Franz Joseph Haydn. (Have you practiced the piano today?)

This is Poinsettia Day.

On this day in 1843, *A Christmas Carol* by Charles Dickens was published.

Humbug!

Since we're moving quickly toward Christmas, it won't be long till you'll see a version of *A Christmas Carol*. You probably know the story well. It features Bob Cratchit, Jacob Marley's Ghost, Tiny Tim, and the Ghosts of Christmases Past, Present, and Future, through whom Scrooge learns the real meaning of Christmas.

Do you remember Scrooge's famous phrase? That's right—"Bah! Humbug!" he would say whenever someone tried to get him in the Christmas spirit.

Have you ever felt like Scrooge? Have you grown tired of all the carols and crowds, or run short of money with presents still to buy? Are you afraid you won't be getting what you really want for Christmas? Are you stressed with the added activities and responsibilities? Are you tempted to say, "Humbug"?

That's when we need to remember Christmas past. No, we don't need a visit from a fictional ghost; we just need to remember the *true* meaning of Christmas and why we celebrate.

Our verse for today says it all: "God with us." Christmas celebrates the greatest gift ever given—God himself in human flesh. The wise men presented gifts to baby Jesus. And for centuries Christians have exchanged gifts in his honor.

Christmas is all about the *giving*, not the getting. And when we give to family, friends, and others, we should expect nothing in return. Our giving should be a response, not a habit or a way to *get*.

So get through those humbug feelings and find the truth in this season. And don't forget to "Thank God for his Son—a gift too wonderful for words!" (2 Corinthians 9:15).

to do ☑

BUY AN EXTRA GIFT FOR SOMEONE WHO REALLY NEEDS IT. GIVE IT ANONYMOUSLY (WITHOUT PUTTING YOUR NAME ON IT). AND DON'T EVER LET HIM OR HER KNOW THAT YOU WERE THE GIVER.

Look! The **virgin** will conceive a **child!** She will give **birth** to a **son**, and he will be **called Immanuel** (meaning, **God** is **with** us). [Matthew 1:23]

also on this day

✳ This is Bicycle Built for Two Day.

✳ The first music store in America opened. **1759**

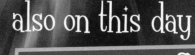

• **2000** U.S. Vice President Al Gore conceded the 2000 Presidential election to Texas Governor George W. Bush.

good grief!

On this day in 1999, Charles M. Schultz announced that he was retiring his *Peanuts* comic strip.

Good grief!" says Charlie Brown, commenting on his latest misadventure. Charlie, his sister Sally, his friends Linus, Pigpen, Lucy, Schroeder, and Peppermint Patty, and his dog Snoopy are characters featured in the *Peanuts* comic strip.

Your newspaper may still carry *Peanuts*. Although it officially ended after 18,000 strips on February 13, 2000, many newspapers reprint it. Charlie the lovable loser never seems to get it right, whether playing baseball, kicking a football, picking a Christmas tree, or trying to impress the mysterious little red-haired girl. And with each misadventure he exclaims, "Good grief!" The comic strip was wildly successful probably because most people could identify with Charlie. We all have days when nothing seems to go right, and we sigh, "Good grief!"

That's a strange expression, isn't it? What could possibly be good about grief? Grieving means loss and sorrow and tears. It seems to be the opposite of good. Putting those two words together is like combining *high low*, *empty full*, or *friend enemy*. Right?

Well, yes and no. The Bible points out how sorrow can actually be good for us.

Consider today's verse in which Paul explains that "God can use sorrow in our lives" for good. If you've been punished for doing something wrong, for example, you know that your sorrow and bad feelings taught you a valuable lesson. Or if you have been injured while doing something and then realize it could have been much worse, then you actually feel glad about the injury, even though it hurts. So grief can be good after all, especially if it pushes us away from sin and toward God.

For God can use sorrow in our lives to help us turn away from sin and seek salvation. We will never regret that kind of sorrow. But sorrow without repentance is the kind that results in death. [2 Corinthians 7:10]

also on this day

This is Yuletide Lads Day in Iceland, so if you're traveling there, be prepared to celebrate.

1799
George Washington died at the age of 67.

VE WOMEN THE VOTE

1918
For the first time in Britain, women voted in a general election.

to do ☑

THINK BACK OVER THE PAST YEAR AND LIST THE "SORROWS" THAT HAVE BEEN GOOD. WHAT LESSONS DID YOU LEARN? IN WHAT WAYS WAS YOUR GRIEF GOOD? REVIEW ROMANS 8:28.

heat up or cool down

On this day in 1654, a meteorological office established in Tuscany, Italy, began recording daily termperature readings.

How often does your family check the weather forecast? It's virtually impossible to miss because all the radio stations give regular updates. And you can get the latest from the meteorologists on TV. If you're really into temperatures, fronts, and isobars, you can watch the Weather Channel.

Knowing the weather helps us prepare. If a winter blast is predicted, complete with ice, snow, and howling winds, we bundle up from head to toe and stock up on hot chocolate for when we come in from the cold. And in the summer when we learn of a coming heat wave, we wear shorts, make sure the air conditioning is working, and get those cold drinks and ice ready.

Today's verse isn't about weather, but it does touch on temperatures. Maybe you've found it confusing. So switch gears here and think of hot and cold drinks.

Let's say you've been out in the cold, shoveling snow. You're freezing and tired. You come in and your mom says, "How'd you like some hot chocolate?" You eagerly take the mug and put it to your lips expecting the sweet hot liquid to warm you up. But it's lukewarm instead. How awful!

Or imagine it's summer and you've finished playing ball. You reach into the cooler, pull out a juice bottle, and take a swig. It's lukewarm—yuck!

God wants believers to be "hot" or "cold"—fully committed. Lukewarm just doesn't cut it. But sometimes followers of Jesus are just that—lukewarm. Blah. Bored. Blended into society.

So what's your temperature? How do you think you "taste" to God?

to do ☑

MAKE YOURSELF A CUP OF HOT CHOCOLATE OR HOT TEA. AS YOU DRINK IT, ASK GOD TO HELP YOU BE HOT FOR HIM.

"I know all the things you do, that you are neither hot nor cold. I wish you were one or the other! But since you are like lukewarm water, I will spit you out of my mouth!" [Revelation 3:15, 16]

also on this day

1939

The movie *Gone With the Wind,* based on the novel by Margaret Mitchell, premiered at Loew's Grand Theater in Atlanta.

This is One Day! Day.

This is National Bill of Rights Day.

How much do you like chocolate? Some people call themselves "chocoholics" because they are almost addicted to the sweet treat. They grab anything chocolate and have trouble controlling the urge. They would love this day. To them, "chocolate covered anything" sounds wonderful.

But is it? Chocolate covered nuts are OK. And cherries. And just about everyone likes cake, cookies, or ice cream covered in chocolate. But how would you like to bite into a chocolate covered onion, or cockroach, or dirt ball, or brussels sprout? Eeeewww! As your tongue hits the chocolate, you think, *This is great*. But then you reach what it covers and you spit it out faster than you can say Willie Wonka. What's on the inside matters; in fact, it's more important than the sweet covering.

Life can be like that too. It's good to be sweet and nice on the outside. And we should try to be positive, pleasant, and fun to be around. But sometimes an appealing exterior can hide a difficult person. And if we are fooled by a phony exterior, when we learn the truth we can feel hurt and cheated.

One day Jesus encountered a group of religious leaders who were giving him a hard time and trying to trip him up. They looked great on the outside, all dressed up and saying all sorts of good-sounding religious words. But inside they were pretty bad. So Jesus told them the truth about themselves. Read his harsh language in today's verse.

The lesson is clear: we should be careful about what's on the inside of our lives, even more than the outside. God wants genuine people—no phonies—whose hearts are right, who truly love and obey him.

How are you on the inside?

How terrible it will be for you teachers of religious law and you Pharisees. Hypocrites! You are like whitewashed tombs—beautiful on the outside but filled on the inside with dead people's bones and all sorts of impurity. [Matthew 23:27]

This is National Chocolate Covered Anything Day.

to do ☑

IN HONOR OF THIS DAY, GET YOURSELF A CHOCOLATE COVERED TREAT. AS YOU ENJOY THE CANDY, THINK OF HOW YOU CAN BE MORE CHRIST-LIKE IN YOUR THOUGHTS, MOTIVES, AND ATTITUDES.

also on this day

1773 Colonial patriots, dressed like Indians, dumped nearly 350 chests of tea into Boston Harbor. This is now known as the Boston Tea Party.

The Tale of Peter Rabbit by Beatrix Potter was printed for the first time. **1901**

chocolate covered

ONE WAY

one way!

On this day in 1791, New York City established the first one-way street.

After getting your driver's license you'll become very aware of traffic signs: Stop, Yield, No U-Turn, Construction Zone, and many more. These signs keep traffic orderly. One of the most important is One Way. Certain streets have been given that designation to allow more vehicles to go faster in one direction. It's a terrible mistake to drive the *wrong way* on a one-way street. It's frightening and dangerous to suddenly have all the cars coming toward you.

Since 1791, most drivers are OK with one-way streets. But many people have trouble accepting the idea of having a single way in other areas of life, especially in spiritual matters. Someone might say, "There are many ways to God" or "It doesn't matter what you believe as long as you're sincere." That may sound good, but it's sincerely wrong.

You remember Jesus saying, "I am the way, the truth, and the life. No one can come to the Father except through me" (John 14:6). Clearly he was claiming to be the *one* way, the *only* way. But to many that seems narrow and just not right. They don't want *anyone*, especially Jesus, to make that claim because they want to make their own way.

What if you drove like that? You come to a street marked One Way and you say, "Oh, no you don't—I'm going my way!" Or you come to a bridge marked, "The only way across the river," and you say, "I don't believe it! I'm going downstream five miles and cross there!" Possible consequences are a collision with another car, a traffic ticket, or wasted time getting lost or backtracking.

Instead of rebelling against God's one way to Heaven we should say, "Thank you, Lord, for providing a way, the *only* way!" Then drive God's way.

But the Scriptures have declared that we are all prisoners of sin, so the only way to receive God's promise is to believe in Jesus Christ. [Galatians 3:22]

also on this day

This is Aviation Day.

1903

Orville and Wilbur Wright made the first successful gasoline-powered airplane flight near Kitty Hawk, North Carolina.

to do ☑

GO TO THE MALL AND BUY A ONE WAY SIGN (THAT LOOKS LIKE A TRAFFIC SIGN). OR YOU CAN MAKE ONE, USING WHITE CARDBOARD AND A BLACK FELT-TIP PEN. HANG IT IN YOUR ROOM TO REMIND YOU THAT JESUS IS GOD'S "ONE WAY."

don't be half-baked

This is Bake Cookies Day.

Yum! Yum! Nothing beats Christmas cookies right out of the oven. Which ones are your favorites: gingerbread men? peanut blossoms? sugar? shortbread? spritz? jam thumbprints? pecan tassies?

If you've ever made cookies, you know the steps. First you get all the ingredients together. Next, you mix them in the right order (dry first, and then wet). Then you form the cookies. Finally, you bake them. Then you're ready for the best step—you eat them.

But have you ever bitten into a cookie that was half-baked? Not too good. They have to spend time in the oven, just the right time, to be perfect.

Not only does heat help us prepare food to eat; but heat also helps make steel, form diamonds from coal, and remove impurities. The Bible uses that last one as an illustration of how believers can grow strong in their faith.

We can experience many kinds of "heat" in life. Persecution is one kind. That's when people make fun of us or even try to hurt us because of our faith. Another kind of heat involves the challenges of living, like the pressure you feel in school before a big test and when you have to make an important decision. Heat can also come from life's troubles—sickness, setbacks, injuries, broken possessions and relationships.

Life's heat can help us become all that God intended. The heat can remove impurities, like purifying gold. It can make us strong and durable, like in forging iron and steel. And it can make us appealing and tasty, like a Christmas cookie.

So instead of running from troubles or whining about them, look for what God is doing with you in his kitchen.

to do ☑

ASK A PARENT OR OLDER SIBLING TO MAKE COOKIES WITH YOU. THEN MAKE SPECIAL ONES FOR THE FAMILY AND A FEW DOZEN MORE TO GIVE TO PEOPLE IN THE NEIGHBORHOOD. USE THE EXPERIENCE TO REMIND YOU OF GOD MAKING YOU JUST RIGHT.

also on this day

1936

Su-Lin, the first giant panda to come to the U.S. from China, arrived in San Francisco, California. It was sold to the Brookfield Zoo in Illinois for $8,750.

Kenneth LeBel jumped 17 barrels on ice skates.

1965

For **everyone** will be **purified** with **fire**.

[Mark 9:49]

1898 A new automobile speed record was set at 39 mph.

This is Oatmeal Muffin Day.

Taste Trust

Yesterday was cookies, and today it's muffins. What is this, baking week?

Most kids probably would say that oatmeal muffins don't sound too appetizing. They think of oatmeal as a bland and mushy breakfast cereal. Besides, oatmeal muffins are probably good for you, right? That means they must taste bad.

You've been down this road before—being told about something you *should* eat, even if it doesn't sound very tasty. Certain vegetables, liver, and bran all fit in this category. For some kids, eating those foods is like taking medicine. But at least with medicine you see results. The benefits of eating the right foods may not be seen for many years.

That's why you eat in *faith*. You pop those brussels sprouts in your mouth, trusting that what your mother, father, or grandparents says is true. You know they love you and want the best for you (and they have more experience and knowledge), so you grimace and eat.

We can face a similar situation in relation to God. The Bible explains that certain experiences and actions are important for our spiritual health—like telling the truth even if it hurts, admitting when we're wrong, spending time every day reading the Bible, befriending the unpopular kid, praying for our enemies, and so forth. They may be hard to swallow, like an oatmeal muffin, but we do them anyway, in faith. God loves us, so we can trust him to give us only what's best for us, even if it seems distasteful at the time.

to do ☑

THE NEXT TIME YOUR MOM OR DAD TELLS YOU TO EAT SOMETHING BECAUSE "IT'S GOOD FOR YOU," SAY "THANK YOU," AND EAT IT WITHOUT COMPLAINING. WHEN THEY GET OVER THE SHOCK AND ASK WHY YOU HAD SUCH A GOOD ATTITUDE FOR A CHANGE, EXPLAIN THAT YOU ARE "EATING BY FAITH."

That is **why** we **live** by **believing** and not by **seeing**.

[2 Corinthians 5:7]

also on this day

1777 General George Washington led his army of about 11,000 men to Valley Forge, Pennsylvania, to camp for the winter.

1887 Jake Kilrain and Jim Smith fought in a bare knuckles fight that lasted 106 rounds and 2 hours and 30 minutes. The fight was ruled a draw and was halted due to darkness.

Way before the Internet, letters were hand-written and hand-delivered. And if you lived in the country off a snow-covered road, you'd have a tough time getting your mail. If you were expecting only a pile of bills and ads, that might be OK. But if you depended on the postal service to deliver important documents or letters from someone you loved, you wouldn't be satisfied waiting till spring. And think how you'd greet the mail-delivering dog sled driver! You see the sled in the distance—beautiful! You throw on your coat, hat, boots, and gloves, and run to meet the dogs and driver. It would make your day.

Today's verse sounds funny because we don't usually think of feet as beautiful. Isaiah isn't saying that the person's feet are physically attractive. When he writes, "How beautiful . . . are the feet of those who bring good news," he is highlighting what the person is bringing—good news. It would be like you living in the Maine boondocks and seeing the dog sled saying, "What beautiful dogs!" because they were bringing you essential letters.

In this case, the good news on the mountain is God's peace and salvation. Those words would sound good to anyone, but especially to the people of Israel who had been living as conquered captives.

These days we aren't living in an occupied land dominated by a foreign dictator. But people are captive in other ways—to sin and to Satan. So God's message of freedom is wonderful, welcome news. And get this—God has given us, his people, the great privilege of delivering that news. We don't need dog sleds; we just need to tell others about Jesus when we get the chance.

When we do that, we'll have beautiful feet!

to do ☑

WHEN YOU PUT ON YOUR SHOES OVER THE NEXT FEW DAYS, THINK OF HOW BEAUTIFUL YOUR FEET ARE WHEN YOU DELIVER THE GOOD NEWS ABOUT CHRIST.

How beautiful on the mountains are the feet of those who bring good news of peace and salvation, the news that the God of Israel reigns!

[Isaiah 52:7]

beautiful feet!

On this day in 1928, mail delivery by dog sled began in Lewiston, Maine.

also on this day

1606 ✷

The *Susan Constant*, *Goodspeed*, and *Discovery* set sail from London. Their landing at Jamestown, Virginia, was the start of the first permanent English settlement in America.

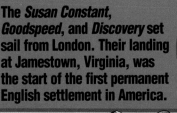
This is Games Day. ✷

it's important

On this day in 1620, the Mayflower landed at Plymouth Rock, Massachusetts.

What would it take for you to pack up all your belongings, leave your home and way of life, and make a dangerous journey to a distant land?

For those travelers from England about 400 years ago, religious freedom was their reason. They knew nothing about the land we now call America—no maps, travel brochures, Internet, or newscasts. It was vast and mysterious. And they didn't have huge ocean liners or airplanes that could transport them safely and comfortably in a matter of hours. No, they had ships of dubious safety, and they had to endure many days of dangerous ocean travel. But that just shows how important it was to them to have the freedom to worship God as they wanted. They risked *everything*!

Even today some people still do not enjoy religious freedom. Christians are beaten and even killed in China, Indonesia, Pakistan, Sudan, Iran, and many other places simply for following Christ.

In America we have no official religion and we can worship Christ freely. In fact, most of our cities and towns have many types of churches in beautiful facilities. We can find a worship service of almost any style that we like.

Yet we often take this freedom for granted, sometimes not going to church because we're sleepy or the weather's bad or we just don't feel like it. Don't you wonder what those pilgrims would have said about that? What about the people in other lands who desperately seek fellowship, worship, and Bible study?

Thank God for your freedom of religion, and freely worship him!

to do ☑

AT CHURCH THIS WEEK, MAKE A LIST OF EVERYTHING YOU APPRECIATE ABOUT YOUR CHURCH—THE WORSHIP SERVICE AND THE OTHER PROGRAMS—AND THANK GOD FOR EACH ITEM ON THE LIST.

But the time is coming and is already here when true worshipers will worship the Father in spirit and in truth. The Father is looking for anyone who will worship him that way. [John 4:23]

also on this day 1937

Walt Disney debuted the first full-length animated feature in Hollywood, California—*Snow White and the Seven Dwarfs.*

This is Humbug Day.

X-ray vision

On this day in 1895, German physicist Wilhelm Röntgen made the first X-ray image.

What's the first X ray you can remember? Maybe it was at the dentist's office to check for cavities in those pearly whites. Hopefully you haven't had to have a leg or arm X-rayed because of an injury. X rays are extremely useful if you need them. In a matter of minutes, the doctor can spot a hairline crack in a bone, a foreign object in the stomach, or a problem in a joint. So Dr. Röntgen sure invented an amazing, lifesaving machine.

It's neat to be able to see inside a person, through clothes and skin. Just imagine if you could make your eyes work that way! In the comics, Superman is said to have X-ray vision, so he can spot criminals as he looks through walls.

God sees all that and much more. He sees inside our minds and hearts. He sees right through to the *real* person on the inside. God knows what we're thinking and feeling—our motives and fears, hopes and dreams. That's why we can pray silently, thinking our prayers to him.

So how does that make you feel? Guilty? Afraid? It can be scary to know that we can't hide from God. And the Bible reminds us that "God knows all hearts, and he sees [us]. . . . And he will judge all people according to what they have done" (Proverbs 24:12).

Even though he knows all about you, God still loves you and wants the very best for you. And he's always close! Also, as today's verse reminds us, God continually looks for those who trust him and want to follow him. Is that you?

> God looks **down**
>   from **heaven** on the
>   entire **human** race;
>   he **looks** to see if there is
> **even one** with **real**
>   **understanding**, one who
> **seeks** for **God**. [Psalm 53:2]

also on this day

This is Abilities Day.

1882
Thomas Edison created the first string of Christmas tree lights.

1958
The "Chipmunk Song" reached #1.

to do ☑

ASK YOUR MOM OR DAD IF THEY HAVE ANY X-RAYS IN THE HOUSE (PERHAPS IN AN OLD MEDICAL FILE). IF YOU CAN, PUT ONE IN YOUR ROOM WHERE YOU CAN SEE IT TO REMIND YOU OF GOD'S UNLIMITED KNOWLEDGE AND CONSTANT CARE.

'Twas the Night

On this day in 1823, the poem "A Visit from St. Nicholas" by Clement C. Moore was published.

This poem by Clement Moore is still popular after almost 200 years. You probably know it best by the first line: "'Twas the night before Christmas . . ." A lot of what we think about Santa Claus and the reindeer comes from it. If you were asked to name Santa's reindeer, for example, you'd probably answer, "Donder, Blitzen, Comet, Cupid," and so forth—right out of the poem. And everyone can identify with the children "nestled" in their beds, dreaming of Christmas day. But what's the deal with the "visions of sugar plums"?

Christmas Eve, the night before Christmas, is an exciting time for everyone in the family, especially children. They can hardly get to sleep for all the excitement, wondering what Santa will bring. No wonder they have such weird dreams.

Anticipation. Expectation. Nothing's quite like it as we eagerly wait for the wonderful event. Besides Christmas, we eagerly anticipate birthdays, vacations, other celebrations and holidays, and incredible reunions with loved ones.

But the greatest event could come at any moment—and it's also a reunion—the Second Coming of Jesus. That's right. One of these days Jesus will return, to judge the world and to bring his people home.

The Bible says that we should watch for Christ's return—sort of like kids on Christmas Eve. This doesn't mean spending our time looking to the clouds (the Bible also says that no one knows the timing of this great event). Instead, it means that we should be ready. Here's a question that can help. We can ask, "Is this something I would want to be doing if Jesus were to return today?" We might live differently if we expected Christ to arrive at any moment.

Are you excited and ready? It'll be better than Christmas!

to do ☑

GET OUT A COPY OF CLEMENT MOORE'S FAMOUS POEM AND READ IT ALOUD FOR THE WHOLE FAMILY. IF YOU HAVE A BIG AND COOPERATIVE FAMILY, YOU COULD EVEN ACT IT OUT TOGETHER.

also on this day

❋ In Mexico, this is Night of the Radishes.

❋1888

Following a quarrel with Paul Gauguin (another painter), Dutch painter Vincent Van Gogh cut off part of his own earlobe. Gogh figure!

"What I **say** to **you** I **say** to **everyone**: **Watch** for his **return!"**

[Mark 13:37]

This is Christmas Eve.

Yesterday we discussed the night before christmas, but now that day is actually here. Do you have all your shopping done or do you have to make one more, last-second trip? And what gifts are you hoping for?

Even though we like to *receive* gifts, Christmas is all about *giving*. That's the whole reason for this holiday—God gave his Son, the greatest gift. So we celebrate his birth, and we honor him by giving gifts to others.

The gift-giving didn't end in Bethlehem, however. In today's verse, we hear Jesus talking with the disciples, his closest followers. Do you see the gift he promises to them? It's "peace of heart and mind." And notice that this peace differs from the kind they could expect to find in society. It's deep. It's lasting. It's real. Peace of heart involves security and joy. Peace of mind involves understanding and believing that God is real and in control.

Soon after hearing that promise, immediately following Jesus' crucifixion, the disciples would be scattered and then hunted and persecuted. Jesus knew that he would be resurrected from the dead, but he also knew that he would leave the disciples again and that they would face difficult times in the world. So he promised them peace. He offers us the same gift today.

What a Savior we serve! He just keeps giving gifts. And what an amazing gift this is: peace of heart and mind.

No matter what your life is like and regardless of what you are going through this holiday season, God has a gift for you—his Son, Jesus. Jesus has a gift for you, too—peace. It comes from trusting in him, the Prince of Peace.

to do ☑

ON A PIECE OF PAPER, MAKE TWO COLUMNS. LABEL ONE "HEART" AND THE OTHER "MIND." UNDER HEART, LIST THE FEELINGS YOU EXPERIENCE THAT ARE ANYTHING BUT PEACEFUL (ANXIETY, FEAR, AND OTHERS). AND UNDER MIND LIST THE SITUATIONS OR THOUGHTS THAT THREATEN YOUR PEACE (CRIME, DISASTERS, DOUBTS, AND SO FORTH). THEN THINK OF HOW KNOWING CHRIST CAN CALM THOSE FEELINGS AND EASE THOSE CONCERNS. AND THANK GOD FOR HIS GIFT OF PEACE.

also on this day

1818 Franz Gruber of Oberndorf, Germany, composed the music for "Silent Night" to words written by Josef Mohr.

This is National Eggnog Day.

the giving of gifts

merry christmas!

This is Christmas Day.

The day is finally here. Hopefully you've already had a great time of giving and receiving and celebrating Christ's birth.

But do you really understand Christmas?

It's all about *incarnation*. This word simply means "in the flesh," and it describes what Jesus did. John 1 says that Jesus is fully God and has always existed, and was even involved in creation. But then John says, "the Word became human and lived here on earth among us" (John 1:14). Today's passage from Philippians puts it even more dramatically: "He made himself nothing; he took the humble position of a slave and appeared in human form."

Imagine that you created a colony of ants in your yard. You love those ants and do your best to protect, feed, and help them. You want to communicate your love for them, but everything you try just frightens them. After all, they see you as gigantic and hear your voice as a roar. So what can you do to get through? Write a big sign? Radio the message? Grab one or two and try to get close to them? They just wouldn't get it.

The only way to communicate effectively would be to become an ant yourself, to somehow put aside your size, power, and prestige and become a tiny insect crawling around in the dirt.

That's exactly what Jesus did. He left his heavenly home and put aside the unlimited use of his divine powers and shrunk himself to our size, becoming a mere speck in the vast universe that he had created. He became a baby human.

And Jesus did this because of love—for you and everyone else on earth. That's Christmas.

Though he was God, he did not demand and cling to his rights as God. He made himself nothing; he took the humble position of a slave and appeared in human form. And in human form he obediently humbled himself even further by dying a criminal's death on a cross. [Philippians 2:6-8]

also on this day

1896

John Philip Sousa titled his melody "The Stars and Stripes Forever."

1914

During World War I, British and German troops observed an unofficial truce and even played soccer together on the Western Front.

to do ☑

TAKE A FEW MINUTES AND LIST ALL THE GIFTS YOU HAVE RECEIVED FROM GOD, BEGINNING WITH THE INCARNATION. THEN THANK GOD FOR EACH ONE.

serve no whine

This is National Whiners Day.

Whoever made up this day probably did so because of so many people complaining about Christmas gifts. Besides the verbal complaints, this is one of the busiest days of the year for stores because of all the presents being returned or exchanged.

Gifts are supposed to be unexpected and undeserved—just given out of love. But the world tells us that we should expect to receive as much as we give. Advertisers would have us believe that we deserve to receive quality gifts. Then, when we don't get exactly what we want, we often pout or whine.

The only way to break this bad habit and poor attitude is to remember God's gift of Jesus and salvation. "God showed his great love for us by sending Christ to die for us while we were still sinners" (Romans 5:8). "Salvation is not a reward for the good things we have done, so none of us can boast about it" (Ephesians 2:9). Salvation is totally free, a gift (Romans 6:23). All we have to do is accept it.

That's the most important gift of all. Anything else we receive from parents, friends, or anyone else is a bonus. So today, instead of being disappointed in your gifts and letting everyone know those feelings, adjust your attitude to gratitude. Rejoice in your greatest gift, and be thankful for the others too.

Be content.

to do ☑

TODAY, BEGIN WRITING THANK-YOU NOTES FOR ALL YOUR CHRISTMAS GIFTS.

Yet **true religion** with **contentment** is **great wealth.**

[1 Timothy 6:6]

also on this day

1927

The East-West Shrine college football bowl game featured numbers on both the front and back of players' jerseys.

This is Boxing Day in Canada and Britain.

The Man of the Year in *Time* Magazine was a computer. This was the first time a non-human received the honor.

1982

This is National Bingo Month.

Bingo!

You yell, "Bingo!" because you were the first to fill in the squares on your card vertically, horizontally, or diagonally (or the four corners). Winning this game feels good, but you know it's mostly just luck. Your success in this game is determined by how the letter and number combinations drawn match what you have.

Many people feel the same way about life, that it's all about luck and chance. Good things happen to a person, they believe, simply because he or she is in the right place at the right time. They believe that's how bad stuff happens too.

Others say that everything depends on our *choices* in life. We control our own destiny—everything depends on what we choose to do or not do.

The Bible presents a much different view—God is in control. Nothing happens without his knowledge and his permission. Proverbs 16:9 states, "We can make our plans, but the LORD determines our steps."

This is wonderful knowledge, especially when everything going on around us seems crazy. Knowing that God is all-powerful and all-knowing gives a great feeling of security.

Remember when you were little and got scared at night? You would go into your parents' bedroom and sleep with them. You could relax and sleep peacefully knowing that Mom and Dad were with you and would take care of you.

That's how it is with God. He's right with you, watching out for you. Your life doesn't depend on luck—it depends on him. And that's true on both good and bad days.

to do ☑

WATCH TELEVISION NEWS, AND DURING EACH STORY THINK, "GOD IS IN CONTROL." WATCH HOW THAT TRUTH AFFECTS YOUR ATTITUDE.

also on this day

But the **LORD's plans** stand **firm forever**; his **intentions** can **never** be **shaken**.

[Psalm 33:11]

* This is National Fruitcake Day.

✳ 1938

The first snowmobile course in America opened in North Conway, New Hampshire.

flavor that lasts

On this day in 1869, William E. Semple of Mt. Vernon, Ohio, patented chewing gum.

People chew gum for many reasons. Some think it helps digestion. Some chew to fight bad breath. Others like to blow bubbles. But most people enjoy chewing gum because of the taste. Whether mint, cinnamon, or fruit flavor, the taste brightens the mouth without filling the stomach. So it's frustrating when a piece of gum loses its flavor and becomes stale and gooey.

Way back in 1959, English musician Lonnie Donegan released a pop song with the title and musical question, "Does Your Chewing Gum Lose its Flavor on the Bedpost Overnight?" Eventually it reached number five on the U.S. charts. The song was catchy but silly; yet it touched on the problem of gum losing its flavor, whether in the mouth or stuck and saved somewhere else.

All of our pleasures seem to end way too soon— having fun with a friend, consuming an ice cream cone, playing on a snow day off from school, enjoying a vacation, watching a favorite TV show, and having perfect weather. We want the flavor to last and last.

Days come and go. Pleasures fade. Friendships change. And, eventually, every person dies. Nothing lasts forever— nothing, that is, except *everything* connected with God. In Genesis 17:19, God tells Abraham, "I will confirm my everlasting covenant." Deuteronomy 33:27 promises, "The eternal God is your refuge, and his everlasting arms are under you." Yesterday's verse highlights "the Lord's plans." First Corinthians 13:13 says, "There are three things that will endure—faith, hope, and love—and the greatest of these is love." And think of all the verses that speak of eternal life.

So for flavor that lasts, stick with God.

But the love of the LORD remains forever with those who fear him. His salvation extends to the children's children. [Psalm 103:17]

also on this day

In Mexico, this is Day of the Innocents.

1945

The United States Congress officially recognized the Pledge of Allegiance.

to do ☑

BUY A FEW PACKS OF GUM AND PASS OUT STICKS TO FAMILY AND FRIENDS. EACH TIME SAY SOMETHING LIKE, "GOD'S FLAVOR LASTS!"

stylin'

Don't you wonder what possessed Emma to wear pants when she knew it was forbidden? Maybe she just had a stubborn streak. Perhaps it was a demonstration; she wanted to show that she didn't agree with the weird law. Or maybe she just wanted to be a trendsetter.

Clothes aren't usually so controversial, but we sure spend hours thinking about them and deciding what to wear. Clothes protect us from the weather, keeping us warm and dry. Clothes also protect us from rough ground, prickly plants, mosquitoes, and sunburn. And, of course, we wear clothes out of modesty.

Over the years, clothes have become much more than coverings. They have become statements of who we are or who we'd like to be. The fashion business is humongous because everyone wants to be in style. Often we wear clothes *only* because they're fashionable. Some fashions make no sense, but a designer has an idea and a celebrity or two picks up on it, and soon everyone is wearing it.

Today's verse says that Christians shouldn't "copy the behavior and customs of this world." Some kids find that confusing. Does this mean we shouldn't wear clothes that are in style? Not really. It's all right to look good and to be fashionable. The problem comes we become so focused on stylin' that we take our eyes off God and forget who we really are. And it's OK to spend money on clothes, but not too much—not at the expense of tithing and helping others.

A popular phrase says, "Clothes make the person." But that's wrong. Who you are is much deeper than what you are wearing. God loves the real you and he wants you to conform to *his style* on the inside.

Don't copy the behavior and customs of this world, but let God transform you into a new person by changing the way you think. Then you will know what God wants you to do, and you will know how good and pleasing and perfect his will really is. [Romans 12:2]

to do ☑

GET OUT AN OLD PHOTO ALBUM WITH PICTURES OF YOUR PARENTS WHEN THEY WERE TEENAGERS. CHECK OUT THE CLOTHING STYLES. ASK YOUR MOM OR DAD TO EXPLAIN WHY SHE OR HE WORE THOSE CLOTHES.

also on this day

1848 U.S. President James Polk turned on the first gaslight at the White House.

The first Young Men's Christian Association (YMCA) was organized in Boston, Massachusetts. **1851**

The Mask

On this day in 1809, wearing masks at balls was forbidden in Boston.

Yesterday it was a woman wearing pants in public, and today it's wearing masks at balls. What's the deal with Boston and weird laws?

Wearing masks is popular at Halloween, Mardi Gras, and costume parties. Hiding behind a mask and pretending to be someone else or just clowning around can be fun. You could wear a mask and pretend to be George Bush, Mickey Mouse, Little Orphan Annie, a gorilla, Spiderman, Oprah, Hillary Duff, Aslan, LeBron James, or some other person or character.

People wear masks in other ways, even without putting anything over their faces. They pretend to be a different kind of person by acting a certain way or by trying to look the part. They might try being funny or tough or cool because they want to be friends with a certain group. Some people just don't like the way they are; they want to be more outgoing or better looking. Others are trying hard to be popular. That's why some intelligent kids pretend to be dumb. Have you ever known anyone who did that?

Maybe you've worn a mask. Probably you discovered that we may fool ourselves and others for a while, but we never fool God.

God knows you, the *real* you, and everything about you. He sees through and behind your masks. Not only that, he loves you the way you are. So it makes no sense to try to hide from him or to trick him.

Drop the mask and be honest with God. Be yourself with others too.

to do ☑

FOR FUN, PLAY A LITTLE GAME WITH YOUR FAMILY AT DINNERTIME. EXPLAIN THAT WHEN YOU SAY AN EMOTION OR AN ATTITUDE, EACH PERSON OUGHT TO MAKE A FACE THAT EXPRESSES IT. YOU COULD SAY WORDS LIKE, SAD, COOL, HORRIFIED, TOUGH, SHY, IN LOVE, SPIRITUAL, AND SO FORTH. THEN YOU COULD EXPLAIN TODAY'S DEVOTION TO THEM.

O **God**, you **know** how **foolish** I am; my **sins** cannot be **hidden** from **you**.

[Psalm 69:5]

also on this day

This is Universal Human Rights Month.

We received the first picture of a comet from space. **1973**

1953 The first color TV sets went on sale for about $1,175 (that would be more than $8,330 today).

rearview mirror

On this day in 1907, for the first time a ball dropped at Times Square to signal the new year.

This is the last day of the year—New Year's Eve. Are you going to a party? Do you plan to stay up late to watch the ball drop and ring in a new year?

We celebrate this night because we made it through another 52 weeks. It's the end! But it's also the beginning. So we think of starting fresh and we make resolutions.

It's good to look ahead and set goals for the next 12 months. But this day also provides a great opportunity to look in the rearview mirror, to see where we've come from. We need to know where we've been before deciding on where to go.

The Bible tells of the people of God reflecting on all that God had done for them in the past. Deuteronomy 32:7 says, "Remember the days of long ago; think about the generations past. Ask your father and he will inform you. Inquire of your elders, and they will tell you." Remembering God's great works would give the people hope for the future. And they would keep in mind the lessons learned back then. Past experiences would help guide their future actions.

We can also learn from what others went through. That truth is emphasized in the verse for today in which Paul explains the importance of reading the Bible. Then he says, "If you think you are standing strong, be careful, for you, too, may fall into the same sin" (1 Corinthians 10:12).

So take a few minutes to reflect on this past year. What victories and defeats did you experience? What lessons did you learn from those events? In what ways did you see God work in your life and in your family?

Then thank God for being with you each step of the journey.

to do ☑

ASK EACH FAMILY MEMBER WHAT HE OR SHE CONSIDERS TO BE THE HIGHLIGHT OF THE PAST YEAR. ALSO ASK WHAT LESSONS WERE LEARNED FROM THOSE EXPERIENCES.

All these events happened to **them** as **examples** for **us**. They were **written** down to **warn** us, who **live** at the time **when** this **age** is **drawing** to a **close**.

[1 Corinthians 10:11]

also on this day

1784

This is Make Up Your Mind Day.

This is also Unlucky Day.

Sarah Knauss died at the age of 119 years. Born on September 24, 1880, she was the world's oldest person.

1999

index

reference	title	date
Luke 21:36	Be On the Lookout	May 4
Luke 23:33	Breathing Free	October 28
Luke 23:43	Unconditional Pardon	September 8
Luke 24:49	A True Superhero	March 1
John 3:2	The Mark of a Great Teacher	May 7
John 3:3	Flat As A Pancake	February 27
John 4:14	A Thirst Quencher	November 24
John 4:23	It's Important	December 21
John 5:8	Overcoming Obstacles	November 4
John 6:9	Go M.A.D.	October 27
John 6:51	Bread of Life	November 3
John 8:32	The Truth will Set You Free	March 16
John 8:36	True Freedom	June 17
John 8:45, 46	It's the Truth!	June 4
John 9:39	The Blind Will See	January 9
John 10:10	Surprise!	February 19
John 12:35	Walk this Way	February 29
John 13:34, 35	Daring to be Different	May 25
John 14:6	True North	August 8
John 14:16	Disney's Dream World	May 27
John 14:27	The Giving of Gifts	December 24
John 15:13	The Real Deal	July 11
John 17:21	Together	April 5
John 20:27	Show Me	August 10
Acts 1:8	Plugged In	February 11
Acts 1:8	The Ends of the Earth	October 17
Acts 4:12	The Real Lifesaver	January 30
Acts 4:36	What a Nice Thing to Say	February 6
Acts 13:22	Real Heroes	May 26
Acts 17:6	Upside Down	October 18
Acts 17:11	Reel Life	April 23
Acts 22:14	The Real St. Patrick	March 17
Romans 2:4	Random Acts of Kindness	November 13
Romans 5:1	Give Peace a Chance	November 27
Romans 5:3, 4	Don't Give Up the Ship!	June 1
Romans 5:8	The Greatest Sacrifice	November 11
Romans 5:12	Getting Antzy	June 18
Romans 8:6	Mind Matters	October 3
Romans 8:15	Twice Free!	December 6
Romans 8:24	Free At Last!	August 28
Romans 8:29	First!	May 9
Romans 8:37	"I Have Not Yet Begun to Fight"	July 6
Romans 8:38, 39	Everywhere and Always	April 17
Romans 9:17	Fame!	August 31
Romans 10:9	Beachhead	June 6
Romans 10:10	Entrance Exam	November 12
Romans 11:6	Undeserved Favor	September 29
Romans 12:2	Stylin'	December 29
Romans 12:7	Help!	April 27